Jane Egginton
and John Howell

Buying a property
EASTERN EUROPE

CADOGANguides

Contents

Part B: Countries

About the authors

Jane Egginton is an award-winning travel writer and photographer who has been writing and editing guide books for more than 15 years. A member of the British Guild of Travel Writers, she produces glossy, highly illustrated coffee-table books and comprehensive, fact-filled publications, as well as destination articles for international and national magazines and newspapers. Jane has travelled extensively throughout the world, writing about everything from adventure travel in Central America to country walking in Britain for publishers such as Reader's Digest, Insight, Berlitz, Thomas Cook and the AA. She has a tendency to stay near the sea, whether circumnavigating India by rail, visiting Britain's seaside resorts, flying around Brazil's coastline or Caribbean island-hopping. Although she originally planned to buy a ramshackle property on Croatia's Adriatic Coast, she plumped instead for a purpose-built apartment on Bulgaria's Black Sea, which proved easier to let out. Jane is also the author of *Working and Living: Australia*, also published by Cadogan Guides.

John Howell established John Howell & Co in Sheffield in 1979 and by 1997 it had become one of the largest and most respected law firms in the north of England, employing over 100 lawyers. On moving to London in 1995, John Howell has gone on to specialise in providing legal advice to clients buying a property in France, Spain, Italy and Portugal and more recently Turkey and Croatia.

Titles available in the *Buying a Property* series

Buying a Property: Abroad
Buying a Property: Retiring Abroad
Buying a Property: France
Buying a Property: Spain
Buying a Property: Italy
Buying a Property: Portugal
Buying a Property: Ireland
Buying a Property: Florida
Buying a Property: Greece
Buying a Property: Turkey
Buying a Property: Cyprus
Buying a Property: Eastern Europe

Related titles

Working and Living: France
Working and Living: Spain
Working and Living: Italy
Working and Living: Portugal
Working and Living: Australia
Working and Living: New Zealand
Working and Living: Canada
Working and Living: USA

Forthcoming titles

Starting a Business: France
Starting Business: Spain

Conceived and produced for Cadogan Guides by
Navigator Guides Ltd, The Old Post Office, Swanton
Novers, Melton Constable, Norfolk, NR24 2AJ
info@navigatorguides.com
www.navigatorguides.com

Cadogan Guides
2nd Floor, 233 High Holborn,
London, WC1V 7DN
info@cadoganguides.co.uk
www.cadoganguides.com

The Globe Pequot Press
246 Goose Lane, PO Box 480, Guilford,
Connecticut 06437–0480

Cover designs: Sarah Rianhard-Gardner
Cover photographs: © Tim Mitchell
Series editor: Linda McQueen
Editor: Susannah Wight
Proofreader: Ali Qassim
Indexing: Isobel McLean

Printed in Finland by WS Bookwell

A catalogue record for this book is available from
   the British Library
ISBN 1-86011-180-7

The author and publishers have made every effort
to ensure the accuracy of the information in this
book at the time of going to press. However, they
cannot accept any responsibility for any loss,
injury or inconvenience resulting from the use
of information contained in this guide.

Please help us to keep this guide up to date. We
have done our best to ensure that the information
in it is correct at the time of going to press. But
places are constantly changing, and rules and
regulations fluctuate. We would be delighted to
receive any comments concerning existing entries
or omissions. Authors of the best letters will receive
a copy of the Cadogan Guide of their choice.

Introduction

01

Around a million and a half of us in Britain own property abroad. It's no secret that home ownership is the nation's new obsession, nor that we are looking farther than the familiar neighbouring countries of France, Spain and Italy. Thirty years ago, there were derelict farmhouses in Tuscany and Provence, which property-hungry Brits began to look at tentatively and eventually snapped up; now these regions have reached saturation point and property prices are beyond most people's reach. Now, with relative peace in Eastern Europe, greater accessibility with the rise of cheap airlines and accession to the European Union (EU), personal investors are looking at the region afresh. The fall of the Iron Curtain has opened our eyes to the grand old cities and the tranquillity of the countryside of Eastern Europe. The seaside resorts of Bulgaria and Croatia have been compared to Italy in the 1950s, while the capital of Slovenia is said by some to be like Dublin 10 years ago. A recent poll of top US firms revealed that 46 per cent consider Eastern Europe their preferred location for investment.

View this book as a companion, as if your best friend were giving you all the essential information you need to buy your perfect property. We take you step by step through the whole procedure, from choosing your country right through to the all-important tax breaks. Whether you are looking for a heavenly place to retire to or a sure way to make an investment, this guide leads you through the property maze, from the tourist centres of Prague and Dubrovnik to the rural peace of the Slovak and Bulgarian countryside. You will find advice on how to make the best of business opportunities, and on your financial situation if you decide to retire in Eastern Europe. From renovating a Slovakian shack to buying a luxury serviced apartment, we give you legal and financial advice and tell you what to consider in terms of facilities, even advising you on the food available to eat.

Buying a property in Eastern Europe can be nearly – but not quite – as safe as buying a property in England, France or the USA. It can also be an excellent investment – your opportunity to get into a market ahead of the majority of people and to enjoy the rewards reaped by those who invested in, say, Nice or Marbella 50 years ago. Or it can be a disaster: you could buy an overpriced property with no legal title and no planning permission; the house is bulldozed; the land is repossessed by its true owner. You lose your shirt.

On reading a book such as this – which must explain the potential pitfalls if it is to serve any useful purpose – buying a property can seem a frightening or dangerous experience. But if you go about the purchase in the right way it is not ridiculously dangerous and should not be frightening. True, the danger is greater than when buying in England or other, more established, markets, that is inescapable. Some risks that can be eliminated in the established markets cannot be completely excluded in the emerging markets. Some enquiries that can be made, for example, in England cannot or are not made in Eastern Europe. But by taking sensible precautions and professional advice, those dangers can be reduced to an acceptable level, commensurate with the potential rewards on offer.

In general the same or similar dangers arise when buying a house in any market. Is what you have been told about the property true? Is the property in good physical condition? Does it have proper legal title? Does it have all the necessary planning consents? Are there any restrictions on my freedom to use the property? Is the way I am thinking of owning the property – the proposed legal structure of the ownership – going to minimise my tax and inheritance problems? The difference is that in other – more mature – markets these dangers have been recognised for many years and are better understood and controlled.

If you are in any doubt as to the dangers that exist even in an ancient and well regulated market such as that in England, look briefly at a textbook on English property law. You do not worry about those dangers because you are familiar with them and, more importantly, because you are shielded against contact with most of them by your lawyer.

The same should be true when buying abroad. Read this book to understand the background and why some of the problems exist. Ask your lawyers to advise you about any issues that worry you and leave them to avoid the landmines! You will then know that the transaction is being looked after by someone who understands the dangers and the ways of avoiding them – and (if they are English solicitors) who has insurance that will pay you compensation in the unlikely event that they makes a negligent mistake. One thing is clear: unless the money you are spending is 'fun money' – money that you are prepared to lose completely – you should *never* buy property in these markets without getting specialist and independent legal advice.

East or West?

This book focuses on the emerging markets in Eastern Europe and covers Bulgaria, Croatia, the Czech Republic, Estonia, Hungary, Latvia, Lithuania, Montenegro, Poland, Romania, Slovakia and Slovenia. It does not cover all of Eastern Europe, in particular Albania, Belarus, Bosnia, Serbia or the Ukraine; there is little demand for property in these countries at present.

The definition of the term 'Eastern Europe' is not without problems. Traditionally, it was an area in the east of the continent – that is to the western border of Russia. In Western Europe we tend to use it to mean all European countries that were previously under Communist rule – that is, the Eastern Bloc countries. But this is a complex region. Croatia and Montenegro were never Communist, for example, and in fact the origins of the definition are very recent. Historically,

Europe was divided north from south so that countries on the Mediterranean formed a separate half from the Atlantic Ocean and Baltic Sea countries. The term came about in the 18th century to loosely categorise those countries that were falling behind economically. Geographically, Bulgaria, Croatia and Montenegro are, strictly speaking, southeastern Europe, while the Czech and Slovak Republics, Hungary and Slovenia are Central Eastern Europe.

The European Union

The motivation for creating the EU has its roots in the Second World War, when no one wanted to see such destruction ever happening again. Winston Churchill hoped to create a 'kind of United States of Europe'. Initially, the EU consisted of just six countries: Belgium, Germany, France, Italy, Luxembourg and the Netherlands. Denmark, Ireland and the UK joined in 1973, Greece in 1981, Spain and Portugal in 1986, Austria, Finland and Sweden in 1995. In May 2004 the biggest-ever enlargement of the EU took place, with 10 new countries joining, including many in Eastern Europe; certain transitional arrangements may still apply in the case of these countries. Although to begin with much of the co-operation between the EU countries was about trade and the economy, now the EU deals with many other subjects of importance for our everyday life, such as rights, job creation, development and environmental protection.

In January 2005 the European Union (EU) contains the following: Austria, Belgium, Cyprus*, the Czech Republic*, Denmark, Estonia*, Finland, France, Germany, Greece, Hungary*, Ireland, Italy, Latvia*, Lithuania*, Luxembourg, Malta*, the Netherlands, Poland*, Portugal, Slovakia*, Slovenia*, Spain, Sweden and the United Kingdom. The countries marked * joined on 1 May 2004.

EU membership offers political stability and economic growth and eases residence for EU nationals. Money is pouring into the Eastern European countries, aimed at stimulating economic growth and improving the infrastructure. EU funding is a key issue: the newcomers are waiting to benefit from investments from companies based in Western Europe and from EU funding. Tariff and quota barriers have all but been abolished for new members, but they must agree to the *acquis communautaire*, which means applying 80,000 pages of EU law to legal and administrative structures.

The **European Economic Area (EEA)** comprises the EU countries plus Iceland, Liechtenstein and Norway.

Candidate Countries

As at January 2005 the countries awaiting possible accession to the EU are Bulgaria, Croatia, Romania and Turkey. Dates for becoming members have not yet been fixed and it is still possible that these countries may not meet the eligibility criteria for membership. If these countries join it is likely to be, in the case of Bulgaria, in 2007/8, in the case of Croatia, in 2007/8 and in the case of Romania in 2010. The joining date for Turkey is less clear; probably not before 2011/12. An application to join the EU has also been received from the former Yugoslavian Republic of Macedonia, but this is still at a preliminary pre approval stage.

Euroland

Otherwise known as the euro zone, this is the group of countries that have replaced their old national currencies with the new single European currency, the euro (€). In January 2005 these countries were: Austria, Belgium, Finland, France, Germany, Greece, Ireland, Italy, Luxembourg, the Netherlands, Portugal and Spain. Strangely, Montenegro (which is not an EU member or candidate country) also uses the euro as its currency; this is because it used to use the German Deutschmark.

A Short History of Eastern Europe

After the First World War, many countries in Eastern Europe were created for the first time. Although the idea was that they become fully fledged democracies, these young entities were knocked by the depression of the 1930s and were not strong enough to withstand other outside influences. Caught between Nazi Germany and the Soviet Union by the time of the Second World War, countries such as Hungary and Bulgaria aligned themselves with the Nazis while the former Yugoslavia strongly resisted.

By the time the war ended, the Soviet Union occupied much of Eastern Europe. Post-war poverty, unemployment and economic collapse had paralysed these countries and demoralised the people. Stalin promised Churchill and Roosevelt that the Soviet-occupied countries would be permitted to be full democracies. Instead they were subjected to full-blown Communism brought in from the east. Stalin died in March 1953 and in 1955 the Warsaw Pact was formed between the Soviet Union and the majority of the Eastern European countries. When in 1956 the Hungarians revolted against the Communists, the Soviet Union rolled in with tanks and killed thousands of people, shocking the rest of the world.

Daily Life under Communism

Housewives became used to queuing several hours a day for a limited range of goods. There would be one brand of soap and one flavour of ice-cream, and that was if they were in stock at all. No one had bank accounts and everything was paid for in cash. Although everyone was guaranteed a job, these jobs were often menial and wages were minimal. Housing was incredibly overcrowded and in very short supply. Local transport was good but it was against the law to travel outside the Eastern Bloc. Education and healthcare was available to all. Crime was low but corruption rife. There was no freedom of speech and religion was suppressed. There were secret police and trials were rigged. One writer who tried to describe the effects of daily degradation is the Romanian Norman Manea, who wrote of the 'terrible derailments of history, of society, of the psyche' that afflicted these countries first under fascism and then under Communism. 'A whole nation subjugated, hungry, humiliated, and forced to celebrate the crime ceaselessly. Life is a series of postponements, a tumour-like growth of mistrust and fear, an all-encompassing schizophrenia. A step-by-step reduction of private life, and finally its abolition... You would gradually stop seeing your friends because the buses ran very infrequently and were overcrowded...and because you...were sick of repeating the same lament for the billionth time, and because you didn't want to face the other's defeat – marked each time by new wrinkles – and recognise it as your own.'

Life in Eastern Europe Today

Inevitably, there is a certain amount of nostalgia for the Communist years. Many people miss the days when everything was black and white and when, as long as you kept quiet you had a job, food on the table and paid-for holidays. Since the series of revolutions in 1989, Communist parties have been voted back into power in most of these countries and consistently get around 15 per cent of the vote. In Prague there is even a Museum of Communism above McDonald's.

In rural communities in countries such as Hungary and Slovakia, there are concerns that EU regulations and the cutting back of subsidies to as much as one-quarter could sound the death knell for small farmers. In addition, agricultural changes pose a huge threat for wild and bird life on the undeveloped coasts and in the flower covered meadows and dense forests.

However, some are convinced that it is worth the price. 'I can't stop rejoicing that I live in this time and can participate in it – whether potatoes will be more expensive seems negligible compared to this,' Vaclav Havel the playwright and former Czech president who led his country out of Communism, told the world.

In terms of industry, car production in Eastern Europe is set to increase by a third, and sales by 50 per cent, according to a recent report. The Economist Intelligence Unit (EIU) predicts that the Eastern European economy will be boosted by car production, with output increased from 2.3 million cars in 1999 to 3 million in 2005. However, this doesn't mean that the car market will be swamped by old-fashioned Ladas and the like. The big companies have been investing in Central and Eastern Europe to build facilities to produce cars for the rest of the world too. Daewoo, Peugeot-Citroën and Toyota have interests in the Czech Republic as well as several other Eastern European countries. However, analysts suggest that it is unlikely that the car manufacturers will shift much more of their production eastwards in the near future, given that their Western European factories have excess capacity.

The Justice System

As a hangover from the days of Communism, all the countries in this guide have at best creakingly slow justice systems; at worst they are corrupt. Bribery is still rife and the grip of the mafia is still strong. Polls in some countries show that as few as 30 per cent of people actually trust the justice system in their country and that a staggering 60 per cent think they would need to bribe individuals in a court proceeding. In one court, one out of five people had seen a judge being bribed. In the Czech Republic over 3,000 cases are over seven years old, a sad testament to the fact that things have improved little since the days of Kafka immortalising the terrifying social systems of his country. Investigations by the International Monetary Fund showed that Czech judges had little understanding of the latest financial and commercial law.

Why Buy in Eastern Europe?

Most people thinking of buying property in Eastern Europe are attracted by relatively cheap property prices compared with the UK. But beyond that, unless you are simply making an unemotional investment, you are likely to have some kind of affinity with the country you choose. It may be that you saw a travel article and something about the landscape appealed, or there may be practical reasons: you have family there, or you want to retire with a higher standard of living. Whatever the reason, you need to be clear about what you want to get from your property. It is no good buying a tumble-down stone house on a Croatian island to fulfil a romantic ambition if you are never going to visit or renovate it; although you may be able to sell it on several years down the track, you will not be able to let it out in the meantime.

Investment

In 2004, just three months after joining the European Union, property prices in the new Central and Eastern European member countries have stabilised following steep price rises in 2003. The massive increases were in anticipation of and even panic about money to be made by following these nations joining the EU. Some experts say that prices in parts of the Czech Republic have doubled over the last year and that the case was much the same in Hungary. Well-chosen property in popular destinations offers huge potential.

As badly constructed postwar Communist housing is literally disintegrating, the supply of new housing will soon become extremely important. Some experts say that about a third of the new EU member states' population will have to be rehoused in the next 20 years, and 24 million people will need somewhere to rent or buy.

While Croatia and Prague seem to have to boomed already in terms of property prices, countries like Bulgaria, Slovenia and Slovakia appear like fledgling birds ready to turn into swans. But making money from property in this region is by no means a sure thing, and you have to pick your country and property carefully. While there seems to be a growing trend in this country and around the world to believe in property as a substitute for a pension, it is worth remembering that the days of negative equity, when people lost fortunes and their homes, were only around 10 years ago.

A Second Home

Not everyone who is looking to buy property in this region is interested solely in investment. Some will be enticed by the generally slower pace of life, where there is more emphasis on family and less on work. Choosing Eastern Europe as a second home may perhaps be more adventurous than buying in Italy and Spain. When British people first started buying in Spain 20 or so years ago, it was thought incredibly risky and daring. Now it seems that everyone is doing it; there is also a large expatriate community of British holidaymakers in countries such as Spain and Italy, which you will not find in 'New Europe'.

Although some people in the larger cities and tourist areas of Eastern Europe speak some English, because the largest group of tourists to those countries to date have been German, this is the most commonly spoken foreign language. Also, the food, language and culture is largely foreign. Despite the fact that the countries dealt with in this book have either joined or are about to join the EU, Western European standards clearly can't be expected. Indeed, the attitude of people in Eastern European countries to environmental issues, the treatment of animals and corruption may shock you.

Don't Believe the Hype

This book comes with a warning. Thanks to television programmes like *Get a New Life*, people are following a dream. But according to some reports, as many as 35 per cent of people are coming back, having found their chosen country too hot, difficult or lonely – and that includes countries with large expatriate communities. Some experts say that as many as 90 per cent of the people looking to relocate overseas have something wrong in their life and are expecting their country of choice to solve all their problems. In many cases they are seeking something unattainable, and are risking everything by moving to a place that they know nothing about.

Starting a Business

During the early 1990s there was a somewhat frenzied surge in investment in Eastern Europe, resulting in burnt fingers for many hopeful people. But since 2000 the economies of these countries have in some ways outperformed those in the West. However, despite incredible move from Communism to capitalism, potential entrepreneurs considering setting up a business in the area may have to face endemic corruption, inadequate business regulation and generally poor organisation.

How is Buying in Eastern Europe Different from Buying at Home?

Because You Are a Pioneer!

If you are a foreigner buying a property in, say, Spain, the path is well trodden. Literally millions of other foreigners have already done it. Every estate agent, lawyer, notary, tax office and town hall has dealt with dozens – if not hundreds – of sales. As a result, officials have established guidelines to regulate how they interpret the rules. There are still potential dangers and pitfalls but they are well understood. The solutions to most of the common problems were worked out many years ago and many lawyers are familiar with them. That does not mean that your transaction will automatically go without a hitch, but the problems are set in a context that is well understood and, generally, stable.

By contrast, if you are buying a home in Montenegro or Slovakia you could be the first foreign buyer that the person dealing with you has ever come across. That is true for the real estate agent, the lawyer, the notary and the officers at the tax department or Land Registry. As a result they will, probably, not know what to do. They may ask for information over and above what was asked for last time you dealt with the same office or they may impose their own procedure. They may interpret the law differently from the way their colleague at the next desk did last week. The rules they have to follow may not fit the case of foreigners neatly or clearly. Some of the documents needed by local people may not exist in the case of foreigners, or they may not know the special rules that apply to foreigners. They will not be familiar with 'international' documents – such as a power of attorney prepared in another country and authenticated under the Hague Convention.

In many cases you are dealing with low-paid public officials, many of them still deeply embedded with the old Soviet era mentality of not rocking the boat, not doing anything to draw attention. This is particularly the case in rural areas rather than in the big cities, which are the more prestigious posting for the career minded official. Many of the officials you deal with might, therefore, not be trained to the level you have come to expect when dealing with people in equivalent positions in the UK. As a result, one of three things happens:

- **They might simply find a reason why they can't deal with the problem today, hoping that when it comes back someone else will be on duty; sometimes a small financial payment is required to focus their mind.**

- **They may just refuse to accept the application or a document, despite the fact that is perfectly valid and was probably accepted by their colleague in the same office last week. Refusal is usually easier and less dangerous than making what your boss considers to be the wrong decision.**

- **They might let it go through, despite the fact that it is patently wrong. At best this approach leads to unnecessary delay and to wasted time. At worst it can put you in breach of a contractual deadline and threaten your deal.**

As a result, sometimes UK buyers and their solicitors have to redo many times documents already accepted, have to rethink the strategy to fit in with the official's requirements, end up in cul-de-sacs, make unnecessary detours, or stand their ground and confront the official with the law and the practice of his colleagues. On other occasions it is faster, easier and cheaper for our clients to give in and do things the way the official wants.

This is all part and parcel of being a pioneer! You have to accept the bumpy bits. Just like the settlers travelling across America to the Wild West you will have to put up with a bit of discomfort. You do this knowing that the country-side is beautiful and there are untold riches just over the horizon.

Language

At a pinch, if you buy a house in Spain or France you can get by without speaking a word of the local language – and thousands of buyers do just that. Even in these countries, speaking the language will pay huge rewards and you will get a lot more pleasure out of your property but so many people speak English – especially in the main tourist areas – that this is not essential.

In these emerging market countries you cannot expect everyone to speak English. Surprising numbers do but, in most Eastern European countries you cannot expect the official at the tax office, the taxi driver or the shop assistant to at the builders' merchants to speak (fluent) English.

Disregard for the Rules and Little Redress

In every country there is a certain amount of rule-bending, but in many Eastern Europe countries it is unusual for the rules to be followed at all. This is seen in many different areas of life, in particular the acceptance of black (under-the-counter, unofficial, undeclared) money and the tendency to build first and get permission later.

In more developed markets there is usually a fairly sophisticated and functioning system of legal redress if things go wrong. Nobody wants to go to court, but if it is necessary to do so you go there comforted by the fact that the process will be reasonably fast and fair. In some of the emerging market countries this is not so and imost of them the court system is very slow and unreliable. This is made worse because, up to now, there have been few foreigners owning property and so few disputes that have needed to go to court. As a result the courts and lawyers concerned have little experience of dealing with foreigners. This makes it even more important to get things right at the outset, for example by drafting a contract in a way that minimises misunderstandings or circumvention.

You Probably Don't Know The Countries Well

Most people buying a home in, for example, Spain or France already know the area quite well. They may have been there for many holidays. They will have read about it and seen lots of programmes about it on television. They probably know not only that area but other areas in the country and other areas in other countries, so that they are in a position to decide which area is going to best suit their particular requirements. Eastern European countries are less well known. Most have only been accessible as tourist destinations for the last few years and, even then, have been little visited by tourists. In addition, many people buying in these emerging market destinations are buying primarily for investment purposes, attracted not so much by the thought of a particular place in a particular country as by the potential for growth and revenue that each presents; *see* pp.7–8.

Summary

Buying in the emerging markets is not for a person who gets upset if the train is 10 minutes late. So why would you want to buy there? There are a number of reasons. Many are buying as an investment. Others love the country, the people and the lifestyle. They are buying *because* it is still authentically 'foreign'. For them the investment potential is, at best, a side issue and, at worst, a threat to the qualities they love in the place. Some are simply buying superb property in stunning locations for their own use at prices they could not afford elsewhere.

Although this is no different from buying in a foreign country elsewhere in the past, clients' expectations are now far higher than they were 25 years ago, enlarging the gulf between what they expect and what can be delivered. However, although the system is different in Eastern Europe countries and less sophisticated than what you might be used to, thousands of local people buy property each year and obtain 'clean' title to a property built with the necessary planning consents, and which is free from debts, charges and other burdens.

Money, Law and Terminology

In this book **prices** are given in local currencies with an approximate conversion into sterling. Exchange rates vary wildly over time and in a few years the figures given will probably be treated with either nostalgia or amusement. At the time of writing, €1 = c. £0.68. Prices quoted are usually only rough estimates.

This book is intended primarily for people from England and Wales and comparisons are therefore drawn with **English law**. Scots law is somewhat different. Where the points apply also to Scots law, depending on the context, reference is made either to UK or British law. There are several references to the US legal and tax system, which gives rise to a number of language issues, as the terminology used by Americans is, in some cases, different from that used on the other side of the Atlantic. In some places two terms are used (e.g. 'You need to arrange for a survey or inspection'). In other places this doesn't work too well. The law is intended to be up to date as at 1 January 2005.

Most English people are bad at languages so wherever possible or sensible we use **English terms**, often accompanied by the local term. Be careful when trying to translate legal and financial terminology, because it can relate to institutions, systems or procedures that do not have an equivalent in the other country. In these circumstances translations can give a false sense of familiarity.

We use standard terminology in this book to make it easier for you to understand the steps being taken, especially relating to the signing of contracts. The **reservation contract** is the document you may sign at the outset of the transaction; *see* p.75. This is, in some respects, similar to an English option contract. The **preliminary contract** is the contract that you sign to commit yourself to the purchase of the property; *see* pp.75–6. This is, in some respects, similar to the English purchase contract. The **final contract** is the document that finalises the sale of the property to you; *see* p.82. This is in some respects similar to an English property transfer form or deed of conveyance.

Travel and Tourism in Eastern Europe

Financial experts suggest that air traffic will increase by 20 per cent more a year on routes to new EU countries. The pound has fallen about 10 per cent against the euro in the year from May 2004 to April 2005, and, as a result, already high hotel rates in the euro zone have risen even further, making countries new to the EU more appealing than ever. Tour operators say that many four-star hotels in Bulgaria and Croatia are about the same price as three-star hotels in Spain, Portugal, France and Italy.

Part of the appeal of Eastern European countries is the curiosity factor; it is not just about getting value for money. In 2004 the budget airline easyJet announced an extension of its Eastern European services. The carrier has established daily flights to Budapest from Newcastle and Bristol airports and has estimated that it will carry more than 2 million passengers on its Eastern European routes over the next 12 months (to May 2006). The Bratislava-based airline SkyEurope is rapidly increasing its services, and Hungary's Wizz Air took off towards the end of 2004. A report published by holiday firm Thomson in 2005 predicts that Slovakia and cities in Slovenia will be among the top tourist destinations in 20 years' time.

From 2007 to 2015 there will be further widening of travel routes within the European Union, and journeys through EU countries have become progressively easier over the years with the removal of most passport and baggage formalities, and with the introduction of the euro in 12 of the EU countries. A borderless system all the way from Donegal to Dubrovnik has been created, and visitors, can now compare prices directly and no longer have the cost and inconvenience of exchanging money.

If you are buying with the intention of letting to holidaymakers, these statistics make Eastern Europe particularly attractive in investment terms.

How to Use This Book

This book is divided into two parts. The first part deals with the things that are (more or less) the same in each of the countries covered. These include, for example, the preparations you should be making before you begin to look for property, how to go about finding property, special factors to consider when buying investment property, the UK tax treatment of your ownership of overseas property and so on. The second part has chapters on each country in turn, and describes any points that are particular to them.

It may well be worth reading the first part of the book from beginning to end (ignoring any sections that obviously don't apply to your situation) before reading whichever of the country-specific sections are of interest to you.

Disclaimer

Although we have done our best to cover most topics of interest to the buyer of a property in these markets, a guide of this kind cannot take into account every individual's personal circumstances and the size of the book means that the advice cannot be comprehensive. The book is intended as a starting point that will enable people who are thinking of buying property to understand some of the issues involved and to ask the necessary questions of their professional advisers. *It is no substitute for professional advice*. The author and the publishers cannot accept any liability for any action taken or not taken as a result of this book.

Where in Eastern Europe?

02

If you know only that you want to buy in Eastern Europe, but have no idea in which country, you have a lot of factors to consider. The countries dealt with in this book have been chosen because they represent good locations for investment. Most, apart from Montenegro, either joined the EU in May 2004 or are due to join in the next wave of new members. Narrowing down your search can be done by working out your list of 'musts'. For example, if you decide you definitely want somewhere by the sea, you will not be interested in Hungary, the Czech Republic or Slovakia, and only a tiny part of Slovenia will appeal.

Very broadly, those locations with easy access to Western Europe are more expensive. The Czech Republic is as far west as you can get while still being in Eastern Europe, while Montenegro can seem like another continent. The further east you go, the longer you have to travel from Western Europe and the less attractive it is to travel overland, a factor which is reflected in property prices.

If you are buying for your own use, the choice of location and type of property you buy is down to personal preference. You are probably buying a home overseas because you have been reasonably successful in life. One of the rewards of such success should be the ability to do as you please. It is too easy to forget, as you become immersed in the detailed planning for the purchase, that this whole exercise is supposed to be fun. If you want to throw caution to the wind and buy the house of your dreams, there is nothing wrong with doing so – provided you understand that this is what you are doing. If you are buying as an investment, however, other considerations apply. Personal preference – in the simple sense of 'does it appeal to me' – is then a dangerous distraction. The considerations are dealt with in the chapter on investment property later in this book. In either case, do your research. The time spent will be fun and amply repaid.

Getting to Know the Areas

The best way to find out about the areas is to travel extensively, in summer and in winter. The need to know a place in both seasons cannot be over-emphasised. Some summer resorts close down almost completely in the winter and a climate which was so agreeable in June can be awful in January. The place that was a tranquil 20-minute drive from town in May might well involve a two-hour nose-to-tail ordeal in August.

A fair substitute for an initial visit is a bit of reading. General travel guides to the various countries, such as those listed in the country-specific parts of this book, can give you a reasonable feel for what a place will be like. Follow that up with reading about the areas that interest you, television programmes and so on, and you will be ready for a productive exploratory visit. Libraries, the internet and tourist boards are good sources of information.

Most people know within a few minutes of arriving in a town whether it is somewhere they would like to live. A two-week self-drive holiday, using some inexpensive small hotels, can cover a lot of ground. Take a large-scale map or motoring atlas. Be a vandal. Write your comments about the places you visit on the page, otherwise you will never remember which was which. Buy some postcards to remind you of the scenery or take a video or digital camera. Pick up a copy of the local paper. Even if you do not speak the language, it will give you some idea of what goes on in the area and also supply details of local estate agents and so on. Visit the local tourist office for more information about the area and an idea of what goes on throughout the year. Look in estate agents' window and make a note – again on the map – of the sort of prices you will have to pay for property of the type that interests you. But *don't go inside*. Make it an absolute rule that you will not look at any properties. If you do you will be caught in the classic trap of focusing on bricks and mortar rather than the area. What matters most is the area where you are going to live. There are nice houses in every area. Provided the initial look at prices doesn't make you faint, if you like the town, mark it on the map with a big tick and move on to the next place. If it is not for you, mark the map with a big cross and move on.

If you are looking for somewhere to live, rather than a pure investment, once you have shortlisted your two or three most likely places visit them in summer and winter. Spend a little time there. Make contact with estate agents and look at property to your heart's content.

For information about choosing a property with the intention of letting it, *see* 'Letting Your Property', pp.118–21.

Climate and Geography

Most British people buying abroad are motivated in large measure by the thought of a better climate. What is 'better' depends on your personal perspective. If the property is for retirement, the buyers will want a climate that is acceptable all year round. If the property is a holiday home the buyers will be looking for a climate that appeals to them at the time is when they are most likely to use the property. If the property is for investment and for letting to holidaymakers they will be looking for a long rental season.

From the heights of the Czech Republic's Bohemian massif to the warm shores of southern Croatia, the geography of the countries covered in this book is hugely varied and the climate may surprise you. For example, despite being close to north and central Europe, Hungary enjoys long hot summers. Bulgaria's beach resorts have high temperatures from June to September but in winter are often freezing with local airports closed. While the climate in the north of

Croatia is more similar to that of its northern neighbours, high temperatures in the south can make you feel as if you are in a different country entirely. For specific details of climate and geography, see the 'References' sections of the respective countries.

Remember that temperature and rainfall charts do not tell the whole story. Wind, lack of shelter, altitude and other factors can greatly influence your perception of the climate, which is what really matters. A place where it rains a bit on 200 days per year will *seem* wetter than a place with the same amount of rainfall but where it only rains for 120 days. Figures can also conceal substantial daily variations. As always, the best advice is to go and visit your short-listed areas in both summer and winter. Key indicators are the monthly maximum temperatures, the monthly minimum temperatures, the monthly rainfall pattern and the monthly hours of sunshine.

Access

Second only to climate in most people's decision-making process is the question of access to the property. How will you travel there? How will your family and friends travel? How will you get about whilst visiting?

Getting There

For those who live in the southern part of England, travelling to the nearer parts of Eastern Europe by car ferry or tunnel is increasingly popular. The roads in Western Europe are good and those in Eastern Europe are rapidly getting better. At least the early part of your journey can be fast or picturesque and interesting, at your choice. Travelling by car from the north of England may be less pleasant. There is interesting research in the tourist industry that suggests that if visitors have a journey of more than an hour by road at either end of their journey, 25 per cent will not bother to travel. More than 1½ hours and 50 per cent won't bother. This may not concern you, but it is worth bearing in mind as far as family and friends are concerned. It is even more relevant if you are thinking of letting your property to the British market.

Most people travel by air, and there are now a number of budget carriers that fly to many – but not all – destinations in Eastern Europe. To use these services easily you will need Internet access. Budget airlines are changing the way people are looking at this part of the world. If **Ryanair** or **easyJet** fly to an airport near you, it can make a huge difference to the value of your property, and new flights are being added all the time. In 2004 **easyJet** began flying into Slovenia's capital, opening the country up to many who had never considered visiting it before. If such airlines are about to introduce new routes, and you buy a property before they begin operating, you may find yourself a bargain. Watch out for agents promising that budget flights are about to be introduced, though. It may just be a sales tactic; and budget routes get dropped as often as they get started, which has caught out a lot of people buying holiday homes in France. Be aware that there are often restrictions with cheap flights; you may find that British Airways or the national carrier of the country you are going to can offer competitive prices and take you to more mainstream destinations.

Not all airports will have the facilities you require. In some smaller towns and cities there may be limited services. In some places– such as those on Bulgaria's coast – regional airports may even close down altogether out of season. Don't just look at airports in the country you are considering. Because of the geography of Eastern Europe, all of the countries in this book have several neighbours and there may be a convenient airport just across the border. For example, a number of parts of Slovenia are easily accessed from Austria; the Slovak's Republic capital is only 30 miles away from Vienna; and Istria in the north of Croatia is just a couple of hours' drive from Trieste in Italy. Although Ryanair flies into Trieste, this last option is not without its disadvantages if you don't have your own transport; bus and train connections are tricky.

Just as there is evidence of the maximum distance people are happy to travel at each end of their air journey, there is some evidence about the maximum distances people are prepared to actually fly without protest. People travelling abroad for a weekend do not usually want to travel more than a maximum of three hours and would prefer to travel no more than for two hours. For longer-duration holidays, the preference is to travel for no more than five hours.

It is also worth paying particular attention to the ease of access to the destination during the winter months. One of the penalties of being a pioneer is that, in the early years, communications are less developed than they will be in a few years' time. For example, for the moment it is not possible to fly directly from the UK to Dubrovnik in Croatia during the winter months; you have to fly via Zagreb, which adds several hours to the journey time. There are similar problems when flying to the Black Sea coast of Bulgaria. As the situation in these countries stabilises, they will become more popular and this should lead to more flights being provided.

Getting Around Once You Have Arrived

If you are buying a home for retirement, is it in a place that will still be accessible in 20 or 30 years' time? Or will you be uncomfortable driving up the twisting mountain access road at the age of 85? Is there any public transport? There will be times when you will need it. Your car may need repair. You may have broken a leg. You may be invited to a boozy party.

Think about travel once you have arrived by air or train. Most people either hire a car or own their own 'local' car, which they leave at the house or (better) in the airport car park waiting for their next visit. It is worth doing a careful price comparison. Surprisingly often, the cost of insuring, taxing and maintaining a local car plus airport parking and the depreciation in its value can amount to nearly as much as – or more than – renting a new, clean car on each visit, which requires no 'management' on your part. Renting also means you can choose the type of car you need for that particular visit. Look at cheap, local car hire companies as well as the big names, who sometimes have surprisingly good deals available.

If you do not have a car, local transport is key. How easy is it for you to get to the nearest shops and how far will you have to carry your shopping? Without your own vehicle, the proximity of the nearest bus stop is important. One woman who bought a cottage in Slovakia based her choice partly on the fact that her home would be on a bus route with a good service which was unlikely to be cut back because it supplied a local factory.

Finally, how will your children or visitors travel when they arrive in the area? Will they have to or be able to rent a car? Remember that many car hire companies have a minimum age limit of 25. Is there any public transport? Will you be an unpaid taxi service for the duration of anyone's visit?

Facilities

Your future happiness in the home you buy will depend on the facilities in the area. Each person will have different requirements. Are you a golfer? If so, just one or two golf courses in the vicinity is unlikely to satisfy you for long. Are you thinking of retiring to the area? If so you will need a major shopping centre within an hour or so by car. Do you visit the theatre or opera? What is available? Are you sociable? Is this an area where you will find 'your kind of (English-speaking?) people'? Do you expect your teenage children to visit? If so, is there anything for them in the area?

If you are planning actually to live in the country concerned, you are not just choosing a property but a lifestyle. Those with children need to make sure local education is of a good enough standard, which for the vast majority will mean finding an international school as few will have children who speak the local language. Health facilities are another crucial factor, especially if you are moving to retire and have ongoing medical complaints. Shopping opportunities are important, too. Don't forget that Communism has not been gone long and during those days food was very much a necessity rather than a luxury. Local people had to make do with what was available and generally accepted the situation; even today, standards are not the same as we are used to in the West. You make feel as if you have died and gone to heaven when you purchase a lovely old stone house with its own mooring on a Croatian island. Messing about on your boat and sipping leisurely coffees in beachfront cafés may be your dream life, but when you find out that the local shops (there are no real

Case Study: Food for Thought

As a confirmed bachelor and hardworking architect, Dave Healey never cooked his own food at home. 'I would invariably leave the office late and come home to put a pre-prepared meal in the oven. It was usually something from Marks & Spencer – chicken with dauphinoise potatoes, say, or beef bourguignon. I might steam some green beans to have with it, but dessert would be a ready-made trifle or something similar. During the weekends, I ate at good London restaurants.' When he bought a villa on the shores of Hungary's Lake Balaton Dave got a shock. Nearby shops stocked no pre-made foods and there were no beans from Kenya or fruits out of season. 'I wasn't really prepared for the difference in what was available. I had found out a lot about the culture and landscape of the country, but I just hadn't considered the local food. To begin with, I got quite depressed and even considered going back to London. Good food is an important part of my life and not something I think of as a luxury. When friends came to visit I made sure they were laden down with supplies from Waitrose or M & S. They had to bring one suitcase for their things and one suitcase full of supplies for me. It wasn't just obvious things like Marmite that I missed, it was everything.'

This went on for several months, with Dave going to local restaurants in the evening and becoming more used to the local food. He visited one restaurant in particular quite frequently and became friendly with the manager, Eva – so friendly that he married her. 'The funny thing is that Eva doesn't really like to cook, and anyway, working in a restaurant all day means it is the last thing she wants to do when she gets home.

'She began taking me to the market and gave me a cookery book for my birthday with recipes for Hungarian dishes. It makes much more sense economically, and some say even medically, to eat local foods in season. It is quite obscene that in the UK we fly green beans all the way from Kenya in winter and expect to have South African grapes all year round. Now I really enjoy picking the freshest local produce and I can cook up a mean goulash, complete with paprika, and a delicious stew using locally caught fish.'

limited and expensive supply of food – most supplies need to be shipped from the mainland, which increases costs – you may feel like packing it all in. The choice of produce in rural areas throughout this region is often limited. Most local people have a relatively basic diet, eating dishes made with regional foods, with few exotic or convenience foods.

City-dwellers who have decided to make the move to the country have even more to consider. Are you really prepared for rural life in a foreign country? It is easy to be driven into the ground by the traffic and pollution in London, but how much do you take for granted? Most people living in central London have within walking distance a choice of bus or tube transport and a corner shop open late into the night. There are all kinds of galleries, theatres, restaurants and bars and you are never far away from another human being. Relocating to the country may seem to represent some peaceful utopia in which all the stresses of modern life disappear. You may fondly imagine that being sur-rounded by green hills will instantly soothe you and that the tranquillity will be good for your soul, only to find the lack of excitement is killing you. Even if you do fall in love with rural life, it will bring its own problems. You won't be able to pop round to a neighbour for a chat and a coffee. If there is any kind of emergency, help is much further away and you can easily feel isolated.

It may be that you decide that you are happy to live in a remote location but that you will make regular journeys into the city. One couple built their own wooden house in the countryside in the Czech Republic but it was only just over an hour's drive to Prague. They made the effort to travel in at least once a week to shop, eat out and take in cultural events. It was worth the couple of hours in the car to give them their fix of city life.

Going to the cinema may be important to you but the chances are films will not be shown in English. You may have to content yourself with hiring DVDs or videos, in which case a local video shop is a necessity. One tip if you are a film buff is to subscribe to an online service that regularly delivers the DVDs of your choice to your home – you return the ones you have watched by post.

Expatriate Communities

Some people looking for a location in a foreign country will want to be near to an expat community; others will want to be as far away from Brits as possible. Of course, if you are looking for a property to let to holidaymakers, you will be seeking somewhere that is popular with tourists and that will have at least some foreign residents.

There are two camps of individuals who want to buy abroad. The first intends to immerse him or herself in local culture, learn the language and live as a local. The second wants some reminders of home and other Brits to talk to and socialise with. Eastern Europe is not like Spain or France, where you find large numbers of English people who seem to overwhelm the local way of life. They go to English pubs, eat Heinz baked beans and never learn the language. You may find small pockets of Brits in cities such as Prague and in some parts of the south of Croatia, but they are generally assimilated into local life. In Budapest there is a large community of Irish natives, while in summer it can feel as if Dubrovnik is home to more foreigners than locals.

If you pick somewhere where there is an existing foreign population, the price of property will already be somewhat inflated. Interest from people overseas may suggest you have identified an attractive location, but this will be reflected in the amount you have to pay for the privilege of purchasing property there.

Selecting a Property

03

Once you have narrowed down your choices to a country, and ideally a town, city or area within that country, only then is it time to start researching individual properties.

Fixing a Budget

Fix a budget for the operation. What is the maximum that you are prepared to spend to end up with a house ready to live in? Include the cost of purchase, any essential repairs or improvements and all the taxes and fees payable. If you are buying a new property or one that does not need major repair, this is fairly simple. If you are buying a house in need of repair, fixing a budget is clearly more difficult. You will always underestimate the cost of the repairs. No job ever finishes exactly on budget! That is as true in an Eastern European country as it is in England.

Buyers create a rod for their own backs by their unrealistic costings. Often the extent of repairs needed goes far beyond what is obvious. It is just as expensive to repair a roof or rewire in Bulgaria as it is in Dorset. If you are buying a property that needs major work, do not commit yourself until you have had a survey and builders' estimates for the work shown to be necessary. If you are told that there is no time for this and that you will lose the property if you can't sign today, this week or before Easter, walk away.

Unless you are in the happy position that money is no object, do not exceed your budget. It is too easy, after a good lunch and in the company of a silver-tongued estate agent, to throw your financial plans to the wind. 'Only another £30,000' is a statement you may later come to regret.

When to Visit to Search for a Property

House-hunting is possible year-round, but it makes sense to see properties during the country's most popular season, especially if you will be letting it out. So, if you are looking for somewhere on the coast in Montenegro go in the summer months. In the same way, if you are considering buying in a Bulgarian ski resort, make a visit in the winter. Going during the 'shoulder' season – at the beginning or end of the most popular periods – when you will be charged lower prices and find fewer crowds.

If you have children you may be limited to school holidays when travelling and accommodation costs are usually higher than in term. Take into account public holidays, which are listed in the References section for each country. Not being able to make contact with estate agents and other companies even for just one day will be a waste of time.

Research and Information Sources

The Press

Individuals place advertisements in the 'For Sale' section of the local paper. In some towns and in popular tourist areas in the countryside there are free local newspapers – 'freesheets' – similar to those in the UK or USA. In some places there are specialist free property papers. All are likely to have adverts.

National newspapers tend to carry advertisements mainly for more expensive properties or new developments. In some areas there are specialist magazines which exist primarily to carry advertisements from private individuals selling their property. Some have just a local coverage, others a regional or even national coverage. Browse through a couple of newspaper kiosks and see what is on offer. Buy them all; they will give you a good general guide to prices. There are also several more glossy 'lifestyle' publications, covering property (particularly more expensive property) in some popular tourist areas. Again, buy the lot. They will be full of useful information.

Private individuals advertise in the main specialist British property press such as *Homes Overseas*, *World of Property* and *Private Villas*. Also try more general publications such as *Daltons Weekly* and *Exchange & Mart*, especially for cheaper property. You may also find advertisements from private sellers in *The Sunday Times*, weekend *Telegraph* and *Mail on Sunday*. Generally speaking, private individuals advertising in the British press are British.

The Internet

Many people will start their search on the Internet – *see* the information for each country for more on this subject. There will be at least two or three estate agents with information in English for all the countries covered in this book, many of which are listed in the resource section for each country. The sites vary in their searchability, standard of photographs and level of English, but most are reasonably good and carry detailed information about the properties for sale.

There is a huge amount of property available for private sale on the Internet. Finding it can sometimes be tricky. Remember that you should search (if you can) in the local language as well as in English. For example, in Bulgaria, the following combinations in the search box have been proven to work in Google:

+property + 'for sale' + Bulgaria
+house + 'for sale' + Bulgaria
+apartment + 'for sale' + Bulgaria

You can further limit the geographical area by typing in the name of the place where the property is located, but this has very mixed results because of the various different ways people enter the details of the property they are selling.

The best bet is probably to use a province or city as the limiter:

+apartment + 'for sale' + Burgas
+house + 'for sale' + Bansko

Always try the Internet. It is full of useful information. But do not fall in love with a property you find there. All too often you will find that it has been sold and not removed from the website. Treat the Internet as a way of finding what types of property are available in any area and at what price. If what you find has not sold, treat it as a big bonus.

Property Exhibitions

Although the focus of property exhibitions is predictably on countries like Italy and Spain, more and more of them are representing Eastern European sellers. Most of those in England will have a representative from each of the countries covered in this book, although of course it makes sense to check. They take place throughout the country, but especially in London. Entry is normally free, and these exhibitions are a good way of seeing several agents at once, although they are not a substitute for an inspection visit. Financial advisors and solicitors are usually well represented, too. Often there is a programme of seminars covering key regions and properties; these can be very informative.

Bear in mind that they will be about 'finding your dream', with smooth-talking salesmen in suits who have plastic models of their apartments or plots of land for off-plan buildings. No one will be telling you about the pitfalls of buying property abroad and you will not necessarily be given independent advice.

Some property exhibitions (all of which tend to have very similar names) include the **Property Investor Show** at London's ExCel Exhibition Centre, the **Invest in Property** exhibition at London's Earl's Court and the **International Property Show** in the east of London.

Seminars include topics such as 'How to Build a Property Portfolio' or 'Building Wealth Through Property'. They might focus on a particular region – such as the emerging markets or Eastern Europe – or deal with a buying property in one country. Seminars are usually led by estate agents and so the tone is invariably upbeat. Most seminars are free, although there may be a small fee charged and you normally need to put your name down in advance.

Some of the international property shows have a section where private individuals can post details of property for sale. Contact the show organisers.

Estate Agents

Estate agents catering to the international market are new in most Eastern European countries. The market itself has only existed in any volume for the last two years, so you could not expect anything else. There are some good, reliable estate agents in Eastern Europe; they can be a mine of useful information and knowledge about the area and provide practical help. Most of them are genuinely enthusiastic about property in their country and about your joining their community. Take advantage of what they have to offer, form a rapport with them, become their 'friend' (after all, they will pretend to be yours), buy a property through them...but get everything checked by your legal adviser just as you would in Britain.

Be wary of estate agents who say that their fees include services for checking out the title of the property on your behalf. Some local agents offer this service. It is dangerous. Many agents, particularly the foreign agents, know little or nothing about the intricacies of the law relating to title, or of the interaction between the East European country and the English legal system. Even if their intentions are entirely above board and honest, will you really have the confidence that they will alert you to any problems when, if you do not proceed, they will lose their commission? Remember that the Eastern European estate agent's commission is typically 5 per cent and, in the case of a foreign agent, often 15 per cent of the price of the property. That is several years' salary for the average East European. Always take independent advice.

As a preliminary step, check out all the websites you can find to get an idea for the prices and types of property available. Remember that not every agent will sell the same property at the same price. On the other hand, if you are looking for a 'different' property, possibly one inland or a project for restoration, you may well find it useful to recruit the services of a local property-finder (*see* pp.34–5).

Many of the principles that apply to selecting a property at home are the same as when looking further afield. Take all information sources with a pinch of salt. Think, 'What is the aim of this company or resource?' whether it is an estate agent or a website. However nice sales people are, their aim is to make a sale and that may involve trying (subtly) to intimidate or manipulate you. If you feel yourself on the point of panic-buying (along the lines of, 'If I don't buy this, someone else will get it and I will lose out' or 'There are only a limited number of apartments and this is my last chance'), take stock. Just like that so-called 'bargain' coat in the sales that you buy under pressure, the property that you purchase under pressure may turn out to be a bad buy. If the country, area or apartment block is such a sure thing, there will be other opportunities. Estate agents in Eastern Europe know very well that they have a lot of their clients over a barrel because they don't know the region, the market or even the language. That, coupled with the fact that you may be on a viewing trip for just a few days, makes their leverage all the stronger. So talk to as many different sources as possible. Ask your estate agent to put you in touch with previous clients. Talk to locals, people in your hotel, shop-owners.

Pick your estate agent carefully and only go with one you trust. Your decision will be a personal one, and may be based on something as simple as his or her style of selling. Some people love a smooth talker with a gift of the gab, others just want to be told the straight facts with no embellishment. Remember you are paying the agent a fee, and if you are not happy with any aspect of his or her service, say so.

You might decide to use a foreign agent, especially if you are buying some-where off the beaten track, but remember that local agents tend to have a deeper knowledge about the regions and the properties on sale. If you go to an agent in the town or area you are thinking of buying in, there may be someone who knows about important factors very specific to that location. Most foreign agents in larger tourist destinations will have an English-speaking agent, but in the countryside this is less likely. Check that the company is accredited.

Local Estate Agents

The role of the local estate agent is, superficially, similar to the role of a British estate agent. Their job is to find buyers for properties entrusted to them by a seller. But there the similarity ends.

Estate agency is a new profession in most Eastern European countries. Most have only been in business for, at the most, 10 years. Estate agents selling to foreigners are even newer. For example, in Slovakia foreigners have only been allowed to own property since 1 May 2004. As a result there is generally little tradition of service and usually little in the way of professional qualifications.

Many local agents, especially those outside the main tourist areas, will have little or no experience selling to foreigners. Few will speak good English. The agent or his staff may speak English well enough to tell you which is the bathroom and which is the kitchen but they are unlikely to be able to have an in-depth discussion with you about the proeprtry, local schooling, local healthcare provision and so on.

There are, however, still significant differences from English practice. Generally agents are rather less proactive than they are in England. This is particularly true in rural areas, especially non-tourist rural areas. You will seldom find printed property particulars or be supplied with photographs. Still less will you find usually plans or room dimensions in most estate agents' offices. They see their role as 'capturing' property to sell and then showing buyers around that property.

Many agents are either 'one-man bands' or in small firms with a limited range of property on their books. This is especially true in rural areas, but if you walk through Prague or Dubrovnik you will see evidence of the large numbers of small agents offering services to the public. This can make it difficult to get a comprehensive view of what is on the market in a locality.

There are few local or national groupings of agents and no concept of the multi-listing service. Once you have experienced this service it is hard to understand why it is not universal practice. In these countries there is little sense of co-operation and no sense of wanting to share their commission with one of their arch competitors. So you are left to trudge from agent to agent, or accept 'second best' – a property you like but don't love. Or a property that is a good investment but not superb.

Only about half the property in Eastern Europe is sold through estate agents. The rest is sold in a number of other ways. In rural areas – where there are only a small number of transactions in the year – a common method is by word of mouth. Everyone knows that Mrs Smith has died and that her house is for sale. No one from outside the areas is likely to be interested. Why do you need an estate agent? In such areas your best way of finding out what is available could be to ask at the local bar or baker's.

One of the reasons that a lot of property bypasses estate agents could be the fees that they charge. By UK (though not US) standards they are high. Generally estate agents fees are 4–10 per cent of the purchase price, depending on the value of the property and the country and area where it is located. Cheaper properties generally pay more commission than more expensive properties and properties in main tourist areas tend to pay more commission than in less sought after (and generally poorer) areas. Remember that you, the buyer, unlike in the UK, may end up paying all or part of this commission, so the level of charges is important to you.

You are probably best off starting to look for property by using an estate agent in the immediate vicinity of the place where you are looking. Many rural and some city agents will only cover an area about 20km in diameter. If you are still uncertain where precisely you intend to buy, try several adjoining agents or, if there is one in your area, one of the big chains. Local newspapers will give you an indication of which agents are advertising, and so active, in your area. You can also get names out of the local Yellow Pages. The Yellow Pages for popular areas are kept in many big city libraries in the UK. Many agents also advertise in both the local and UK specialist property press.

Estate agents also often operate as property management companies and as property letting agents. In order to do this they, generally, need a separate licence and mandate from the person letting the property. Give priority to agents who speak English.

UK-based Estate Agents

There are growing numbers of people based in the UK who sell property in Eastern Europe, and most popular areas are covered. Although under English law they are entitled to call themselves estate agents, it is important to note that in most cases they are not licensed local estate agents in the countries where licensing is required.

They very often work in association with one or more local agents, generally covering a wider area than a single local agent would cover. They tend to choose properties from the 'book' of those local agents that they think will be of particular interest to the British buyer. They then either obtain the descriptions and photographs necessary to sell those properties (if none exists) or translate the existing materials. They market the properties through exhibitions, etc. and then act as an intermediary between the potential buyer and the local estate agent – who may not speak English and may not understand either the culture or requirements of the overseas buyer. Because they deal with British buyers all the time, they should be able to anticipate some of the common problems that can arise and smooth the progress of the transaction.

Generally they should share the commission of the local agent – who is very pleased that they can expand his potential buyer base by introducing foreign buyers. Thus their services should cost you nothing extra. These people can be very useful, particularly if you have little experience of dealing with the country in which you want to buy property and don't speak the local language.

However, some charge substantial amounts of extra commission for their services, which they may not disclose to the buyer. There is nothing wrong with paying someone who is doing a useful job some commission, but you should be told that you are expected to do so. You can then decide whether the convenience of dealing with someone in Britain is worth the extra cost. Always ask for confirmation that the price you will be paying is exactly the same as you would have paid locally or, if there is an extra charge, the amount of the charge.

Some UK-based agents advertise their prices as a global price including the price of the property, tax, notary's fees and all commissions. This can be very useful for the British buyer unused to these transactions but it can also, in the hands of the unscrupulous, be a way of hiding a large element of hidden commission. Mrs Smith has agreed to sell her cottage for €50,000. Commission has been agreed at 5 per cent (€2,500) Notaries fees and taxes will amount to, say, 8 per cent (€4,000). An all-inclusive price of €60,000 therefore gives an extra hidden charge of €3,500 – well over £2,000. If you are offered property on this basis, check what the price includes.

Many of these UK-based sellers are highly experienced and very reputable. Before deciding which to use, ask about their level of experience. How many properties have they sold in the country? How long have they been in business? It is more difficult to assess whether they are reputable. A good starting point is to see whether they are members of the **Federation of Overseas Property Developers, Agents and Consultants (FOPDAC; t** (0870) 350 1223, **www.fopdac.com**). This is a non-profit organisation that agents and developers can join if they are experienced in the field, prepared to be scrutinised and willing to abide by its code of conduct.

Briefing the Estate Agent

Be as specific and honest with your agent about your needs and concerns. They will want to help you but can only go on the information you have given them. Treat them with the respect that you expect to be given yourself. If you make an appointment, keep it or cancel in good time. Establishing a good relationship with your agent makes the whole experience of purchasing property more pleasant for everyone.

Try to give estate agents a clear brief as to what you are looking for. This will help them help you and avoid your time being wasted by them showing you totally inappropriate properties. Always discuss your requirements with the local agents who are helping you find a property rather than dictating those requirements to them. They may well say that what to are asking for is not obtainable in their area – but that something very similar is, and at reasonable cost. Make sure they have a very clear specification of what you are interested in and be clear about your budget. Most agents work on the assumption that if somebody says they have a £150,000 to spend, they actually have £200,000. Because they are paid commission as a percentage of what you spend, they will therefore try to show you the more expensive properties. It is very helpful if you make it quite clear to the agent that the amount you have specified is your maximum spend and that you will not spend anything more. Alternatively, if you do have some in reserve, it would be sensible to say that you are trying to find a property for £150,000 but for the right property might be prepared to go to £200,000.

Do not be afraid to change your mind. It is quite common for people to start off looking at cottages for restoration and to end up deciding that, for them, a new property is a better bet. Or, of course, the other way round. If you do change your mind, you must tell the estate agents you are working with. Better still, you should be discussing your developing views with them and getting their confirmation that what you want is do-able.

Viewing Trips

More and more agencies are offering inspection trips, which typically last two or three days and involve being escorted by estate agents to various properties. Agents are usually English, out for the season, or expatriates. In some cases, the agents may be locals who speak English fluently. Trips can take a variety of forms. Sometimes the cost of the trip is deducted from any property you buy; sometimes the agency makes all the arrangements, charges you in the same way as a travel agency but asks for a daily fee for an agent to show you around. The main advantage is that you can be very focused on viewing properties and not waste any time.

However, you may feel pressurised and it always makes sense to go to several sources for information before committing. Some visits are heavily subsidised by the company concerned, and you may be put under real pressure to purchase; no business wants to spend money for nothing. Many companies make clients sign a declaration saying they are genuinely interested in buying

Case Study: Going it Alone

Mark Maidment and his wife Virginia were considering buying somewhere in Bulgaria, but they had no knowledge of the country. Virginia was very impressed with the agent they had approached and trusted him, so when she found out that the company organised inspection trips, she seriously considered it. 'I didn't want to go on a package deal. I didn't like the idea. The price of the deal offered by the agent seemed fair and on top of that we only had to pay around €50 a day for the driver. I liked the idea of being independent and the fact that the driver was being paid would, I imagined, make us feel less pressurised,' says Virginia.

In the end, though, the Maidments decided to go it alone. Mark explained, 'If we were going to go all that way we wanted to have a holiday as well. And enjoying ourselves and going on trips was a good way of finding out about the country we were potentially going to be spending a lot of time in.' So Mark found a good package deal, which included a nice hotel on the beach, and managed to persuade Virginia to put aside her prejudices. They spent several days of their trip on the beach, visiting other places, and then arranged with the agent in the location to pick them up at a time that suited them.

something. In other cases, the cost may be refundable if you buy a home. But the chances are that the cost of the visit has just been added on to the price of the property anyway. There is no such thing as a free holiday. Remember the time-share sales tactics of the 1980s and 1990s? Potential clients were lured with free cocktails, bottles of brandy or a hire car for the day and in return had to endure a lengthy presentation by a sales person. If companies need to persuade their clients to listen to them, something is probably wrong. Providing free meals with plenty of alcohol is not just to create a good atmosphere, but a way of subtly making it less likely that objective decisions are made.

Agents may meet visitors at the airport on arrival and spend as much time as possible with them. If they monopolise your time, spending all day and even dinner with you, you will not have a chance to see other company representatives. However, most agents know that many people are put off by a hard sell and have learned that the best way to close a deal is to let the client make up their own mind.

Viewing trips need not be a sinister approach to making you part with your money. They can be a convenient way of getting you out to the country concerned and giving you the maximum amount of time to see appropriate properties. Some estate agents say that these kinds of trips are tailored so that clients only see the best buildings in the best locations, though in many cases clients will be taken in a group in a minibus, making it unlikely that individual needs have been catered for. This has the advantage that you get a chance to speak to other people in the same situation as you, and is a good way to feel less isolated in your decision.

Some people are nervous about arriving in a strange country and prefer the idea of an inspection trip, but you could just as easily arrive on a package holiday and be picked up from the airport and taken to your hotel. Then, on settling in, you can arrange on the ground for your agent to take you around. The great thing about arranging your own trip, even though it will invariably be more work, is that you will not have to let yourself be steered to where the agent wants to take you. It also makes it much easier to combine it with a relaxed holiday, as you can schedule in side trips and days off.

However you decide to do things, if you don't see the property you want, don't be forced into buying.

If you do decide to go on an inspection visit, don't expect it to be a holiday. Travelling around in the heat inspecting pieces of land and building sites or wandering around newly built apartments for hours on end can seem like a real chore when the cool sea is beckoning. Try to do as much research as possible beforehand about the country and to look at a variety of properties on the Internet. Take a camera with you; once you have seen several properties a day over a period of a week, you will find it hard to remember which is which, especially if they are not yet built and just building sites.

Make a note of the references of any properties that take your fancy in advance on agents' websites and check that they are still available when you make your trip. Properties can sell quickly and agents don't always update their sites regularly – sometimes deliberately, as the more properties they advertise, the greater their chances of generating interest.

Questions to Ask

Once you get closer to buying a property, there are some specific points to consider. Ask yourself and/or your agent the following questions to help clarify the situation and ensure you don't rush into something you might later regret.

- **Where is your money coming from?** A lot of people in England are releasing equity from their homes to buy overseas. This is especially true for people buying in Eastern Europe where mortgages are not yet readily available, although this will change in the next few years. If you are planning to cover the cost of borrowing by renting out the property, make sure you are realistic about potential revenue.

- **Are you using a licensed estate agent?**

- **What will be the costs of any repair or renovation?** Making improvements to your property can soon eat into your budget. Be pessimistic rather than optimistic about any such charges.

- **Are there any outstanding charges?** Your solicitor should check that there are no debts or unpaid taxes on the property which you would be liable to pay once you owned it.

• Are there any outstanding bills on the property? Make sure that all utilities are paid up to the date you take ownership of the property, otherwise you could find yourself having to pay for gas, electricity, water or telephone from the previous owner.

• How is the water supplied? In remote areas there may not even be a direct water supply, or it may come from a shared well, which you need permission to use.

• Who is the owner? In some cases the owner may actually be a family and permission will be needed from all members. There have been situations in Eastern Europe where the Mafia have bought out a desirable flat from an elderly person and sold it on to a foreigner who only later discovers the paperwork is not in order and he or she is not the legal owner.

• Is there a tenant in the building? If there is a tenant, you need to decide whether you want that person to remain, in which case a new lease needs to be drawn up. Otherwise, the legal procedure giving the tenant adequate notice has to be followed.

• What taxes or fees are you liable for? Hidden charges and unknown taxes can rapidly push up the cost of your property.

Other Ways to Find Property

Property-finders

In Britain we are used to the idea that the estate agent is paid by the seller. This is not always so in some of the Eastern European countries. It is commonplace for the fees of the estate agent to be paid in part by the seller and in part by the buyer. In other places a developer will tell the agent how much he wants to receive for the property and the agent will add his fees to that price, effectively making them payable by the buyer. Of course this is all a little theoretical; if the seller were to pay all of the fees he would simply increase the price. Nonetheless, it is worth clarifying who is paying the agent and how much.

The fact that you may be expected to pay all or part of the estate agent's fee and the fact that, in many places, a local person will secure a better price than an obvious foreigner has led to the emergence of the property-finder. This is somebody who acts on the behalf of the buyer and locates properties to meet a certain specification. Their role varies somewhat from place to place. Sometimes they merely gather and sift the information. Other times, they will preview the properties and make a shortlist of the best properties.

Property-finders have existed in busy markets (where property only remains on sale for a very short period of time), such as Paris for some time. They have always been used by busy people. In Eastern Europe, using a local property-finder as a scout can be a sensible move. The property-finder may have access to properties that you would not otherwise encounter. These would include the many properties on offer privately and often unadvertised.

Their fee is usually 2–5 per cent of the price of the property. Some of property-finders advertise. Otherwise your lawyer might well be able to put you in touch with a suitable person.

Developers

A developer is the person or company arranging the building of and often then selling new property. They do not need to be licensed as estate agents (provided they are only selling their own property). Many developers sell via third-party estate agents. Others sell direct. Some carry out marketing and sales campaigns in Britain.

Auctions

Property in can be bought at auction, just as in England, but it is rare for foreigners to buy in this way. You will need legal advice.

DIY Sales

If your language is good enough, you may decide to buy direct from the seller. Some people welcome not having to be in the hands of a middle man. Properties may be advertised in the local press or on the Internet; *see* p.25.

In Eastern Europe far more property is sold 'person to person' than in the UK. Depending on area this can be 15–50 per cent. As you drive around, you will see a number of DIY 'For Sale' signs, usually with a contact telephone number. To take advantage of property offered in this way you have to be in the area and you will probably need to speak the local language. If you do not speak it, it is worth a trial phone call. You never know your luck! If the person who answers doesn't speak English there may be a local English-speaking person – perhaps in your hotel – who would make contact on your behalf. As a last resort phone your lawyer. He or she should be able to find out the necessary details for you and, if you wish, make arrangements to view. He or she will, of course, charge for this work but the saving of estate agents fees will make his charges look cheap.

Temporary Accommodation

If you are going to be looking for a property for any length of time – this is particularly likely if you are seeking a property to move into yourself – then hotels can be expensive, although if you are staying in a popular tourist area there are likely to be some good package deals which include a flight and hotel. One option in cities is to rent an apartment, which can usually be done by the day. This makes good sense if you are a family and cooking facilities will be available, which will bring down eating expenses.

Renting Before Buying

If you are after a home rather than a property to let or to take holidays in, then you will want to make sure you like the area as well as the building. It can be difficult enough to find somewhere to live in England – a place you are familiar with – but in a foreign country the task can seem overwhelming.

For many people it makes sense to rent somewhere before buying. It is a good way to test to see if you like an area, the country and everything that goes with it, such as the culture and way of life. It also allows you to discover important factors you might not know about if you were just buying through an estate agent. For example, it might turn out that there are plans for extensive building work in the area, that the location has a bad reputation locally or that there is good sense of community.

There are various options for finding somewhere to rent. Either you can go through an agent, which will invariably mean paying a fee but has the advantage of being easier to arrange from overseas. You could also go through the Internet or get someone in the country to check the local press. The ideal approach is to use local contacts.

Whichever way you choose, the normal procedure once you have found a property is to pay one month's rent in advance and one month's rent as deposit. Contracts typically last for a year, although they can sometimes be six months or occasionally as little as three months. If you are not sure how long you intend to stay, it might be possible to arrange a clause in which you are allowed to leave before the contract expires at one month's notice. Otherwise, if you need to move out, if you find another tenant for the property, the terms of the lease may not need to be followed and you will be allowed to leave. Agents and individual owners will usually ask for two references, bank statements and a letter confirming employment. Don't rule out the possibility of bargaining the price down. Many Eastern Europeans assume everyone from Western Europe has pots of money and will automatically put the price up – sometimes by a large amount. Usually rent is payable monthly and by direct debit.

Properties are usually furnished but you may be able to find unfurnished accommodation if you committed to the move and want to bring the contents of your household from home. If furnished, an inventory detailing all the items, right down to the number of glasses, will be given to you to sign. If anything is lost or broken, the cost of it will be deducted from your deposit on departure. Before signing anything, check that the inventory is correct and that all appliances work. Once you have moved in, it can be hard work to get the owner to arrange the repair of a washing machine, or to provide missing equipment. If an inventory is not drawn up for you, it is wise to make one yourself and get the owner or agent to sign it.

The costs of any services are paid by you, the tenant. It can be a time-consuming business to get all the utilities put into your name, and setting up a phone line is often a very lengthy and frustrating business. If you are not yet a resident of the country concerned, providers can get nervous that they can't check your financial status easily and that you may leave the country without paying the bill. In some circumstances there may be additional charges, for example for the porter and cleaning of communal areas in serviced buildings.

Choosing the Right Property

In the emerging market countries of Eastern Europe, most people living in cities live in flats. Many British buyers are reluctant to contemplate this, yet there can be many advantages to apartment living, particularly if you do not have young children and you are looking for a holiday home. The purchase cost will probably be cheaper. It will cost less to run. You will not be responsible for organising the maintenance and repair of the outside of the property. You may have shared facilities such as tennis courts or a pool. And, at the end of your holiday you can simply turn off the water and electricity and leave. Flats also and often provide you with a ready-made community of neighbours who can look after your property in your absence and leave a loaf and milk in the fridge for your arrival. Of course, there are drawbacks. For the majority of us the most obvious is the lack of a private garden. There is also, usually, less space – particularly storage space – than in a house.

If you are not ready for such a revolutionary change to your lifestyle, there are a wide variety of types of house available. From small workers' cottages to luxury villas, something will take your fancy and suit your pocket. Think, though: if you are buying a holiday home for use, say, two weekends per month and twice per year for longer periods, who is going to look after your two hectares of land? Who is going to maintain your glistening pool – and at what cost?

Think about your current and future requirements. In Britain, we are used to moving frequently. We buy a house to suit our present needs and, as they change, we sell it and buy another. In many Eastern European countries this is a very expensive thing to do.

Property Types

Apartments

Eastern Europe has some monstrous post-war blocks, modern concrete high rises that tend to be in city suburbs, constructed as cheap accommodation for the masses. Severely lacking in character, these types of property are unlikely to appeal to foreign investors. But there are also plenty of attractive newer urban apartments. There are also a large number of apartments outside major towns and cities, either on the coast or in the countryside. They may be built in the traditional style or in modern resort complexes. Often they benefit from having shared facilities, such as parking and even swimming pools.

Castles and Manor Houses

Some splendid castles and grand houses in Eastern Europe are so appealing that they have caught the interest of people such as American film stars. They may be in a poor state of repair at the time of purchase, as the owners have not had the cash for their upkeep. Unless they are on the small side, they mostly attract investors who want to convert them into hotels or resort complexes.

Rural Cabins or Cottages

There is a culture in Eastern Europe of owning a rural property, which can be anything from a basic cabin to a cottage and is normally used just at weekends and holidays. Often lacking in facilities and services – some may not even have running water – these kinds of buildings can be a bargain.

Villas

Villas can be modern or traditional in style. Usually in desirable locations with good views of the sea or the countryside, they typically have land attached.

New-build Properties

With the growth of the European Union, lots of contemporary housing is being built. Many agents in the 'New Europe' are selling new-build off-plan properties, where the buyer pays a deposit and the rest in instalments until the construction is completed.

Land

Most plots are available in rural areas, although it is still possible to buy a piece of land on the coast. Buyers are attracted to this kind of investment because it means they can design their own building to their individual specifications.

Commercial Properties

Shops, restaurants, hotels, offices and other types of commercial properties are available throughout the region. It is important to clarify that the building is licensed for commercial activity and that the business is still viable.

Space

Most people underestimate the space they will need in their overseas home because they underestimate how popular they will become once they have a home abroad! The combination of your own accommodation needs, the needs of visitors and the requirement for storage space means that, if the budget permits, it is worth thinking of buying one more bedroom than you thought of.

Especially if you are buying a property for retirement you will also need to think about adequate space for 'stuff'. Most of us are very bad at throwing things away, particularly items of sentimental value.

Fortunately, in most Eastern European countries space is still fairly cheap. It doesn't cost that much more to buy a house with four bedrooms rather than one with three.

Heating

Eastern Europe is not warm. Even the best bits can be as cold and wet as it is in Britain. Most is worse. Even in the warmest parts of the east of Bulgaria or the Croatian coast you need a decent heating system because there are numerous days each year when heating will be needed. It may, in the summer, be a lot warmer than it would have been in Edinburgh, but if you have been used to daily temperatures of 21°C then a drop of a few degrees will make you feel cold. In the winter, all these countries are cold.

Piped gas is rare in rural areas. Bottled gas is too fiddly to be genuinely convenient. Installing large tanks for gas can be problematic from a town planning point of view. Solid fuel has all the drawbacks we forgot about in the UK 30 years ago. Solar heating – particularly solar water heating – works well in sunnier areas but cannot be relied on as the sole form of heating and can never be relied on in winter. For many people this leaves oil and electricity as candidates. Whichever you choose, installing a good centrally controlled heating system will be money well spent, especially when you are building a new house, where the extra cost can be very small.

Air-conditioning

We recommend that everyone buying a home abroad should install at least some minimal air-conditioning. With predicted global warming, summer temperatures are likely to rise. You may not need it often, but when you do, you really need it. For people buying a home for retirement, or with elderly relatives who will visit, it is worth remembering that, as we get older, we gradually lose our ability to adjust to extremes of temperature. Temperature that is unpleasantly hot for a 55-year-old can be life-threatening for a 90-year-old.

Whether to install full air-conditioning, possibly combined with a heating system using some of the efficient modern technologies such as heat pumps, or a stand-alone portable system will depend on the location of your property, your preferences and your wallet. With portable units available for £300–400, getting something makes a lot of sense.

Parking

If you have a nice car and want to keep it secure, private off-street parking is an asset in any country. Much property is sold without any dedicated parking space, and spaces can cost a surprising amount if bought separately.

New or Old?

Traditionally Eastern Europeans, except for the wealthy, have scorned older, restored property in favour of new build. This left the market open to the British to buy up the older homes for a pittance, love them, restore them and live happily ever after. Things have changed. In many areas the local people have developed an interest in older 'character' property. A visit to a Bulgarian DIY store will show you that it is not just the British who spend money on home improvements.

For those interested in cheap rural property, there is a seemingly inexhaustible supply of houses and cottages abandoned as a result of rural depopulation after the Second World War. Remember that the similarly 'inexhaustible' supply in France has almost run out in some areas, bought not just by thousands of British and other foreigners but by local people, and prices are rising. This will probably also happen in Eastern Europe, particularly in the skiing areas and the pretty parts within easy travelling distance of big cities, though in the real rural areas it is likely to take many years.

When considering whether to buy new or old property, consider the features of each type of property in the light of your own personal preferences. Most people are clear from the outset which they prefer.

New Property in Eastern Europe
Advantages

- The technical specification and design will be better than in an older property. This is particularly so in areas such as insulation and energy-efficiency.
- It will have been inspected and built to known standards.

- Most people prefer new kitchens, which get more sophisticated each year.
- It will probably have a reasonable heating system.
- Electrical and plumbing installations will be to a superior standard.
- Few people will have used the bathrooms.
- Provision will probably have been made for car parking.
- You may share the cost of expensive common resources such as pools or tennis courts with other people.
- The building will require a lot less maintenance than an older property, certainly for the first few years.
- It should be cheaper to run.
- You can design your own property or, at least, often fine-tune the design to your special requirements.
- The fabric will be guaranteed.
- If you buy 'off plan' you may see some pre-completion growth in value.

Disadvantages

- The building will be new and brash, not mellow.
- It can be hard to envisage what you are going to get from a plan.
- You will have to sort out all the small snags inevitable in any new building. You may spend all your holidays chasing the builder or doing this. You probably don't speak the local language.
- You will have to sort out the garden.
- You may have to decorate.
- Although technical design may have improved, the aesthetic appeal may be less than that of an older property and the detailed workmanship less rewarding than that of a time when labour was cheap.
- As a rental property most (British) people wanting to rent in a rural area prefer a traditional cottage, and those renting in the city prefer a character historic' building; this is not so true on the coast

Older Property in Eastern Europe

Advantages

- The property has 'character'. Its design may be classically beautiful and the detailed workmanship will probably be superior to today's product.
- The garden will be mature.
- It may occupy a better site than a newer property – on the basis that the best were often built on first.
- It may be a more attractive rental proposition than a new property, especially in rural areas.

- You will feel that you are living in a 'foreign' property.
- What you see is what you get. You turn on the taps, there is water. You can see the room sizes and how the sun lies on the terraces. You can see the views and the distances to adjacent properties.
- It may be cheaper than a comparable new property.
- It will probably have more land than a comparable new property.

Disadvantages

- Older properties can need a lot of maintenance and loving care.
- It will be more expensive to heat and run.
- You may need to spend significant sums on, say, the kitchen and bathrooms to bring the property up to modern standards.

Investment Potential

Capital Growth

One of the great attractions of owning a property is the potential for the asset to grow in value while, at the same time, you enjoy the use of it. For some people the choice of place to buy a property – or the selection of which of several places to choose – is governed by likely capital growth. The British view property as an investment as well as a home. We expect our house to rise in value, if not year by year, at least over time. Until recently this was not really a consideration for the Eastern Europeans. As a result there has been a perception that property in Eastern Europe does not increase in value – or, at least, not to any significant extent. That perception is, generally, false. There is a grain of truth in relation to some very rural areas where there is still a lot of property left over after the massive depopulation of the 20th century. The thousands of rural homes they abandoned in their flight to the city and large towns lay empty for many years. This will continue to depress rural property prices. In popular areas – and, in particular, in popular tourist areas – there has been great property inflation. Accurate and comprehensive statistics are hard to come by.

Rental Potential

Not all properties will perform equally for rental purposes; *see* 'Letting your Property', pp.118–21. There are good, long-term investment opportunities in Eastern European countries, but in some of them the market has been talked up and sold to speculators at inflated prices. How do you tell which is which? There are two real tests. They apply whether you are buying the property to keep and rent out or whether you are buying it to 'flip' – sell on at a profit before actually completing the purchase and taking title.

• **Who is going to rent or buy the property?**

To make money from rentals there needs to be a ready supply of potential tenants. There are lots of potential groups of tenants: students, expat businessmen, the local middle class or tourists. You will need to choose which market to address as you cannot be all things to all men. Does that market exist right now where you are thinking of buying? Will it exist when you take delivery of the property? In some of the emerging markets these tenants do not exist – at least at present. You are investing in the expectation that they will exist by the time your property is finished. You should either do some research or seek advice about whether this change in the market is likely to happen.

The same considerations apply if you are buying to sell. Some properties stand out as being the pick of the bunch. They have the best views in the complex, or a better internal layout, or a corner plot. These are properties are the ones that will sell or let well even in a thin market. In these markets these are, even more than normally, the properties to buy. *See* individual country sections for more particular information about buying properties for investment.

• **What type of person is now buying the properties?**

Are your fellow buyers mainly people who are buying to use the properties themselves as holiday homes or for retirement? Are they people who have identified the property as satisfying a potential letting market? Or are they speculators, intending to sell on at a profit as soon as the properties have been finished? If they are speculators then there will be a large number of these properties coming on the market about the time the complex is finished. Will the market be strong enough to absorb them? You need to be in the position to be able to complete the purchase, by paying over the balance of the price and taking delivery and title, if you cannot sell when you wish to do so. Otherwise

Case Study: Sibling Rivalry

Siblings Jemima and Dimitri Calum decided that they wanted to buy a property in Bulgaria, but couldn't agree on which kind and where. Jemima is a writer, for whom aesthetics are crucial, while her brother's financial background makes him much more practical. Dimitri recognised Bulgaria as a country with a lot to offer, while Jemima favoured chic Croatia. They decided to make a trip out to the Black Sea coast, where Jemima expected to find inedible food, grey buildings and general misery. Instead, she encountered smiling people, beautiful countryside and a cuisine she couldn't get enough of.

They managed to agree on San Vlas, an undeveloped part of Sunny Beach, but Jemima instantly plumped for a one-bedroom flat in a five-star complex with an infinity pool right on the beach. Her more sensible sibling suggested a two-bedroom, three-star apartment just behind, with views out to sea. Unable to agree, they spoke to the helpful director of Bulgarian Dreams, also with a financial background, who echoed Dimitri's views, and the deal was set.

you will have to make a crisis sale, at a very low price, and you will be lucky not to lose money instead of making a profit.

Renovating a Property

Renovating a property is fraught with problems. How often have you had a leak or problem in you own home, called out a plumber or builder and had it fixed within a reasonable time scale at a reasonable cost? You have to have a strong will and an iron resolve to take on renovating a property overseas. There are the logistics of organising it all from home, not having builders you know or trust and not speaking the language. All that is compounded by the fact that most Eastern European builders are going to assume you have loads of money and that time is not important. Beware...

You should not expect to recoup the cost of any renovations, let alone to make your fortune. Many experts would advise buyers not to purchase somewhere in need of repair with the sole aim of selling it on at a profit. Only consider such a project if it is going to be a labour of love. Agents are likely vastly to under-estimate the extent of any work needed. 'In need of repair' probably translates as a property that is quite literally falling down. Somewhere that is 'partially restored' is likely to be a building without basic facilities such as electricity.

Roof repairs in particular can cost more than the actual property. If the structure is not intact, then it is probably best to forget it. Get all structures and foundations checked. Dampness can be identified by bubbling or discoloured walls but a professional can spot it before it even gets to this stage. Once damp has set in it can be difficult to stop. The electrical system needs to be looked over – apart from being costly to repair, faulty electrics can be highly dangerous. The source of water must be checked: if it is a well, confirm its cleanliness and reliability as well as whether it is shared with other properties.

On a more positive note, labour costs in Eastern Europe are a fraction of those in the UK. In fact, with more and more labourers from these countries coming over here to work, you may even manage to make contacts for labourers at home. Building materials are cheaper, too, although watch you are not over-charged. Check that there are no restrictions on improvements to the property. Conservation areas are less common in Eastern Europe, but there are protected buildings and whole cities are UNESCO sites. If any permission is needed, be sure to obtain it before you buy; the process can be lengthy and expensive .

There is a strong tradition of corruption in these Eastern European countries, which continues today despite the collapse of Communism and the cleaning up of illegal practices for EU membership. If you resort to making unofficial payments to speed things up, make sure you know exactly what you are letting yourself in for. Make sure you get a guarantee for any work done in case of future problems. It is a good idea to get a translator and, if you are not going to

Case Study: A Labour of Love

It was the realisation of a dream when William and Samantha Sarne found a three-storey house in a street in Budapest. The ground floor had been used as a fast-food outlet but the newly married couple wanted to turn it into an upmarket restaurant. The whole building had to be completely redecorated and because of lack of funds they were forced to live on the upper floors when work was being carried out. The fact that they had a one-year-old son, Saul, made it all the more stressful. 'We knew there was a demand for an eatery that served food fast but was healthy. We spent a lot of time researching the market and the location,' explains William.

The Sarnes' main concern was to get the necessary work completed as soon as possible. They knew they had to get the business up and running quickly in order to recoup their investment. 'Luckily we had English friends who had done something similar, so we took all the advice we could from them and they put us in contact with local workmen with a good reputation who could be trusted,' says Samantha.

The foreman spoke excellent English and they all worked around the clock. A disabled toilet had to be built at great expense, which ate into the size of the ground floor, but within six months the restaurant was complete. The builders were still there on the evening of the launch and it was touch and go whether they would open at all. But the night was a great success, the reports in the press the next day glowing and just a week later the restaurant was packed. Samantha says, 'It really is a labour of love and we could not be happier.'

be around, a professional to oversee the work. It is asking for trouble to pay workers to carry out a project without checking progress frequently. The chances are your property will be ignored for weeks at a time.

Don't ask estate agents for recommendations of builders, as they tend to take commission. Local papers are a good source of tradespeople, although some argue that those who need to advertise are not the best workers – if they were any good they would get all their work through personal recommendations, and this is undoubtedly the best route to finding a company or individual to carry out the work. Approach several builders to get at least three quotes, but don't necessarily go for the cheapest – take into account their level of professionalism, as the last thing you want is a job badly done.

Some people bring a workforce out from the UK, especially if they have workmen they know and trust. This has the advantage that one can communicate with the workforce in English, but it is expensive. Not only are labour costs much higher in the UK, but there are also the costs of keeping the workers in the country concerned while they complete the work.

Some workmen charge by the hour, others by the square metre and others by the job. Try to avoid additional costs being added for a job taking longer than expected by getting a guarantee in writing as to the final costs. Confirm how the payments are to be made. You are likely to be asked for a deposit and then weekly or monthly payments. Never pay more than 20 per cent in advance and always get a receipt. As in the UK, in some cases paying in cash gives a discount. Establish the completion date, too, and get it in writing

Standards will invariably be different. Eastern European homes – even those in major cities – are very different from those in this country. Carpets are much less common, for example, central heating does not come as standard, and in rural areas there may not even be electricity or running water. Building styles and decoration techniques are likely to be different, too. Where open-plan properties are popular in the UK, there are few in the countries covered in this book. Be cautious about bringing too many modern ideas to your plan. A highly contemporary look may look ridiculous in rural Hungary. Using local materials and perhaps a traditional style with a modern twist may work better.

If you have the skills and commitment you may decide to take on the process yourself, but this still involves liaising with locals to buy materials, arrange items such as skips and, unless you are a professional, an electrician. If you decide to go for this option, be prepared for a long, hard slog. It is definitely not a choice for the faint-hearted.

Just as there are sites telling you how to make 'guaranteed' income on property purchase, there are several informing you on how you can be sure to 'triple' your property investment profits'. Treat any claim of how much your property will increase in value after renovation with extreme caution and always get several opinions. In America it is sometimes called 'sweat equity' – the idea being that the amount of work you put into the building work will be equal to the amount of profit you make. Not necessarily.

Building from Scratch

Building from scratch is another story altogether but becoming more and more popular in areas where there is not much development. Plots of land are increasingly becoming available for purchase, and the advantage is that you can buy the land and keep it until you are ready to build your property. This has been made to seem less daunting by TV programmes about building your dream property in the sun. Although they focus on disasters, too, these can make it seem as if there is nothing more natural than getting yourself some land or tumbledown building, hiring a designer and creating a palace.

To make a costing, establish what the price per square metre would be. You can get a quote for the basic work or, for a completely finished building, to include decoration. Usually an architect can recommend a team of workers – including carpenters, builders, decorators, plumbers and electricians. You may also need to hire the services of a landscape gardener to complete your project.

Making the Purchase

Arranging Finance

In these days of low interest rates many more people are taking out a mortgage in order to buy property abroad. But often their own money would be better employed in their business, or other investments, than in a home overseas. If the property is viewed simply as an investment, a mortgage allows you to increase your benefit from the capital growth of the property by 'leveraging' the investment. If you buy a house for £200,000 and it increases in value by £50,000, that is a 25 per cent return on your investment. If you had only put in £50,000 of your own money and borrowed the other £150,000 then the increase in value represents a return of 100 per cent on your investment. If the rate of increase in the value of the property is more than the mortgage rate, you have won. In recent years, property in most popular areas has gone up in value by much more than the mortgage rate. The key questions are whether that will continue and, if so, for how long.

If you decide to take out a mortgage you can, in most cases, either mortgage (or extend the mortgage on) your existing UK property or you can take out a mortgage on your new Bulgarian property.

Many people buying property in an Eastern European country will look closely at fixed rate mortgages so they know their commitment over, say, the next 5, 10 or 15 years. Again there are advantages and disadvantages.

UK Mortgages

Ini this context, UK mortgages mean a mortgage of your UK property. At the moment there is fierce competition to lend money and there are some excellent deals to be done, whether you choose to borrow at a variable rate, a fixed rate or in one of the hybrid schemes now on offer. Read the Sunday papers or the specialist mortgage press to see what is on offer, or consult a mortgage broker. Perhaps most useful are mortgage brokers who can discuss the possibilities in the UK and Eastern European countries.

It is outside the scope of this book to go into detail about the procedures for obtaining a UK mortgage. A number of people have found that, in today's climate of falling interest rates, re-mortgaging their property in the UK has reduced the cost of their existing borrowing so significantly that their new mortgage – *including a loan to buy a modest overseas property* – has cost no more, in monthly payments, than their old loan.

Mortgaging a UK Property: Advantages
- **The loan is likely to be very cheap to set up.**
  You will probably already have a mortgage. If you stay with the same lender there will be no legal fees or land registry fees for the additional loan. There may not even be an arrangement fee.

If you go to a new lender, many special deals mean that the lender will pay all fees involved.

• You will pay UK interest rates which, at the time of writing (Jan 2005), could be lower than some local rates.

UK rates are about 5 per cent variable. Local rates in Eastern European countries vary from 3.8 to 8 per cent variable, so some are higher than UK rates. Make sure you compare the overall cost of the two mortgages. Crude rates (which, in any case, may not be comparable as they are calculated differently in the two countries) do not tell the whole tale. What is the total monthly cost of each mortgage, including life insurance and all extras? What is the total amount required to repay the loan, including all fees and charges?

• The loan repayments will be in sterling.

If the funds to repay the mortgage are coming from your sterling earnings, then the amount you have to pay will not be affected by fluctuations in exchange rates between the pound and the euro or other local currency. At the time of writing (Jan 2005), most experts predict that the pound will fall further in value against the euro. Equally, if sterling falls in value, then your debt as a percentage of the value of the property decreases. Your property will be worth more in sterling terms, but your mortgage will remain the same.

• You will be familiar with dealing with British mortgages and all correspondence and documentation will be in English.

• You can take out an endowment or PEP mortgage or pension mortgage or interest-only mortgage, none of which is available in Eastern Europe.

None of these is available in most emerging arket countries. Normally only repayment mortgages are available in Eastern Europe. Sometimes no mortgages are available.

• You will probably need no extra life insurance cover.

If you had to take out more cover this could add considerably to the cost of the mortgage, especially if you are getting older.

Mortgaging a UK Property: Disadvantages

• The loan could be comparatively expensive to set up. It would not be unusual for mortgage set-up costs to be about 4 per cent of the amount borrowed.

• You will pay UK interest rates which, at the time of writing (Jan 2005), could be higher than some local rates.

UK rates are about 5 per cent variable. Local rates in Eastern European countries vary from 3.8 to 8 per cent variable, so some are lower than UK rates.

Make sure you compare the overall cost of the two mortgages. Crude rates (which, in any case, may not be comparable as they are calculated differently in the two countries) do not tell the whole tale. What is the total monthly cost of each mortgage, including life insurance and all extras? What is the total amount required to repay the loan, including all fees and charges?

• If the rate of sterling increases in value against the euro or other local currency, a mortgage in euros would become cheaper to pay off.

A loan of €60,000, worth about £40,800 at €1 = £0.68, would cost only about £30,000 to pay off if the euro rose 20 per cent to £0.50.

• If you are going to let the property, it will be difficult or impossible to get local tax relief on the mortgage interest.

• Many people do not like the idea of mortgaging their main home – a debt they may only just have cleared after 25 years of paying off a mortgage.

• You will not be using the equity in your overseas home and will, perhaps unnecessarily, be eating up the equity in your UK home.

• Some academics argue that, in economic terms, debts incurred to buy assets should be secured against the asset bought and assets in one country should be funded by borrowings in that country.

Taking out a UK mortgage is generally the better option for people who need to borrow relatively small sums and who will be repaying it out of UK income.

Local Mortgages

In most but not all of the emerging market countries, mortgages are available for foreigners buying property in that country. Local mortgages are those taken out on your property overseas from a local bank (or other lending institution) or from a British bank that is registered and does business in that country. You cannot take a mortgage on your new overseas property from your local UK branch of a building society or high street bank. It is likely that anyone contemplating taking a mortgage on a property still in the course of construction will be paying an interest rate lower than that currently available, but this cannot be guaranteed.

Because mortgages are new, the rules are evolving rapidly. Hardly a week goes by without some new product or variation appearing in the marketplace. It is sensible to get independent advice about what is available and what might suit you best. You need to make sure that the funds will be available in time for the signing of the final contract. If you are unable to pay the money at that stage, you will lose the deposit that you have paid.

The basic concept of a mortgage is the same in these emerging market countries as it is in the UK. It is (usually) a loan secured against land or buildings. Just as in England, if you don't keep up the payments the bank will repossess your property. If they do this they will sell it and you are likely to see it sold for a pittance and recover little if anything of the equity you built up.

Mortgages in these countries are, however, different in many respects from their English counterparts. It is important to understand the differences, which are explained in the country-specific sections of this book.

Differences Between a Mortgage in the UK and in Eastern Europe

• Local mortgages are almost always created on a repayment basis in Eastern European countries. That is to say, the loan and the interest on it are both gradually repaid by equal instalments over the period of the mortgage. Endowment, PEP, pension and interest-only mortgages are not generally known.

• The formalities involved in making the application, signing the contract subject to a mortgage and completing the transaction are more complex in Eastern European countries and stricter than in the UK.

• Most local mortgages are granted for 15 years, not 25 as in England. Normally the mortgage must have been repaid by the mortgagee's 70th (sometimes 65th) birthday.

• The maximum loan is generally 70–80 per cent of the value of the property in Eastern European countries. Valuations by banks tend to be conservative – they are thinking about what they might get for the property on a forced sale if they had to repossess it. As a planning guide, we suggest that you think of borrowing no more than two-thirds of the price you are paying.

• Fixed rate loans – with the rate fixed for the whole duration of the loan – are more common than in England. They are very competitively priced.

• In Eastern European countries the way of calculating the amount the bank will lend you is different from in England. As you would expect, there are detailed differences from country to country and bank to bank, but most banks are not allowed to lend you more than an amount the monthly payments on which amount to 30–33 per cent of your net disposable income. *See* 'How Much Can I Borrow?', p.52.

• There will usually be a minimum loan (say £20,000) in Eastern European countries and some banks will not lend at all on property of less than a certain value. Some will not lend in rural areas.

• In Eastern European countries the way of dealing with stage payments on new property and property where money is needed for restoration is different from in England. *See* below.

• In Eastern European countries the way the paperwork on completion of the mortgage is different from that common in the UK. There is (usually) no separate mortgage deed. Instead the existence of the mortgage is mentioned in your purchase deed.

Generally speaking, a local overseas mortgage will suit people letting their property regularly.

How Much Can I Borrow?

Different banks have slightly different rules and slightly different ways of interpreting the rules. Generally they will lend you an amount that will give rise to monthly payments of up to about 30–33 per cent of your net available monthly income.

The starting point is your net monthly salary after deduction of tax and National Insurance but before deduction of voluntary payments such as to savings schemes. If there are two applicants, the two salaries are taken into account. If you have investment income or a pension this will be taken into account. If you are buying a property to let, even with a track record of letting income, this will not generally be taken into account. If you are over 65 your earnings will sometimes not be taken into account, but your pension and investment income will be. If your circumstances are at all unusual seek advice, as approaching a different bank may produce a different result.

e.g.	Mr Smith – net salary per month, after tax and NI	£3,000
	Mrs Smith – net salary per month, after tax and NI	£2,000
	Investment income per month	£1,000
	Total income taken into account	£6,000 per month

The maximum loan repayments permitted will be 30 per cent of this sum, less your existing fixed commitments

i.e.   Maximum permitted loan repayment £6,000 x 30% = £1,800 per month

Regular monthly commitments would include mortgage payments on your main and other properties, any rent paid, HP commitments and maintenance (family financial provision) payments. Repayments on credit cards do not count. If there are two applicants, both their commitments are taken into account.

e.g.	Mr and Mrs Smith – mortgage on main home	£750
	Mr and Mrs Smith – mortgage on holiday home in UK	£400
	Mrs Smith – HP on car	£200
	Total pre-existing outgoings	£1,350 per month

Maximum loan repayment permitted = £1,800 – £1,350 = £450 per month. This would, at today's rates, equate to a mortgage of about £60,000 over 15 years.

If you are buying a property for investment (rental) the bank may treat this as commercial lending and apply different criteria.

Repayment Mortgage: Monthly Repayments per £1,000 Borrowed

Period of Repayment	2%	3%	4%	5%	6%	7%	8%
5 years	17.50	17.92	18.36	18.79	19.24	19.69	20.14
10 years	9.19	9.63	10.09	10.56	11.05	11.54	12.05
15 years	6.42	6.89	7.37	7.88	8.40	8.94	9.49
20 years*	5.05	5.53	6.04	6.57	7.13	7.71	8.31
25 years*	4.23	4.73	5.26	5.82	6.41	7.03	7.67

Rates vary depending on formula used by the bank.
*Not usually available

Applications for a Local Mortgage

The information needed varies from country to country and from bank to bank, and also depends on whether you are employed or self-employed. Applications can receive preliminary approval (subject to survey of the property, confirmation of good title and confirmation of the information supplied by you) within a few days. A formal letter of offer will take a couple of weeks from the time the bank has received all of the necessary information from you. A fee will be payable.

The documents you will are likely to need are:

- **a completed application form.**
- **a copy of the passports of all applicants.**
- **proof of outgoings such as rent or mortgage.**
- **a copy of the last three months' bank statements.**
- **a cash-flow forecast for any expected rental income.**
- **proof of income (usually three months' pay slips or a letter from employer on official paper); self-employed applicants may be asked to provide audited accounts for the last three years and the previous year's tax return and proof of payment of tax.**

Allow at least 4 weeks from the date of your application to receiving a written **mortgage offer**, as getting the information to them sometimes takes a while. Once you receive the offer you will generally have 30 days from receipt of the offer in which to accept the offer. You cannot accept it for 10 days from the date of receipt so as to give you a 'period of reflection'. This is very frustrating if the offer has taken ages to arrive and you are in a hurry! Have the mortgage explained in detail by your lawyer. Not all banks will finance **property that needs restoration**. If you have enough money to buy a property but need a mortgage to renovate it you must apply for the mortgage before buying the property as it can otherwise be difficult to find a lender.

You will probably be required to take out **life insurance** for the amount of the loan, though you may be allowed to use a suitable existing policy. You may be required to have a medical. You will be required to insure the property and produce proof of insurance – but you would probably have done this anyway.

The offer may be subject to **early repayment/redemption penalties**. These must be explained in the offer and cannot exceed the penalties laid down by law. The details of these rules vary from time to time. Early payment penalties are of particular concern in the case of a fixed rate mortgage.

The Exchange Rate Risk

If the funds to repay the mortgage are coming from your sterling earnings then the amount you have to pay will be affected by fluctuations in exchange rates between sterling and the euro or other currency involved. Do not underestimate these variations, as they can make a tremendous difference to your monthly mortgage repayments. At the time of writing (Jan 2005), most experts are predicting that the pound will fall further in value against the euro. See the country-specific sections.

The UK Tax Trap

In certain circumstances your local overseas mortgage can give rise to a liability to UK tax. This is because, unless the paperwork complies with UK and local law, the interest charges paid to the local bank can give rise to the need to pay **withholding tax** to the UK Inland Revenue. Worse still, the local mortgage documentation may not give you the right to deduct any such tax paid. This means that, if you make the deduction, you will fall into arrears, with all the risks that that entails. This is not a common problem, but check the position with your lawyer or accountant.

Saving Money on Your Mortgage Repayments

Your mortgage will usually be paid directly from your local overseas bank account. Unless you have lots of rental or other local income going into that account, you will need to send money from Britain in order to meet the payments. Every time you send a payment you will face two costs: on the price of the currency, which depends on the exchange rate used to convert your sterling, and on the charges that will be made by your UK and local banks to transfer the funds, which can be substantial.

There are steps that you can take to control both of these charges. As far as the exchange rate is concerned, you should be receiving the so-called 'commercial rate', not the tourist rate published in the papers. This is a much better rate, but rates vary from second to second and so it is difficult to get alternative quotes; by the time you phone the second company, the first rate has changed. In any case, you will probably want to set up a standing order for payment and not shop around every month.

There are various organisations that can convert your sterling into other currencies and your bank is unlikely to give you the best exchange rate. Specialist currency dealers will normally better the bank's rate, perhaps significantly. If you decide to deal with a currency dealer, deal with one that is reputable; ask your lawyer for a recommendation.

As far as the bank charges are concerned, different banks make different charges, whether in the UK or overseas. Discuss bank charges with them. In the case of your UK bank there is usually room for some kind of deal to be done. In the case of the overseas bank the level of these charges will probably – after the ability to speak English – be the most important reason for choosing one bank over another. Some local lenders may offer you a facility to pay the monthly payments into their UK branch and transfer the funds free of charge. The deals available change quickly. If this is offered, it is a valuable feature. If it is not, ask for it. Who knows what the response might be? If you are using a **currency dealer** to convert your sterling into euros or other currencies it is usually most economical to get them to send the money overseas, as this saves an additional set of bank charges. Some dealers have negotiated special rates with overseas banks to reflect the high volumes of business they do. Again, if you are using a UK lawyer, ask for a recommendation.

Another possibility for saving money arises if you '**forward-buy**' the currency that you are going to need for the year. See 'Forward-buying', pp.79–80.

Bearing in mind the cost of conversion and transmission of currency, it is always better to make fewer rather than more payments. You will have to work out whether, taking into account loss of interest on the funds transferred but bank charges saved, you are best sending money monthly, quarterly or every six months.

Foreign Currency Mortgages

It is sometimes possible to mortgage your home overseas but to borrow not in euros but in sterling – or any other currency. There may be some attractions to borrowing in sterling if you are repaying out of sterling income. The rates of interest will be sterling rates, not euro rates, and this will currently mean paying more. Usually the rates are not as competitive as those you could obtain if you were remortgaging your property in the UK, as the market is less cut-throat. You will have all the same administrative and legal costs as you would if you borrowed locally in local currency –about 4 per cent of the amount borrowed.

This option is mainly of interest to people who either do not have sufficient equity in their UK home or who, for whatever reason, do not wish to mortgage the property in which they live.

Other Types of Loan

Many people may not need to incur the expense of mortgaging their property overseas. Very often a buyer intends to move abroad permanently, has already paid off their UK mortgage and their UK home is on sale. They have found the perfect place in, say, Bulgaria, and have, say, £180,000 of the £200,000 purchase price available from savings and pension lump sums. The balance will be paid from the sale of their UK home, but they are not sure whether that will take place before they are committed to the purchase of the house in Bulgaria in a few weeks' time.

It is unnecessarily complicated to mortgage the UK home for such a short period, and indeed, it could be difficult to do so if the bank knows you are selling and if you are, say, 65 years old and not working. In this case it is often simplest to approach your bank for a short-term loan or overdraft. This might be for the

£20,000 shortfall or it could be that you don't really want to sell some of your investments at this stage and so you might ask for a facility of, say, £50,000.

Some people choose to take out formal two- or three-year UK loans for, say, £15,000 each while still resident in the UK before leaving for an Eastern European country to cover a gap such as waiting to receive a pension lump sum. Despite the high interest rates on such loans, the overall cost can be a lot less than taking a short-term mortgage on the Bulgarian property and paying all of the fees relating to that mortgage.

In other cases, the property in an emerging market can be so inexpensive that taking a personal loan – or even using a credit card – can prove, overall, the cheapest way of financing the purchase, despite the much higher interest rates payable. Be sure to research all options.

Surveys and Valuations

Whatever property you are thinking of buying, you should think about having it inspected (surveyed) before you commit yourself to the purchase, though new properties are usually covered by a guarantee for a fixed period.

Whichever type of report you buy, and whether it is from an architect or a surveyor, you will find that it is different from the sort of report you would get from an English surveyor. Many people find it a little thin, with too much focus on issues that are not their primary concern. It will be in the local language so you will probably need to have it translated. Translation costs amount to about £100 per thousand words. Incidentally, always use an English native speaker to translate documents from the local language into English. An alternative to translation of the full report would be to ask your lawyer to summarise the report in a letter to you and to have translated any areas of particular concern.

A few local surveyors and architects, mainly in the popular areas, have geared themselves to the foreign market and will produce a report rather more like a British or German survey. They will probably also prepare it in bilingual form or at least supply a translation of the original document. Most surveys are provided within 7–10 days.

Check For Yourself

There are several things that you can do yourself, which will help you decide when to instruct a surveyor to do a proper survey and help direct him or her to any specific points of interest. Here is a checklist of points to look out for:

Title

- **Check that the property corresponds with its description, including the number of rooms and plot size.**

Plot

- Check the building density permission for the plot.
- Ask the vendor or developer whether the plot is within the building zone and what building permission the surrounding land has. If the same developer owns it, what are their plans for it?
- Identify the physical boundaries of the plot.
- Is there any dispute with anyone over these boundaries?
- Is there anything suspicious-looking on your plot such as pipes, cables, drainage ditches?
- Is the plot connected to the mains and does it have sewage disposal or a septic tank?
- Is the plot connected to the electricity network? Are there any unsightly cables or posts that you will need to have moved?
- What access is there to the plot? Does anybody else have access across your land?
- Is there somewhere to park a car?
- Is the plot noisy? If you are buying near an airport, are you under the flight path?
- If you are buying in town, are there any bars or nightclubs nearby which may disturb you?

Garden

- Is there anything in the garden that is not being sold with the property, potted plants, fountains, etc.?
- Is the garden overlooked?

Swimming Pool

- What size is the pool? Is it clean?
- Does the filtration system work?
- When was it installed?
- Who maintains it and how much do they charge?

Walls (this is particularly important when buying an older property)

- Are the walls vertical?
- Are there any obvious cracks?
- Is the stone in good condition?
- Are there any recent-looking repairs to the walls?
- If you are buying an older property, has it been built to withstand earth tremors?

Roof

- Is the roof in reasonable repair?
- If it is tiled, are there any tiles missing?
- Is the water tank on the roof in good condition? How old is it?
- Are the solar panels on the roof in good condition? How old are they?
- If there is a satellite dish, is it included in the sale of the property?

Guttering and Downpipes

- Is everything present? Are the gutters securely attached? Are there any obvious repairs?

Enter the property

- Does it smell musty?
- Does it smell of dry rot?
- Are there any other strange smells?

Doors

- Do the doors close properly?
- Do the locks work?

Windows

- Do the windows have flyscreens?
- Do the windows close properly?
- Do the locks work?

Floor

- Does the floor appear in good condition – without chips or cracks in stone or marble, and no cracked or warped wooden boards?

Underfloor

- Can you get access under the floor?
- If so, is it ventilated?
- Are the joists in good condition?

Attic Space

- Is it accessible?
- Can you see daylight through the roof?
- Will you be able to turn it into an extra room if required?
- How hot is it?
- Is there anywhere to put a window or a skylight and would you get permission to do this?

Woodwork

- Is there any sign of wood-boring insects?

Interior Aalls

- Is there any sign of recent repair or redecoration?
- Are there any significant-looking cracks?

Utility Bills

- Are you responsible for your own or are they shared with other tenants in the building?
- Are there any other communal costs you should know about?

Electricity

- How old is the electricity meter?
- Does the wiring look safe?
- Are there enough power points?
- If you have a plug tester, does it show good earth?

Lighting

- Do all the lights work?
- Which light fittings, if any, are included in the sale?
- If you are buying an old house, turn the lights off to see how dark the interior is likely to be during the day.

Water

- Is the property connected to the mains, or does water come from a well? If so, who owns the well and how much will you be charged for water?
- Do all the hot and cold taps work?
- Is there enough water pressure?
- Do the taps drip?

Gas

- Where are the gas bottles stored?
- If you are buying a rural property, can you get gas delivered?
- Does the property have sufficient ventilation?

Central Heating

- Is the property fitted with central heating?
- If you are buying off-plan, is central heating included in the price?
- If so, does it work?

- Is there heat in all the radiators?
- Do the thermostat appear to work?
- Are there any signs of leaks?

Fireplaces

- Are the chimneys unblocked and in good order?

Air-conditioning

- Does the property have central air-conditioning or individual units in some of the rooms?
- If you are buying off-plan, is air-conditioning included in the price?
- Are individual units included in the sale?
- Does the air-conditioning work and is it quiet?
- Do any of the rooms have ceiling fans?
- If there is no air-conditioning, is there a provision for it?
- If you do not intend to have air-conditioning, is there a good flow of air through the house when the doors and windows are open?

Telephone

- Is there a phone?
- Does the phone work?
- Is it included in the sale?
- Is the area suitable for a broadband Internet connection?
- Is there a mobile phone signal?

Satellite TV

- Does the property come with a satellite dish?
- Does it work?
- Is it included in the sale?

Drainage

- If there is a septic tank, how old is it?
- Who maintains it?
- When was it last serviced?
- Is there a smell indicating drainage problems in the bathrooms or toilets?
- Does the water drain away rapidly from sinks and showers?
- Do the drains appear to be in good condition?

Kitchen

- Do the cupboards open and close properly?
- Is the tiling secure and in good order?
- Are there enough power points?
- What appliances are included in the sale?
- Do they work and how old are they?
- If you are buying off-plan, is there a good choice of kitchens offered by the developer? If not, why not?

Bathroom

- Is the tiling in good condition?
- Does the shower work properly?
- Is the bathroom adequately ventilated?
- If you are buying off-plan, is the developer offering you a decent choice of bathroom fittings?

Furniture

- Is any of the furniture included in the sale? Remember to ask about garden furniture as well.

Repairs and Improvements

- What repairs have been carried out in the last two years?
- Have any improvements being made to the house?
- If changes have been made, was permission granted and are there builders' receipts and guarantees?
- Is there building consent or planning permission for any further additions or alterations?

Defects

- Is the vendor aware of any defects in the property?

Valuations

There are two main ways of having your property valued (appraised): professional valuers and local real estate agents. There are professional valuers in most countries. Often, their main role is to value property for official or court purposes. Sometimes those valuations are of little help to the buyer of property as they may reflect a 'technical' valuation rather than a market value – which is what the buyer wants to know. Prices for valuations vary by country.

Sometimes a more sensible valuation can be obtained from a local estate agent. Obviously, you choose one who is well respected, experienced and with no involvement in this transaction. The agent can be asked how much he or she thinks the property would sell for if the seller wanted a reasonably quick sale. That is, generally, the figure you want to know. This type of valuation is usually cheaper than a formal valuation – perhaps £200 or so.

Inspections by Professionals

Mortgage Lenders

This is no substitute for a proper survey. Many lenders do not require an inspection and, where they do, it is normally fairly peremptory, limited to a check on whether the building is about to fall over and whether it is worth the money the bank is lending you.

Local Builders

If you are going to do a virtual demolition and rebuild then it might make more sense to get a builder to do a report on the property. A reputable and experienced qualified builder will also be able to comment on whether the price is reasonable for the property in its existing state. Ask for a binding written quotation for any building work proposed, but in many countries you will not get one. As in any country, it is as well to get several quotes, though in rural areas this can be tricky.

Local Surveyors

There is no single profession of 'surveyor' in most Eastern European countries as we have in England. Instead, different professionals carry out surveys that are different from each other and appropriate in different circumstances. Seek advice about which to use in your case. In most rural areas there will be limited choice but, for obvious reasons, it is perhaps better not to seek a recommendation from the estate agent selling the property. If you are using UK lawyers, they will probably have a recommendation. If you prefer, you can select someone from a list of local members supplied by a professional body.

The survey from a surveyor will focus on measurement and valuation, but will also cover the essential issues relating to the structure of the property.

Architects

An architect's survey will tend to focus on issues of design and construction although it should cover all of the basic subjects needed in a survey. The body to contact for a list of local architects is the architects' professional body, the College of Architects. Costs vary depending on the size and complexity of the house and the distance from the architect's base.

UK Qualified Surveyors Based Locally

A number of UK surveyors – usually those with a love of the country – have seen a gap in the market and have set themselves up locally in some emerging market countries to provide British style structural surveys. As in this country, they usually offer the brief 'Homebuyers' Report' or the fuller 'Full Structural Survey'.

This is not as simple as it would first appear. To do the job well they must learn about local building techniques and regulations, which are different from those in Britain; without this knowledge the report will be of limited value. Prices are generally slightly more expensive than for a local report, but it will be in English and so avoid the need for translation costs. Your UK lawyer should be able to recommend a surveyor able to do a survey in your area. Alternatively, look for advertisers in the main property magazines.

Check that the surveyor has indemnity insurance covering the provision of reports in that country. Check also on the person's qualifications and experience in providing reports on property in that country and get an estimate. The estimate will only be an estimate, because the surveyor will not know for sure the scope of the task until they visit the property, and because travelling time means that visits to give estimates are not usually feasible.

UK-based Surveyors

Some UK surveyors provide reports from a base in the UK. These can be very good but travelling time often makes them impractical – especially in remote areas – and expensive. Make the same checks as for a UK surveyor based in the country.

Contracts 'Subject to Survey'

This is unusual. Legally there is usually nothing to stop a local preliminary contract containing a get-out clause stating that the sale is conditional upon a satisfactory survey being obtained. It is unlikely to meet with the approval of the seller, his agent or lawyer unless the transaction is unusual, for example, the purchase of a castle where the cost of a survey could be huge. In an ordinary case the seller is likely to tell you to do your survey and then sign a contract. This exposes you to some risk, as the seller could sell to someone else before you get the results of the survey. You may be able to enter into a reservation contract (*see* p.75) to take the property off the market for a couple of weeks and so avoid this risk. Alternatively, you may make a (probably) unenforceable verbal agreement that the seller will not sell to anyone else for the next two weeks and so allow you to have your survey done. It helps if you have established a good relationship with the seller or his agent and have shown you are a serious player, perhaps by having already placed the deposit money with your lawyer. The seller is reluctant to place a get-out clause in the contract because of the difficulty of deciding what is a satisfactory survey. The problem exists in England too.

General

Whichever report you opt for, its quality will depend in part on your input. Agree clearly and in writing the things you expect to be covered in the report. If you do not speak the local language (and the surveyor doesn't speak good English) you may have to ask someone to write on your behalf – your UK lawyer for example. Some of the matters you may wish to think about are set out below and will involve you in additional cost. Ask what will be covered as part of the standard fee and get an estimate for the extras.

Who Should Own the Property?

This section needs to be read in conjunction with the country-specific sections of the book, as the law and tax issues vary from place to place. What follows contains the core elements. The decision as to who should become the legal owner of the property you are going to buy is the most important decision that you will make in connection with the purchase for two reasons: getting it wrong can have unintended consequences, and if you get it wrong it is usually expensive to correct the error later on.

Am I Free To Choose?

Sometimes you will have no choice. For example, in the Czech Republic at present the law requires foreigners buying property to buy in the name of a Czech corporation or limited company. However, even in this situation there is still a choice to be made; it simply moves from the choice of who should own the property to who should own the shares in the company, which gives rise to many of the same issues and problems as the question of who should own the property itself does in more liberal regimes.

In most countries, however, you will be able to choose freely the structure of ownership that best suits your immediate and long-term needs.

The Consequences of Making the Wrong Decision

These vary somewhat from country to country but, generally, there are two main problems. The first is that substantial **tax consequences** flow from the decision as to who should own the property. Where will you pay the income tax due if you rent out the property? Will there be any capital gains tax when you sell it? Will there be any inheritance tax owed when you die? When thinking about tax you have to think not only about the country where the property is located but also about the tax liabilities that may arise in your own country.

Changing the owner of the property will change the tax consequences of ownership. For example, a company is taxed differently from a private individual. Putting the property into your wife's name can mean that the income and capital gains are hers and not yours, which can often reduce your tax bill, for example if she does not work and so is not already a taxpayer. Putting the property into the name of your children means that, as far as the tax authorities in the country where the property is located are concerned, there will be no inheritance tax to pay when you die, as the property has always been theirs.

There are many other options available to you. Picking the right option – one that works well both in the country where that property is located and in the country where you normally live and pay tax – can save you, quite literally, tens or hundreds of thousands of pounds. Recently someone came to see me who was buying a £200,000 property in Croatia. We changed, slightly, the way in which she intended to structure the ownership of the property and saved at least £80,000 in tax liabilities. Even on a modest holiday home costing only £30,000 or £40,000 the tax savings can be significant.

The second problem is that, in many countries, people do not have complete **freedom to do as they please with their assets when they die**. In many countries the law dictates that certain of your relatives have certain automatic rights to inherit a certain proportion of your estate. In these countries you cannot simply write a will and leave the property to, for example, your mistress. If you do this then the people with the protected rights (the so-called 'protected heirs') will still be entitled to inherit, whatever your will might say. Your will is only effective in dealing with the part of your estate that does not pass automatically to the protected heirs. If you put the property in the wrong names then the wrong people will have the right to inherit. For example, if the law states that your children must inherit the bulk of your estate, if you put the property into the name of your second wife it will be only her children and not your children who will have the benefit of that inheritance. This will include the children of any previous marriage of hers. Your own children will effectively have been disinherited. The inheritance problem does not apply in every country, and in some countries it applies to citizens of that country but not to foreigners. The inheritance problem is, generally, of particular concern to those who are in a second marriage or who are living with someone to whom they are not married.

Can I Correct a Wrong Decision?

In the UK, if, for example, a man and his wife buy a property and for some reason only put it in the man's name this is not a big problem. If, a few years later, they decide that what they have done was foolish, it is simple and inexpensive to correct the decision and to put the property in both of their names.

In most continental European countries this is more complicated and more expensive. The gift by one partner to another will, in most cases, be a taxable event. The rate of tax varies from country to country but in the case of an unmarried couple can rise to 82 per cent of the value of the property transferred. On top of the tax there are legal fees and other expenses to pay in connection with the transfer.

Buying in any name and putting it right later is, therefore, not a sensible choice. It is important to get the ownership correct at the outset. This means deciding who should be the legal owners of the property, at the very latest, by the time you come to sign the final contract or title to the property. It is much better if it is decided before you have even signed a reservation agreement in respect of the property, for two reasons. First, in some countries, even the transfer of the benefit of the reservation agreement will be an immediately taxable event, so reserving the property in your name and later lying in the name of you and your wife could incur unnecessary taxation.

Just as importantly, there is now a trend whereby clients agree to buy a property before consulting tax planners. They agree to buy it, for example, in their own joint names. After speaking to an adviser it may become obvious that it would be much more tax-efficient if the property was bought, for example, in the name of their children. Sometimes sellers then state that if the client wants to change their contract the price of the property will increase, because they realise that the change is to save the buyers' money and they want to take some part of it. Although this phenomenon is at present fairly rare, it can be expensive and is therefore best avoided.

The Main Options

One of the options set out below will suit each buyer of a home overseas perfectly. Another might just about make sense. The rest would be an expensive waste of money. The trouble is, it is not obvious which is the right choice. There is no one size fits all. You need in every case to take advice. If your case is simple so will be the advice. If it is complex, the time and money spent will be repaid many times over.

Sole Ownership

In some cases it could be sensible to put the property in the name of one person only. If you run a high-risk business you might want to put the property into your husband's sole name to protect the asset if the business goes bust. If you are 90 and your wife is 22, putting the property in her name will probably make sense – unless you think she will run away with the milkman as soon as she has her hands on your assets. If you intend to let the property and want all the income to be yours for tax purposes in the UK it might also be worth considering. It is seldom a good idea from the point of view of tax or inheritance planning.

Shared Ownership

If two people are buying together they will normally – though not always wisely from a tax and inheritance point of view – buy in both their names. There are two ways of doing this, although in some countries only the first is available. The first is separate ownership and the second is by way of a loose equivalent to an English 'joint tenancy'. The choice you make is of great importance.

If you buy with **separate ownership** then your half is yours and your fellow owner's is theirs. On your death, each half will be disposed of in accordance with the rules laid down by local law. These may permit you to leave the property by your will, as you please. In some countries, as explained above, there are restrictions on your freedom to do so. If you decide to buy with separate ownership then, in certain cases, it can make sense to split the ownership other than 50/50. If, for example, you have three children and your wife has two, then to secure each of those children an equal share on your death you might think about buying 60 per cent in your name and 40 per cent in your wife's name.

Each country has laws regulating the rights of the separate owners as between themselves and as between themselves and third parties. If, instead of buying with separate ownership, you buy with **joint ownership**, then your part of the property will pass automatically to your fellow joint owner or joint owners on your death. This does not necessarily mean that the gift will be tax free. *See* the country-specific sections of this book for more details.

Adding Your Children to the Title

If you give your children the money to buy part of the property and so put them on the title now, you may save them quite a lot of inheritance tax. On your death you will only own (say) one-fifth of the property rather than half. Only that part will be taxable. It may be such a small value as to result in a tax-free inheritance. This generally only works if your children are over 18. There are drawbacks; for example, if they fall out with you they can insist on the sale of the property and receiving their share.

Putting the Property in the Name of Your Children Only

If you put the property only in the name of your children then the property is theirs. The idea also works with other intended beneficiaries. On your death there will be little or no inheritance tax and there will be no need to incur the legal expenses involved in dealing with the inheritance. Those expenses alone can amount to £1,500 or so.

For the right person this can save huge amounts of tax. If you are over the inheritance-tax-free threshold in your own country (currently £275,000 in the UK, $1,500,000 in the USA) then you will pay lots of tax on the excess. In the UK it is 40 per cent. If your home overseas is worth, say, £300,000 then there is a saving of £120,000 by getting it out of your UK estate. Even if your property is only worth £60,000, the saving will be £24,000. These are serious sums of money and if you can avoid paying them, all to the good. Giving the property away can, in the right circumstances, also help reduce income tax and capital gains tax. This all sounds attractive. Remember, however, that you have lost control. It is no longer your property. You may need this money later on. If your children divorce, their husband or wife will be able to claim a share. If they die before you without children of their own, you may end up inheriting the property back from them and having to pay inheritance tax for the privilege.

You might also think of putting the legal ownership of the property in the name of your children (or other preferred beneficiaries on your death) but reserving for you and your co-owner a life interest over the property (*usufruct*). This is the right to use the property for their lifetime. So, on your death, your rights would be extinguished *but* your second wife or partner, who still has a life interest, would still be able to use the property. Only on their death would the property pass in full to the people to whom you gave it years earlier. This device can not only protect your right to use the property but also save inheritance tax, particularly if you are young, the property is valuable and you survive for many years. As ever, there are also drawbacks, not least being the fact that after the gift you no longer own the property. If you wish to sell you will, in most countries, need the agreement of the 'owners', who will be entitled to their share of the proceeds and who would have to agree to buy you a new house.

If you intend to go down this route, it is vital to structure the purchase properly. For example, in some countries, if you give the person the property, that will create an instant liability to gift tax. In those countries you will need to make sure that you have given the people the money – in the UK – and they have then used their own money to buy the property. This will need to be documented. Your lawyer can do this for you.

Even if you give your children the money, this is not the end of the matter. The gift will only be fully free of UK inheritance tax if you survive for seven years – though there is a sliding scale of tax reduction that will start saving you tax if you survive for two years. You will also need to make sure that the gift does not fall foul of the rules on 'gifts with reservation of benefit' (in which case they will be ineffective for tax purposes) or the new pre-owned assets tax, introduced in the UK in April 2005. *See* the section on UK tax in Chapter 05 for details.

You will also need to make sure that the gift will be effective as a tax-saving device in the country where the property is located and that it will, overall and taking into account the tax systems in both countries, prove a cost-effective solution to your problems.

Limited Company

For some people, owning a property via a limited company can be a very attractive option. It can provide privacy, shield the assets from creditors, be useful in getting the status of permanent resident in non-EU countries, and help when you come to sell the property. You own the shares in a company, not a house. If you sell the house you can do so by selling the shares in the company rather than transferring the ownership of the property itself. This can save the acquisition costs that the new owner would otherwise have to pay (often 5–10 per cent of the value of the property) and so, arguably, allow you to charge a bit more for the property.

Owning property via a limited company also help reduce your taxes and problems with inheritance laws. When you die, you do not own 'immoveables' – land and buildings – in the country but 'moveables' – loosely the equivalent of UK 'personal property', and so you may not run into the difficulties that can arise as a result of any local fixed inheritance laws, which (as far as foreigners are concerned) usually only apply to land and buildings.

Local Commercial Company

A local commercial company can be useful if you are going to use the property primarily as an income-generator, especially if it is one of several properties owned. You will be taxed as a company and the overall taxes paid can be lower than would be the case for an individual. Set-up costs can be high and there will be annual management and maintenance costs. In some cases, however, the management and funding issues and the savings in later inheritance and capital gains taxes can outweigh these disadvantages.

Buying through a company gives rise to a host of potential problems as well as benefits. The plan needs to be studied closely by your advisers so that you can decide whether it makes sense in the short, medium *and* long term.

UK Company

It is rare for a purchase through a UK company to make sense for a holiday home or single investment property. This is despite the fact that the ability to pay for the property with the company's money without drawing it out of the company and so paying UK tax on the dividend is attractive. There are still times when it can be the right answer. Once again, you need expert advice from someone familiar with the law of both countries.

Offshore (Tax Haven) Company

The viability of using a tax haven company depends almost entirely on the tax rules in the country concerned and your tax status in the UK. Ownership in this way has most of the same advantages and disadvantages as ownership by other types of company, with the added disincentive that you will, in some countries, have to pay a special tax of a percentage of the value of the property every year. This is to compensate the local tax department for all the inheritance and transfer taxes that they will not receive when the owners of these companies sell them or die. Even in countries that do not yet have this special tax, you need to take into account the likelihood of such a tax being introduced. It is very tempting for governments.

For a person who is (or intends to be) resident in the country for tax purposes, there can be additional advantages and disadvantages. Needless to say, anyone thinking of buying through an offshore company should take detailed advice from a lawyer familiar with the law and tax systems of both countries.

General Points about Companies

The downsides to owning via any form of company is that the company will cost, perhaps, £1,500 to set up and there will be an ongoing cost each year to keep it going. If the Inland Revenue sees you as a director or a 'shadow director' of the company (someone who is not listed as a director but 'pulls the strings') and you use the property as a holiday home he can argue that you have received a 'benefit in kind' from your directorship of the company, which will be taxable under UK law – probably at 40 per cent of the rental value of the property. The local tax inspector can also challenge the arrangement as a sham or fiscal fraud. Despite all this, if you follow the right procedures the company can be a very useful tool – especially for the property investor, the person intending to live overseas (whether or not in the country where the property is located) or where several friends are buying a house together.

SIPPs (Self Invested Pension Plans)

At the time of writing this book the UK government has announced a major revision to the range of pensions available in the UK and to the way in which UK pensions are to be administered. One of these changes is the Self Invested Pension Plan or SIPP.

The detailed regulations for the use of these SIPPS for buying international property have not yet been published, but SIPPs are likely to be a popular and extremely tax-efficient way of owning international real estate for people who view that real estate as a long-term savings programme intended to replace or supplement their regular pension.

A person will be able to set up a SIPP with a regulated and registered SIPP provider. If they are employed, their employer will be able to invest, subject to certain rules, up to £215,000 per year into the SIPP. If they are self-employed they will be able to invest, effectively, up to the amount that they have drawn from their business. The SIPP will then be entitled to invest the monies put into the scheme in a number of different classes of investments, of which real estate is one. Currently (2005) only commercial real estate is permitted but from April 2006 residential real estate will also be permitted, subject to certain rules. The SIPP can also leverage the investment by borrowing up to 50 per cent of the entire SIPP fund.

The advantages of investing in the SIPP, and through the SIPP in real estate, are that the money placed into the pension fund will be tax-deductible (meaning that, for people paying higher-rate income tax, the tax man will subsidise 40 per cent of the cost of buying the property) and that the income and capital gains are generated by the SIPP will be tax-free in the UK.

To take advantage of this opportunity it is necessary to make sure that the purchase is particularly carefully structured so as to minimise the income and capital gains tax liabilities in the country where the property is located. Otherwise the tax paid there could negate the tax savings in the UK.

SIPPs will not be right for somebody who wishes to use the properties for trading purposes or who wishes to draw out parts of the fund for their own personal use before the age of 55.

Trusts

Trusts can be a very useful way of reducing taxation in many countries, especially in continental Europe where there is generally no concept of trusts and, as a result, little in the way of legislation to limit their potential for tax saving. These advantages vary from country to country. See the sections on the individual countries and the section on trusts.

As a vehicle for owning a property, trusts are, generally, of little direct use, however. The law does not, in most countries, recognise the trust, and so the trustees who are be named on the title as the owners of the property would be treated as private individual owners, having to pay all of the income, wealth and inheritance taxes applicable in their case. In a few cases this could still give some benefit but there are probably better ways of getting the same result.

This does not mean that trusts have no place for the owner of property overseas. A trust could still, for example, own the property via a limited company if this fitted the 'owner's' overall tax- and inheritance-planning objectives. Again, careful specialist advice is essential.

Buying the Property: General Procedure

The general legal procedure when buying a property in the countries covered by this book is similar because they have legal systems based on the continental civil law or Napoleonic law. The country-specific sections deal only with the ways in which the local system differs from the general model described below.

The general procedure when buying a property also seems, at first glance, similar to the purchase of a property in England: sign a contract; do some checks; sign a deed of title. This is deceptive. The English legal system is not based on the civil law system and has many different features. These make the procedure very different and even the use of the familiar English vocabulary to describe the very different steps in, for example, Croatia or Bulgaria, can produce an undesirable sense of familiarity. This can lead to assumptions that things that have not been discussed will be the same as they would in England. Work on the basis that the system is totally different.

Agreeing the Price

The price can be freely agreed between the parties. Depending on the economic climate there may be ample or very little room for negotiating a reduction in the asking price. At the time of writing (Jan 2005) the scope was limited for popularly priced properties in the main cities and tourist areas in the emerging markets, for two reasons. Properties are in short supply. Many of these markets are emerging not only as markets but also from a 'socialist' era lasting 50 years or so. There is, therefore, a huge pent-up demand for good homes. The second reason is that these are red-hot as investment destinations for people who see fantastic value for holiday or retirement homes and/or the scope for considerable medium-term growth in value. There is still some scope for negotiating on the price if buying, for example, in undiscovered Montenegro or rural Hungary, especially if the property needs repair.

There is also scope in the case of more expensive properties, many of which have been 'marked up' considerably by a seller selling to a foreign buyer. In every area there are also properties that have 'stuck' on the market, usually because they are overpriced and/or in a poor location. Find out when the property was placed on the market. Ask to see the agent's sale authority (mandate). Negotiating a reduction is always worth a try, but if your advances are rejected do bear in mind the probability that it is not mere posturing but a genuine confidence that the price asked is achievable. If you want to negotiate, start a little low and test the water. You can always increase the offer if the first is rejected. Don't pitch the price too low as, in these markets, this can make a genuine local seller feel offended and that you are not serious. They may then refuse to deal with any increased offer.

If you are unsure of the value of the property – and you may well be, especially if you are buying during a short trip to the country – it is often possible to obtain a valuation (*see* p.61). This is unusual, but useful in the case of properties, especially in rural areas, where there may few obvious similar properties on the market to use for price comparisons. The estate agent may also be able to give you some guidance as to comparative values, but he is, in most cases, being paid by the seller to sell the property, and receiving a commission based on the amount he receives so treat his input with caution. A recommendation from your lawyer will be more independent.

Above all, don't get carried away. There is always another property. Fix a maximum budget before you set off on your visit – and stick to it. Make ample allowance for the likely cost of repair or refurbishment. If you are buying as a rental investment, do some research into the likely rent achievable (in high and low season), the number of weeks you will potentially be able to let the property, likely returns, expenses and management costs before committing yourself (see **Letting Your Property**, pp.117–26).

Which Currency?

In most countries you are free to agree a price for the property in whatever currency you like. In others, for example, Croatia, the price must be agreed in the local currency. In many emerging markets it is commonplace to price properties in major currencies such as the euro or sterling. The currency used will reflect the main buyers in that area. This use of 'foreign' currencies is a hangover from an era, generally now passed, when the local currencies were weak and prone to high levels of inflation. This agreement only affects you and the seller. The price of the property will be recorded in the deed of sale in the local currency.

This use of a currency other than the local one would involve the buyer paying and the seller receiving the currency of their choice, which might be useful if, for example, both were British and living in the UK, as it will remove the risk of exchange rate fluctuations for both parties.

If you are worried about exchange rates between sterling and the currency chosen, it might be more beneficial to enter into a 'forward contract' to buy or sell the currency. See the section on transferring the funds, pp.78–80.

How Much Should be Declared in the Deed of Sale?

For many years there was a tradition in most countries of under-declaring the price actually paid for a property when signing the deed of sale. This was because the taxes and notary's fees due were calculated on the basis of the price declared. A lower price means fewer taxes for the buyer and less capital gains tax for the seller. This still applies in many of the emerging market countries, but under-declaration is generally foolish; it may cost you more in the long run, with higher capital gains tax to pay when you sell because on paper you have made more profit. However, some form of under declaration is almost inevitable in most of these markets.

There is scope for, quite legitimately, for reducing the price declared and so reducing tax. For example, if, as sometimes happens, your purchase of a holiday home includes some furniture, a boat or a car, there is no need to declare the value of those items and pay stamp duty on the price paid. You can enter into a separate contract for the 'extras' and save some money. There is also a semi-legitimate 'grey area' for manoeuvre, rather like doing 40mph in a 30mph limit. It is wrong but you will not get into serious trouble. Seek advice.

Try to avoid arrangements, usually as part of an under-declaration, where part of the money is handed over in cash in brown-paper parcels. Apart from being illegal, it is dangerous at a practical level. Buyers have lost the bundle – or been robbed on the way to the notary's office. Sometimes there is even a suspicion that the seller, who knew where you were going to be and when, could be involved.

General Enquiries and Special Enquiries

Certain enquiries are made routinely in the course of the purchase of a property. These are not the same as the enquiries that would be made in the UK. Typical UK enquiries would, in many cases, be inappropriate in the country where the property is located. Even if made they would not be answered; the seller, his lawyer, the town hall and the land registry would think you were crazy. Equally, the enquiries made locally sometimes include enquiries about things that would not be asked about in the UK. In practice, thousands of local people quite satisfactorily buy houses using the local system. Sometimes additional enquiries and precautions are needed but, generally, if buying a property in a country you will need to follow the system in that country and not try to superimpose on it elements of your 'home' system.

These regular enquiries vary from country to country but generally include a check on the planning situation of the property. This will reveal the position of the property itself but it will not, at least directly, tell you about its neighbours and it will not reveal general plans for the area. If you want to know whether the authorities are going to put a prison in the village or run a new railway line through your back garden (both, presumably, bad things) or build a motorway access point or railway station 3km away (both, presumably, good things) you will need to ask. There are various organisations you can approach but, just as in England, there is no single point of contact for such enquiries. If you are concerned about what might happen in the area then you will need to discuss the position with your lawyers at an early stage. There may be a considerable amount of work (and therefore cost) involved in making full enquiries, the results of which can never be guaranteed.

Normal enquiries also include a check that the seller is the registered owner of the property and that it is sold (if this has been agreed) free of mortgages or other charges.

In order to advise you what other enquiries might be appropriate, your lawyer will need to be told your proposals for the property. Do you intend to let it out? If so, is it on a commercial basis? Do you intend to use it for business purposes? Do you want to extend or modify the exterior of the property? Do you intend to make interior structural alterations? Agree in advance the additional enquiries you would like to make and get an estimate of the cost of those enquiries.

Reservation and Preliminary Contracts

Reservation Contracts

In many cases, particularly if you are dealing with an international estate agency, you will start off by signing a reservation contract. As its name suggests, this contract reserves a particular property for you, typically for 30 days. It does not commit you to the purchase of the property.

When you sign the reservation contract you will pay over a small deposit – typically £2,000/€3,000. During the reservation period your lawyers can check out the property, you can get surveys done and you can arrange your finance. If, within the reservation period, you go ahead and sign a preliminary contract to buy (see below) then the deposit paid will be counted as part of the price of the property. If you do not go ahead simply because you have changed your mind you will, generally, lose your reservation deposit. This will depend on the terms of your contract. If you do not go ahead because your lawyers find a genuine legal problem you should be entitled to the refund of the deposit.

There are dangers involved in signing these contracts:

- **Sometimes, although the document says it is a reservation contract it is actually, when read by a lawyer, a full purchase contract giving the seller additional rights against you if you do not go ahead with the purchase.**

- **Sometimes the contract will limit (or eliminate) the circumstances in which your deposit is repayable.**

- **Once you have parted with the money to the seller or the seller's agent it is always harder to get it back, whatever your legal rights.**

Unless you are absolutely clear about the effect of what you are signing it is always sensible to get even a reservation contract checked over by your lawyer before you sign it. Nonetheless, reservation contracts are the best way to start the purchase of a property in an emerging market country, as you secure the property for only a modest sum of money.

Preliminary Contracts

Most sales start with a preliminary contract. This is similar in concept to the sort of contract you sign when buying a property in the UK or the USA, and the details vary from country to country. Signing a preliminary contract has far-reaching legal consequences, which are sometimes different from the consequences of signing a similar document in England. Always seek legal advice before signing.

Key Points to Check Before Signing a Preliminary Contract

Property in the Course of Construction	Existing Property
Are you clear about what you are buying?	
Have you taken legal advice about who should be the owner of the property?	
Have you taken legal advice about inheritance issues?	
Are you clear about boundaries?	
Are you clear about access?	
	Are you sure you can change the property as you want?
	Are you sure you can use the property for what you want?
	Is the property connected to water, electricity, gas, etc.?
	Have you had a survey done?
Have you made all necessary checks *or* arranged for them to be made?	
Have you included 'get-out' clauses for all important checks not yet made?	
Is your mortgage finance arranged or a get-out clause inserted in the contract?	
Is the seller clearly described?	
If the seller is not signing in person, have you seen a power of attorney/mandate to authorise the sale?	
Are you fully described?	
Is the property fully described? Identification? Land registry details?	
Is the price correct?	
Are there any possible circumstances in which it can be increased or extras described fully?	
Are the stage payments fully described?	
Do stage payments meet any legal restrictions?	
Is the date for completion of the work agreed?	
Does the contract say when possession will be given?	
Is there a receipt for the deposit paid?	
In what capacity is the deposit paid?	
Is the date for signing the final contract/title agreed?	
Does the contract provide for the sale to be free of charges and debts?	
Does the contract provide for vacant possession?	
Is the estate agent's commission dealt with?	
What happens if there is a breach of contract?	

If you have signed a contract before seeking legal advice and it turns out that it has deficiencies that, though not legally sufficient to cancel the contract, cause you concern, it may be possible to renegotiate the contract. The sooner you attempt to do this the better.

Powers of Attorney

Very often it will not be convenient for you to have to go to the country to sign the final contract in person. Sometimes there may be other things that, in the normal course of events, would require your personal intervention but where it would be inconvenient for you to have to deal with them yourself. Just as often you will not know whether you will be available to sign in person. Completion dates are notoriously fluid and so you could plan to be there but suffer a last-minute delay to the signing that makes it impossible.

The solution to this problem is the power of attorney. This document authorises the person appointed to do whatever the document authorises on behalf of the person granting the power. The most sensible type of power to use will be the local style of power that is appropriate to the situation. In theory an English-style power should be sufficient, but in practice the cost and delay associated with getting it recognised will be unacceptable.

The type of power of attorney that you will need depends on what you want to use it for. Your specialist English lawyer can discuss your requirements with you and prepare the necessary document. Alternatively you can deal directly with the local notary, who will ultimately need the power.

The power must be drafted in express terms clear enough to leave no doubt that the person appointed has the authority to do what he is going to do. This is not always simple. For example, the purchase of a property could also involve the person drawing a cheque on your local bank account. The power will in that case have to authorise both activities.

The power of attorney will generally need to be signed in front of a notary; it will cost about £50–60 for the notary to witness a simple power of attorney. The power will then need to be authenticated for use overseas by being stamped by the UK Foreign & Commonwealth Office. This process is known as 'having the apostile affixed'. This is required under the Hague Convention, which governs the international use of such documents. It sounds complicated but your lawyer will arrange it quickly. It currently costs £12 in fees payable to the FCO.

A power of attorney can specifically state that it cannot be revoked for a certain period. If it is not stated that this is the case, the power can be revoked in a number of ways. It can, specifically, be time-limited. That is, you could grant it in such a way as it was only valid for six months from the date of signing it. Alternatively it can be cancelled by giving written notice to the person appointed. Recorded delivery post is the best way of doing this. The power ceases to be valid on the death or mental incapacity of the person granting it. It cannot, therefore, be used in the same way as an English enduring power of attorney to look after the affairs of an elderly person who has lost his or her mental capacity.

The power of attorney is a powerful tool. It gives the person appointed great power to do things on your behalf that could prove very costly. So it should only be given to people you trust implicitly, such as a close member of your family or your lawyer. If an English lawyer misuses the power he or she will be struck off and you will receive full compensation.

Even if you intend to go to to an Eastern European country to sign the final contract, it is sensible to think about granting a power in case of emergency. It is not something that can be done at the last moment. From decision to getting the document to Bulgaria will take at least 7 and, more likely, 10 days. If you are able to go, the power will not be used.

Even if you have granted a power of attorney, if you get the opportunity to go at the time of the signing, it is worth doing so in order to check the house to make sure that everything is in order before the final contract is signed.

Getting the Money There

There are a number of ways of getting the money to its destination.

Electronic Transfer

The most practical is to have money sent electronically by SWIFT transfer from a UK bank directly to the recipient's bank overseas. This costs £20–35 depending on your bank. It is safer to allow a week for the money to arrive in a rural bank, despite everyone's protestations that it will be there the same day.

Europe has introduced unique account numbers for all bank accounts, which incorporate a code for the identity of the bank and branch involved as well as the account number of the individual customer. These are known as IBANK numbers. They should be quoted, if possible, on all international currency transfers. You can send the money from your own bank, via your lawyers or via a specialist currency dealer.

For the sums you are likely to be sending, you should receive an exchange rate much better than the 'tourist rate' you see in the press. There is no such thing as a fixed exchange rate in these transactions. The bank's official inter-bank rate changes by the second and the job of the bank's currency dealers is to make a profit by selling to you at the lowest rate they can get away with. Thus if you do a lot of business with a bank and they know you are 'on the ball' you are likely to be offered a better rate than a one-off customer. For this reason it is often better to send it via your specialist UK lawyers, who will be dealing with large numbers of such transactions. This also has the advantage that their bank, which deals with international payments all the time, is less likely to make a mistake causing delay to the payment than your bank for which such a payment might be a rarity.

You or your lawyers might use a **specialist currency dealer** to make the transfer of funds instead of a main UK bank. Such dealers almost always give a better exchange rate than an ordinary bank. Sometimes the difference can be significant, especially compared to your local branch of a high street bank. This can be worth 1 per cent of the price of the property. This means that changing your currency in this way can save you £1,000 on the price of a £100,000 property. Although these dealers use major banks actually to transfer the funds, you need to make sure that the dealer you are dealing with is reputable. Your money is paid to them, not to the major bank, so could be at risk if the dealer is not bonded or otherwise protected.

However you make the payment, make sure you understand whether you or the recipient is going to pick up the receiving bank's charges. If you need a clear amount at the destination you will have to make allowances for these deductions, either by sending a bit extra or by asking your UK bank to pay all the charges. These can be substantial, sometimes a couple of hundred pounds or more. Even if you do ask your bank to pick up all the charges, often additional charges are levied at the far end and erode the amount sent, so a margin for safety should always be included in the payment.

Make sure you have the details of the recipient bank, its customer's name, the account codes and the recipient's reference precisely right. Any error and the payment is likely to come bank to you as undeliverable – and may involve you in bearing the cost of it being converted back into sterling.

Forward-buying

Using a currency dealer you can also 'forward-buy' the currency needed. This can be attractive because you will know accurately how much, in sterling, your house will cost you when you take delivery of it in, say, 18 months' time. In times when exchange rates are volatile this can be comforting. Recently, for example, the pound has been worth €1.72 and it has been worth €1.30. A €200,000 house would therefore have cost you anywhere between £116,279 and £153,846 – a difference of £37,597. That is a lot of money. You will, most likely, be paying it out of a salary paid in sterling, so the difference is real.

Many people want to eliminate this risk, but we do not have a crystal ball and so cannot predict what the future holds as far as exchange rates are concerned.

If you think it likely that sterling will fall against the euro (or any other currency you might need) then you could buy all of the money you need today. If you are unsure what might happen and want to hedge your bets you could buy half of what you need now and the rest when it is needed. That means that, whatever happens to the exchange rate, you will neither win nor lose. The increase in value of one currency you hold balances out the fall in the other.

There are two ways of forward-buying. If you have the sterling amount already available, you can simply buy the currency you need now. However, it can be cheaper to keep that invested and to enter into a forward-buying contract with a currency dealer. This is a contract with a currency dealer under which you agree to buy a certain amount of money on or before a certain date. For example, if you need €200,000 in 18 months time you can agree today to buy that from a dealer at an exchange rate that is agreed today. It is, generally, fairly close to the rate prevailing today. This is because of various complicated ways in which the dealers buy, sell and invest currency. Under the contract, buyers generally pay 10 per cent of the price today and the rest when they take delivery of the money.

If you need to pay stage payments you can either take out several contracts or one contract permitting you to draw down any part of the amount agreed at any point up to the end date on the contract. This has a number of attractions. You do not need to have the money available today. You know the cost of the house. It is simple. It also has drawbacks. These include all the potential problems of all dealings with currency dealers plus the danger that the company could go bust in the period between signing the contract and taking delivery of the money. Make sure you deal with reputable bonded dealers.

Banker's Drafts

You can arrange for your UK bank to issue you with a bankers draft (bank certified cheque) which you can take to the country you are buying in and pay into your bank account. Make sure that the bank knows that the draft is to be used overseas and issues you with an international draft.

Generally this is not a good way to transfer the money. It can take a considerable time – sometimes weeks – for the funds deposited to be made available for your use. The recipient bank's charges can be surprisingly high. The exchange rate offered against a £ sterling draft may be uncompetitive as you are a captive customer. If the draft is lost it can, at best, take months to obtain a replacement and, at worst, be impossible to do so.

Cash

This is not recommended. You will need to declare the money on departure from the UK and on arrival in the country where the property is located. Even then, if you declare £200,000 or so they will think you are a terrorist or drugs dealer. That suspicion can have far reaching consequences in terms of listings in police files and even surveillance. To add insult to injury, the exchange rate you will be offered for cash is usually very uncompetitive and the notary may well refuse to accept the money in his account. Don't do it.

Exchange Control and Other Restrictions on Moving Money

There is, generally, no longer any exchange control when taking money to or from these countries. There are, however, some statistical records kept showing the flow of funds and the purpose of the transfers. When you sell your property you will be able to bring the money back to England if you wish to do so.

Final Checks

All of the points outstanding must be resolved to your satisfaction, as must any other points of importance to you, before you sign the final contract. This includes identifying any 'snagging' problems on a new property.

The date stated in the preliminary contract for signing the final contract could be described as flexible or aspirational. More often than not it will move, if only by a day or so. For this reason it is not sensible to book your travel or send your furniture until you are almost sure that matters will proceed on a certain day. That may mean a few days before signing.

Checklist of Steps to Take Before Completion

Property in the Course of Construction   Existing Property

Prepare power of attorney

Check what documents must be produced on signing the final contract

Check that any official permission needed to buy has been granted

Confirm all other important enquiries are clear

Receive draft of proposed final contract – one month in advance if possible

Confirm arrangements (date, time, place) for completion with your lender
if you have a mortgage

Confirm arrangements (date, time, place) for completion with notary
if you have a mortgage

Send necessary funds

Receive rules of community of owners if any (*see* below)

Insurance cover arranged?

Sign off work or list defects   Proof of payment of community fees

Proof of payment of other bills

The Community of Owners

This is a device familiar in continental Europe but more unusual in the UK. It is similar to the Uk concept of 'commonhold'.

The basic idea is that when a number of people own land or buildings in such a way that they have exclusive use of part of the property but shared use of the rest, then a community is created. Houses on their own plots with no shared facilities will not be a member of a community. In a community, the buyer of a house or an apartment owns his own house or apartment outright – as the English would say, 'freehold' – and shares the use of the remaining areas as part of a community of owners. It is not only the shared pool that is jointly owned but (in an apartment) the lift shafts, corridors, roof, foundations, entrance areas, parking zones, etc. The members of the community are each responsible for their own home. They collectively agree the works needed on the common areas and a budget for those works. They then become responsible for paying their share of those common expenses, as stipulated in their title.

The community is managed by an elected committee and appoints a president and secretary – both of whom are residents in the community. Day-to-day management is usually delegated to an administrator. Charges are divided in the proportions stipulated in deed creating the community. You will pay the same community fees whether you use the place all year round or only for two weeks' holiday.

The Final Contract

This must usually be signed in front of a notary in the country where the property is located, either by the parties in person or someone holding power of attorney for them. The terms of the document itself vary by country.

The signing of the final contract is not the end of the matter. Your taxes must be paid to the state. Once the taxes are paid, your title and any mortgage should be presented for registration at the Land Registry. Do this as quickly as possible, as there is a danger of someone registering another transaction (such as a debt or judgement) against the property. Those who register first get priority.

Key Points When Buying Property

Property Under Construction

- Make sure you understand exactly what you are buying. How big is the property? What will it look like? How will it be finished? What appliances are included? What facilities will it enjoy?

- Think about who should own the property so as to minimise tax and inheritance problems.

- Make sure the contract has all of the necessary clauses required to protect your position.

- Be clear about the timetable for making stage payments.

- Think about whether you should forward-buy currency (*see* 'Getting the Money There', pp.79–80).

- When you take delivery of the property consider carefully whether it is worth incurring the expense of an independent survey to confirm that all is in order with the construction and to help draft any 'snagging list'.

Resale Properties

- Make sure you understand exactly what you are buying. Are the boundaries clear? What furniture or fittings are included?

• Think about whether to have the property surveyed, especially if it is an older property and your statutory guarantee will soon be expiring.

• Think about who should own the property so as to minimise tax and inheritance problems.

• Make sure the contract has all of the necessary clauses required to protect your position.

• Think about whether you should forward-buy currency.

• When you take delivery of the property make sure that everything agreed is present.

Old Properties

• Are you having a survey? Not to do so can be an expensive mistake.

• Are you clear about any restoration costs to be incurred? Do you have estimates for those charges?

• Are you clear about any restrictions over the use of the property or rights that have grown up over the property?

• Are there any planning problems associated with any alterations or improvements you want to make to the property?

• When you take delivery of the property make sure that everything agreed is present.

Rural Properties

• Such properties have often acquired a number of rights and obligations over the years. Are you clear about any obligations you might be taking on?

• Do any people enjoy any rights of pre-emption over the property?

• You are probably buying for peace and quiet and the rural idyll. Are you sure that nothing is happening in the vicinity of your property that will be detrimental?

• If you have any plans to change the property or to use it for other purposes, will this be permitted?

City Properties

• City properties will usually be apartments; see over.

• Unless you are used to living in a city – and, in particular, a continental city – do not underestimate the noise that will be generated nearby. If you are in a busy area (and you are likely to be) this will go on until late at night. How good is the sound insulation?

• Are your neighbouring properties occupied by full-time residents, are they weekday-only *'pieds à terre'* or are they holiday homes? Think about security issues.

• If you intend to use a car, where will you park?

Apartments and Houses Sharing Facilities

• Have you thought about having a survey of the property carried out? Will it include the common parts?

• Read the rules of any community of owners – *see* p.81.

• Make sure you understand the charges that will be raised by the community.

• Make contact with its administrator. Ask about any issues affecting the community. Are there any major works approved but not yet carried out? Make sure that the contract is clear about who is responsible for paying for these.

• Make contact with other owners. Are they happy with the community and the way it is run? Remember that no one is ever fully happy!

• Understand how the community is run. Once you are an owner try to attend the general meetings of the community.

First Things to Do after Completion

• Insure the property and its contents.

• Make a full photographic record of the property, useful in the event of an insurance claim and for your scrapbook.

• Make arrangements for your bank to pay water, electricity and other utility bills.

• Make a will in the local form covering your assets in the country, which will usually involve making small changes in your existing UK will as well.

Financial
Implications

Taxes

All tax systems are complicated and the systems in the emerging markets are no exception. They are often made more complicated because these countries have, generally, only just emerged from relative isolation and so until the last few years there was little interaction with other countries as far as private individuals and their taxation are concerned. As a result the rules are less well understood than, say, the rules in France or Spain. The good news is that they are often not understood by the tax administration either!

Fortunately, most people will only have limited contact with the more intricate parts of the system. For many non-resident owners of holiday homes their contact with the system will be minimal.

It is helpful to have some sort of understanding about the way in which the system works and the taxes that you might face. Be warned: getting even a basic understanding will make your head hurt. You also need to be particularly careful about words and concepts that seem familiar to you, but which have a fundamentally different meaning in the country where your home is located from in England. And be aware that the rules change every year.

There are several points in this book where I have said that the contents are only a general introduction to the subject. There is nowhere where this is more true that in this section. Books (and long ones at that) have been written about the subject of international taxation. This general introduction does little more than scratch the surface of an immensely complex subject. It is intended to allow you to have a sensible discussion with your professional advisers and, perhaps, to help you work out the questions that you need to be asking them. It is not intended as a substitute for proper professional advice.

Your situation when you have a foot in two countries – and, in particular, when you are moving permanently from one country to another – involves the consideration of the tax systems in both countries with a view to minimising your tax obligations in both. It is not just a question of paying the lowest amount of tax in, say, Poland. The best choice in Poland could be very damaging to your position in England, and vice versa. The task of international advisers and their clients is to find a path of compromise. There is no one perfect solution to most tax questions, though there are a great many bad solutions.

Each individual will have a different set of priorities when deciding which course to pursue. Some are keen to screw the last halfpenny of advantage out of their situation. Others recognise that they will have to pay some tax but simply wish to moderate their tax bill. For many the main concern is a simple structure, which they understand and can continue to manage without further assistance in the years ahead. Just as different clients have different requirements, so different advisers have differing views as to the function of the adviser when dealing with a client's tax affairs. One of your first tasks when speaking to your financial adviser should be to discuss your basic philosophy concerning the payment of tax and management of your affairs, to make sure that you are both operating with the same objective in mind and that you are comfortable with his or her approach to solving your problem.

Are You Resident or Non-resident for Tax Purposes?

The biggest single factor in determining how you will be treated by the tax authorities in any country is whether you are resident in that country for tax purposes. This concept of tax residence causes a great deal of confusion. Tax residence can have different meanings in different countries.

Tax residence is nothing to do with whether you have registered as resident in a country or with whether you have obtained a residence permit or residence card (though a person who has a card will usually be tax resident). Nor does it have anything to do with whether you have a home (residence) in that country – although a person who is tax resident will normally have a home there. Nor, in most countries except the UK, is it much to do with your intentions. Tax residence is a question of fact. The law lays down certain tests that will be used to decide whether you are tax resident or not. If you fall into the categories stipulated in the tests, then you will be considered tax resident whether you want to be or not and whether it was your intention to be tax resident or not.

It is your responsibility to make your tax declarations each year. Part of that declaration will be whether or not you consider yourself resident. The decision as to whether you fall into the category of resident is, in the first instance, then made by the tax office. If you disagree with the decision you can appeal through the courts. Because people normally change their tax residence when they move from one country to another, the basis on which decisions are made tends to be regulated by international law and to be fairly, but not totally, consistent from country to country.

Tax Residence in the UK or Overseas

You will have to consider two different questions concerning tax residence. The first is whether you will be treated as tax resident in England and the second is whether you will be treated as tax resident in the country where your overseas property is located. For the purposes of this section I will call that place Bulgaria, as it is simpler.

It is outside the scope of this book to go into any details about United Kingdom taxation but I will have to deal with some basic points in order that the explanation of international taxation makes any sense. In England there are two tests that will help determine where you pay tax and how much tax you will pay. These are your domicile and your residence. This is important terminology. Some taxes are only paid by people *domiciled* in the UK. Some are paid by all who are *tax resident* here, some are paid by people who are *ordinarily resident* in the UK.

Residence falls into two categories. Under English law there is a test of simple residence and of ordinary residence.

Residence

Whether you are resident for tax purposes is a question of fact, to be decided in the light of all the circumstances of your case. It depends on a combination of how much time you spend in the UK and your intentions in being there. Most of our readers will have lived in the UK all of their lives and will intend to continue to do so. They are clearly tax resident in the UK – short absences abroad do not alter your tax residence. If you go abroad for a full tax year, your tax residence will come to an end – or, at least, be suspended pending your return to the UK. If you go abroad intending to stay away for a protracted or indefinite period, by concession you will be treated as ceasing to be tax resident from the date of your departure.

Persons are generally be treated as resident in the UK if they spend 183 or more days in the UK during the tax year (6 April to 5 April). Visitors are treated as resident if they come to the UK regularly for less than 183 days per year and yet spend significant time here. If on average they spend, over a period of four or more years, more than three months in the UK per year they are treated as tax resident. If you come to the UK intending to stay for two years or more you will be treated as being tax resident in the UK from the date of your arrival.

Ordinary Residence

Once again, most of our readers will have lived in the UK all of their lives. They will be treated as ordinarily resident in the UK. Persons can continue to be ordinarily resident in the UK even after they have stopped actually being resident here. Persons are ordinarily resident in England if their presence is a little more settled. The residence is an important part of their life and it will normally have gone on for some time.

This phrase means what it says. Ordinary residence is residence in the UK that is not casual or uncertain. You are ordinarily resident in the UK if you live here in the ordinary course of your life. This is a common sense test. For example, if you have lived in the UK for years but then go to live abroad for two years you will no longer be resident in the UK but, if you intend to come back or are still based here, you may still be 'ordinarily resident' in the UK.

The most important thing to understand is that, once you have been ordinarily resident in this country, the simple fact of going overseas will not automatically bring that residence to an end. If you leave this country in order to take up permanent residence elsewhere then, by concession, the Inland Revenue will treat you as ceasing to be resident on the day following your departure. But it will not treat you as ceasing to be ordinarily resident if, after leaving, you spend an average of 91 or more days per year in this country over any four-year period.

Domicile

Domicile is the test of belonging and is very difficult to change. You start off with a domicile of birth, generally the domicile of your father. The test of domicile is the test of where you consider your real home, your roots. It used to be expressed as the place you would choose to go home to if you knew you were dying. You can change that domicile, but it is difficult to do so. It can be very worthwhile to do so in tax terms, however, especially for inheritance tax.

You cannot escape the effects of domicile just be expressing a wish to do so. You will be deemed to be domiciled in the UK, even if you have broken your actual links of domicile, if you have been tax resident in the UK for at least 17 of the last 20 years. In other words, even if you do everything needed to break your domicile (*see* below) you will not escape until after you have been living out of the UK for at least three years.

Tax Residence in More Than One Country

Remember that you can be tax resident in more than one country under the respective rules of those countries. For example, you might spend 230 days in the year in Bulgaria and 135 days in England. In this case you could end up, under the rules of each country, being responsible for paying the same tax in two or more countries. This would be unfair, so many countries have signed reciprocal double taxation treaties (*see* 'Double Taxation Treaties', p.94).

Changing your Residence

Changing your residence is straightforward. You need to establish a residence of some kind abroad, remain out of the UK for a complete tax year, refrain from returning to the UK for more than 183 days in any one tax year and make sure that you do not spend more than an average of 91 days per year in the UK.

Changing your Domicile

Changing your domicile is much more complicated. Detailed consideration of the necessary steps is outside the scope of this book. In summary, however, the more of the following steps you take, the more likely it is that the Inland Revenue will accept that you are no longer domiciled in the UK.

- **Make clear your intention to change your domicile to as many people as possible.**
- **Live abroad for a long time.**

- Buy a home abroad. Failing that, at least enter into a long-term lease on a home abroad.
- Take your immediate family to live with you.
- Put your children through the local education system rather than sending them to an expat school.
- Make long-term investments there.
- Set up or relocate your business there.
- Resign from all clubs, professional institutions, political societies, churches and the like in your old country and join similar organisations in your new country.
- Marry a local person.
- Vote in your new country.
- Make a will respecting the laws of your new country.
- Arrange to be buried in your new country.

Decisions When Planning Tax Affairs

The most basic decisions that you will have to make when planning your tax affairs is whether to cease to be resident in the UK, whether to cease to be ordinarily resident in this country and whether to change your domicile to another country. The second consideration is when in the tax year to make these changes. Seek proper professional advice before making these decisions. You will need advice from specialist lawyers, accountants or financial advisers all of whom should be able to help you.

UK Taxes for People Resident in the UK but Owning Property Abroad

The mere ownership of property overseas has no tax consequences in the UK. Making money by letting it, selling it at a profit or leaving it to someone by way of inheritance does. The nature of those consequences depends on whether you are tax resident, ordinarily resident and/or domiciled in the UK.

Income Derived From Overseas Property

In practical terms, for most readers who normally live in the UK, you will pay UK tax on your letting income but receive a credit for any tax on the same income already paid in the country where the property is located.

Other Overseas Income

This could, for example, be interest from any bank accounts you have abroad. Once again, you pay any necessary tax overseas and receive a credit for that tax against the corresponding tax due in the UK.

'Benefits in Kind'

If you choose or are obliged to own your property abroad through the vehicle of a limited company of which you are either a director or a 'shadow director', you will face the possibility of being taxed in the UK on any fringe benefits that you receive from that company. These benefits will include the right to occupy the company's house rent-free.

A shadow director is a person who effectively pulls the strings in a company and controls it despite the fact that he or she is not officially a director of a company. If you own a home abroad through a company you are almost certainly going to count as, at least, a shadow director.

If you use the company's property in order to do your job – for example, if you are asked to decorate the property – you should not have to pay any tax in relation to that period of occupancy. On the other hand, if the company allows you the use of the property for your holidays then you will face UK income tax on the market rental of that property for the period for which you occupied it. For many people who pay higher-rate tax, that tax will be at 40 per cent.

If this situation applies to you, you therefore have the choice of either paying the company that owns the property (in effect, yourself) the market rental for the weeks you have used, or paying the UK Inland Revenue the tax. In many cases you may need to pay the company some money in order to pay the expenses of the property, so paying the rent could be the better option. Also, in many cases the company will have sufficient expenses to set off against its income that there will be no tax payable in the country where the property is located or where the company is located. In other cases, however, there may be no allowable deductions against rental income and so the money you pay would be taxed in the country where the property is located. Obviously, it is then a question of working out whether the tax payable to the Inland Revenue here is greater or less than the tax that you would have to pay abroad.

Capital Gains

You hope that when you sell your property overseas you will make a substantial profit. These gains will generally be taxed in the country where the property is located, though some countries do not charge capital gains tax. See the country-specific sections of this book for more details.

Gains will also be taxable in the UK if you are UK-domiciled *and* either tax resident or ordinarily resident in the UK. The tax rates are 10 per cent, 20 per cent and 40 per cent – as for investment income. Calculating the amount of your taxable gain is not entirely straightforward. The detail of how to do this is beyond the scope of this book but a general indication of the process will probably be helpful. The consideration – value – that you are deemed to have received for each of your disposals will be either the actual sale price obtained or, in the case of gifts made to or transfers to connected persons such as business partners or close relatives, the open market value of the assets. The gain is then calculated as follows:

Step	Cost	Example
Calculate the consideration received for the item		£300,000
What was the cost of the item?	£50,000	
Was the item bought before 31 March 1982? If so, use its value on that date.	£100,000	
Deduct actual or deemed acquisition cost		–£100,000
Deduct expenses of acquisition and disposal		–£25,000
Deduct cost of any capital improvements to the asset		–£15,000
Deduct indexation allowance up to 5 April 1998 on cost, expenses and improvements in accordance with RPI increase – March 1982 = 79.4%, April 1998 = 162.6%		–£146,700
Net Gain		**£153,000**
Deduct taper relief from 6 April 1998 – asset owned 6 full years since 1998 – non business asset 20 per cent, business asset 75%		20%
Net taxable gain		**£122,400**

To calculate the applicable tax rate you take your total gains and losses for the tax year, deducting any allowable capital losses brought forward and the annual exemption of (in 2004/5) £8,200. You then add your taxable income – your income after reliefs and allowances. The resulting sum is taxed as follows:

Capital Gains Tax Rates 2004/5

Total income and gains up to £2,020	10%
Balance up to £31,400	20%
Over £31,400	40%

Most people, therefore, will be paying at 40 per cent. Subject to any more favourable arrangements in the specific double taxation treaty concerned, you will receive a credit for any tax paid on the same gain to the government of the country where the property is located.

Inheritance Tax

Most countries charge inheritance tax on any real estate (land or buildings) owned in that country. When you die, inheritance tax (IHT) is paid in the UK on the value of your property overseas if you are UK-domiciled or deemed to be so. This is an important point, particularly if you have gone to live in a country where there is no inheritance tax. In these cases you should seek advice as to whether, in your case, steps can be taken to end your UK domicile and so avoid having to pay IHT. This tax amounts to a lot of money if your estate exceeds the tax-free allowance of £263,000. The tax is 40 per cent of the excess over the tax-free allowance. Double taxation relief is available, in the absence of a more generous arrangement under the treaty concerned, by way of giving you a credit for any similar overseas against your UK IHT liability.

UK Taxes for People Living Abroad

Detailed treatment of this subject is outside the scope of this book, but the significance of these residence rules is that you will continue to be liable for some British taxes for as long as you are either ordinarily resident or domiciled in the UK. Put far too simply, once you have left UK to live abroad:

- **You will continue to have to pay tax in the UK on any capital gains you make anywhere in the world for as long as you are ordinarily resident *and* domiciled in the UK.**

- **You will continue to be liable for UK inheritance tax on all of your assets located anywhere in the world for as long as you remain domiciled in the UK. This will be subject to double taxation relief. Other, more complex rules apply in certain circumstances.**

- **You will always pay UK income tax (Schedule A) on income arising from land and buildings in the UK – wherever your domicile, residence or ordinary residence.**

- **You will pay UK income tax (Schedule D) on the following basis:**

  - **Income from 'self-employed' trade or profession carried out in the UK (Cases I and II) – normally taxed in the UK in all cases if income arises in the UK.**

  - **Income from interest, annuities or other annual payments in the UK (Case III) – normally taxed in the UK if income arises in the UK and you are ordinarily resident in the UK.**

  - **Income from investments and businesses outside the UK (Cases IV and V) – normally only taxed in the UK if you are UK-domiciled *and* resident or ordinarily resident in the UK.**

  - **Income from government pensions (fire, police, army, civil servant, etc.) in all cases.**

  - **Sundry profits not otherwise taxable (Case VI) arising out of land or building in the UK – always taxed in the UK.**

- **You will pay UK income tax on any income earned from salaried employment in the UK (Schedule E) only for earnings from duties performed in the UK unless you are resident and ordinarily resident in the UK – in which case you usually pay tax in the UK on your worldwide earnings.**

Double Taxation Treaties

A double taxation treaty determines what happens if, under local tax law and UK tax law, you are deemed to be liable to pay tax in both countries. The general principle behind all double taxation treaties is that it is unfair that you have to pay the same tax twice, so the rules are designed to help the two countries decide which of them should get what.

The detailed effect of double taxation treaties depends on the two countries involved – although treaties may be similar in concept they can differ in detail. The following countries have basic double taxation treaties with the UK: Antigua, Argentina, Australia, Austria, Azerbaijan, Bangladesh, Barbados, Belarus, Belgium, Belize, Bolivia, Botswana, Brunei, Bulgaria, Burma, Canada, Chile, China, Croatia, Cyprus, the Czech Republic, Denmark, Egypt, Estonia, the Falkland Islands, Fiji, Finland, France, Gambia, Germany, Ghana, the Gilbert Islands, Greece, Grenada, Guernsey, Guyana, Hungary, Iceland, India, Indonesia, the Republic of Ireland, the Isle of Man, Israel, Italy, Ivory Coast, Jamaica, Japan, Jersey, Jordan, Kazakhstan, Kenya, Korea, Kuwait, Latvia, Lesotho, Lithuania, Luxembourg, Malawi, Malaysia, Malta, Mauritius, Mexico, Mongolia, Montserrat, Morocco, Namibia, Netherlands, New Zealand, Nigeria, Norway, Oman, Pakistan, Papua New Guinea, the Philippines, Poland, Portugal, Romania, Russia, Seychelles, Sierra Leone, Singapore, Slovakia, Slovenia, the Solomon Islands, South Africa, Spain, Sri Lanka, St Kitts and Nevis, St Lucia, Sudan, Swaziland, Sweden, Switzerland, Taiwan, Thailand, Trinidad and Tobago, Tunisia, Turkey, Uganda, Ukraine, the USA, the Russian Federation and former members of the USSR not otherwise dealt with, Uzbekistan, Venezuela, Vietnam, Zambia and Zimbabwe.

If there is no treaty between the country you are interested in and the UK, you may be allowed unilateral relief by the Inland Revenue under which any sum is paid in respect of the same income overseas will be deducted from your UK tax liability on that income.

Only the following countries have double taxation treaties that deal with inheritance taxes: France, India, Ireland, Italy, Netherlands, Pakistan, South Africa, Sweden, Switzerland and the USA.

If there is no treaty for inheritance taxes between the country you are interested in and the UK, you may be allowed unilateral relief by the Inland Revenue under which any sum is paid in respect of the same inheritance will be deducted from your UK tax liability on that inheritance.

Tax Planning Generally

Do it and do it as soon as possible. Every day you delay will make it more difficult to get the results you are looking for. There are many possibilities for tax planning for someone moving overseas. Some points worth considering are:

- **Time your departure from UK to get the best out of the UK tax system.**

- **Think, in particular, about when to make any capital gain if you are selling your business or other assets in UK.**

- **Arrange your affairs so that there is a gap between leaving UK (for tax purposes) and becoming resident overseas. That gap can be used to make all sorts of beneficial changes to the structure of your finances.**

- **Think about trusts. Although the legal system where you are going to live may have more restrictions on their effective use, they can still be very effective tax planning vehicles.**

- **Think about giving away some of your assets. You will not have to pay wealth tax on the value given away and the recipients will generally not have to pay either gift or inheritance tax on the gift.**

Any money spent on tax planning is likely to be rewarded many times over.

Investments

Most of us don't like making investment decisions – they make us face up to unpleasant things like taxes and death. We don't really understand what we are doing, what the options are or what is best. We don't know who we should trust to give us advice. We know we ought to do something, but it will wait until next week – or maybe the week after. Until then our present arrangements will have to do. But if you are moving to live overseas you *must* review your investments.

Most of us are, in financial terms, worth more than we think. When we come to move abroad and have to think about these things it can come as a shock. Take a piece of paper and list your actual and potential assets in the table overleaf. This will give you an idea as to the amount you are worth now and, just as importantly, what you are likely to be worth in the future. Your investment plans should take into account both figures.

You may already have an investment adviser and be very happy with the quality and service you have received, but UK advisers are unlikely to be able to help you once you have gone to live in an Eastern European country. They will almost certainly not have the knowledge and are unlikely to know about investments in the country you are moving to or of the offshore products that might be of interest to someone no longer resident in the UK. Even if they have some knowledge of these things, they are likely to be thousands of miles from where you will be living.

What Are You Worth?

Asset	Value (local currency)	Value (£)
Current Assets		
Main home		
Holiday home		
Contents of main home		
Contents of holiday home		
Car		
Boat		
Bank accounts		
Other cash investments		
Bonds, etc.		
Stocks and shares		
PEPs		
Tessas		
ISAs		
SIPPs		
Investment (real estate)		
Value of your business		
Value of share options		
Other		
Future Assets		
Value of share options		
Personal or company pension – likely lump sum		
Potential inheritances or other accretions		
Value of endowment mortgages on maturity		
Other		
TOTAL		

Nor is it a simple question of selecting a new local adviser once you have moved. They will usually know little about the UK aspects of your case or about the UK tax and inheritance rules that could still have some importance for you. Choosing an investment adviser competent to deal with you once you are living abroad is not easy. By all means seek guidance from your existing adviser. Ask for guidance from others who have already made the move. Do some research. Meet the potential candidates. Are you comfortable with them? Do they share your approach to life? Do they have the necessary experience? Is their performance record good? How are they regulated? What security, bonding and guarantees can they offer you? How will they be paid for their work? Fees or commission? If commission, what will that formula mean they are making from you in 'real money' rather than percentages? Above all, be careful.

Where Should You Invest?

For British people the big issue is whether they should keep their sterling investments. Most British people will have investments that are largely sterling-based. Even if they are, for example, a Far Eastern fund, they will probably be denominated in sterling and they will pay out dividends, etc. in sterling.

Once you move, you will be spending euros or some other currency. As the value of the euro or that currency fluctuates against sterling, the value of your investments will go up and down. That, of itself, isn't too important because the value won't crystallise unless you sell. What does matter is that the revenue you generate from those investments (rent, interest, dividends, etc.) will fluctuate in value. It is therefore preferable to hold investments that pay out in euros if you live in a euro country. If you are living in a non-euro country with a stable currency the same considerations apply, but the conclusion is a little less clear-cut because of the lower profile of the currency. Perhaps some form of 'halfway house' is the best compromise.

If you are going to live in a country with an unstable currency, think about splitting your investments into a part generating income in euros, a part in sterling and a part in US dollars. All this requires detailed advice.

Trusts

Trusts are useful to those who live overseas. Legislation has been introduced in some countries to limit the abuse of trusts as devices to conceal income and assets but it is still limited in scope and effectiveness. Trusts offer the potential benefits of:

- **allowing you to put part of your assets in the hands of trustees so that they no longer belong to you for wealth tax or inheritance tax purposes.**

- **allowing you to receive only the income you need (rather than all the income generated by those assets), so keeping the extra income out of sight for income tax purposes.**

- **allowing a very flexible vehicle for investment purposes.**

To set up a trust, after leaving the UK (and before moving abroad), you reorganise your affairs by giving a large part of your assets to 'trustees'. These are normally a professional trust company located in a low tax regime. The choice of a reliable trustee is critical.

Those trustees hold the asset not for their own benefit but 'in trust' for whatever purposes you established when you made the gift. It could, for example, be to benefit a local hospital or school *or it could be to benefit you and your family.* If the trust is set up properly in the light of the requirements of local law then those assets will no longer be treated as yours for tax purposes.

On your death the assets are not yours to leave to your children (or whoever), and so do not (subject to any local anti avoidance legislation) carry inheritance tax. Similarly the income from those assets is not your income. If some of it is given to you it may be taxed as your income, but the income that is not given to you will not be taxed in the country where you are living and, because the trust will be located in a nil or low-tax regime, it will not be taxed elsewhere either.

The detail of the arrangements is vitally important. They must be set up precisely to comply with local tax law. If you do not do this they will not work as intended. Trustees can manage your investments in (virtually) whatever way you stipulate when you set up the trust. You can give the trustees full discretion to do as they please or you can specify precisely how your money is to be used. There are particular types of trusts and special types of investments that trusts can make that can be especially beneficial in the country where you are going to be living.

Trusts can be beneficial even to residents of modest means – say, £350,000. It is certainly worth investing a little money to see if they can be of use to you, as the tax savings can run to many thousands of pounds. If you are thinking of trusts as an investment vehicle and tax-planning measure, you must take advice early – months before you are thinking of moving abroad – otherwise it will be too late.

Keeping Track of Your Investments

Whatever you decide to do about investments – put them in a trust, appoint investment managers to manage them in your own name or manage them yourself – you should always keep an up-to-date list of your assets and investments and tell your family where to find it. Make a file. By all means have a computer file but print off a good old-fashioned paper copy. Keep it in an obvious place known to your family, with your will and the deeds to your house. Also keep in it either the originals of bank account books, share certificates and so on, or a note of where they are to be found.

Life in Eastern Europe

06

See individual country chapters for information about the language, home utilities, media, money and banking, shopping, crime and food and drink for the individual countries. Sections in this chapter apply generally to all the countries covered in this book.

Emergencies

To contact the emergency services in any EU country, call **t** 112.

Mobile Phones

You can use your mobile phone anywhere in Europe thanks to the EU's GSM technical standard. Before travelling, however, contact your network provider to make sure that your phone is enabled for international roaming. Coverage will vary and the costs will depend on your provider but are usually extremely high. Don't forget that there can be charges for *receiving* calls abroad for you and the caller. If your phone is not locked to a network, i.e. you bought it SIM-free, it will work out cheaper to buy a new local pay-as-you-go SIM card abroad.

Banking

In most countries, anybody can open a bank account. You will need to prove that you are over 18 and provide the bank with proof of your identity, your status, your local address and the various other bits and pieces of information that will vary from country to country and bank to bank. In these days of international terrorism anything to do with the movement of money from one country to another gives rise to enquiry.

The type of bank account you open will depend on whether you are resident on non-resident in the country. For most practical purposes there is little difference between the two types of account. Most people will operate a simple current (chequing) account and will ask the bank to make payments of the electricity, water and other bills by direct payment from that account. There are no cheque guarantee cards in most Eastern European countries, yet cheques are still sometimes accepted because of the severe penalties that result from abuse of a cheque. In most places, however, payment in cash is still the norm.

If your needs are more sophisticated than this, study carefully the various types of account available to you. These, and the terms of conditions of use, differ substantially from the accounts you may be familiar with in England.

Banking needs vary dramatically from person to person. If you are retiring or running a business you may need a full and fairly sophisticated banking service, but if you are a tourist with a holiday home your banking needs are likely to be very simple. Most British people fall into this category. For them there is virtually no difference between the services offered by any of the major banks. The three major considerations when choosing between foreign banks will be the convenience factor – whether the bank is located near your property, the question of whether the staff at the bank speak English and whether the bank provides internet banking – preferably in English.

In many small towns you will have no choice of bank and there are advantages to dealing with a local bank, as it will make the local community feel that you want to be part of them. Who knows, your bank manager might even take you for lunch!

If you have the luxury of a choice between various convenient banks where the staff speak English, perhaps the most significant factor to take into account would be the bank's charging structure for receiving money. Banks charge for nearly everything, but some charge a lot more than others for the simple task of receiving money that you send from the UK.

There is no reason why you should not also retain a **UK bank account**, even after you have moved permanently. It will probably be convenient to do so.

Offshore accounts are the subject of considerable mystique. Many British people resident overseas think that by having an offshore bank account they do not have to pay tax in the country where they are living. This is not true. They only do not pay the tax if they illegally hide the existence of the bank account from the local tax man. There is no reason why you should not have an offshore bank account either as the owner of a holiday home or as a person resident overseas, but you should only do so for good reason.

Property Insurance

Most owners of property abroad take out a multi-risk household policy, which covers the fabric of the building, its contents and any civil responsibility landing upon the owner of the property other than in certain specified circumstances such as liability incurred in connection with the use of a motor car. Requirements vary from country to country. Premiums are, not surprisingly, comparatively cheap in rural areas, more expensive in big cities.

Just as in England, if you under-insure the building and the worst happens, the company will not pay you out for the full extent of your loss. The amount for which you should be covered as far as civil liability is concerned should be a minimum of €1 million and preferably higher. Because the risk of a claim under this category is small, the premiums for this part of the insurance are low and so high levels of cover can be provided at low cost. The amount of cover you should have for the building itself should be the full cost of reconstruction of the building.

If you own an apartment, then the cost of the buildings insurance for the whole block of apartments should be included in your service charge. You will then only need contents and public liability insurance. Once this insurance value has been established, it should be increased each year in line with the official index of inflation of building costs.

Make a detailed estimate of the value of your furnishings and possessions likely to be in the property at any time. Remember to allow for items such as cameras that you may take with you on holiday. Pay particular attention to the details of this policy and study the small print about what you have to specify when taking out the insurance and any limitations on claims that can be made against it. Notice in particular whether there is a requirement to stipulate items of high value. If you have any items of high value it is worth having them photographed and possibly valued. The insurance company might specify security measures that must be in place in your home. If you do not use them you may find that you are not covered.

If you are using the property as holiday accommodation you must specify a policy which is a holiday home policy. If you do not, you are likely to find that one of the conditions of the policy is that cover will lapse if the property is empty for 30 or 60 days. Premiums will be higher for holiday homes because the risk is higher.

If you intend to let your property you must notify the insurance company and comply with any requirements of the insurance company with regard to the lettings. Otherwise your cover could be void. Your premiums will be higher.

There are some UK-based insurance companies that offer cover for properties overseas. The main advantages in dealing with a UK company are that the documentation is likely to be in English and that if you have to make a claim the claim will be processed in English. There are some local companies that also have the facility for dealing with claims in English. This should not be underestimated as an advantage. Unless your knowledge of the language in which you live is fluent, you would otherwise have to employ somebody to deal with the claim on your behalf or to translate what you have said, which is costly and never entirely satisfactory.

If you have to make a claim, note that there are usually time limits for doing so. If the claim involves theft or break-in you will usually have to report the matter to the matter to the police, which should normally be done immediately after discovery of the incident and in any case within 24 hours. The claim should be notified to the insurance company without delay. Check the maximum period allowed in your policy, which could be as little as 48 hours. As with all important documents, the claim should be notified by recorded delivery post.

Management Charges

Management charges are not taxes but charges for those who live in an apartment complex or in a group of buildings that share a common facility (such as a swimming pool) to cover the cost of providing those common facilities. In the case of a block of apartments, charges cover the cleaning and electricity for the general areas, any gardening, the maintenance of pools, lifts, car parking areas and so on. The cost of the management charge depends on the quality and number of facilities provided.

Health

If you are an EU national and you are suddenly taken ill or have an accident during a visit to any EU country, you can get free or reduced-cost emergency treatment if you have completed an E111 form (available from any post office) as evidence that you are entitled to these benefits. Bear in mind, though, that does not mean treatment is free. The Department of Health has a leaflet called Health Advice for Travellers summarising healthcare provision in the countries covered in this book, including exactly how to access health services; ask for it at a post office. A passport is often enough to get medical treatment in many countries, however. From December 2005 a European health card will replace the E111, making procedures much simpler and reimbursement of costs more rapid; even if you have an old E111, make sure you change it for the new card.

If you need special medicines, carry your prescription with you and check with your doctor if you require medicines while abroad; the list of medicines requiring a prescription may vary between European countries.

Entitlement to UK Benefits While Living Abroad

Use of the NHS

The National Health Service is paid for from your National Insurance contributions and from general taxation and is residence-based, that is, the only people entitled to use it are people ordinarily resident in the UK or persons who are entitled by special exemption to use the health service (such as certain students). Entitlement has nothing to do with nationality, nor does it have anything to do with previous contributions or previous or current payment of tax in the UK. People may not use the NHS just because they used to be ordinarily resident in the UK. Anyone who is not presently ordinarily resident is subject to the NHS (Charges to Overseas Visitors) Regulations 1989. These regulations place a responsibility on NHS hospitals to establish whether a person is ordinarily resident, exempt from charges under one of a number of exemption categories or liable for charges.

As a person resident in another EU country you will have the right to emergency treatment in the UK in just the same way that, as a person resident in the UK, you presently have the right to emergency medical treatment in, say, France. This does not permit you to come back from, say, the Czech Republic *in order to* take treatment in the UK.

UK Social Security Benefits

People can qualify for welfare benefits in one of three ways – by enforced reciprocal EU/EEA rules, under the rules of the country where they pay social security contributions or under the rules of the country where they live.

The idea behind the EU/EEA rules is that a person exercising his or her right to move from one EU/EEA state to another should not lose out on welfare benefit rights by doing so. The people covered by the EU/EEA rules are:

- **employed and self-employed nationals of EU/EEA states.**
- **pensioners who are nationals of EU/EEA states.**
- **subject to certain restrictions, members of the families of the above, whatever their nationality.**
- **civil servants of EU/EEA states and members of their families, provided they are not covered by an enhanced scheme for civil servants in their own country. This is generally not a problem for UK civil servants.**

Note that the EU/EEA rules do not include cover for the economically inactive (people retired early, students and so on).

EU/EEA rules include:

- **sickness and maternity benefits.**
- **accidents at work.**
- **occupational diseases.**
- **invalidity benefits.**
- **old-age pensions.**
- **widow's and other survivors' benefits.**
- **death grants.**
- **unemployment benefits.**
- **family benefits.**

The rules do not replace the national benefits to which you might be entitled, but they co-ordinate the national schemes. They decide in which of several possible countries a person should make a claim and which country should pay the cost.

Apart from the basic principle that you should not lose out by moving within the EU, the other principle is that you should only be subject to the rules of one country at a time. The law of a member state cannot – except in the case of unemployment benefit – take away or reduce your entitlement to benefit just because you live in another member state. If you remain entitled to a, say, a UK benefit while living in Bulgaria, payment of benefit to which you were entitled in your original member state can be paid in a number of different ways, depending on the state and benefit concerned:

- **by the benefit authorities in the member state in which you now live, acting on behalf of the benefit authorities in your original country**
- **directly in your new country by the benefit authorities in your old country.**

There are two main factors for deciding which rules apply to you: the country that insures you and the country in which you live. You are insured in the country where you carry out your work. If you work regularly in more than one member state, you are insured in the country where you live. Short-term posting (less than one year) to another country is ignored. Retired people who have only worked in one member state remain 'attached' to that state for pension and other purposes for the rest of their lives. People who work in several states will build up pension entitlements in each member state in which they work for more than one year.

Some benefits flow from your presence in a country. Each potential benefit, in the UK and abroad, has associated rules stipulating which categories of people are entitled to benefit from it.

What UK Benefits Can You Claim?

Welfare benefits in the UK are divided into 'contributory' and 'non-contributory' benefits. The former are benefits to which you only become entitled if you have paid (or been credited with) sufficient National Insurance contributions to qualify you for payment. The latter do not depend on paying any National Insurance contributions.

In the UK there are various classes of National Insurance contributions. Not all rank equally for benefits purposes, and some types of National Insurance contributions cannot be used to qualify payments for certain benefits. The categories are:

- **Class 1: paid by employees and their employers; a percentage of income up to a certain maximum.**
- **Class 2: a flat-rate payment paid by self-employed people.**
- **Class 3: voluntary payments made by people no longer paying Class 1 or Class 2 contributions; these protect their right to a limited range of benefits.**

- **Class 4: compulsory 'profit-related' additional contributions paid by self-employed people.**

The table below shows the different benefits that are allowed depending on what NI contributions have been paid.

	Class 1	Class 2/4	Class 3
Maternity Allowances	Yes	Yes	No
Unemployment Benefit	Yes	No	No
Incapacity Benefit	Yes	Yes	No
Widows Benefit	Yes	Yes	Yes
Basic Retirement Pension	Yes	Yes	Yes
Additional Retirement Pension	Yes	No	No

As well as being categorised as 'contributory' and 'non-contributory' benefits, benefits are also categorised into 'means-tested' and 'non-means-tested' benefits. The former are paid only if you qualify under the eligibility criteria for the benefit in question and are poor enough to qualify on financial grounds – generally covering income and savings. The latter are paid to anyone who meets the eligibility criteria, irrespective of their wealth. Means-tested UK benefits are likely to be of little interest to residents in Eastern European countries.

Sickness and Maternity Benefits
See 'Use of the NHS', p.103.

Accidents at Work
Any benefits you presently receive from the UK benefits system as a result of an accident at work should remain payable to you despite your having moved overseas.

Occupational Diseases
Any benefits you receive from the UK benefits system as a result of an occupational disease should remain payable despite your moving overseas.

Invalidity Benefits
Any National Insurance benefits you receive from the UK benefits system as a result of invalidity should remain payable to you despite your having moved overseas. Attendance Allowance, Severe Disablement Allowance and Disability Living Allowance are not usually payable if you go to live abroad permanently.

Retirement Pensions
See 'Retirement and Pensions', pp.108–12.

Widow's and Other Survivors' Benefits
Any benefits you receive from the UK benefits system as a result of being a widow should remain payable to you despite your having moved overseas.

Death Grants

The position is complex. Seek advice.

Unemployment Benefits

You may be able to get contribution-based Jobseeker's Allowance in the EEA for up to 13 weeks if you:

- **are entitled to contribution-based Jobseeker's Allowance on the day you go abroad.**

- **have registered as a jobseeker for at least 4 weeks before you leave; this can be less in special circumstances.**

- **are available for work and actively seeking work in Great Britain up to the day you leave.**

- **are going abroad to look for work.**

- **register for work at the equivalent of a Jobcentre in the country you are going to within 7 days of last claiming Jobseeker's Allowance in the UK; if you do not, you may lose benefit.**

- **follow the other country's system for claiming benefit.**

- **follow the other country's benefit rules, such as being available for and actively seeking work, that would have applied if you had stayed in the UK.**

Employment

The latest wave of EU member states created the largest single market for trade and investment in the world, with around 500 million consumers, making it bigger even than the USA and Japan combined. The expansion is expected to create more than 300,000 extra jobs, but no one seriously believes there will be a flood of British people rushing to find work in Eastern Europe, although the region suffers from a shortage of skills, particularly in engineering and finance.

As a national of an EU country, you have the right to work in any other member state, without the need of a work permit. You also have the same rights as nationals of your destination country in terms of conditions and pay.

But before you pack your suitcase and go off to look for work in the new EU, bear in mind that work restrictions placed on workers from Eastern and Central Europe entering the UK have meant that some of the new members have introduced tit-for-tat measures. For example, Hungary says it will match restrictions placed on its nationals applying for work in the rest of the EU. Also, not all professional qualifications are recognised across the EU and some professions have employment restrictions. Language skills and fluency levels may also be important when seeking work.

Since the collapse of Communism in 1989, many multinational companies have cashed in on cheap labour costs. Since May 2004, several European companies have moved east, bringing in expatriate workers working in senior management positions to train local employees, normally for three years. This represents an opportunity for skilled workers from the UK, particularly in the areas of investment banking, the advisory and financial professions and retail. Because of the amount of building work that needs to be done, there is also a demand for engineers. In addition, some places, such as the capitals of Hungary and Slovakia, are important centres for the manufacture of cars and parts.

Education

The Education Act 1996 imposes a duty on local education authorities to provide sufficient schools for people resident in their area but does not oblige them to provide for children of parents living in, for example, Croatia. Overseas students should not expect to be subsidised by the British taxpayer.

Students are classified as 'home' students (and thus not subject to payment of fees as an 'overseas student') if they can demonstrate that they were settled in the United Kingdom within the meaning of the Immigration Act 1971 and that they have been ordinarily resident in the UK for a specified three-year period preceding their course. They must also demonstrate that no part of that period of residence was wholly or mainly for the purpose of receiving full-time education. This is a complex area and you should seek early advice.

Retirement and Pensions

More and more British people are tempted by the idea of spending the end of their days languishing in the sunshine sipping sangria or the equivalent local brew and having a much higher standard of living than they have in the UK. A recent survey by Alliance and Leicester showed that 13 per cent of people about to retire were considering moving abroad, almost double the number from the previous year. But before you rush into anything, make sure you do your research. **Age Concern, t** 0800 009966, **www.ace.org.uk**, produces a useful fact sheet on retiring abroad. As a UK national, you have the right to retire in any country that is a full member of the EU. But first consult the British consul in the relevant country and its foreign consulate in the UK.

Moving Abroad Before Retirement

If you have not yet retired and move to, say, Bulgaria (whether you intend to work in Bulgaria or not), your entitlement to your **UK state pension** will be frozen and the pension to which you are entitled on the basis of your contributions record at the time of your departure will be paid to you at UK retirement age. If you have only worked in the UK for two-thirds of the normal contributions period, you will only receive two-thirds of the pension – but it is a little more complicated than that. This freezing of your pension can be a disadvantage, especially if you are still relatively young when you move to Bulgaria. This is because you need to have made a minimum number of NI contributions (44 qualifying years, or, for women retiring before 2010, 39 qualifying years, increasing by one year until 2020 until they also need 44 years) in order to qualify for a full UK state pension. If you have not yet done this but are close, it may be worth making additional payments while you are resident overseas. You may choose to pay either Class 2 or Class 3 contributions.

You may pay Class 2 contributions if you:

- **are working abroad.**
- **have lived in the UK for a continuous period of at least three years during which you paid NI contributions and you have already paid a set minimum amount of NI contributions.**
- **were normally employed or self-employed in the UK before going abroad.**

You may pay Class 3 contributions if you:

- **have at any time lived in the UK for a continuous period of at least three years.**
- **have already paid a minimum amount in UK NI contributions.**

Class 2 contributions are more expensive but, potentially, cover you for maternity allowance and incapacity benefits. Class 3 contributions do not. In both cases, you apply in the UK on form CF83. The decision as to whether to continue to make UK payments is an important one. Seek advice.

If you have been paying National Insurance contributions in the UK, you will usually be sent a claim form from the Pensions Service four months before you reach the UK pensionable age. It will ask you if you want to claim a UK retirement pension and for details of any periods of residence and state insurance you have in other countries. If you have an enquiry about your pension when you are abroad, you can either complete the online form or contact the **Pension Service International Pension Centre**, Tyneview Park, Newcastle-on-Tyne NE98 1BA, **t** (0191) 218 7777, **f** (0191) 218 3836.

If you have a **personal or stakeholder pension** taken out while still a resident of the UK, then you can leave the country and continue to contribute to that pension for another five years, in addition to the remainder of the tax year in which you started the pension. After that you must stop paying into it.

Drawing Your Pension Abroad

The **UK state retirement pension** can be paid in full **anywhere in the EU** and will be **increased regularly according to inflation**. This will not include the pension credit. Around one million people from the UK currently claim the state pension abroad. The pension will either sent to you by means of a cheque, paid into a chosen non-UK bank account or paid to a designated agent on your behalf. You will be paid without deduction (except remittance charges if sent overseas). Widow's or bereavement benefits are paid in full and war pensions can be paid anywhere in the world, but many other benefits cannot be paid to people living permanently outside the UK. You will be able to claim local benefits and social assistance in the country you have moved to, but these are likely to be much less than those in the UK.

If you have established an entitlement to a **state retirement pension in other EU countries** by virtue of working in them for periods of time, all the pensions will be payable to you wherever you finally live. Once again they will be paid without deduction (except remittance charges) and your pension will be updated whenever the pensions in those countries are updated.

Normally, **company and personal pensions** will be paid in full when you lve abroad, including any increases. But check, and be aware of any costs of transferring the money between currencies, and the fact that the value of your pension is subject to fluctuations in the exchange rate. If you have a company pension it will be paid wherever the pension scheme rules dictate. Some permit the administrators to pay the money into any bank anywhere and others, ostensibly for security reasons, insist on the money being paid into a UK bank account. If yours does this you can simply ask the bank to send it on to you in the country where you are living (for which you may have to pay a fee). Bank transfer costs mean that it is probably best to do this only three or four times per year. You can also make an annual arrangement with some currency dealers whereby they will send the money at an exchange rate that will apply for the whole year, which provides certainty of income.

If you have a **government pension** it will still be taxed in the UK. Otherwise the pension should be paid gross (tax-free) and it will be taxed (if it is taxed at all) locally where you are living.

Warning: if you are **retiring to a non-EU country** (such as Montenegro) then, in some cases, your UK state pension will be **frozen as of your date of departure** and only be paid at the rate applicable when you leave, not the enhanced rates that will be paid to allow for inflation as the years go by. There are different rules depending on the country you move to. There are general 'reciprocal arrangements' with some non-EEA countries, including Australia, Barbados, Bermuda, Canada, the Isle of Man, Israel, Jamaica, Jersey and Guernsey, Mauritius, New Zealand, the Philippines, Turkey and the USA. However, these arrangements do not guarantee the index-linking of pensions; in Australia, Canada, New Zealand and South Africa, for example, your pension will be paid only at the level it was at the time of retirement. On the other hand, if you live in Barbados, Bermuda, Bosnia-Herzegovina, Croatia, Guernsey, Israel, Jamaica,

Jersey, Macedonia, Mauritius, the Philippines, Sark, Turkey and the USA, index-linking will apply.

On Arrival

When you get to your destination country, register with the local authorities to give you any access to its local welfare services. Also register with the British consulate in the case of an emergency abroad and even just for general assistance. Open a non-resident bank account. Then once you have a residence permit – usually after six months – you can open a normal account, into which your retirement pension can be paid.

Consult the **Association of Retired and Persons Over 50 (ARP/O50)**, Greencoat House, Francis St, London SW1P 1DZ, **t** (020) 7828 0500, **f** (020) 7233 7132, **info@ arp.org.uk**, **www.arp.org.uk**, for more information about retiring abroad. **Laterlife, www.laterlife.com**, gives advice about moving and living abroad for those aged over 50.

The Cost of Living

The cost of living in most emerging market countries is much lower than in the UK, so UK pensioners can live well on the basic state pension. To get some idea of the relative cost of living, look at the GDP per capita figures in the country-specific sections of this book and compare them with the figure for the UK. This is not a direct indicator of the relative costs of living, but it gives a pretty good feel for the position.

Checklist

If you are thinking about retiring to another country, first consider the following points:

- **Work out what your retirement income will be. You can ask for a forecast of the UK state pension you can expect to get up to four months before you reach the UK pension age. The forecast will tell you what your pension is now and whether or not you can get more by the time you retire. The Retirement Pension Forecasting and Advice Unit, t (0191) 218 7585, can give you a state pension forecast. Also see www.thepensionservice.gov.uk.**

- **The Inland Revenue can give you information about entitlements when abroad and can also tell you about tax liability on any income over the UK personal allowance, which will depend on where you decide to live.**

- **If you are already living outside the UK you will need to contact the Inland Revenue Centre for Non-Residents, Room BP1301, Benton Park View,**

Newcastle-on-Tyne NE98 1ZZ, for pension forecasts or questions about your National Insurance contributions.

• If you are in the UK you can telephone or fax the Centre for Non-Residents (Newcastle) helpline, **t** 0845 915 4811, **f** 0845 915 0067.

• Find out about your welfare rights abroad as some UK benefits are not payable outside the UK, while others apply only in the EU or in countries which have agreements with the UK.

• Make sure you inform your Social Security office or the Inland Revenue National Insurance Contributions Office (International Services) and the Department for Work and Pensions when you move and provide them with your contact details abroad.

• Establish healthcare costs in the country you want to retire to. The Department for Work and Pensions, **www.dwp.gov.uk**, will be able to advise you on your rights in EU countries. It is wise to take out health insurance to cover private medical and dental treatment.

• Find out about your tax liability abroad, whatever your age. Even if you retire abroad you will still have to pay UK tax on income you receive from the UK.

Coming Back to England

You are free to return to England at any stage, but very few people do. Many people wonder whether they should preserve an escape route by, for example, keeping their old house and letting it out until they are sure of their intentions, but this may prove a bad idea. The house will be a worry and a distraction. How do you manage it? Might tenants be ruining it? It may not be ideal for investment purposes and may generate less than you could get by selling and putting the value elsewhere. It may not be in an area with good capital growth and the income (and capital value) will be at the mercy of exchange rate fluctuations. The house might not even suit your requirements if you do return to England. It also encourages you to look backwards instead of forwards.

Death and Burial

Deaths should be registered within 24 hours, usually at the town hall. The death of British people should also be recorded at the British consulate. Burial is much more common than cremation in Eastern European countries as land is plentiful and crematoria are expensive to build. Crematoria are usually only found in larger towns and cities. Funerals are just as ridiculously expensive as in the UK; taking the body of a dead person back to the UK is possible but complex and even more expensive.

Driving

A driving licence issued in an EU country is valid throughout the EU. If driving your own car, in some countries you will need to have your vehicle registration document with you in addition to carrying a valid driving licence.

There are age limits for hiring a car – usually 21 is the minimum age. Normally, wherever you are in the EU, your car insurance policy will automatically provide the minimum cover (third-party liability) required by law. Vehicle breakdown insurance is also a good idea. Your insurer can give you a European accident statement form, which makes it easier to make a claim if you have an accident in another country. Motorists will find it straightfoward to get compensation for accidents wherever they are in the EU.

Passport Controls

There are no longer any frontier controls at the borders between most EU countries as they are covered by the Schengen Agreement, which is part of EU law. Always carry a valid passport or ID card when travelling in the EU, however, because you may be required to prove your identity. Also, make sure that any children travelling with you either have their own separate passport or ID card or are registered on yours.

If you are not a UK citizen and so obtain a visa for any EU country (except Ireland and the UK) or for Iceland or Norway, also known as the 'Schengen countries', it will automatically allow you to travel freely throughout the Schengen area. The Schengen rules are the part of EU law that aim to remove all internal border controls, but put in place effective controls at the external borders and introduce a common visa policy. Ireland and the UK do not participate in the aspects that relate to frontiers.

Taking Your Pet

Amazingly, a flight for your pet can cost as much as for you, or more (as much as £700) and within the EU you pay VAT on freight if your pet is sent as cargo. You can either go through the airline directly, which can be a complicated process given the different rules of each airline, or you can use a specialist company. Shop around if you are using a company, as many of them charge extortionate fees and airlines charge each company the same – there are currently only eight of them in the UK. Some airlines only allow animals to be transported through a company and not with an individual. Because airlines have lots of minimum charges, the chances are that costs will be reduced if you are transporting more than one animal.

You must make sure that you meet the usually strict regulations of the airline. For example, British Airways allows a dog and a box of less than 40 kilos to travel if it fits under your seat. There are plenty of horror stories of people being told at check-in that their pet couldn't fly with them because the box was too small or they had wrong licence. Airlines do not bend these rules because they may be fined and the animal impounded or even worse. Budget airlines don't allow pets because their turnaround time is too short. You, or the company you choose, need to arrange:

- airline documentation.
- the flight.
- an import and export licence.
- custom and excise documentation.
- a pet passport.
- IATA container approved for air travel.

Animals usually travel in the hold – this part of aircraft is separate from where luggage is stored and has the same pressurisation and temperature as that in the passenger section; the only difference is that is dark, which can frighten some animals. The director of **Jets4Pets**, **t** 0845 408 0298, **www.jets4pets.com**, which specialises in transporting animals, recommends that if you decide to arrange transportation yourself you should talk to the airline and see if it can transport the pet as excess baggage, which may be possible only if it can fit under the seat. Ask for the size of container necessary. Find an agent to provide the export licence (definitely) and import licence (maybe). If you don't feel looked after either by the airline or the agent on the phone, the chances your pet won't get to fly, as the necessary criteria won't be met.

The Pet Passport and the Pet Travel Scheme

The Pet Passport allows you to bring your pet back into the UK without quarantine if it has been to certain EU countries and meets certain criteria. See the **DEFRA** website (**www.DEFRA.gov.uk**) for more information on this.

None of the countries covered in this book is yet part of the **Pet Travel Scheme** (**PETS**), but they are likely to join in years to come. Check with DEFRA at the website above, or the **Department for Environment, Food and Rural Affairs**, Area 201, 1a Page Street, London SW1P 4PQ, **t** 0870 241 1710, **f** (020) 7904 6834.

To be part of PETS (once the country you move to joins the scheme), your pet must be microchipped, vaccinated and blood-tested. All vets who are local veterinary inspectors can carry out these procedures, for which they will make a charge. They will give you an EU Passport which will verify that these procedures have been carried out.

Animal Transport

- **Jets4Pets, t** 0845 408 0298, **www.jets4pets.com,** can help you, whether you want to arrange for your goldfish to be taken to Hungary or 400 high-bred Welsh pigs to be transported to Montenegro.
- **Animal Airlines, t** (01625) 827414, **www.animalairlines.co.uk,** will transport your animal overseas.

Taking Your Car

Don't. It will be much better to buy a 'new' car when you arrive there. It is much safer to drive a car with the steering wheel on the left-hand side. This is particularly so if you are driving in towns or in country areas without the benefit of a passenger to help you check for oncoming vehicles when overtaking. You will also find that it is much easier to get spare parts. Even if you think your present car is sold throughout Europe, you will find that there are many parts that at different on the UK model because it is a right-hand drive. It is also widely reported that a local car makes you less visible in the community and thus less likely to be burgled.

Cars may also be cheaper than in the UK, so selling your car here and buying another one when you arrive could even prove beneficial. The rules permitting foreigners to own cars in Eastern European countries vary from country to country and the process of buying and registering a car is seldom simple. Seek advice if you are thinking of buying a car. If you do buy a new car, it will be just like any other local car – taxed, insured and tested in that country. This will mean paying local vehicle tax (if any).

If you insist on taking your British car you will, generally, be able to use it on local roads for a maximum of six months a year without converting it to a local car by officially importing it, having it tested and re-registered locally. Note that it can only lawfully be used on local roads when it complies fully with the requirements necessary for use on British roads, including the requirements that the vehicle is tested and taxed. Insurance will only be available from British insurance companies and you will have to disclose to the company the fact that the vehicle is used primarily abroad. If you intend to keep the vehicle in the country for more than six months in any year you *must* officially import the vehicle, which can be an expensive bureaucratic nightmare.

Taking Your Furniture

As a British (or other EU) citizen you will be able to take your possessions with you to any other EU country and, usually, to other countries too. You do not need permission nor do you need to pay taxes or customs duties if you are going to an EU country. You do need permission and you will probably need to pay taxes or customs duties if you are going to a non-EU country.

The most practical way to move the furniture is to use a specialist removal company, who will charge about £3,000 for taking the contents of a medium-size house from the UK to Croatia, about £4,000 to Bulgaria.

Internation Removal Companies

- **www.intlmovers.com**. Has a searchable database; for example, if you type in UK and Bulgaria, five companies are listed from whom you can request quotes.

- **Simpsons UK, t** 0800 515930, **www.simpsons-uk.com**. Covers most countries in Europe, operating regular road services, either full or part load, also air freight.

- **Monarch UK and International Movers, t** 0800 954 6474, **www. theeuropeanmovingcompany.com**. Provides a complete service to any destination in mainland Europe, by road transport or sea or air freight.

- **EMS Hansard,t** (01304) 241616. Provides overseas removals and storage either to or from the UK.

Letting Your Property

07

Buying an overseas property to let, either to foreign tourists or to locals, has become increasingly popular now that the buy-to-let market in England has reached saturation point. As a foreigner you are in a good position to understand the needs of tourists, particularly those from the UK. You have the advantage of speaking their language and having access to publications in the UK for advertising, and you can promote the property to your friends and family.

Providing that you buy wisely, once the business has been established buying to let can be a good and easy way to make money. There are some serious pitfalls to avoid, however. First, serious research into the rental market is necessary. There is no point buying somewhere you like where there is a limited demand for property. Be very clear about who your potential clients might be and aware that in some places in Eastern Europe the buy-to-let market has already reached bursting point. After the collapse of Communism in these countries, large numbers of Western companies moved in and as a result there was a demand for housing for their expatriate workforce. When the local workforce had been trained, many of the foreign workers returned home, and this section of the rental market declined.

Joining the EU will bring new changes, making the region volatile in terms of rental potential. As a relatively unknown quantity, Eastern Europe buy-to-let investment represents much more of a risk than more established markets.

Choice of Property and Rental Potential

Choice of Property

It is important to be clear what you want to get out of your property purchase. Do you just intend to cover your costs or want to make an income from it? Is it just a way of making money or do you really desire a dream home for yourself? It is no good buying a romantic tumbledown house in the Hungarian countryside that you have fallen in love with if you intend to let it and you never actually go there. If you are going to let out the property for just part of the time, work out when you want to be there. You may choose the peak of summer but then you need to calculate the rental you will lose. Once you have established the expectations from your proposition, then you can begin to look at places which will give the highest rental yield.

That old, old cliché about location, location, location still holds true. Choosing the best position for your price can be hard enough in an area you know, but when buying abroad the prospect can seem impossible. The obvious, boring answer is to do your research.

Location begins with the country you decide on. You will probably want to learn as much as possible about the country's background, look at photographs and generally get a feel for the place.

Then consider very carefully the area around the property as well as the building itself. If it is not obviously appealing, there is a high chance that the property will remain vacant. When considering buying in a city, take into account your potential client. A business man or woman or even just a regular resident is going to want convenient access to the main business area, as well as proximity to shops, transport hubs and other facilities.

While older buildings may have more obvious charm, there are a number of advantages of new builds. Those who buy off-plan can benefit from extended payment terms, often over as much as a year. In addition, new-build properties usually come with a guarantee of 5 or 10 years. New properties tend to have more built-in facilities and need a lot less maintenance and may be more likely to appeal to those with children and those who value practicality over aesthetics. Younger and older couples without children might be more attracted to a characterful property in the middle of the country.

Rental Potential

Be careful of agents promising substantial letting income. There are no guarantees. Plenty of people in the UK have been stung by buying rental flats to find the bottom had fallen out of the letting market. It is crucial to study the market and to find out from an independent source what the demand is and what the rental income is likely to be.

Factor in regular potential losses. For example, in some beach resorts, the rental market will only last over the summer period. Even if you do get rental income all year round – say, from a city apartment – there could very well be a few weeks or even months of the year when it is empty and between tenants. Additional costs such as maintenance, advertising and administration need to be worked in. As a rule, be pessimistic rather than optimistic about your likely returns.

The Local Market

Compared with Britain, Eastern Europe has incredibly low rates of owner-occupation. The relatively recent collapse of Communism has opened up this area but mortgages have not yet become commonly available to local people. Many of the post-war apartment blocks were built on the cheap and are falling apart, creating a high demand for housing. According to some predictions, as many as 30 per cent of the population of the new EU members will require new housing over the next 20 years.

However, letting out to permanent residents will not necessarily provide a significant profit. Do your research and make sure your information is up to date. A few years ago Budapest was crying out for accommodation for Westerners who had come over to work in the post-Communist environment. That is no longer the case. While you don't want to be the first in the area it is no good picking one that is already saturated.

Buy-to-let propositions cover the whole range of accommodation – from luxury apartments in Prague aimed at the business population to wooden villas in Bulgarian ski resorts. Some experts are saying that the middle-class market will be big, with professionals looking for new homes

The Holiday Market

There are potentially a large number of holidaymakers looking for self-catering apartments, villas and houses. More and more of us are shunning package deals for independent holidays.

If you are aiming at the holiday market, you will need to consider different factors from letting as a residence. As a general rule, the holiday market is not going to give you year-round revenue; at a beach destination you would only have tenants in the summer months. Climate is a major factor: there are few locations in Eastern Europe that are warm outside the summer months, and winters can be very cold. In Bulgaria, for example, the airports on the Black Sea close in winter and temperatures reach almost freezing. That said, more resorts are working at having year-round appeal; one major ski resort in Bulgaria is investing millions in building a racetrack, swimming pools and walking trails in a bid to attract visitors outside the skiing season. Cities may have appeal in most months, but will visitors want to stay for a whole week? City breaks tend by definition to be shorter.

For overseas visitors, access – the distance of a property from an airport – is crucial. Most visitors, according to research, do not want to travel more than an hour from an airport. The transport to and from the airport is also something to be considered as not everyone will hire a car and a taxi both ways could add another £100 on the total cost of a holiday. It is important to visit the country you are thinking of buying in so that you can get a sense not just of the culture and property but also its position.

Also important to consider is the property's proximity to tourist attractions, which may be natural features or man-made ones; and to a few shops, bars and restaurants.

You may be tempted to offer your property to friends and family for nothing, but think about whether you can afford to do this, as you could lose weeks of income if the place is popular. Don't forget to include the cost of cleaning, caretaking and so on, for that period, which could mean that you are actually paying for someone else's holiday. You might consider scheduling in two weeks off-season for free holidays for your friends and family, and offering them to whoever books in first.

Finally, decide on restrictions – will you accept pets, smokers or small children?

Equipping the Property

Buying the property is only the first step. The next is to get to work on getting it ready for letting, which is almost as crucial. First check that the exterior of the building and any garden or pool area is in good condition. Expectations from people renting are often higher than normal. Your property really should be spotless. The advantage of employing a management company (*see* pp.124–6) is that the staff will take care of all these aspects for you, although they will charge for it. Normally they will employ a cleaner once a week (fortnightly if it is not being rented out) who will ensure that toilet roll, washing-up liquid and so on (if stated in the contract) is supplied. In some cases, the cleaner can also act as caretaker and local contact, checking that there is no damage, monitoring the inventory, returning deposits and delivering the keys when visitors arrive.

- **Furnishings**: Although you don't want to go overboard, the standard of furnishings will in some ways dictate how much you can charge in rental fees. Inevitably there will be some breakages, so prepare an inventory – you can get a template for one from an agent or the Internet. Go for hard-wearing furniture and furnishings which are easy to clean, and pick neutral colours which are less likely to offend personal tastes. In warmer countries, floors are likely to be tiled or wood, which are much easier to clean. Ensure there is enough storage space in each room and adequate lighting.

- **Kitchen**: The kitchen should be modern and fully equipped, with every-thing in full working order. The basics are a fridge, oven, hob, microwave, cutlery, crockery and cooking equipment.

- **Bedrooms**: Beds should have new mattresses and be comfortable. Provide two sets of bed linen, which allows for one set to be washed. There should be adequate hanging and storage space.

- **Bathroom**: A bath is uncommon in many Eastern European countries; a good shower should suffice. Liquid soap is more practical than bars, and providing towels is a nice touch.

- **Living areas**: Often a sofabed in the sitting area is a good idea, as it allows for flexibility of sleeping arrangements.

- **Heating**: Check out what is usual locally. If everyone else has heating, you will want it too.

- **Laundry facilities**: A washing machine and a dryer are extras, but providing somewhere to put wet beachwear will be appreciated.

- **Air-conditioning**: In most cases air-conditioning is a luxury, and though it doesn't cost a fortune to install, it can run up large electricity costs.

- **Swimming pool**: Of course a pool is highly desirable and can increase the appeal of your property considerably. However, maintenance costs can be enormous and they do need to be cleaned regularly.

- **Welcome pack**: Supplying basic groceries such as tea, coffee, milk, sugar, bread, butter and fruit is becoming standard practice. It's also welcoming – and needn't be expensive – to leave a bottle of local wine.

- **Information pack**: Send out clear and precise instructions of how to get to the property to visitors when they book. No one wants to get lost on the way to their holiday residence. The problem of foreign signs and not being able to speak the language could quickly turn the arrival into a very unpleasant experience. An information pack with details of nearest shop, attractions and restaurants is easy to put together with information gathered from the local tourist office. A comments book is a good idea. This will give you all important feedback, but also contact details if you are letting through an agency, which you can then use in the future if you decide to go it alone (ask for e-mail addresses and phone numbers). Emergency numbers including an electrician and plumber are essential.

Marketing

Marketing is crucial. The first few years of letting a new property require more effort than later on when you can rely on your existing client base and word of mouth. This is a key reason for making sure everyone who does rent from you is entirely satisfied, so that they make return visits or recommend you to friends and family. Don't go overboard in spending a lot of money on putting adverts in glossy magazines. The best bet is to concentrate all your efforts into responding well to the enquiries you do get.

In general, before shelling out any money on marketing, do some research and pick the media that best suits your potential tenants. For example, if you are expecting to rent to young families there is not much point in placing an ad in an expensive fashion magazine. Before advertising in the country concerned, speak to local people about what they would advise.

When queries come through, follow them up immediately. If people are contacting you via e-mail, make sure to check it at least every day during the week and reply immediately. Answer all questions, and make a follow-up call if necessary. The following year, before the main season, send a new brochure with your details, with a friendly note, as a gentle reminder.

Directories and Web Directories

Before creating copy for entry in a directory, look at other entries and think about what would make you choose a property. Make sure all the selling points are included and succinctly described. A photo or two will make all the difference but try to imagine what they will look like on the screen when they have been reduced in size. Many travel sites have space for property marketing.

Resources

• **www.daltonsholidays.com** in 2005 had one entry each for Bulgaria, Croatia and Czech Republic but this is likely to increase quickly. The site has good details for properties as well as activities and facilities, with a quick link to the owner of the property, availability and price.

• **www.apartmentsabroad.co.uk** is another good site, offering villas and apartments (as well as hotels). It has a sophisticated search engine and covers all the main areas in Bulgaria, Croatia and Hungary.

• **www.holiday-rentals.com** advertises over 8,400 privately owned vacation rentals from all over the world.

• **www.privatevillas.co.ul** is a site for upmarket villas.

• **www.europerealestatedirectory.com** has a list of agents in Europe and letting agents.

Personal Website and E-mail

Rather than rely on someone else's website for advertising, why not set up your own? It needn't cost much and can be simple to create from a template. A website is your shop window to the world, which can even include a booking system so that visitors can check availability and you can charge your fee from credit cards. Prioritise great photos of inside and out over lots of text, as a picture paints a thosand words.

E-mail can also be a powerful tool, which allows you to target people quickly and cheaply by sending them an electronic 'brochure'.

Doing Deals

There are two kinds of 'mutual aid' deals that can be helpful to independent owners, both of which work best in slightly out-of-the-way areas. The first is to make contacts with local people in business, so that they advertise your service. Someone who runs walking holidays may want to accommodate visitors in your property, for which you pay them a commission from the profits. It is worth contacting others who are letting property in case you have double bookings, so that contacts for potential clients can be passed on. The second type of deal involves co-operating with other people in the area who let properties, assuming there are any. One of the frustrations of marketing your property is when you have four lots of people who all want to rent it for the same week. Getting together with others in a mutual assistance group will allow you to pass excess letting to one other.

Your Own Contacts

Tell everybody at home about your new property, including friends of friends of friends. You could contact everyone on your email list and even your children's email list. Putting a card up in your local gym or crèche or on your work noticeboard will probably have a better result than expensive press advertising.

Management Agencies

On the whole, the people who are most successful over a period of time in letting their second homes are those who find their tenants themselves. This, however, requires a level of commitment that many people simply cannot afford. For non-resident owners who cannot dedicate much time to keeping track of their property, it is far simpler to use a local letting agency. Agencies – or at least good ones – will be able to attract local clients as well as those of different nationalities. You will have to pay them a sizeable commission, but they will argue that this will be recovered by the extra lettings that they make during the holiday season. This may or may not be true. Resist being wowed with claims of how much money an agent will make you and the extra business they will bring in. Consider the possibility that an agent abroad could let your luxury apartment but never tell you and pocket the money. Also consider the likelihood that, while the agent might not be out to rob you, they may just not be very organised, and much keener to let out another property where they know the owner, or they have done it before.

It is necessary to be very clear about what the services of letting agencies involve and exactly what the service charges are. They may make restrictions so that you are not able to use the property when you wish. A key aspect of their service is advertising, so make sure you are given guarantees of what will be done and through which media. Agents rarely vet potential tenants, though they may check basic references. The service normally includes meeting guests with keys and checking the property on departure. It may also include arranging emergency repairs. An agency will market the property for you, take the booking enquiries and organise the payments. This is the best solution if you do not want to take the bookings enquiries yourself. It also means you do not have to bother with foreign payments, as the booking agency will simply transfer the money into any bank account you specify – less their commission, which is usually between 15 per cent and 20 per cent plus VAT.

One advantage of using a letting agency is that it may only require availability 'on request'. This means you can block off availability for yourself at any time. .

Selecting an Agency

In major tourist areas, management agencies are easy to find – often through local estate agents. Alternatively, find one at home. Again, it comes back to research. Make as many checks as possible on any agent you are thinking of using. Look at testimonials, go and talk to several different employees in the office. Try to get in touch with another owner who has used them. All in all, be sceptical. The amount of money to be lost in using a bad agent is considerable. Ask agents for their professional qualifications and how long they have been trading. Assess the premises, their advertising tools and their commitment to marketing your property.

Ask as many questions as you want to, particularly about expected revenue and fees. Look at information packs and promotional material sent to clients and decide your reaction if you received something similar. Check how much advertising space your property would get and how many photographs would be shown. Take a look at other properties on their books. Check and re-check the contract and possibly get a lawyer to look at the details. Ensure that you are able to cancel the contract at short notice.

Controlling the Agency

Make sure your contract specifies details, including notification of availability, the commissions that will be taken, when deposits and full payments will be made, the cancellation policy and complaints-handling procedures

Contracting an agency is just the beginning. Regular checks are necessary. You should:

- **Check the reports you receive from the agency and that the money you receive corresponds to the amounts shown in them.**

- **Let the agency know, in the nicest possible way, that you and all of your friends in the area check each other's properties every time you are there, and compare notes about which are occupied and the performance of your letting agencies. If they believe you, this is a good deterrent to unauthorized lettings.**

- **Telephone your property every week. If someone answers the phone make a note, and make sure that there is income shown for the week of the phone call.**

- From time to time, have a friend pose as a prospective customer and send for an enquiry pack.
- If you get the chance, call to see the property without warning, to check its condition.

Letting through a Holiday Company

The main advantage of letting through a holiday company is that they do all the marketing for you through their brochure and they let your property for the whole season. They may have certain criteria that the building needs to meet – for example, safety regulations and providing neutral furniture.

Formalising the Lettings

Rental agreements tend to be fairly standard but they are not always transferable from country to country, so take legal advice. Furnished property normally gives the owner more security and rights if they want to evict the tenant. Although eventually the EU will demand a uniform standard of law, it is going to take time before this is implemented.

Tenants should be supplied with a copy of any community rules in apartment blocks, or at least the part of them that is relevant. In the rental contract you should also stipulate what things are going to be covered by your insurance and what are not – typically, for example, tenants' personal possessions would not be covered under your policy.

Check what rights your tenant would have in case of dispute.

References

Resources in the UK

- **National Association of Estate Agents, t** (01926) 496800, **www.naea. co.uk**. The largest professional estate agency organisation in the UK. Representing nearly 10,000 members, the association can also advise property buyers. It says: 'Before considering buying property abroad – as a holiday home or main residence – find out if the area has the facilities you need. Accessibility, medical support, infrastructure and climate are just some of the points you'll need to be clear about. Members of the NAEA who specialise in selling properties abroad are well qualified to help you in your research. They will give you "best advice" based on the knowledge they have amassed over the years. This consultation is usually free.'

- **Law Society of England and Wales, www.lawsociety.org.uk**. Has a database of solicitors in this country who are registered European lawyers. You can search for the country you are interested in.

- **Foreign Office, www.fco.gov.uk**. Has a directory of English-speaking lawyers, translators and doctors in all the countries covered in this book.

- **Confederation Européenne d'Immobilier**. Represents over 25,000 estate agents in Europe, including Hungary and Slovakia, who have agreed to its code of conduct.

- **Europe Regional Directory**. A useful large directory of sites from each European country, including links to education, health, business and the economy, society and culture, travel and tourism and many other resources.

- **Federation of Overseas Property Developers, Agents and Consultants (FOPDAC), t** (0870) 350 1223, **www.fopdac.com**. A body representing estate agents, developers and consultants who work in the international property markets.

- **Architects' Council of Europe**. Represents architects throughout the EU and has a directory of contacts.

- **Royal Institute of Chartered Surveyors, www.rics.org.uk**. Branches throughout Europe including the Czech Republic and Hungary. The RICS website has links to contact details for each individual country's branch.

- **Inland Revenue , www.inlandrevenue.co.uk**. Produces a range of leaflets giving tax advice for those looking at moving abroad and can also give guidance.

- **Harlon Management Services Ltd, t** (020) 8944 9538, **f** (020) 8404 7003, **www.harlon.co.uk**. Works with partners in Hungary, Croatia and Bulgaria to manage properties.

- **CEREAN** (Central European Real Estate Associations Network), **www. cerean.com**. A registered non-governmental, not-for-profit organisation, concerned with the development of ethical and professional real estate markets in the member countries, including Bulgaria, the Czech Republic, Slovakia and Hungary.
- **International Consortium of Real Estate Associations (ICREA).** An alliance of estate agent organisations in the world's major markets, and assists buyers and sellers in locating properties outside their country and in getting in touch with an estate agent who agrees with their code of ethics and can best meet their individual needs.

Useful Websites

Europa is the site for the European Union (**www.europa.eu.int/**). It provides up-to-date coverage of European Union affairs and essential information on European integration. Users can also consult all legislation currently in force or under discussion, access the websites of each tourist office and get information about living and working in each country. Other useful websites are:

- **www.bbc.co.uk/worldservice/europe/neweurope** has up-to-date news and articles about the region.
- **www.bbc.co.uk/languages/community** details experiences of people who have moved to a different country and learnt the language.
- **www.ebuild.co.uk** is a directory and provides links for building and renovating your home.
- **www.direct.gov.uk** gives information about health, pets, retirement and moving.
- **www.arp.org.uk** is an association of retired and persons over 50 years old.
- **www.xpatloop.com** is a good community source with personal stories.
- **www.eubusiness.com**.
- **www.nationsonline.org** includes maps, media, the arts and education.
- **www.nationbynation.com** has good, basic, general introduction, information.
- **www.ori-and-ricki.net** created for 'mobile' children aged 9 to 12, with country information, and contributions from its 'readers'.
- **www.contactexpats.com**.
- **www.expatexchange.com** has a question and answer section and country profiles; provides subscription service by e-mail.

- **www.support4learning.org.uk** has information about working abroad, with lots of practical advice.

- **www.stepstone.co.uk** gives a directory of jobs in Hungary, Slovakia and the Czech Republic.

- **www.expats.cz** is a resource for finding flats, jobs and resources for the expatriate community in Prague and the Czech Republic. It also offers relocation information and advice.

Further Reading

Rough Guides publishes a range of country and city maps which are comprehensive as well as rip-proof and waterproof, including The Rough Guide Map – Croatia, Scale: 1:325,000 and The Rough Guide Map – Czech Republic, Scale: 1:350,000.

Rates of Exchange, Malcolm Bradbury. A comic novel about the misadventures of an English academic in the imaginary Communist state of Slaka.

On Foot to the Golden Horn, Jason Goodwin. A personal account of a journey through Eastern Europe on foot.

The History of Eastern Europe for Beginners, Paul Beck – an irreverent tour of recent Eastern European history in comic-book style.

The Walls Came Tumbling Down, Gale Stokes – authoritative and interesting account of the collapse of Communism in Eastern Europe.

Exit into History, A Journey Through the New Eastern Europe, Eva Hoffman. A personal report from Polish-born Hoffman, outlining the collapse of the Soviet Union in Poland, the Czech Republic, Hungary, Romania and Bulgaria

Bury Me Standing: The Gypsies and Their Journey, Isabel Fonseca. Fascinating stories and photographs of the author's four years spent with Gypsies from Albania to Poland.

Bulgaria

09

Why Buy in Bulgaria?

Bulgaria has outgrown its post-Communist image and is full of surprises, but sadly we don't have many positive images of the country. Bulgaria was the evil land with the dictatorial king and terrifying child-catcher in *Chitty Chitty Bang Bang*. It was also the homeland of womble Great Uncle Bulgaria. The eccentric head of the Wimbledon burrow, aged between 300 years and eternity, insists on his daily copy of *The Times*, resists modern technology and happily sings the 'Always Behind the Times' song.

But the country has changed dramatically in the last few years. Two Peace Corps workers returning after six years exclaimed, 'The country is now developed!' and were amazed that they could no longer find a room at the beach in peak season. Out of all the countries in Eastern Europe, the Bulgarian market has the best opportunities to buy coastal properties. All other countries with a significant coastline in this area already have an established market, and Croatia in particular is comparatively expensive.

The surprise agreement that Bulgaria is set to join the EU in 2007/8 (it was previously thought this would not happen until the following wave of countries to join) only adds to the phenomenon. While prices of £5,000 for a house are often bandied about, this kind of bargain is only available inland and for

Brigitte's Bears

Bulgaria's dancing bears are a hideous hangover from medieval times, and there are only a handful left. A park, built with the help of French actress Brigitte Bardot, now pays owners several thousand dollars for their bears and rehabilitates them before releasing them into the wild. Some locals are shocked that it costs nearly double their monthly income to feed the bears and have started joking, 'Oh, how wonderful to be a bear in Bulgaria.'

buildings that need maintenance. For popular coastal areas, the figure is upwards of £35,000 for an apartment.

In many ways at the crossroads of Europe and Asia, Bulgaria is bounded to the north by Romania, to the east by the Black Sea, to the south by Turkey and Greece and to the west by Serbia and the Former Yugoslav Republic of Macedonia. Bulgaria borrows cultures and cuisine from its neighbours, and Istanbul is only a bus ride away.

Tourism

While Germans, Scandinavians and richer Eastern Europeans – mainly Russians – have been coming here on holiday for years, Bulgaria is still largely unknown by the British. For these other nationalities, prices are cheap and it is as close to them as Spain is to us. But now that prices have risen in Spain – for holidays and properties – the UK market is taking off. Prices in the euro zone have risen, and as a result Bulgaria offers particularly good value for money.

In 2004 several large British holiday companies began offering packages to Bulgaria, and there has been a shortfall in available accommodation, so opportunities for letting are extremely good. A spokesperson for First Choice Holidays, which has offered package holidays to Bulgaria since 2000, said that the country was its 'star performer'. The company reported that, while most holiday bookings had dropped by 25 per cent, sales of holidays to Bulgaria had rocketed by 100 per cent in only the second week in January 2004, while the *Washington Post* named Bulgaria as one of the world's top ten international destinations of 2004. The cost of living in Bulgaria is extremely cheap; according to Thomas Cook the average cost of a pint of beer is 50p, while a three-course meal is £6. In Spain, the corresponding prices are £1.76 and £11.

Bulgaria is the fastest-developing tourist destination on the 'Old Continent', says the European Tourism Commission. The number of tourists from the EU visiting Bulgaria rose by nearly 50 per cent in the summer of 2004 according to the *Sofia Morning News*, with British tourists increasing by a massive 75 per cent. Greece tops the list of those most interested in Bulgaria for holidays, with visitors numbering more than half a million, and tourists from Germany and Macedonia were hot on their heels.

Tourism and Property Investment: Pros and Cons

In 2005 there is a huge interest in the purchase of property in Bulgaria and there is always a danger in such an explosion in demand. Is this a real change in the market, or is it a bubble? There are good signs and bad signs.

The good signs are that there is a genuine and large increase in the number of British and other Western European tourists who are visiting the country – Bulgaria has been discovered. There are many people who like Bulgaria simply because it is not Spain. It is not yet as developed, though it is rapidly heading in that direction. Of those tourists there will be a percentage who like it so much that they decide to buy a holiday home in the area. They may well be nudged in that direction by the realisation that prices are likely to rise because of the increasing demand, because Bulgaria may join the European Union in 2007/8 and because of the impact of the bid to host the Winter Olympics in 2014.

Current rental yields are reasonable, though not stunning, but they should improve as more tourists become familiar with Bulgaria and become more adventurous, prepared to rent privately rather than going on a package deal. They may then diminish as the large amount of new building coming on-stream hits the market. For rental yields to remain static there needs to be a continuing rise in tourist levels. That is entirely possible, but the danger is that some other new and cheaper destination will come along and take the shine off the Bulgarian market. The contestants are already lining up. For example, the Cape Verde Islands offer comparable prices with a year-round superb climate. They are 2hrs' further flying time and 2–3 years behind in the development curve.

The bad news is that a very large percentage of the people who are buying now are buying as an investment. They have little or no interest in personal use of the property. They intend to flip (sell it on before completion) at a profit. This creates an obvious danger: if too many people want to do this, there will *be* no market. There will be no one to buy, or, at least, not be enough buyers to generate any profit for those wanting to sell. Our advice to anybody wanting to do this remains the same: you should not buy a property with the sole intention of flipping it. You should buy it as a medium-term hold because you think it is outstanding either as a place to live or as a place to let out. If, when it is ready for delivery, somebody then makes you an offer that you cannot refuse, feel free to take it and rejoice. All in all, however, it is likely that the ski areas in particular will offer a long-term good investment yield.

Also note that the UK is still a small player in the Bulgarian tourist market. The main sources of tourism in Bulgaria are from relatively low-income countries, which will have an impact on the likely rental levels achievable if you are hoping to let to people from outside the UK, German or Scandinavian markets. However, in 2000 the British were the ninth most numerous incoming tourists in Bulgaria, in 2001 the eighth, and from 2002 onwards the fifth; British tourism to Bulgaria has increased by 33.5 per cent in 2001, 60.26 per cent in 2002, 43.68 per cent in 2003 and 62.60 per cent in 2004.

Tourists to Bulgaria in 2004 Compared with 2003, by Country

	Country	Number	% Increase
1	Greece	707,453	+ 29.17
2	Tfyr Macedonia	655,974	− 2.44
3	Serbia and Montenegro	576,965	− 2.50
4	Germany	565,337	+ 5.75
5	UK	259,092	+ 62.60
6	Russia	120,523	− 0.67
7	Czech Republic	102,045	+ 30.17
8	Poland	99,684	+ 61.25
9	Sweden	96,131	+ 36.43
10	Romania	91,539	+ 19.43
11	Israel	79,172	+ 14.65
12	Slovakia	75,253	+ 17.74
13	Finland	58,463	+ 19.72
14	Denmark	52,594	+ 23.15
15	France	48,634	+ 35.98
16	USA	39276	+ 26.18
17	Turkey	37,600	+ 13.92
18	Hungary	33,028	+ 51.17
19	Austria	32,219	+ 38.79
21	Ukraine	29,793	− 29.71
22	Italy	28,337	+ 15.28
23	Netherlands	25,874	+ 19.09
24	Norway	21,403	+ 37.15
25	Switzerland	20,085	+ 39.43
26	Cyprus	13,400	+ 52.93
27	Belarus	12,037	− 1.38
28	Slovenia	11,824	+ 73.40
29	Ireland	11,460	+ 83.39
30	Spain	9,638	+ 40.27

The Economy

In the early 1990s, as a result of the loss of the Soviet market, Bulgaria's economy dropped significantly and the standard of living fell by about 40 per cent. Sanctions by the UN against Yugoslavia and Iraq also had a damaging effect. The economy picked up in the mid-1990s, but collapsed in 1996. From 1997 it improved again, and there has been steady growth in the last few years.

Unemployment is relatively high and the standard of living low, with the average annual income around £1,000, and 80 per cent of the population thought to be living below the poverty level.

Bulgaria became a full member of NATO in 2004, and has its currency pegged to the euro. The country looks set to be admitted into the European Union in 2007/8, and already the EU has invested millions of money to upgrade its roads and airports.

The Exchange Rate

One of the key indicators of any country where investment is likely to prove successful is an exchange rate that is either stable or slowly improving against other major currencies. A common pattern for emerging market countries is that when they first get their independence the exchange rate sinks rapidly, improves slowly and then stabilises or, if the country is doing well, slowly gains ground.

The figures in the table below have been adjusted to take into account a devaluation of 1,000 per cent that took place in 2001. In other words, the exchange rate in 2000 was 3,084.73 to the pound and in 2001 this was revised to 3.10 to the pound. Today it is around 2.80 to the pound.

Exchange Rate – Bulgarian Lev

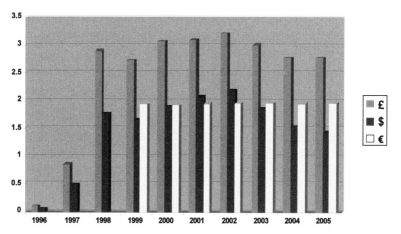

Notice how the lev has been rock-solid against the euro for a number of years. This is all part of the Bulgarian preparations for coming into the European Union and, they hope, soon into the euro zone. The currency has varied slightly against the dollar and the pound in the same way that the dollar and the pound have varied against the euro. Given the general feeling that the euro will strengthen in value against the pound over time, this is a promising background for the currency of a country in which you are thinking of making an investment.

Visas and Permits

Citizens of the UK and any other members of the EU do not require either a visa or return ticket to enter Bulgaria for up to **30 days**, but they must be in possession of a passport valid for at least three months beyond departure. They can only visit Bulgaria once in any six-month period. If you wish to visit for longer than 30 days or more often than once every six months, obtain a Type C visa from the Bulgarian consulate in the country where you live or download an application form from **www.bulgarianembassy.org.uk**. The formalities are minimal. The visa will allow you to remain in Bulgaria for up to 90 days in any six-month period.

In theory, anyone visiting Bulgaria must register as a foreigner within 48 hours. Your hotel or hostel will do this for you, but if you are staying with friends, go to the local police station with your passport, the host and their ID. In return, you will get a registration slip – be prepared to show this at any time and give it up when leaving the country.

From 1 December 2001 all foreign and stateless persons visiting Bulgaria have been required to have **medical insurance**, covering them for the entire length of their stay.

If you are going to be in Bulgaria for more than 30 days you will need a **foreign identity card**. This is issued by the local passport office of the Ministry of the Interior in the place where you are staying, on presentation of a passport with three passport photos and a birth certificate.

There are two sorts of **residence permit**, both of which are easy to obtain after a certain amount of paperwork. The first is a **temporary permit** that lasts for one year. In order to obtain such a permit you need to obtain a Type D visa from the Bulgarian consulate in your country of residence before you travel to Bulgaria. You need to show proof of health insurance and that you have sufficient funds to support yourself in Bulgaria. This generally requires you to demonstrate that you have about £1,000 deposited in a Bulgarian bank. This permit can be renewed annually. After five years it can be converted into a **permanent residence permit**.

Before applying for Bulgarian **citizenship** you must have:

- **been granted permission for permanent residence in the Republic of Bulgaria not less than five years previously.**
- **an income that allows you to support yourself.**
- **a command of the Bulgarian language.**

Profile of Bulgaria

Recent History and Politics

In 1946, with Bulgaria under Communist rule, King Simeon II was forced into the exile at the age of nine. When Communism famously collapsed across Europe in 1989, Bulgaria became a democracy and in 2001 the former king became prime minister. He is still largely admired for sound financial policies.

The Roma

The Roma people have experienced – and continue to experience – extreme segregation and discrimination. Under Communism they were unable to call themselves Gypsies or express certain aspects of their culture, but democracy has done little to redress the balance. The size of the country's Gypsy population is unknown, but thought to be around 500,000, or nearly 7 per cent of the population. Unemployment is high – around 70 per cent – while an astonishing 91 per cent of the general Bulgarian population believe that Roma are predisposed to criminal behaviour.

Religion

More than 85 per cent of the population is Eastern Orthodox and 13 per cent is Muslim; the remaining percentage are Roman Catholic and Jewish. The Bulgarian Church is autonomous and headed by a Patriarch. Although the country officially converted to Christianity in the 9th century, according to a Gallup poll as many as half of its people are deeply superstitious. The evil eye, horoscopes and tarots are just some of the beliefs that are hangovers from pagan times.

Climate and Geography

Because of the country's incredibly varied landscape, temperatures and weather are extreme. Bulgaria enjoys four very distinct seasons. While summers can be hot (although rarely uncomfortable or humid), providing beach playgrounds on the coast, winters can be icy, offering ideal conditions for skiers in the mountains. In the mountains and during the evenings, temperatures drop an average of 5°C. Sofia's daytime temperatures average 27°C in July and August, but plunge to 2°C in January. On the coast, summer temperatures are about the same as in the capital. The average annual temperature is 5°C, and in winter about 0°C. Rainfall is generally high in spring and autumn.

See pp.163–4 for climate charts, and log on to the **Bulgarian National Institute of Meteorology and Hydrology**'s website, **www.meteo.bg**, for the national weather forecast.

Regional Profile

Despite being roughly half the size of Britain, with a population of just 8 million, Bulgaria is incredibly varied and one of the least populated countries in Europe. The Black Sea 'Riviera' has some of Europe's largest beaches. The main resort of Sunny Beach, and to a lesser degree Golden Sands, are lively, even brash, but only half an hour's drive away you will see horse-drawn hay carts. Inland there is dense forest, broken by coloured plains, swaths of sunflowers and pockets of vines. To the west there are mountains, lakes and international ski resorts, with historic towns in the centre and Sofia, the more sophisticated capital. Romans splashed in the ancient hot springs, which are now modern spa resorts used by sophisticated visitors.

As a result of the decline in agriculture, countries such as Bulgaria are trying to increase rural tourism as a means of regenerating country areas socially and financially. Fresh air and a slower pace of life, along with lower property prices and activities from bee-keeping to horse-riding, are obvious attractions for foreign and Bulgarian tourists.

Sofia

Despite being the country's largest city and its capital, Sofia is not high on most visitors' list of places to see. But it has a blend of building styles from Greek to Turkish, including pretty churches, important museums and galleries, and a cultural scene you would expect from a capital city. Sofia makes a good base for exploring the pleasant surrounding area, which includes the World Heritage Site of Rila monastery, Vitosha National Park, and various ski resorts.

A certain number of post-Communist grey blocks, a workaday atmosphere and the fact that Plovdiv – the old capital, which has stunning Byzantine and Renaissance architecture – boasts much more history and charm means that Sofia is often ignored. Bear in mind that Sofia is the hub for international and domestic flights and the home of Bulgaria's foreign diplomatic missions; there are many people requiring accommodation to let.

The Black Sea Coast

Bulgaria's 354km of Black Sea coastline includes wide bays with long golden beaches backed by verdant hills. The main resort of **Sunny Beach** has unkindly been compared to Blackpool; its sloping woodland and mostly low-rise buildings are nothing like the British resort, but it does have a flavour of the good old days of seaside holidays, with fairground rides and games and street food.

This is the mecca for Bulgarian beach package holidays; there are already over a hundred hotels with more being constructed all the time, along with an

Golf Playgrounds

'Golf playgrounds green up Bulgaria,' screamed the headline in the *Sofia Morning News* in May 2004. The newspaper reported how the international game was coming to Bulgaria, with the second golf course in the country at Sliven, 100km from the Black Sea. The 'playground', which covers a huge area, is partly owned by Bulgaria's Air Sofia – which also owns the country's first golf course at Ihtiman. Investors have planned a minimum of five such 'playgrounds' and the airline has wasted no time in readying itself to create a third course in the town of Razgrad, in the northeast.

Beautiful Bulgaria

Thanks to the UN-funded 'Beautiful Bulgaria' programme, Western volunteers have restored many of the country's impressive monasteries, churches and castles. Sofia dates back to the 4th century BC, with buildings showing many architectural traditions including Greek, Roman, Byzantine, Bulgarian and Turkish. EU funding is paying for roads to be upgraded and environmental concerns addressed.

increasing number of self-catering apartments. And upmarket elements of Sunny Beach are developing, such as the all-inclusive Elenite resort, the quieter village of **San Vlas**, and the glitzy, Las Vegas-style hotels on its northern edge. Across the bay is **Nesebâr**, designated a World Heritage Site because of its traditional wooden houses. There is not much of a beach here; accommodation is limited and high-priced; and in peak season it gets overrun with day-trippers.

The nearest airport in the area is in **Burgas**, around half an hour away from Sunny Beach. Essentially a port, the city is pleasant enough, with street cafés, pedestrianised shopping areas and breezy, green sea gardens. Southeast of Burgas is the less developed and natural **Sozopol**, a tiny peninsula connected to the mainland by a skinny strip of land with a number of surrounding camp sites. Sozopol itself has narrow, winding streets lined with lovely traditional wooden houses, ancient churches and modern art galleries. It became the biggest fishing centre on the Black Sea coast before developing tourism around its main beaches – Tsar, Raiski, Kavatsite and Harmanite. An ancient necropolis was discovered here in 1993 and excavations continue today.

South of Sozopol is almost unknown territory. Only hardened travellers – or those making their way down to Turkey – come here, and there is very limited public transport. North, towards the border with Romania, is **Varna**, another pleasing city with an airport and sea gardens. The coast's second major resort, **Golden Sands**, is north of here, with all the facilities of Sunny Beach but on a smaller scale.

Ski Resorts

Bulgaria has a well-established reputation as a ski destination. Its resorts offer great value for money for western European visitors and they are being developed all the time – both to improve their ski facilities and to make them true year-round destinations. In winter, visitors from all over the world come to enjoy the consistently snowy conditions, and in summer they arrive to hike across the mountains through swathes of wild flowers.

Upmarket **Pamporovo**, in the heart of the Rhodopi mountains, is the mythical home of the singer Orpheus. At 1,650m it gets lots of sunshine as the most southerly ski resort in Europe. **Borovets,** surrounded by ancient pine woods, is the oldest international mountain resort in the country. At the foot of the Rila mountains, it is well established with British skiers, at 1,350m above sea level,

The Travel Foundation

The First Choice Winter Sun brochure, which promotes Bulgarian ski resorts, features information on the charity the Travel Foundation. First Choice, along with other travel companies, is asking every customer to donate 10 pence per adult and 5 pence per child to the Travel Foundation when booking a holiday. The charity will use this money to try prevent the harmful effects of tourism by protecting the natural environment, traditions and culture of these resorts, and improving the wellbeing of local families.

with pistes as high as 2,600m. In 2004 the local mayor announced plans for the resort: it will have 100km of pistes, no fewer than 17,000 beds, and lifts able to transport 35,000 skiers over 90 minutes. By 2009, he says, the resort will spread from the town of Samokov to the village of Beli Iskar and be divided into three levels, with a hierarchy of accommodation offered 'according to the financial status' of the tourist.

Bansko is the younger sibling of the old favourites. In the southwest of the country, in the foothills of the Pirin mountain, it sits at 925m above sea level. The historic buildings, with a generous sprinkling of cultural monuments, make it a World Heritage Site. The resort has a variety of ski slopes and good *après-ski*, with nearly 100 taverns. In 2003 the numbers of visitors doubled from the previous year, partly the result of huge investment in the village, which included the installation of a gondola lift, modern lifts and new pistes. Over the next few years a golf club, boating lake, stables with race track and sports facilities are being created to give visitors a reason to visit when the snow has all melted.

Veliko Târnovo

Ask Bulgarians where to visit inland and they will invariably come up with **Veliko Târnovo**, reciting the name like some kind of litany. The magical medieval town at the base of the Balkan mountains became a centre of the Bulgarian Uprising against Byzantine domination in 1185. Over the next couple of hundred years, it became the most significant political, economic, cultural and religious centre in the country.

Name a Famous Bulgarian

Vasil Levski is Bulgaria's national hero (at least according to one 19-year-old girl). His surname is actually a nickname meaning lion-like, because he was once a monk and led the revolt against Ottoman rule.

Ivan Vazov is the author of the most famous example of Bulgarian literature. *Under the Yoke* was published in 1893, and tells the story of the Ottoman oppression of the country.

Christo, the artist, lives in California now, but is known internationally for wrapping up large objects and buildings, including the Pont Neuf in Paris.

Selecting a Property

Getting There

Bulgaria's national airline is **Balkan-Bulgarian Airlines**. Other airlines serving Bulgaria include **Air France, Alitalia, Austrian Airlines, British Airways, KLM, LOT Polish Airlines, Lufthansa, MALEV Hungarian Airlines, Olympic Airlines** and **Swiss**. It is usually cheaper to take a package deal than buy separate flights and accommodation, but this will change as the budget airlines move in over the next few years. It is only a matter of time before budget airlines such as **Ryanair** and **easyJet** start flights to the country.

Direct international flights are available to the capital, Sofia, all year round. Direct charter flights to the Black Sea (Varna and Burgas) are on offer between mid-May and mid-October; at other times you will need to take a connecting internal flight from the capital. Air space is opening up all the time, with direct flights from Bristol to Plovdiv announced in summer 2004.

Getting Around

By Car

Roads between the main tourist centres have been greatly improved and are generally good, but drivers should be constantly on the alert for unmarked hazards, and signposts are often only in Cyrillic script. *See* 'Settling In', p.159.

By Train

In recent years rail services, operated by **Bulgarian State Railways** (BDZh), **t** 931 1111, **www.bdz.bg**, have been shrunk to almost nothing. Often there are only one or two services a day, even on major routes, and they are painfully slow. The chances are – unless your sign language is particularly good – that you will need the help of someone who speaks Bulgarian in order to get timetable information and to buy a ticket, although international services are printed in the Roman alphabet, rather than Cyrillic.

By Bus

Buses in Bulgaria are generally faster and more efficient than trains. Services are operated by private companies, so in towns and tourist areas there may be several terminals and information may be hard to come by, as companies only want to tell you about their own operations. When you are catching a bus that started its journey elsewhere, tickets are often only sold when the bus arrives. In rural areas, tickets are often bought from the driver.

Choosing a Location

The Black Sea Coast

The Black Sea coast has long been popular with tourists from Bulgaria and from other parts of Eastern Europe. It is easy to see why. It is still inexpensive as a holiday destination – prices are much the same as they were in Spain 20 years ago. It has some good beaches and an agreeable summer climate.

This coast is a second-division destination, however: it is not the new Spain and never will be. This is for several reasons. First, the climate is simply not quite good enough. The temperatures are almost identical to those in Spain during the summer but there is a lot more rain and humidity, and in winter the temperatures are on a par with London. Many people wish to make use of their holiday home during the winter months, particularly if they come from a cold climate, and this is simply not a realistic option on the Black Sea coast. Secondly, there isn't as much to do as there is in Spain. There are few tourist attractions, golf courses, world-class cities or social activities, and even fewer where the staff speak English. Thirdly, for the British buyer or traveller there is the additional disadvantage that flying to Bulgaria takes (in the summer) 4½ hours rather than 2½ hours to Spain.

This does not mean that the Black Sea coast is necessarily a bad investment. If you are looking for a holiday home for use in summer you will find one that is relatively inexpensive. If you are looking for an investment there still seems to be considerable room for upward movement of prices before they become anything like comparable with those in Spain. Just do not delude yourself that your apartment will become as valuable as an apartment in Marbella.

The main areas of interest are towards the southern end of the coast. Look at the area around Sunny Beach and Pomorie. Older developments tend to be lacking in character, as do some newer ones, but there are now more interesting developments being built that are up to the highest standards found elsewhere.

The Ski Areas

By contrast, Bulgaria's ski areas are potentially world class. They need a lot of investment in infrastructure and equipment, but this is coming. Fundamentally, in any case, ski areas are about whether there is good skiing, and the Bulgarian pistes score very well on this test. The quality of the skiing is evidenced by the fact that Bulgaria is attempting to secure the Winter Olympic Games in 2014. Whether they get it or not is another matter, but the mere fact that they are trying speaks volumes for the quality of the skiing available in the area. Purists may think that the skiing in Austria or France is better; whether or not that is true, the huge difference between the price of a good-quality ski apartment in Bulgaria and the same apartment in France means that the Bulgarian apartment offers fantastic value for money. A one-bedroom flat in

Les Arcs in France cost €150,000 in 2005. A similar apartment in Bansko in Bulgaria would cost half this amount. Although the tourist might be prepared to pay more to rent an apartment in Les Arcs, they would probably not be prepared to pay twice as much. Thus the apartment in Bulgaria would be a very cost-effective investment.

Property Types and Prices

In 2003 the average increase in Bulgarian property prices was 24 to 28 per cent (Real Estates National Association). The capital, Sofia, experienced the greatest demand (average price €400 per square metre at end 2003), particularly for apartments between 60 and 80 square metres, which in some areas have increased in price by a massive 100 per cent. The other area in demand was the Black Sea coast, where property prices in Burgas and Varna are 17 per cent higher than the country's average.

The main reasons for the rise in property prices are the low unemployment in Sofia, Varna and Burgas, and the expanding credit market – there was an 80 per cent increase in mortgage-lending in 2003, as Bulgarians have only just been able to take out a mortgage, which has created a domestic property boom.

An enormous amount of building work is going on in Bulgaria. The Black Sea coast and the inland ski resorts in particular are witnessing the creation of modern apartment blocks for the increasing number of foreign visitors visiting the country. These are typically bought 'off-plan', which means you pay in instalments until the building is completed.

Guide Prices

€20,000

- One-bedroom apartment in town centre of Burgas.
- Two-bedroom apartment in a seaside village.
- Villa near Balchik of 100 sq m built up area and plot of 500 sq m.
- Semi-detached house in a village 12km from Burgas.

€30,000

- Small house needing reconstruction with a living space of 80 sq m and a plot of 600 sq m, 5km from Varna.
- Two-storey house in the countryside, 30km from the mountain resort of Borovets.

€45,000

- Two-storey house with sea views and 160 sq m living space and a plot of 612 sq m.

- Summer house near Albena with 90 sq m living space and a plot of 450 sq m, outside shower, toilet and staircase.
- Five-bedroomed villa in spa town of Velingrad, with walled garden.

€60,000

- Fully furnished two-bedroom apartment in the centre of Varna with living space of 92 sq m.
- House on two floors in the old part of Sozopol.
- Stylish old house on two floors in the centre of Balchik.
- Fully renovated house in quiet mountain area of Buinovci.

€80,000

- Brand new two-storey house 20km from Varna, 3,000 sq m garden area.

€100, 000

- New luxurious three-storey house of 300 sq m in Balchik.
- House on three floors near Varna, with garage and parking.

€120,000

- New villa near Balchik, over 210 sq m, with four bedrooms and garage.

What is Available and at What Price?

There is always a huge range of prices in any property market and this one is no exception. You need to remember that, by and large, you get what you pay for. That is to say, a more expensive property is usually more expensive because it has some special quality about it and, conversely, a very cheap property is usually very cheap because it has a very poor location, it is built to a very low standard, it is in a bad state of repair – or all three!

Prices in Bulgaria, January 2005

Place and Type of Property	Low	Mid	High
Sunny Beach: new one-bedroom apartment (60 sq m)		€40,000	€60,000
Sunny Beach: new two-bedroom apartment (100 sq m)		€70,000	€90,000
Sunny Beach: three-bedroom villa (160 sq m)	€70,000		€150,000
Countryside: wooden cottage (42 sq m)	€7,000		
Countryside: two-bedroom apartment (80 sq m)	€33,000		
Countryside: two-bedroom villa (100 sq m)	€40,000		
Bansko: one-bedroom apartment in new hotel-style complex (65 sq m)			€70,000

Price Charts by Square Metre

Information from online Bulgarian real estate magazine *Imoti*.

New Housing in Sofia

Area	€ per sq m
Downtown area	500–1,000
Losenets	600–900
Ivan Vazov	600–950
Beli Brezi	450–600
Manastirski livadi	450–530
Iztok	650–900
Strelbishte	450–550

Apartments in Burgas

Area	€ per sq m			
	1-bedroom	2-bedroom	3-bedroom	larger
Central area and Lazur housing complex, new construction	285–565	315–630	280–800	275–610
Central area and Lazur complex, old construction	340–420	310–475	350–750	360–505
Residential districts Slaveykov, Izgrev, Meden Rudnik, brick masonry	300–450	300–580	295–385	300–370
Residential districts Slaveykov, Izgrev, prefabs	300–440	270–340	290–340	no supply
Meden Rudnik complex, prefabs	260–300	225–270	235–290	no supply

Apartments in Plovdiv

Area	€ per sq m
Downtown, new construction	400–450
Karshiaka, Novotel, Sadiiski quarter, new construction	350–420
Vastanicheski, Smirnenski, new construction	350–360
Trakia, prefabs	250–290

Apartments in Sunny Beach

Type of apartment	€ per sq m
1-bedroom	720–1,000
2-bedroom	720–1,500
3-bedroom	720–1,300
larger	720–900

Apartments in Varna

Area	€ per sq m	% increase on 2003
Downtown	750–900	+ 22
Greek district	750–950	+ 13
Sports hall	600–700	+ 12
Chayka	500–650	+ 11
VINS/Red Square	600–750	+ 11
Generali	600–650	+ 11

Holiday Houses in Varna Area

Area	€ per sq m	% increase on 2003
Trakata	230–550	+ 23
Evksinograd	250–500	+ 24
Sv. sv. Konstantin i Elena	250–500	+ 22
Manastirski rid	150–210	+ 15
Alen mak	150–210	+ 22
Journalist	220–450	+ 24
Galata	100–250	+ 20
Zvezditsa	150–170	+ 20

Building from Scratch or Renovation

Rural areas offer opportunities to purchase older properties for renovation, but consider carefully before taking this route, as the process can be long and costly. As there is not yet much of a market for properties needing huge amounts of work, the problems associated with the renovation project can be huge. Not least will be your inability to speak Bulgarian. If you are contemplating a renovation project, it is vital to get good advice right at the outset.

Building costs are low. A full restoration project is likely to cost about £200 per square metre. If simple repair is necessary you might end up paying about £1 per hour for a skilled labourer, more if you employ a contractor. However, as is the case with many countries, it is very easy to find that, once you have finished your project, the cost of buying the property and the work you have undertaken is more than the value of the property as it stands. Keep control.

Temporary Accommodation

When looking for property in Bulgaria, you may need temporary accommodation. Bear in mind that costs can be as much as five times more expensive for foreigners. Private rooms, available in big cities and along the coast, are often much better value than hotels; local tourist offices can provide information. Small hotels may offer bargains but be of a poor standard. Rates are usually charged per person, and hotels are rated on a star system from one to five.

The Process of Buying a Property

The most important thing to stress about buying a property in Bulgaria is that there is a lot more risk associated with it than by buying in, say, Spain or Scotland. There is a lot of property with either bad title or defective planning consent. Legal advice is essential unless you take the view that the amount you are investing is so small that you can afford to write it off.

Freedom to Buy

You can freely buy apartments in Bulgaria. If you wish to buy land or buildings attached to land, however, you will need to do so through a local Bulgarian company, which will be the owner of the property. This is because only Bulgarians are currently allowed to own land and buildings in Bulgaria. This rule will change no later than 2007/8 when Bulgaria enters the European Union. When you own through a Bulgarian company the property is treated as being owned by a Bulgarian, even if the company itself is 100 per cent owned and controlled by foreigners.

The reason that you are already free to buy an apartment in your own name, without the intervention of a Bulgarian company, is that, technically, the form of ownership of an apartment is slightly short of 100 per cent ownership of land. It is not the same as an English leasehold interest where you only have the rights over the apartment for a limited number of years – your rights as the owner of an apartment in Bulgaria are much fuller – but still not quite the same as the rights you enjoy when you own the land itself.

A number of Bulgarian developers have started to offer the best of both worlds. The land on which the apartments are constructed is owned by a Bulgarian limited company. The apartment is owned by you as an individual. When you buy the apartment you are also sold a share in the limited company. The result is that you and your fellow owners collectively own the land as well as the rights in the apartment. If this can be negotiated, it is the best solution.

Initial Steps

First Contracts

Once you have found a property that you want to purchase, you will be expected to sign some form of contract, generally either a reservation contract or a preliminary purchase contract. *See* p.75 for an explanation of these concepts. Note that the name 'preliminary purchase contract' is misleading: it is actually a full binding purchase contract. We therefore recommend that, wherever possible, you insist on signing a **reservation contract** rather than a preliminary purchase contract at this stage.

Searches and Enquiries

Once you have signed a reservation contract, your lawyer should make various enquiries, such as checking that the contract is fair, that the seller has good title and the right to sell to you, that the area is zoned for residential building and that any building work being undertaken enjoys all the necessary planning and building consents. Depending on the circumstances of your case there could well be other enquiries that also need to be made.

In Bulgaria it is common for work to be started, illegally, before all of these steps are in place. It is also common for property to have a title that is defective. Sometimes these problems should put you off having any involvement in the purchase. On other occasions the risks are minimal and, provided you go into the transaction with your eyes open, might not put you off buying if you really like the property.

Structural Guarantees on New Property

New properties benefit from a 10-year guarantee.

Declared Value

It is common for the value declared in the title to be less than the true value. This is technically illegal but almost universal practice. The reason for this is that the declared value is the value used by the tax office to determine the taxes payable for the purchase.

You should avoid going along with this if possible. The tax payable by you on the purchase (the equivalent of stamp duty) is very low at 2 per cent of the value declared. The main benefit accrues to the seller, who will avoid paying capital gains tax. You will be removing a burden from the seller and landing yourself with a potential capital gains problem later on if you make a significant under-declaration and then, when you sell, your buyer refuses to do the same for you or the rules have been tightened.

In Bulgaria the position is made more complicated because each property has a tax value, a little like our English rateable values, which is often used as the stated value for tax purposes. This is usually roughly half the true value of the property. When buying a property off-plan, you will not know what the tax value is likely to be on completion.

Bank Guarantees

Bank guarantees under which you are repaid the money you have invested if the builder is unable to complete the project are still very much a rarity in Bulgaria. A few developers are now providing them. They are worth having.

Some Problems

The main problems in Bulgaria are defective title and defective planning consents. However, there is a new category of problems that is only just beginning to emerge: problems generated by greed. The difference between the ownership of an apartment and the ownership of land has been described above. Some developers are trying to raise a large charge for the right to use the land on which the apartment stands. They have, no doubt, borrowed this idea from the English concept of a lease and associated ground rent.

Some developers are also trying to charge substantial sums for managing the apartment complex, and are trying to tie in the owners of the apartments into using their services for years. These arrangements are to be resisted.

Signing the Contract and Registering the Title

Once your lawyer has checked out the property and found that everything is in order, you are ready to sign the **preliminary purchase contract**. This commits you and the seller to signing the full contract transferring ownership on an agreed date shortly afterwards, or, if the property is still under construction, once the property has been fully built.

The preliminary purchase contract contains most of the clauses you would expect to see in a UK contract. These will include a description of the property, a statement of the legal title to the property, the price to be paid, how it is to be paid, the deadline for payment and any other deadlines applicable, what should happen in the event of breach of contract, and so on. Many Bulgarian contracts are badly drafted, because there is really no history in Bulgaria of drafting contracts for the sale of land. The problem is exacerbated by the fact that many contracts are drafted in English, which is clearly not the first language of the person doing the drafting. As a result they are unclear or muddled. Specifications tend to be very 'thin'. The contracts tend to be lacking in detail as to what happens if anything goes wrong.

At this point you will normally pay a **deposit** of 10 per cent of the price of the property. In the case of a property under construction ('off-plan') you will start to make **stage payments**, which will vary in size and number from property to property. A typical scheme would provide for an initial payment of 30 per cent followed by two further payments of 30 per cent as construction progresses, followed by a final payment of 10 per cent on delivery. Occasionally schemes are found where there is only one preliminary payment of, say, 30 per cent with the balance being paid on delivery. This is obviously very useful if you are taking out a mortgage.

Once you are ready to take delivery of the house you will sign the **final purchase contract**. This is signed in front of a notary public. It is at this point that the balance of the money is paid across to the seller. You do not need to be present in Bulgaria to sign this document, as your lawyer can prepare a **power of attorney** (*see* pp.77–8) under which you can appoint somebody else to sign on your behalf. This is a sensible thing to do, as it saves the need for you to go to Bulgaria, often at short notice, to sign the final title.

Once you have paid the balance of the price, the seller will authorise you to **register your ownership** of the property in the local title register or land registry. Once this has been done, you – or the local Bulgarian company that you have set up to own the property – will be the full legal owner of the property in much the same way as you would be in the UK. It is likely to take 2–6 weeks for the registered title deeds to be made available to you. How long will depend on how busy the registry is in the place where you are buying. With the current explosion of demand, these periods are getting longer.

The Expenses of Buying Property

The main expenses of buying are:

- tax – the equivalent of stamp duty – 2 per cent of the price.

- estate agent's fees, if these are not paid by the seller – typically 5 per cent of the price if you are using a local Bulgarian agent.

- notary's fees – these will vary from case to case but will typically not exceed £200.

- legal fees – these depend on whether you use a Bulgarian or an English lawyer; English lawyer's fees will inevitably be higher but you will be able to sue them if they get it wrong and they will be able to give you lots of advice, particularly about the vital issues of who should own the property to minimise your tax and other problems, which the local Bulgarian lawyer would not be able to help you with; fees will range from about £350 if you use a local Bulgarian lawyer to £1,500 if you use a specialist English lawyer.

- fees to set up a company – if you are buying a piece of land or a house on a piece of land (but not an apartment) you will need to set up a Bulgarian company; this is likely to cost £500.

Letting Your Property

See the general chapter **Letting Your Property**, pp.117–26.

If you are letting out your property you should make sure that you use a proper **rental contract**. Your lawyer will be able to supply you with a draft that you can amend as necessary. Letting short-term to tourists produces the fewest problems in terms of what you can do if the tenant does not pay the rent or refuses to leave.

Rental yields in Bulgaria are a little uncertain at the moment. Ski apartments and coastal properties produce the highest rental yields and this is likely to continue into the future. In 2005 – and with the substantial qualification that there are huge variations in the marketplace – we would expect to see you let a good one-bedroom apartment on the coast for about £200 per week during high season and a similar apartment in a ski resort for £250 per week. Two-bedroom apartments will, generally, produce a slightly lower return in rental income but, often, a higher return in potential capital growth.

Taxes

Taxes for Non-resident Property-owners

Local Property Taxes

Local property taxes in Bulgaria are very low, and are assessed on the basis of the official tax value of your property which, in itself, is normally only about half its true value. The normal rate of local property tax is 0.15 per cent. This means that if you own an apartment worth £50,000 it is likely to have an official tax value of £25,000 and you will have to pay an annual property tax of £37.50. In addition to this tax, in some areas you will have to pay a local garbage collection tax, which might be £10 per year. Local and national taxes for property ownership vary from €150 a year in the capital Sofia for a two-bedroom apartment to about €80 annually in other parts of the country.

Income and Capital Gains Taxes

The Bulgarian rules for income tax are in the process of being reviewed. Foreign investors can invest in properties in Bulgaria either directly, in their own name, or through a local company.

The tax treatment of a foreign investor depends on whether or not their activities constitute a 'permanent establishment'. The definition of a permanent establishment is very wide. Foreign investors who let out their apartment (except through an independent agent) may well be treated as having a permanent establishment under local Bulgarian law, but the double taxation treaty (*see* p.94) may contain a narrower definition.

If the activities of a foreign person owning property in Bulgaria do not constitute a permanent establishment, the person will be liable for only 15 per cent withholding tax on the rentals and capital gains, unless an even lower rate is applied under their double tax treaty.

If the activities of a foreign person owning property in Bulgaria do constitute a permanent establishment, the taxation is as follows.

• **Rental income on company-owned property.** The basis of the taxable income of a company investing in Bulgarian property is the gross income from the property less any tax-deductible expenses and depreciation. These expenses include any management costs, repairs, maintenance, insurance and interest on any loans used to buy the property. Depreciation is set at a rate of 4 per cent per annum. Real estate acquired for purpose of re-selling is considered as 'investment property' and is not eligible for tax depreciation. It is also subject to annual revaluation of market value.

A municipal tax at a rate of 10 per cent of these profits is also due, but this is deductible in calculating taxable profits.

The corporate tax rate is a flat rate of 15 per cent (incidentally, down from 25 per cent in just two years).

• **Rental income on individually owned apartments.** This is paid only if you are resident in Bulgaria, at rates from 15 to 29 per cent. For non-residents, at present there is only a 15 per cent withholding tax, which can be set off against your UK tax liabilities on the same income. It is soon likely to be clarified that rental income from Bulgarian property will also attract normal Bulgarian tax, even if you are not resident in Bulgaria.

• **Capital gains taxes.** These are treated as part of your income.

Wealth Taxes

There are no wealth taxes.

Inheritance Taxes

These are being abolished for gifts to your spouse or children. There are very low taxes for other recipients and they only apply to your assets in Bulgaria.

Taxes for Resident Foreigners

This is beyond the scope of this book.

Settling In

Learning Bulgarian

Bulgarian is the official language and the Cyrillic alphabet is used, which isn't easy for most foreigners to understand. Unlike the English language, however, letters represent only one sound, and, because most sounds are the same as in the English language, it isn't as difficult as it might first appear.

Traditionally tourists from Germany and Russia were the most common, so these are the main foreign languages spoken by Bulgarians. However, with increasing numbers of British people visiting, this is changing fast.

The Cyrillic Alphabet

А а   a as in 'cat'
Б б   b as in 'bed'
В в   v as in 'vet'
Г г   g as in 'goat'
Д д   d as in 'dog'
Е е   e as in 'egg'
Ж ж   zh as s in 'leisure'
З з   z as in 'zoo'
И и   i as in 'fit' (or 'fee' when at the end of a word)
Й й   y as in 'yes'
К к   k as in 'kite'

Л л	l as in 'last'
М м	m as in 'man'
Н н	n as in 'no'
О о	o as in 'hot'
П п	p as in 'pet'
Р р	r as in 'red'
С с	s as in 'set'
Т т	t as in 'top'
У у	u as in 'rule'
Ф ф	f as in 'fast'
Х х	h as ch in 'Bach'
Ц ц	ts as in 'hits'
Ч ч	ch as in 'much'
Ш ш	sh as in 'wish'
Щ щ	sht as 'shed' in 'wished'
Ъ ъ	u as in 'hut'
Ь ь	softens the preceding consonant
Ю ю	yu as in 'you'
Я я	ya as in 'yard'

Shopping

Prices are extraordinarily low by UK standards, so it is easy to get carried away. Not everything will be a bargain, though, and you should watch out for the many fake goods. Traditional and local products tend to be the best made and the best buys. Go for hand-crafted leather goods, rose oil, embroidery, woodwork and kitchenware, and be aware that prices in the cities (as opposed to the tourist areas) will be lower.

Entrenched in the country (and many others in Eastern Europe) is the two-tiered pricing system, which means a reasonable price for locals and an extortionate (double or triple or more) for tourists. This is changing, though.

Shops are generally open Mon–Fri 10–8 and Sat 10–2. In tourist areas, stalls and shops are often open 10–12 midnight.

Home Utilities and Services

Electricity

Only bigger towns and cities and tourist areas have central heating systems; in rural areas charcoal and wood is used. Charges for electricity are around €30 a month. Bulgaria has invested in solar and wind power and everywhere you travel you can see evidence of this. However, in many ways the country is behind the times – or at least Western Europe – in its attitude to energy and its poor record on pollution. The Kozloduy nuclear power plant supplies around half of Bulgaria's electricity (compared with 30 per cent in Europe as a whole) and earns millions of dollars for the country from electricity exports. But in response to EU demands, the Bulgarians shut the two oldest reactors at the end of 2002 and are under pressure to close the remaining four reactors by 2006. The reform of its energy sector is a condition for Bulgaria's accession to the European Union. As part of the first stage of this process, three foreign companies are currently buying seven domestic electricity distributors. If all goes according to plan, Cez from the Czech Republic will take over power distributors in the capital Sofia; the German company EON will deal with the northeast; and EVN of Austria will look after power in the southeast of the country.

Gas

The gas system is not yet developed in Bulgaria; most locals use electricity for cooking and heating.

Water

Bulgaria's water and sewage system is in serious need of modernisation.

Telephones

For years Bulgaria's telephone system has suffered from lack of investment, although things are improving. In the past the focus has been on business and international calls, so new **public pay phones** (at post offices, important public buildings and larger hotels), which take **phone cards** (sold in post offices and local shops), are of the highest standard. To confuse matters, there are two types of phones – orange (*Bulfon*) and blue (*Mobika*) – which use different cards, so the canny caller carries both kinds.

Alternatively, there are **telephone offices** – really cabins – which are part of post offices and often open as late as 11pm. Because Bulgaria is one of the only countries in Europe that doesn't have peak or off-peak times for dialling, it makes no difference when you dial.

Phone codes for rural areas may be different if you're calling from within a region than if you're calling long-distance. Often the first 0 is substituted for 99. The international operator is **t** 0123. Bulgaria's **country code** is 359; to call Bulgaria from abroad, use the international access codes (UK 00, USA and canada 011), followed by the local area code (e.g. Sofia **t** 02), but dropping the initial 0.

Mobile Phones

Any kind of GSM mobile phone activated with international roaming can be used throughout the country, although you may have reception problems in the mountains. If you are going to spend any length of time in the country, it is worth buying a local phone, otherwise charges for calls within Bulgaria could result in an astronomical bill (as you will be charged for routing via England).

Major mobile operators in the country include **MobilTel** (**www.mobiltel.bg**) and **GloBul** (**www.globul.bg**).

The Internet

There are Internet cafés throughout the country, although in rural areas they may be hard to find. Two major service providers are **GeoEnterprise**, **www. geobiz.com**, and **BOL.BG**, **www.bol.bg**.

Media

The *Sofia Echo* is a weekly English newspaper published in Sofia since 1997. The monthly *Sofia City Guide* (**www.sofiacityguide.com**) is available from major hotels and has useful information on the city for newcomers. **www.bulgaria daily.com** is a comprehensive site, with breaking news. The weekly newspaper, *Sofia News*, is available in English, along with two weekly business publications *Pari* (money) and *Capital*.

The BBC website **www.bbc.co.uk/worldservice** has information about the World Service broadcast on radio in English around the world, non-stop.

Money and Banking

Currency and Cards

The Bulgarian currency is the **lev** (Lv), plural **leva**, which is divided into 100 **stotinki**. Notes come in denominations of Lv 1, 2, 5, 10, 20 and 50. Coins are in denominations of 1, 2, 5, 10, 20 and 50 stotinki.

If you are only planning to be in cities and major resorts, you could get by using ATMs and credit cards, but this would be much more difficult in rural areas, where cash is the best option. Cashpoints or **ATMs** (which can be used with most cards but check with your bank before you leave) are widely available in tourist areas and cities, but much rarer in rural regions. Most **credit cards** are accepted in tourist areas and cities as well as in larger hotels and car hire offices. Only really major hotels and restaurants accept travellers' cheques; many places are reluctant to cash them and there are only one or two places that can issue replacements.

Exchanging Money

Like most places in the world, there is a difference between the exchange rate offered in banks, *bureaux* and hotels. Watch out for apparently good exchange rates with hidden commission charges. The black market was once a thriving

> ### Forged Notes
> Between 2001 and 2004, a staggering three million counterfeit euro notes were confiscated in Bulgaria. Counterfeit travellers' cheques, credit cards and other documents were also confiscated and more than 30 criminal groups involved were disbanded.

business in Bulgaria, but is now best avoided. You will be offered a better rate by street chancers, but you will either be robbed blind or given out-of-circulation notes from pre-1999. When you exchange currency, a receipt known as a *bordereaux* will be given, which shows the amount of currency exchanged; it must be kept until departure.

Banks

Bulbank is the largest and most efficient of the banks. It has branches in most Bulgarian towns and is usually open Mon–Fri 9–4. It is up to you whether you want to open your account in foreign currency or in Bulgarian leva but minimum deposits usually apply. You will need a passport to open an account.

Post

Most post offices are open Mon–Sat 8.30–5.30 . Mail can take 7–10 days to reach Britain and 2–3 weeks to reach the USA, unless sent express or airmail. Parcels are cheap, but you must take items into the post office and have a customs declaration filled out before they are wrapped and weighed.

Working and Employment

Most foreigners coming to Bulgaria don't intend to work. Comparatively low wages and high levels of unemployment, along with the language barrier, frequently make it impractical to do so, anyway, although there are opportunities – particularly in the tourist industry. The increasing number of foreign companies investing in Bulgaria will need local staff, mostly in Sofia.

The following organisations may be useful when seeking opportunities: the **Bulgarian Business and Advertising Network (www.bulgaria.addr.com)**, and **Job Tiger (www.jobtiger.bg)** for job searches in Bulgaria.

The rules for job-hunting in Bulgaria are the same as at home. Ensure your CV is concise and clear and you are focused on the kind of work you are looking for. In this case you may need to get the CV translated for the national market. Make use of local sources and word of mouth, and keep your eyes and ears open. At interview stage, be as well presented as you can possibly be and do your research about the area and the company.

Education

In Bulgaria, education is compulsory for all children aged between 6 and 16. Teaching takes place over a 5-day week, ranging from 22 hours to 25 hours, and the academic year runs from mid-September to the end of May.

Nursery school education is optional and incurs a minimal fee; 95 per cent of pre-primary schools are funded by the state. Many have a music teacher and larger nursery operations employ a psychologist. **Private schools** are slowly being established and beginning to compete successfully with state schools, and more than 40 **higher educational institutions** in the country offer degrees.

There is information on different schools in Bulgaria at **www.schools-be. net/en**, with news and links, in eight languages.

The **Anglo-American School of Sofia**, c/o The American Embassy, 1 Suborna Street, Sofia 1000; **t** + 359 2 974 4575, serves the international community in Bulgaria's capital, teaching around 160 children aged between 3 and 14 from more than 30 countries. The **Indira Gandhi High School**, Sofia 1324, 'Lulin', 710 Street; **t** + 359 2 248 889, **souigandi@abv.bg**, dates back to 1860.

Health and Emergencies

Call **t** 150 for the **ambulance service** (*bârza pomosht*).

Thanks to a reciprocal health agreement with the UK, medical and dental care is given free to UK citizens, although medicines must be paid for. All you need to do is produce a UK passport and an NHS medical card.

For minor problems, take a trip to the local **pharmacy** (*apteka*). Locals are likely to use herbal medicine found in a *Bilkova apteka* but the language barrier could prove a problem here. For a **doctor** (*lekar*) or **dentist** (*zâbolekar*), the best bet is your nearest **health centre** (*poliklinika*) where you should find someone to speak English. Complaints that are more serious require **hospitals** (*bolnitsa*).

As you may expect, standards are below those in the UK, and in certain circumstances you may decide to fly home.

You are not required to have any **inoculations** for Bulgaria, but **vaccinations** against diphtheria, tetanus, typhoid and hepatitis A are advisable. Rabies is present, so if you are bitten, seek medical advice at once. **Tap water** is safe to drink in all parts of the country.

Social Services and Welfare Benefits

Social security contributions are compulsory for all employees of Bulgarian and foreign companies in the country. The rate of social security contributions is 1 per cent for employees, with unemployment fund contributions set at 0.5 per cent. The National Social Security Institute administers cash benefits, while the National Health Insurance Fund is in charge of medical benefits.

Medical benefits in Bulgaria are funded through compulsory health insurance contributions, which all Bulgarian citizens and foreign residents who have permanent residence status have to pay. The rate for these is 6 per cent, split equally between employers and employees.

Cars and Other Private Transport

You can use your national driving licence in Bulgaria for up to six months, but if you are planning to drive through any neighbouring countries, an international licence is required (available from the **AA**, **www.theaa.co.uk**). The Bulgarian equivalent of the **AA** or **RAC** is **Putna Pomosht** (**t** 146). If you intend to stay for a longer period it is also advisable to get an international licence.

Remember to drive on the right – the good news is that international road signs are used. The standard speed limit in towns is 50kph, with a maximum of 90kph for the rest of the country and 120kph on motorways. Mountain roads can be tortuous and add hours to a journey.

Cars

If entering Bulgaria with a car or other vehicle, you must present a document of ownership or registration documents showing you as the owner. If you are taking your own car, bear in mind that spares may be hard to find, so bring your own. On bringing a car into the country, it is given a 'visa tag', which has to be shown on leaving, as a way of preventing foreigners selling their cars in Bulgaria. As in the UK, road tax, insurance and MOT are annual costs (around €50, €30 and €12 respectively). Most cars have LPG systems, which means they run on non-polluting, cheap (around €0.50 a litre) fuel. Car theft is a big problem, so you may want to take out extra insurance. Use car parks with attendants, along with an immobiliser.

Taxis

Taxis are reasonably priced so you may want to consider them for longer journeys that are not served by public transport. Always, always agree a price beforehand and be very clear about it, otherwise you will probably end up with a nasty surprise and an argument. This way is usually cheaper than insisting on the driver using his meter, which means she or he has to declare the earnings. Night rates are double and on the Black Sea coast several times the normal rate.

Crime and the Police

Police, **t** 166.

Gone are the days when every official could be bribed and Bulgaria was known as 'Marlboro country' because cigarettes were the preferred currency for the corrupt. However, it is apparently still necessary for signs to be put up at customs at the airport saying 'no money here'. And corruption is still rife, with stories of schoolteachers being bribed to give their pupils good marks. Statistically, you are less likely to be a victim of crime in Bulgaria than in the UK. There is very little violent or street crime and the country is generally peaceful. That said, it always wise to take sensible precautions and to be aware that by local standards you are very wealthy.

Food and Drink
Food
Bulgarian food is surprising. Greasy stews, grey meat and a scarcity of vegetables might be expected, but instead the cuisine is greatly influenced by Mediterranean cooking. Think rich, slow-cooked soups, tender barbecued fish and lamb, and an abundance of fresh vegetables. The Greek influence is seen in stuffed grape leaves, flaky filo pastry pies, and delicious moussakas. Kebabs are ubiquitous and often a foot long, as are snacks (*zakuski*) – food once eaten in the fields. Vegetarian dishes are amazingly common in Bulgaria, although tourist restaurants may not always serve them; omelette, cheese and stuffed and baked vegetables are the best bets. Much of Bulgaria's locally grown food is organic, as farmers have not been able to afford pesticides and fertilisers.

There seems to be a salad named after every European country you can think of, but *shopska* is the true Bulgarian version, with tomatoes, cucumbers, onions, green peppers and crumbled feta cheese, which the Greeks would call Greek. Soups include the unusual cold *tarator*, made of yogurt and cucumbers, and a spicy bean *bob* soup. Typical Bulgarian cuisine is served in specialist restaurants (*mehanas*) that serve barbecued meat and casseroles of pork or veal in earthenware pots (*kavarma*). Fish (*riba*) is common and usually of much better quality than the meat – from the dubious-sounding sea wolf shark to mountain trout and Danube herring.

Dessert usually means *palachinka* (pancakes), though pastry shops also serve baklava and chocolate cake (*garash torta*). Yoghurt, rumoured to have originated here, is a national speciality, and very good. *Ayran*, a slightly salty and watered-down yoghurt, is a popular drink.

When **tipping**, give the money directly to the waiters rather than leave money on the table.

Drink
Delicious fresh **juices** are found almost everywhere, as is tea. Zagorka and Astika are very drinkable local **beers**. Bulgaria is the fifth largest exporter of **wine** in the world, particularly full-bodied reds such as Cabernet, Melnik, Gamza and Mavrud. These can be very good even when cheap. The best of the whites is

Traminer Han Krum. Local spirits, strong and cheap, include *mastika* (similar to ouzo) and *rakiya*, a fruit brandy best made from plums (*slivova*) or apricots (*kaisieva*). In bars these are sold by the gram, with 50g (*pedeset grama*) equivalent to a double shot.

Bulgarian **coffee** can be very good, especially where *kafe espresso* and *kapuchino* are available, or very bad when just *neskafe*. Cheaper still is *turska* (Turkish coffee), which is an acquired taste.

Bulgaria: References

Directory of Contacts and Resources

Embassies

- **Bulgarian Embassy**, 186–8 Queen's Gate, London SW7 5HL, **t** (020) 7584 9433, **www.bulgarianembassy.org.uk**. Visa Section open Mon, Tues, Thurs and Fri 9.30–11.50am; 24hr Visa Information Service **t** 09065 508950; 24hr fax-on-demand visa application form service **t** 09065 540819; individual enquiries on submitted applications 12.30–1.30pm, **t** (020) 7584 9433.

- **British Embassy**, 9 Moskovska Street, Sofia, **t** +359 2 933 9222, **britembvisa@mail.orbitel.bg**. Visa Section, **www.british-embassy.bg**.

Information and Resources

- **www.bulgariatravel.org**.

- **www.travel-bulgaria.com**.

- **www.RuralBulgaria.com**.

- **www.escapeartist.com/bulgaria/bulgaria.html**.

- **www.bulgaria.com/business**. A comprehensive database of over 14,000 Bulgarian companies in Bulgarian and English.

- **www.bcci.bg**. The website for the Bulgarian Chamber of Commerce and Industry in Sofia, a non-governmental organisation.

- **www.worldbiz.com/bulgaria.html**. How to do business in Bulgaria.

- **www.businessculture.com/bulgaria.html**. Tips on business culture.

- **www.search.bg**. The Bulgarian search engine and searchable directory of Bulgarian web space. It also contains links to business information, news and chat sites, but these links are to pages in Bulgarian.

- **http://britsinbulgaria.com**. Lists everything from builders to removal services, but is not yet well established.

- **www.onlinebg.com**. News, links, exchange rates in English.

Property Companies and Estate Agents

- www.bulgarianproperties.com/best-real-estate-buys.htm.
- www.bulgaria-property.org.
- **Bulgarian Dreams**, 120 Moorgate, London EC2M 6SS, **t** 0800 011 2750 or **t** (020) 7614 1240, **information@bulgariandreams.com**, **www.bulgarian dreams.com**. Unparalleled knowledge, specialises in Bulgaria.
- **Homes in Bulgaria**, **t** 0870 777 3370, **www.homesinbulgaria.co.uk**. Family-run business based in Bournemouth.

Removal Companies

- **Relocation Enterprises**, **t** +39 0682 4060, **www.relocationenterprises. com**. An upmarket company that relocates people around the world.

Holiday Companies

- www.balkanholidays.co.uk.
- www.beachbulgaria.com.
- www.bulgariaski.com.
- www.firstchoice.co.uk.
- www.thomson.co.uk.

Administrative Departments

In 1999 the country was divided into 28 regions: Blagoevgrad, Burgas, Dobrich, Gabrovo, Khaskovo, Kurdzhali, Kyustendil, Lovech, Montana, Pazardzhik, Pernik, Pleven, Plovdiv, Razgrad, Ruse, Shumen, Silistra, Sliven, Smolyan, Sofia City, Sofia Province, Stara Zagora, Turgovishte, Veliko Turnovo, Varna, Vidin, Vratsa, Yambol.

Time

Bulgaria is two hours ahead of GMT (three hours in summer).

Public Holidays

1 January	New Year's Day
3 March	National Day (Day of Liberation)
March or April	Easter
1 May	Labour Day
6 May	St George's Day (Day of Bulgarian Army)
24 May	St Cyril and Methodius Day (Day of Culture and Literacy)

Folklore and Traditions

According to ancient belief, March marks the start of spring. The first day of the month is a national holiday because this is also when the country was founded in 681. Red and white wool dolls known as Martenitsi are given on this day – Marta is a grumpy old woman who is always changing her moods. The colours are worn until a stork is seen as a symbol of the arrival of spring.

The rose has been crucial for the Bulgarian economy for more than three hundred years, although the first festival only took place in 1903. The Festival of Roses occurs in the Rose Valley near the town of Kazanluk at the foot of the Balkan Range on the first weekend of June every year.

6 September	Unification of Bulgaria
22 September	Independence Day
1 November	Day of the Spiritual Leaders of Bulgaria
24–26 December	Christmas

Further Reading

Live and Work in Russia and Eastern Europe, Jonathan Packer (Vacation Work Publications) – covers rights, expectations and responsibilities, and includes personal histories and contacts.

A Concise History of Bulgaria, R.J. Crampton – a very readable illustrated history

Nagel's Encyclopaedia-Guide Bulgaria – history of monuments and attractions.

The Bulgarians from Pagan Times to the Ottoman Conquest, David Marshall Lang – covers medieval Bulgaria with maps and illustrations.

Bulgarian Folk Customs, Mercia MacDermott (Jessica Kingsley).

The Corpse Dream of N. Petkov, Thomas McGonigle (Northwestern University Press) – a fictional account of the last opposition leader to the Communist takeover in Bulgaria.

Bulgaria...in Pictures (Visual Geography), Mary M. Rodgers.

Bulgaria (Enchantment of the World), Abraham Resnick – children's book.

Traditional Bulgarian Cooking, Atanas Slavov (Hippocrene) – 140 authentic recipes, from stews and soups to desserts and soft drinks.

Bulgarian Rhapsody: The Best of Balkan Cuisine, Linda J. Forristal and Angela Eisenbart (Sunrise Pine) – comprehensive and personal.

Climate Charts

Average Seasonal Temperatures

Varna	Jan	Feb	Mar	Apr	May	Jun	Jul	Aug	Sep	Oct	Nov	Dec
Min (°C)	−1	−1	2	7	12	16	19	18	14	11	6	1
Max (°C)	6	6	11	16	22	26	30	29	26	21	13	7

Plovdiv	Jan	Feb	Mar	Apr	May	Jun	Jul	Aug	Sep	Oct	Nov	Dec
Min (°C)	−3	−2	1	5	10	14	16	15	11	8	3	−2
Max (°C)	5	7	12	18	23	28	31	30	26	21	12	6

Sofia	Jan	Feb	Mar	Apr	May	Jun	Jul	Aug	Sep	Oct	Nov	Dec
Min (°C)	−4	−3	1	5	10	14	16	15	11	8	3	−2
Max (°C)	2	4	10	16	21	24	27	26	22	17	9	4

Average Rainfall (mm)

	Jan	Feb	Mar	Apr	May	Jun	Jul	Aug	Sep	Oct	Nov	Dec
Varna	28	30	26	37	26	64	45	37	27	58	35	63
Plovdiv	39	33	37	36	51	65	37	28	32	41	49	44
Sofia	36	28	41	61	87	73	68	64	41	65	48	49

[Source: BBC]

Climate Comparisons with London and Málaga, Spain

Varna

Varna enjoys a most curious climate. During the winter – from November to April – the climate is essentially much the same as that in London as far as maximum temperature is concerned, but during the summer months the climate is almost the same as in Málaga. This makes Varna an attractive summer resort, hence its popularity for many years with the Eastern European market. During the summer the minimum temperature is always quite a lot lower than the minimum in Málaga. During the winter months – and especially during the depths of winter – the minimum temperature is significantly lower than that in London.

Rainfall patterns in Varna are similar to London, and, although the summer temperatures are directly compatible with those in Málaga, there is hugely more rainfall than in the Spanish town.

There are many more daily hours of sunshine than in London for most of the year but nothing like the amount in southern Spain.

Sofia

The key point about the maximum temperature in Sofia and the skiing area around it it is how good it is during the summer months, with summer temperatures nearly as good as Málaga. Of course, this generates the potential for significant summer lettings, which will make the difference between an average-performing and a well-performing skiing investment.

If you avoid April, May and June the rainfall pattern is pretty much what you might expect in southern England. If you come from Scotland and Manchester it looks positively dry.

Croatia

Why Buy in Croatia?

Mention buying a property in Eastern Europe and many people in the UK will think of Croatia. The country was the European playground for years, which came to a halt with the Yugoslav war, but in the last few years it has gone through something of a renaissance. Since the war ended, Croatia has been seen as the chic new destination that outshines all its competitors.

Croatia has a long history of entertaining holidaymakers and has enjoyed the reputation of being a fashionable destination (*see* box, right). Edward VII and Wallis Simpson visited Croatia in the 1930s, and Agatha Christie stayed in the country for her honeymoon. In 2003 food writer Nigella Lawson and art patron Charles Saatchi honeymooned here. Until the break-up of Yugoslavia and the conflict between the Serbs and Croats, around half a million British visitors came here each year. More and more are returning; along with other holidaymakers who are first-time visitors. British tourists in particular have always had a particular connection with the place.

Croatia is a stunning country, with a special geography that gives it numerous wooded islands with old stone towns surrounded by turquoise sea. It is just across the water from Italy and easily accessible from the rest of Europe. Its romance comes from its secluded islands and bays, and a country that is relatively unpopulated, with just five million people. In the south of the country, the road doesn't so much hug the coastline in places as practically fall into it – Croatia tapers to almost nothing at the 'pearl of the Adriatic' that is Dubrovnik. The land in Croatia is generally unforgiving – mostly craggy and barren, allowing only dwarf vine trees. The life is in the sea, where in many places a mooring with a property comes as pretty much standard.

Croatia's seemingly unstoppable popularity with foreign tourists means that it has a good buy-to-let market, with an almost constantly increasing demand from holidaymakers. This is particularly true of Dubrovnik, where a three-bedroom flat near the old town could yield as much as £700 a week. In many

Celebrity Croatia

The French diver Jacques Cousteau was captivated by the clear waters off the Croatian coast, which he described as the cleanest in the world. In the 1970s, film star Elizabeth Taylor came to the country with Richard Burton and declared it one of her favourite spots in the world. Today, a number of millionaire yachtsmen call in at Dubrovnik, along with the likes of Bill Gates, Steven Spielberg and all manner of Hollywood heavyweights. Celebrities are attracted to the quiet bays and islands, free from the prying eyes of the paparazzi.

Although the rumours that Robert De Niro, Sharon Stone and Clint Eastwood have snapped up their very own Adriatic island for anything up to £20 million have turned out to be just that, other celebrities have been quick to buy property in Croatia. American actor John Malkovich, whose family emigrated to America from Croatia in the 19th century, paid £3 million for a run-down villa just outside Dubrovnik which was once used as a summer retreat for the Communist élite under Marshal Tito. The 20th-century stone house has 10 bedrooms, five outbuildings, a private beach and stunning gardens. Although Malkovich first spotted the villa from his yacht in the Adriatic, the purchase has not all been plain sailing. The property is technically in southern Croatia, but has remained part of Bosnia state since the Yugoslav conflict; the actor had to wait for agreement to purchase it from the Bosnian finance minister. Just as many of the gorgeous buildings in the old town were attacked by Serb troops, so also was this historic building, which is in desperate need of repair. The whole house was destroyed by militiamen and has been untouched since the end of the war.

There are few villas like Malkovich's left, and demand far outstrips supply. If you want to follow in his footsteps, you might consider buying an older stone-built estate or a small castle that needs repair. These can be had for as little as £50,000, although the cost of restoration needs to be taken into account.

ways the country has recovered quickly from the scars of the war. Wander around the streets of Dubrovnik today and it is practically impossible to imagine that only 10 years ago the Yugoslav army was senselessly shelling it night and day. The community responded so promptly to the destruction that reconstruction was completed almost immediately.

Wherever you settle, you are more than likely to find some English-speaking people. In Dubrovnik there is a small community of English people, including a family who settled there 20 years ago. In many other coastal places, you are bound to find an English person or two. Croats are generally friendly and decent people and it is unlikely that you will be made to feel unwelcome or taken advantage of in any way.

Tourism

Don't Believe the Hype

In 2004 the *Sunday Times* proclaimed that Croatia has 'better sailing than Turkey, islands to rival those of Greece, and a cuisine to match Italy's: it's the hot spot that came in from the cold'. Yes, the sailing is some of the best in the world – but Greece's inhabitable islands are much more numerous and varied, and Croatian food is generally not very good, with limited menus.

Another paper announced, 'Just as pioneers flocked to the Côte d'Azur in the 1950s, Greece in the 1960s and Tuscany in the 1990s, those on the pulse are now buying into the Istrian coast...' while *The Times* in 2002 told us: 'A wonderful coastline, crystal clear water and a house by the sea: what more could you want?'

We are being told that Croatia is not only the new Tuscany, and Greece before package tourists, but also Spain before the high-rise buildings. But it is worth keeping the media hype in check. If the broadsheets had their way, we would believe that every celebrity worth their salt is either sunning themselves on a yacht off the coast or scoffing oysters in Dubrovnik, and that anyone with a bit of cash to invest is slamming it into property in the area. Take extravagant claims with a pinch of salt.

National Parks

All except one of Croatia's national parks are located by the coast. The Krka River, just outside Šibenik, runs through a canyon and forms lakes, waterfalls and rapids before reaching the sea. The mountainous Risnjak National Park is home to lynx and other wildlife. Paklenica National Park near Zadar has dense forests where reptiles, birds and important flora are found, as well as two spectacularly deep gorges. Plitvice Lakes National Park is the most popular with visitors, and deservedly so. Situated around 200km from the coast, between Zabreb and Šibenik, it has a series of 16 lakes which form breathtaking

> ## A Thousand and One Dalmatians
> There are actually 1,185 Dalmatian islands, but only 50 are inhabited. Low in the clear turquoise waters of the Adriatic, they lie like sleeping giants, forming a beautiful string along the whole coast. Their architecture is a wonderful mix of Baroque, Habsburg, Venetian, Roman and medieval influences, with elegant stone houses along narrow streets running down to the sea.

waterfalls against a backdrop of deep green vegetation. Bears, wolves and deer roam the forest and herons frequent the shore.

Island parks include the Brijuni Islands on the Istrian coast, which is made up of two big islands and 12 much smaller ones, with wonderfully preserved Mediterranean holm oak forests. Kornati Islands National Park includes 140 mostly uninhabited islands, islets and reefs. Mljet, southwest of Dubrovnik, is something of a paradise, with two lakes, and forests which have long been popular with visitors.

All Hands on Deck

As Croatia's coast is one of the most indented on the Mediterranean, providing for seemingly endless bays and numerous ports and marinas, it offers wonderful opportunities for sailors. Its 50 or so marinas, two thousand berths and many beautiful wooded islands give safe haven to visitors, who take to the waters here from all over the world. Vessels range from sleek luxury yachts with their own crew to small basic boats and can be either power-driven or sailing boats.

The ideal months for sailing are May or June, which tend to have good winds and fair weather, followed by July and August, which are more crowded. At other times there can be strong winds and rougher seas. Although the waters around Croatia can be difficult to navigate, holiday companies can advise on the best routes and safest anchorages. Additional watery activities include diving, fishing, windsurfing and waterskiing.

The following UK companies offer mostly inclusive sailing holidays in Croatia:

- **Sailing Holidays, t** (020) 8459 8787, **www.sailingholidays.com**. Mostly inclusive sailing trips.
- **Sunsail Holidays, t** 02392 222 222, **www.sunsail.com**.
- **Blue Yacht Charter, t** (020) 8742 0029, **www.blue-yachts.com**.

Naturism

Croatians claim to have introduced naturism to the world, although they say that British royalty helped kick-start the whole phenomenon. Way back in 1934 the first resort opened on Rab Island and was visited by the Duke and Duchess of Windsor where, according to some reports, they both took a naked swim. The concept really took off in the 1960s when as many as 100,000 holidaymakers enjoyed this kind of holiday every year. There are now around 30 official nudist beaches in the country, and many more where the practice of taking all your clothes off is generally accepted. The largest nudist resort in Europe is Koversada, which has just celebrated its 40th anniversary. One of the most famous nudist beaches in the country is called the Golden Horn. Istria is the focus for naturist holidays, where hotels cater for visitors who want to spend their whole holiday naked and hand over their clothes at check-in. Lopud and Koločep, two islands near Dubrovnik, are other key areas. Two UK companies offering naturist holidays in Croatia are:

- **Peng Travel, t** 0845 345 8345, **www.pengtravel.co.uk.**
- **Dune Leisure, t** (0115) 931 4110, **www.duneleisure.co.uk.**

Take a Hike

Walking has a long tradition in Croatia, dating from the late 19th century when it was deemed a patriotic duty. In spring and early summer, attractive wooded areas offer scenic retreats from the summer heat and the national parks provide environments for walking along with the chance to see local flora and fauna. Croatia was one of the first seven countries in the world to establish a national climbing organisation, and its mountains offer some serious challenges to climbers.

Arrested Development

The countries that have enjoyed enduring popularity with British and other European tourists, such as Italy, France and Spain, have in many ways become a victim of their own success, with an almost unbroken ribbon of development forming along the Western Mediterranean. Croatia is lucky in that it can learn from these other countries' mistakes. On a recent visit to England the Croatian tourism minister pledged to do all she could to protect her country's spectacularly unspoilt stretch of coastline. Croatia is blessed with a government that seems absolutely committed to the preservation of its heritage, its crystal-clear water and its ecological balance. That commitment, coupled with Croatia's natural beauty and its historic heritage, make it a very attractive investment location and an equally attractive holiday or retirement location.

The Economy

Before Yugoslavia was dissolved in 1991, Croatia was relatively prosperous. Although it was part of a Communist system from the 1940s to 1990, there was an element of healthy free enterprise. The country had a healthy agricultural output, with as much as two-thirds of its land being cultivated. Iron and steel production and shipbuilding were also important industries, and there were tourist resorts along the Dalmatian coast. With the outbreak of war in 1991 came a dramatic drop in the country's fortune; the GDP plummeted while inflation rocketed along with unemployment, which reached 17 per cent from 1993 to 1998. Since then Croatia has steadily been picking itself up again; it has been admitted into the World Bank, and EU membership seems set for 2007/8. Tourists from around the world are once again flocking back to its beautiful Dalmatian coast.

The Exchange Rate

In Croatia the currency has for some time been stable when measured against the euro. Its slightly more variable performance against the dollar and sterling simply reflects dollar–euro or sterling–euro exchange rates moving over time.

Exchange Rate – Croatian Kuna

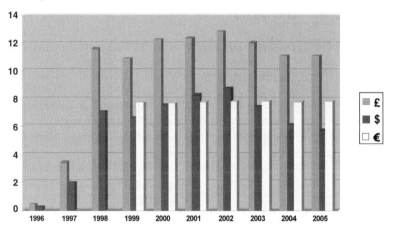

Visas and Permits

Not yet a member of the EU, Croatia nevertheless harmonizes entry regulations with the continent, so holders of full, valid UK, EU, US, Canadian, Australian and New Zealand passports can enter for a period of up to **90 days** without a visa. They can only do this once in any six-month period. If you wish to visit for longer than 90 days you can obtain a visa from the Croatian consulate in the country where you live. The formalities are minimal. This visa will allow you to remain in Croatia for up to 180 days in any year.

If you wish to live permanently in Croatia, without working, you will need to obtain a **residence permit**. The paperwork can be a little tiresome but the permit is not difficult to obtain. You will need to show that you either own property or have suitable accommodation.

Work Permits and Citizenship

If you wish to work in Croatia you will have to obtain a **work permit**. This is a lot more difficult, as you have to be able to demonstrate that you are needed because no local person is capable of meeting the needs of the employer.

To be classed as a **tax resident** is a different matter, which requires the individual to be resident for a period of 183 days, allowing for short breaks, or to have accommodation at their exclusive disposal for 183 days. The **Croatian Embassy** in London, *see* p.195, can provide up-to-date information on formalities and conditions for working visas and residency.

Foreign nationals can acquire **Croatian citizenship** provided that they have had a registered place of residence for at least five years constantly in Croatia and are proficient in the Croatian language.

Profile of Croatia

Recent History and Politics

In less than 80 years, Yugoslavia was created and then dissolved. It was only formed after the First World War when the Croats, Serbs and Slovenes got together to create a new kingdom. After the Second World War, under Marshal Tito, Yugoslavia was transformed into an independent Communist state. When Croatia asserted independence from Yugoslavia in 1991, the once kingdom was fragmented and after four years of war the Serbs were expelled from Croatia.

In 1991 Croatia became an independent parliamentary democracy, and Franjo Tudman its first president. Tudman was criticised for his extreme nationalism and died in 1999. In 2000, Stjepan Mesiać won the presidential elections. He is widely popular and keen to bring modernity to his country.

In 2004 the EU pledged €76 million to help Croatia meet the requirements for future membership. The main focus is to improve democracy, strengthen economic and social development and modernise the political system. As a whole, the local people seem ready to embrace their new future. In 2004, an open-air concert in the capital of Zagreb celebrating their country's impending EU membership was well attended by enthusiastic natives. Most of them are excited about the prospect of Croatia becoming more modern and western.

Why the Croats Have Us by Our Throats

The inventors of the cravat, or necktie, were the Croats and not the French. The word cravat is closely related to the word Croat. Croats wore neckties as far back as the mid-1600s and when soldiers began fighting in different parts of Europe the craze caught on. One story has it that Napoleon admired the scarves tied around the necks of the Croatians fighting with the French in Russia, although the craze caught on way before then, during the reign of Louis XIV.

Timeline

1918   Following the dissolution of the Austro-Hungarian Monarchy after the First World War, Croatia becomes part of the Kingdom of Serbs, Croats and Slovenes, which later becomes Yugoslavia.

1941   German and Italian forces occupy Yugoslavia.

1945   The Republic of Yugoslavia is proclaimed.

1990   The first democratic multi-party elections since the Second World War are held in Croatia.

1991   Croatia and Slovenia proclaim independence, which sparks fighting between Croats and ethnic Serbs.

1991   War breaks out between the Bosnian government and local Serbs, who start the 1992–95 siege of capital Sarajevo.

1992   The Republic of Croatia becomes part of the United Nations. UN forces enter Croatia and fighting subsides.

2000   Slobodan Milosevic concedes defeat in the election. Vojislav Koštunica is sworn in as new Yugoslav president.

2002   Milosevic trial opened as prosecution presents its case against the former Yugoslav leader. UN chief prosecutor accuses Milosevic of being 'responsible for the worst crimes known to humankind'.

Religion

The Croats are overwhelmingly Roman Catholic, while virtually all Serbs are Eastern Orthodox. Roman Catholics were suppressed under Communism in Yugoslavia. Just over 1 per cent of the population are Muslim, with Protestants making up only 0.4 per cent. The capital has a small number of Jews.

Climate and Geography

Croatia is a strangely shaped country. If Italy is a boot, then Croatia is a crescent-shaped offcut of leather, and the many islands the shavings. Istria in the north is practically on the doorstep of Austria and Germany. Just to the south, the gaunt crags of the Velebit Mountains rise sharply 2,000 metres from the sea, making development virtually impossible. But in the south, the Dalmatian coastline and islands offer magnificent scenery, mild winters and some of the clearest waters in the whole Mediterranean. The islands all benefit from dense woodland, charming old stone towns and from being car-free.

Croatia is made up of 30 per cent forest and 40 per cent mountains. Most of the mountainous area is uninhabitable, with dense beech and fir forests where bears, wolves and lynx roam, and otters and trout live in the rivers. The part of the country that is best known and most visited by tourists is the Dalmatian coast and its offshore islands in the Adriatic Sea. This area has a Mediterranean climate with mild winters and warm summers. The coast is backed by the high mountains of the Dinaric Alps.

Summers on this coast are not entirely rainless, and the fine weather is often interrupted by thunderstorms. Sunshine averages some 4hrs a day in winter and 10–12hrs a day in summer. Winters can be cold with a strong wind known as the *bora*, particularly fierce in the north of the Adriatic. In the summer there are occasional thunderstorms on the coast. Inland, winters are cold as much of inland Croatia is mountainous and snow can remain here for long periods.

See also 'Climate Charts', p.198

Regional Profile

Istria

This neat triangle of land is the most developed area for tourists, partly because it is so near to Western Europe, which means property here is relatively expensive. Often called Little Italy, Istria has a landscape very similar to Tuscany, with low rolling hills, lovely towns, olive trees and pretty vineyards. The weather is warm in summer, with cool winters.

Istria takes its name from its first inhabitants, known as the Histri, and there are many remnants of the cultures of the people who have lived here from Roman times. For 400 years it was under Venetian rule, and some towns still have street signs in both Italian and Croatian. It then became part of the Austro-Hungarian Empire before joining the Yugoslav Federation.

The most popular place for tourists is **Poreč**, which has a good infrastructure and a large number of hotels. Poreč was an important Roman colony and still boasts Roman architecture along with some medieval buildings. **Rovinj** has an old town on a peninsula, which was once an island but was linked to the mainland in the 18th century.

The **Brijuni Archipelago** is made up of two large and 12 smaller islands off the west coast of Istria. Together they form an important national park, which contains numerous rare plants and animals. **Pula** lies at the very southern point of Istria. An ancient city, it has a wonderfully preserved 2,000-year-old

Truffle Treasure

Istria lays claim to two prime truffle areas in the woods of Motovun and Buzet. Only a tiny amount of this highly prized fungus needs to be used to impart a sophisticated nutty flavour to dishes. The white truffle is much more highly esteemed than the black variety and commands 10 times the price.

The season starts in September, when specially trained dogs are taken out to sniff out the treasure, and the bounty is of such quality that it is even exported to Italy. Truffle days in the area take place in September and can take on the atmosphere of a festival.

amphitheatre, as well as a number of other historic buildings. As the largest Istria and major port, it has good transport connections and is a thriving business centre.

The Kvarner Gulf

Kvarner is the region adjacent to Istria, with a number of well-known tourist spots that are visited in winter and summer and particularly during the carnival season between January and March. One of them is **Opatija** – once the winter resort for aristocracy from middle Europe and still much-loved. It retains its chic atmosphere, with good restaurants, neat parks and 100-year-old hotels.

The main town is **Rijeka**, which has an airport and reasonable access from Zagreb which is three hours away by road or rail. Its coastal resorts include **Crikvenica**, which is popular with Croats, as well as **Kraljevica** and **Novi Vinodolski**. Property bargains are few and far between, as this area is near to the Croatian interior and therefore sought after by locals.

Dalmatia

The long, skinny tongue of land that forms the the coast of Dalmatia stretches from Zadar in the north to Dubrovnik in the south, 300 miles away.

Nothern Dalmatia has some pretty historic towns, such as Zadar and Trogir, with some small coastal resorts between them, but this is not really a region that keeps visitors for long. **Zadar** is a transport hub and its old town would quite literally be dwarfed by the enormous ferries that call in, if it were not for being built high on its medieval walls. **Trogir**, around 20km west of Split, is a beautiful medieval town on an island of church towers, palaces and a cathedral on rambling cobbled streets around a central square. The modern town has overflowed on to the mainland, which is connected to Trogir by a bridge.

The southern Dalmatian coast and islands are the country's greatest attraction, its clear turquoise waters delighting sailors and swimmers alike. But don't expect beaches – often the term is used loosely to describe any rock or concrete area beside the sea. The **Makarska Riviera** and ancient **Dubrovnik** are among the most popular places, although both these locations are comparatively expensive for property.

The main town is **Split**, which has good transport links by ferry to the Italian port of Ancona and overland to Zagreb by bus or train. It is, as its name suggests, divided, between a hideous concrete jungle and monstrous port, and the cobbled streets and a World Heritage Site of an enormous Roman palace. Most tourists come for just a day, or maybe two. The old town includes the remains of the palace and a cathedral which has sweeping views from its campanile. Street markets, prettily painted buildings and café-filled squares surround the palace, while the waterfront walkway always seems lively and is in many ways the centre of the city.

Hvar is the prettiest island near here, with its purple sheets of lavender fields and gorgeous medieval architecture, but it suffers from sometimes overwhelming numbers of tourists as a result. The country's oldest theatre is here, opened in 1612, and a Franciscan monastery. What it doesn't have is beaches – just concrete platforms which soon become crammed with sun-bathing visitors. Water taxis can take you to wooded islets which are much more peaceful; if you don't want to bare all, avoid Jerolim, the nearest one, which is reserved for naturists.

Brač is one of the country's largest islands and has the archipelago's highest point – Vidova Gora. Pebbled Golden Horn beach always seems to be crowded. **Bol** was once an unassuming fishing village but now has a few large hotels on its outskirts. Further away is the medieval jewel of **Korčula** and **Mljet**, a wooded nature reserve, with walking trails and lakes for boating.

The Makarska Riviera

A string of resorts backed by the **Biokovo Mountains** makes up the Makarska Riviera. What was once a group of low-key seaside villages has sadly become rather overdeveloped, with modern buildings and hotels. **Makarska** sits in the centre of the region and for this reason and its pleasant waterfront makes a good base. Other significant but quieter resorts include **Baška Voda** and **Brela**; all have pebble beaches. It is possible to take the ferry from here to the offshore islands nearby.

Dubrovnik

Dubrovnik simply bewitches. When you step into the old town over a drawbridge where a minstrel is playing a mandolin it feels as though you are walking on to a film set. Its marble streets lined with ancient buildings are just part of its magic, which also comes from its extraordinary combination of being a walled city next to the sea. The old town is incredibly compact, but the city itself, which actually only has 30,000 inhabitants, spreads out over a wide area. Dubrovnik has yachts from around the world, and is a major spot for enormous cruise ships, which appear like high-rise buildings on their sides, some carrying 5,000 people. As many as six ships can arrive at once, swamping the tiny old city with tourists.

The old city has a concentrated wealth of historic buildings, including the splendid cathedral, a Dominican monastery with charming cloisters, a Franciscan monastery with a working 14th-century pharmacy, and a Jesuit church with an over-the-top pink marble Baroque interior. The Placa, or Stradun, is the place to have a leisurely coffee and watch the world go by and marvel at the fact that in the shelling between 1991 and 1992 some 70 per cent of the buildings suffered a direct hit. On the Placa, the Venetian Sponza Palace is home to a display of photographs of those who died during the war.

Lapad is a large suburb of the city, with a couple of beaches where most of the larger hotels are situated. Atlhough there are a couple of town beaches, the best bet is to go to one of the lovely and easily accessible islands. Tiny, tree-covered **Lokrum** is only 15 minutes away by boat, with a disused monastery and rocky beaches, one of which is a well-known tourist spot. The **Elafiti Islands** (often just called the 'Elephant Islands') are a bit further, but worth the journey as they boast sand beaches and have a real out of the way feel. All are covered in trees with attractive stone buildings lining the harbour where the boats come in.

On the Peljesac peninsula, **Orebić** is just north of Dubrovnik. It is relatively unknown and a good place to look at because prices are not as steep as in the old city Although it suffers from being rather isolated, this will change if plans to build a new bridge connecting it to the mainland go ahead. Dubrovnik's residents already know it for its great seafood and pleasant beach.

Cavtat is around half an hour or so by boat or bus south of Dubrovnik. Although a resort in its own right, when accommodation gets booked out in Dubrovnik, some visitors stay here. It has a lively waterfront but is generally very relaxed, despite the fact that it is close to the airport.

Zagreb and the Interior

The inland area around Zagreb and the coast might as well be two different countries. The coast was once Italian, and an Italian attitude to life prevails here, along with the profusion of fish, the more relaxed, slower pace of living and the sea and sunshine. In complete contrast, the region around Zagreb was occupied by Austria, and its people are altogether more reserved and serious. They eat more meat and their relaxation is taken in the coffee shops, not on the beach.

Selecting a Property

Getting There

The best website for checking out the most current travel information, all explained extremely clearly, with up-to-date timestables and contact details, is **www.visit-croatia.co.uk/gettingthere/index.htm**.

At the time of writing there were no budget flights to Croatia, although this looks set to change in the near future. The following airlines fly to Croatia, some routes May to September only:

• **Croatia Airlines, t** (020) 8563 0022, **www.croatiaairlines.hr**. Flights to Zagreb, Split and Dubrovnik from Heathrow, Gatwick and Manchester.

• **British Airways, t** (0870) 850 9850, **www.ba.com**. Flights from Gatwick to Dubrovnik.

• **Ryanair,** UK **t** 0871 246 0000 (10p/min), **www.ryanair.com**. Flights from Stansted to Trieste in Italy (near Istria), but transport connections into Croatia are not good. It can also be difficult to hire a car in Italy to take to Croatia; a tip is to contact the car hire office in Trieste, rather than approaching the company in the UK. Ryanair also flies to Ancona and Pescara on the east coast of Italy, from where you can get an overnight ferry to Split. Cabins are available, but book as far ahead as possible.

Getting Around

By Air

There are flights between Zagreb and Dubrovnik, Split, Pula and Rijeka. In the summer, there is also a service to the island of Brač.

By Rail

Several trains a day, run by national operator Croatian Railways (*Hrvatske Željeznice*), link the major towns. An upgrade of the track between Zagreb and Split allows for new tilting trains, which have reduced the journey time to under five hours. Croatian railways runs trains which are divided into *putnicki* (slow, with lots of stops) and *IC* (faster intercity trains). The overnight service between Zagreb and Split has beds and sleeping cars, but tickets must be booked well in advance.

By Bus

The bus service is good, and even small villages have some sort of bus connection. Express buses cover longer distances and are very comfortable, with toilets and regular stops. The cost of bus travel is a fraction of that in the UK. The network is operated by a number of different companies, so it is best to check with them all when enquiring about times at a bus station. In big city bus stations, tickets must be bought from booths before boarding; in smaller places they can be bought from the driver. A small additional charge is made to store luggage underneath. Try to buy tickets in advance in summer if you can, particularly if you are travelling along the coast.

By Road

There is a good network of roads, but they are not always of good quality off the main routes. There are sections of motorway from Zagreb to Rijeka and Zagreb to Split where reasonable tolls are charged. The main road down the Adriatic coast is frequently choked with traffic in summer.

Some 150km of new motorway have just been opened in Croatia and the new Zagreb to Split motorway is due to be completed 2005, while a motorway to

Dubrovnik is expected to be finished by 2008. There are plans to build a motorway all the way to Greece through Montenegro and Albania by 2015.

See 'Settling In', p.193, for more on driving in Croatia.

By Sea

Jadrolinija (**www.jadrolinija.hr**) operates ferry services down the coast on the Rijeka–Zadar–Split–Korčula–Dubrovnik route at least once a day in both directions between June and August, and two or three times weekly for the rest of the year. It takes 24hrs from Rijeka to Dubrovnik (try to book a cabin or reclining seat in advance). The most scenic section is between Dubrovnik and Split and this journey is always completed in daylight. There are also ferries between Split and the islands of Brač, Hvar, Viš and Korčula, and connections between Split and Zadar to Ancona in Italy, from Pula to Trieste, Italy, and Dubrovnik to Bari, Italy and to Greece.

Choosing a Location

Istria

The coast of Istria has a number of very attractive but somewhat over-developed towns burdened with the aftermath of low-grade development dating back a number of years. Look in Poreč, Rovinj and Novigrad. There are also beautiful areas inland.

The Dalmatian Coast

The northern part of the Dalmatian coast – essentially from the border of Istria down to Trogir, near Split – has received comparatively little attention, though there has been some activity around Zadar and Šibenik. This relative lack of interest is probably a reflection of the fact that the coast is a little less attractive than the coast further south and the climate is not quite as good.

There has been masses of activity in the southern part of the Dalmatian coast. Starting with the lovely and ancient town of Trogir, a few miles west of Split, there is a whole series of small towns and villages that have enjoyed the interest of the property investor. However, the numbers in absolute terms are relatively small.

Dalmatian Islands

Much of the activity in Croatia is on the islands. Croatia has an enormous coastline and a thousand islands – not all of which are habitable. On the main islands there are some substantial developments going on. At least, they are substantial in Croatian terms. They are tiny by comparison with the developments in, for example, Spain.

Island Life

Croatia's islands are arguably its most appealing feature, and properties on its inhabited islands are very much in demand. But locals say the price can double if sellers find out the potential buyer is a westerner. And estate agents report that demand has become so great, it is now outstripping supply, particularly for old stone houses or villas in coastal regions. The largest of the islands are Brač, Hvar and Korčula, which appeal to many potential purchasers, but to get to them you need to travel to Split, then to the ferry port, and then take a ferry. Also, on the islands, public transport is limited, so you will be restricted unless you have a car.

It is worth bearing in mind that the public has access by law to the land up to six metres above the waterline; this has caused some Hollywood stars to withdraw from purchases for fear of lack of privacy. But those who have the cash may look to buy an entire island; the price for one of eight acres with sandy beaches is a cool £1.3 million.

Dubrovnik

Dubrovnik is without doubt the jewel of the Croatian coast. It is divided into the old walled city and newer, but still small, residential areas to the north of the old city. The old city of Dubrovnik is a UNESCO World Heritage Site. Everybody who sees it falls in love with it and would like to buy property there. Given that it is only about 300m across, that means a massive excess of demand over potential supply, which can only lead to rising prices.

Property in the walled city is tiny and generally has no views except across a 6ft-wide alleyway into a neighbouring property. The area is pedestrianised, and getting to many of the houses involves quite a steep climb. For these reasons, some people prefer the newer part of Dubrovnik. There are attractive high-class residential developments about three miles from the old city on the Lapad peninsula. Because the whole of Dubrovnik is geographically constrained by the sea and the mountains and because it is such a popular location for Croatians and tourists alike, even property in the new part of Dubrovnik is in short supply and expensive.

Expensive, however, is a relative concept. Comparable property in, for example, Nice or Marbella would cost several times more. In the future it is likely that people will look back with nostalgia at the prices being charged in Dubrovnik today. This is a world-class destination with a huge long-term potential.

Zagreb and the Interior

As this is the capital, property can get very expensive, although it is still much cheaper than in the rest of Europe. Many smaller towns in northern Croatia have much more reasonably priced property and are close to neighbouring Austria and Hungary.

Property Types and Prices

Most houses are built of old stone, while there are some concrete and high-rise apartment buildings predominate in some city outskirts. Traditional rural housing includes one- or two-storey wooden houses, small cabins and white-washed stone houses. Since the Second World War most rural houses have been built with concrete. Although older property for restoration exists (*see* p.183), it is in short supply anywhere near the coast, and any old property offered for sale is likely already to have been bought by a speculator and sold on at a profit. Many of the old houses in Dubrovnik are in need of renovation, but the new build market is booming. Fortunately there are good restrictions on development and buildings cannot be more than three storeys high or built within 100 metres of the sea.

Prices are not low by Eastern European standards. Prices of property in more popular areas of Croatia have risen by 35 per cent annually in the last 5 years, according to some local agents. A 100-square-metre two-bedroom apartment in Dubrovnik, for example, will cost you about £200,000. The same apartment in one of the small island towns would be about half that amount unless it is literally on the water's edge, when it might cost about £150,000. If Croatia can maintain its focus on quality and policy of limited development, those prices will seem absurdly low in a few years' time.

Buying a plot of land and then building a house usually works out much cheaper than purchasing a property, *see* p.183. The price of a flat in a coastal area can be anything from £800 to £1,400 per square metre. But on some more remote islands you can buy land to build on for as little as £70 per square metre. For example, a plot on the island of Korčula can be bought for €20,000, and a three-bedroom villa with a pool and garden can be built for around €12,000.

Guide Prices

€20,000

- House in need of renovation a short distance inland from Poreč, Istria.
- Old stone cottage with mountain views inland from Poreč, Istria.
- Four-bedroom house in the town of Dugo Selo, 30 miles from the capital, Zagreb.

€50,000

- Two-bedroom stone house 50 metres from the sea in the centre of the old town in Viš, with terrace and boat mooring.
- Two-bedroom apartment in a new block in the coastal town of Bol, on the island of Brač.
- New one-bedroom flat on the coast at Poreč, Istria.

€75,000

- Off-plan studio in a luxury development, overlooking Dubrovnik's yacht harbour.
- Detached stone three-bedroom house, a short distance inland from Poreč, Istria.
- Two-bedroom flat in a new block in the coastal town of Bol, on Brač.

€120,000

- Two-bedroom flat in Dubrovnik, close to the old town with terrace.
- Stone house on the edge of Poreč, Istria, with two studio rooms.
- Three-bedroom flat over three floors.
- New detached three-bedroom cottage on the coast at Poreč.

€150,000

- Four-bedroom house overlooking the sea in Perna, overlooking Korčula island.
- Small stone three-storey house in Vršar, Istria, with harbour and island views.

€300,000

- Two-bedroom flat in good condition with view of old city of Dubrovnik and a shared terrace.
- Restored, 15th-century townhouse in the Istrian hill town of Groznjan, favoured by artists.

€500,000

- Castle for renovation on the outskirts of Dubrovnik, in 16,000 square metres of grounds.
- Four-bedroom flat in Dubrovnik in the old city with business opportunity.
- 500-year-old renovated tower with an old olive mill in need of renovation 70 miles from Dubrovnik with sea views.

What is Available and at What Price?

There is always a huge range of prices in any property market and on the whole you get what you pay for. The more expensive properties are usually more expensive because they have some special quality about them; cheap properties are usually cheap because they have a very poor location, are built to a very low standard, or are in a bad state of repair – or all three!

Prices have been rising rapidly. Some people have seen growth of over 40 per cent in the last year. The table opposite attempts to show some general indication of prices as at January 2005.

Prices in Croatia, January 2005

Place and Type of Property	Low	Mid	High
Istria – Rovinj – four-bedroom house in good order	£200,000	£250,000	£350,000
Istria – Rovinj Old Town – two-bedroom apartment	£150,000	£200,000	
Korčula – apartment in renovated complex with sea views	£90,000	£100,000	£120,000
Brač Island – three-bedroom villa with sea views		£200,000	
Hvar Island – four-bedroom villa with sea views	£250,000	£300,000	£350,000
Dubrovnik – Old Town – two-bedroom apartment of 80 sq m in good condition		£190,000	
Dubrovnik – new two-bedroom, two-bathroom apartment of 100 sq m, near to beach, with sea views			£200,000

Building from Scratch or Renovation

After the war and Yugoslavia's break-up, Croatia's population was around 22 per cent Serbian. When the Serbs fled, Croats occupied their houses and today the Adriatic coastal drive between Makarska and Split is scarred with burnt-out dwellings. But the romance of buying a tumbledown stone house on a pretty Adriatic island quickly dies once the reality of organising the renovation kicks in. Overseeing building projects from afar in a country where you may not be able to communicate in the local language can be a headache. Property companies do offer to provide renovation, building and furnishing options, but of course it will be expensive. Building costs are low, however; a full restoration project is likely to cost about £200 per square metre. If simple repair is necessary you might end up paying about £2 per hour for a skilled labourer, though more if you employ a contractor. Despite this, as is the case with many Eastern European countries, it is very easy to find that once you have finished your project the cost of buying the property and the work you have undertaken is more than the value of the property as it stands.

There is a current trend to build new apartment blocks of individual apartments. Land can also be purchased for those wanting to build their own property, which is advertised by estate agents and particularly in small advert magazines, such as *Mali Oglasnik*. Unless explicitly stated, most of this land will not have a building permit. Because Croatia is very keen to protect its natural and architectural heritage there are very strict regulations concerning building on new land. The further the land is from an urban area, the harder it will be to get a building permit, and for some land it may never be possible. This makes it advisable to buy land which already has a building permit (although it may be permission to build a house that is not to your liking).

Getting planning permission is usually a long process and can take as long as two years. Furthermore, making an application for planning permission is very expensive, and you will also have to pay the costs of getting services like electricity, water and telephone to the property.

Temporary Accommodation

Tourist offices in the region are a good initial source of information for temporary accommodation. If you only need somewhere for a few days, a basic hotel may suffice, but bear in mind that standards may not be the same as at home. Places can get booked up quickly in the summer months on the Dalmatian coast, although you shouldn't need to plan ahead if visiting a city.

The Process of Buying a Property

It is a risky business to buy property in Croatia. Much of it has either bad title or defective planning consent. Legal advice is essential unless you can afford to write off the amount that you are investing.

Freedom to Buy

As a British person you can buy land, buildings or apartments in Croatia, but people of other nationalities can only buy land in Croatia if their country allows Croatians the right to buy land in their country. As a foreigner, you can never buy agricultural land or forestry land, and buying cultural monuments or certain other categories of land requires special procedures.

In Croatia, in order to buy a property you need to seek the authority of the government. This formality is, in essence, a simple confirmation of the fact that Croatian people enjoy the right to buy in the UK, but it can take up to a year to obtain it. This gives rise to problems when, hardly surprisingly, the seller does not want to wait for you to get permission to buy. In this case various safeguards have to be put in place by your lawyers to cover the unlikely eventuality that you do not get permission and to cover the greater risk that, for example, a debt could be attached to the property before you are able to transfer the title into your name.

An alternative to buying in your own name is to buy through the medium of a Croatian limited company. This company could be 100 per cent foreign-owned. In the Croatian context, sometimes the purchase by a company can reduce your overall tax burden – especially if you are buying the property as an investment and for letting – and it will eliminate the need to obtain the official permission to buy the property. Buying through a company involves extra expenditure, however, including the cost of setting up the company (perhaps £1,000 or more) and the annual cost of filing the paperwork and keeping everything in order. *See* pp.69–70 for details of the general advantages and disadvantages.

In Croatia there is a regrettable tendency for agents to encourage you to set up companies in circumstances where they just make no sense but bring a fee to the agent. Before you think about setting up a company, take detailed legal and financial advice. Because of the speed with which you have to move when you see property in Croatia, take that advice before you go looking.

Initial Steps

First Contract

Once you have found a property you want to purchase, you will be expected to sign some form of contract, generally either a reservation contract or a preliminary purchase contract. *See* p.75 for an explanation of these concepts. Note that the name 'preliminary purchase contract' is misleading: it is actually a full binding purchase contract. We therefore recommend that, wherever possible, you insist on signing a **reservation contract** rather than a preliminary purchase contract at this stage.

Searches and Enquiries

Once you have signed a reservation contract, your lawyer should make various enquiries, such as checking that the contract is fair, that the seller has good title and the right to sell to you, that the area is zoned for residential building and that any building work being undertaken enjoys all of the necessary planning and building consents. For apartments, make sure that the building has been officially divided into individual titles for the individual apartment units.

If you are buying an older property, especially one that needs work, consider having a survey carried out. However, in Croatia there is no profession of building surveyor and surveys are comparatively rare. It is possible to arrange surveys either through a local master builder, through land surveyors who have developed an interest in the surveying of the buildings, or through a few specialist UK qualified surveyors who have seen a market opportunity for providing such surveys in Croatia. The UK surveyors are much more expensive.

Depending on the circumstances of your case there could well be other enquiries that also need to be made. In Croatia it is common for work to be started illegally, before all these steps are in place. It is also common for property to have a title that is defective. Sometimes these problems should put you off having any involvement in the purchase. On other occasions the risks are minimal and, provided you go into the transaction with your eyes open, might not put you off buying if you really like the property.

Structural Guarantees on New Property

New property benefits from a 5-year guarantee.

Declared Values

It is common for the value to be declared in the title to be less than the true value. This is technically illegal but is an almost universal practice. By doing this the declared value is the value used by the tax office to determine the taxes payable for the purchase. You should avoid going along with this if possible. The tax payable by you on the purchase (the equivalent of stamp duty) is very low at 5 per cent of the value declared. The main benefit of under-declaration accrues to the seller, who avoids paying capital gains tax. You will be removing a burden from the seller and landing yourself with a potential problem later on if you make a significant under-declaration and then, when you sell, your buyer refuses to do the same for you or regulations are tightened.

Bank Guarantees

It is worth getting a bank guarantee that will repay you any money you have invested if a builder is unable to complete your project.

Possible Dangers

The main problems in Croatia are defective title and defective planning consents. However, there is a new category of problems that is only just beginning to emerge: recent changes to the planning legislation have meant that some plots of land, previously located in places where building could be contemplated, are now not going to permit development. Be very cautious if someone shows you any planning documentation for a plot where building has not started. In addition, there are some properties in Croatia owned by Serbians who fled the country during the war; it is impossible either to contact these people or to secure their agreement to the sale of the property.

Signing the Contract and Registering the Title

Once your lawyer has checked out the property and found that everything is in order, you are ready to sign the **preliminary purchase contract**. This commits you and the seller to signing the full contract transferring ownership on an agreed date shortly afterwards, or, if the property is still under construction, once the property has been fully built.

The preliminary purchase contract contains most of the clauses you would expect to see in a UK contract. These will include a description of the property, a statement of the legal title to the property, the price to be paid, how it is to be paid, the deadline for payment and any other deadlines applicable, what should happen in the event of breach of contract, and so on. Many Croatian contracts are badly drafted and the problem is exacerbated by the fact that many contracts are drafted in English, which is not the first language of the person doing the drafting. As a result they can be unclear or muddled. Specifications tend to be very 'thin'. The contracts tend to be lacking in detail as to what happens if anything goes wrong.

At this point you will normally pay a **deposit** of 10 per cent of the price of the property. In the case of a property under construction ('off-plan') you will start to make **stage payments**. The size and number of these payments varies: a typical scheme provides for an initial payment of 30 per cent followed by two further payments of 30 per cent as construction progresses; this is followed by a final payment of 10 per cent on delivery. Sometimes there is only one preliminary payment of, say, 30 per cent with the balance being paid on delivery. This is very useful if you are taking out a mortgage.

Once you are ready to take delivery of the house, and have obtained your certificate from the Ministry of Foreign Affairs that you are entitled to own property in Croatia, you will sign the **final purchase contract**. This is signed in front of a notary public. It is at this point that the balance of the money is paid to the seller. You do not need to be present in Croatia to sign this document, as your lawyer can prepare a **power of attorney** (*see* pp.77–8) under which you can appoint somebody else to sign on your behalf. This saves the need for you to go to Croatia, often at short notice, to sign the final title.

Once you have paid the balance of the price, your ownership of the property will be **registered** in the local **title register**. Once this has been done, you – or the local Croatian company that you have set up to own the property – will be the full legal owner of the property in much the same way as in the UK.

The Expenses of Buying Property

The main expenses of buying are as follows:

- tax – the equivalent of stamp duty, at 5 per cent of the price; it is payable within 30 days of the sale taking place.

- VAT on new property at 22 per cent – sometimes included in price quoted.

- estate agent's fees, if these are not all paid by the seller; in Croatia it is customary for the buyer to pay part of the estate agent's fees, typically 2–3 per cent of the price if you are using a local Croatian finder or agent.

- notary's fees – these will vary but will typically not exceed £200.

- legal fees – these depend on whether you use a Croatian or an English lawyer; English lawyer's fees will inevitably be higher but you will be able to sue them if they get it wrong and they will be able to give you lots of advice, particularly concerning the vital issues of who should own the property to minimise your tax and other problems, which the local Croatian lawyer would not be able to help you with; fees will range from about 1–2 per cent of the price of the property.

• fees to set up a company, if you are going to set up a Croatian company; this is likely to cost £1,000–£1,500.

Letting Your Property

See the general chapter **Letting Your Property**, pp.117–26.

In order to let your property in Croatia you must obtain a **licence** from the Croatian authorities, which allows you to let property for a certain specified number of months' rental per year. You are then taxed on the period of permitted letting irrespective of actual performance. The system of taxation is different if you are letting through a limited company that owns the property.

If you let your property via a local Croatian agent, that person will be responsible for all the paperwork, for collecting the tourist tax due and for paying other taxes. Their fees will typically be between 15 per cent and 18 per cent of the rental received. Given that a large percentage of the people wanting to rent apartments in Croatia are from Britain, many owners will seek to access that market directly and do so without the necessary permit or registration for rental. Many will not pay their taxes. This is not to be advised, and will undoubtedly become more difficult as the tourist industry develops over the next few years in any case, so do not rely on it in your calculations.

If you are letting property, make sure that you use a proper **rental contract**. Your lawyer will be able to supply you with a draft that you can amend as necessary. Short-term letting to tourists produces the fewest problems in terms of what you can do if the tenant does not pay the rent or refuses to leave.

Rental yields in Croatia are, at the moment, a little uncertain, as the market is still young. In 2005 you could expect to see a rental yield (net of all expenses apart from your finance costs and personal taxation) of about 5 per cent – or 6 per cent in a popular coastal area. There are huge variations in the marketplace, but in 2005 you might expect to let a good one-bedroom apartment on the coast for about £200 per week during the main season. A two-bedroom apartment would let for about £300 per week. In Dubrovnik it will be about 50 per cent higher.

Taxes

Taxes for Non-resident Property-owners

Local Property Taxes

Local property taxes in Croatia are very low.

Income and Capital Gains Taxes

Foreign investors can invest in properties in Croatia either directly, in their own name, or through a local company.

• **Rental income on company-owned property**

The basis of the taxable income of a company investing in Croatian property is the gross income from the property less any tax-deductible expenses and depreciation. These expenses include any management costs, repairs, maintenance, insurance and so on, and interest on any loans used to buy the property. The corporate tax rate is a flat rate of 20 per cent.

• **Rental income on individually owned property**

Non-residents only pay tax in Croatia on income deriving from their presence in Croatia, which includes any rental income that they generate. The tax rates range from 20 per cent to 45 per cent but, in most cases, the 20 per cent rate is applicable to rental income. The taxable amount of the rental income is 70 per cent of the gross rent received.

Capital Gains Taxes

These taxes are treated as income. There is no tax for those who have owned their property for more than 3 years.

Wealth Taxes

There are no wealth taxes in Croatia.

Inheritance Taxes

There is no inheritance tax, but heirs have to pay property transfer tax in order to register their new ownership of the property.

Taxes for Resident Foreigners

This is beyond the scope of this book.

Settling In

Learning Croatian

Croatian is not easy for an English person to learn. A southern Slavonic language, it is closely related to Serbian, Bosnian and Slovene. It is particularly similar to Serbian, but the war ensured that different official languages were created and in 1991 the language of the country, with its three dialects, became known as Croatian. Croatian uses the Roman alphabet, while Serbian uses Cyrillic. Pre-trip tuition can be found on website **www.visit-croatia.co.uk**, which has online audio files of the basics.

Shopping

Croatia has only recently come out of a war and so the retail market is still undeveloped in some places. Many locals were used to travelling abroad to shop, where they had more choice and products were cheaper. But wander around any of the country's major cities and you will see a healthy number of international chains and the occasional shopping mall.

For the freshest food produce, do as the locals do and head for the markets; even the smallest supermarket will have a deli counter for fresh cheese and ham. For souvenirs, look for traditional handicrafts like embroidery, wine, woodcarvings and ceramics.

Shopping hours are generally Mon–Fri 8–8, Sat 8–2. Some shops in cities may now open on Sundays. It is appropriate to bargain.

Home Utilities and Services

Gas and Electricity

The state-owned **Croatian Electricity Company**, or **Hrvatska Electropriveda** (**HEP**), is responsible for the distribution of electricity. Prices rose by 25 per cent in 2003, but are still about 10 per cent lower than in Britain. The electrical supply is 220V, 50Hz, but if you want to use any UK appliances you will need a travel adapter.

Old properties to renovate may well be very cheap but they will often be without any electricity or mains water, so one has to look carefully into the costs of getting these services to your house. With most of Croatia being mountainous and rugged, it can be very expensive. Oil heating is common in many homes, but gas connections can be arranged in larger towns and cities, and cost about €18 per month.

Water

Water supply prices are set by the government. The average bill is around €100 per year.

Telephones

Telephone boxes only accept magnetic-strip **telephone cards** (*telekarta*) which are sold by post offices and newsagent kiosks in credit units (*impulsa*) of 25, 50, 100, 200 and 500. Credits fall at terrifying pace during peak rates between 7am and 10pm. Rates are 5 per cent lower from 4 to 10pm, and Sunday is deemed off-peak (50 per cent off). For international calls, it's usually easier to go to the post office, where you're assigned a cabin and given the bill afterwards.

To **call Croatia from abroad**, dial the country code 385, omit the first zero of the area code, then dial the number. To **call abroad from Croatia**, dial 00 then the country code then dial the number, again omitting the first zero of the area code. Local directory enquiries: **t** 988. International directory enquiries: **t** 902.

Mobile Phones

There are three million mobile phone users in Croatia. Most UK networks function in the country, but make sure you have set up international roaming well in advance of your departure date. It is also wise to check call charges, as you can easily be stung with a huge bill when you get home. Generally, text messages are the cheapest way of communicating. If you plan to use your mobile a lot or over a long period of time, it might be worth renting or buying a phone locally.

The Internet

The internet is becoming more common in Croatia. At the time of writing around a fifth of the population was online and there were six Internet service providers, such as **CARNet** (an academic provider), **HTnet**, and **Globalnet**. Major towns and tourist areas offer Internet access, and e-commerce is increasing.

Media

Croatia's **print media** now operates in an atmosphere of relative freedom following some censorship under Tudjman. *Vecernji list* and *Vjesnik* are two popular dailies; *Feral Tribune* and *Nacional* are major weeklies.

Television is the main source of information for most Croatians. **Croatian TV** is a public, national station, while **Nova TV** is the country's first national private TV network. **Croatian Radio** operates three public national networks. **Radio 101** and **Otvoreni Radio** are two popular commercial stations.

Money and Banking

Croatia's unit of currency is the **kuna** (Kn), which was only introduced in 1994. It is divided into 100 **lipa**. Coins come in denominations of 1, 2, 5, 10, 20 and 50 lipa, and 1, 2 and 5 kuna; and there are notes of 5, 10, 20, 50, 100, 200, 500 and 1000 kuna. The **exchange rate** is currently around £1 = 11Kn; $1 = 5.6Kn; €1 = 7.5Kn.

Money can also be changed in banks and travel agencies. Exchange bureaux may give a slightly poorer rate but tend to have more flexible hours. **Credit cards** are only accepted in the bigger hotels and more expensive restaurants, although you can use them to get cash from **ATMs** and the bigger banks. **Banks** are usually open Mon–Fri 8–5 and Sat 8–12 or 1, except on the coast where some follow shop hours. At the time of writing, the money situation was confusing. **Euros** are accepted in larger establishments – hotels, some bus companies and restaurants, but not usually in shops. You can choose whether you want your change given in euros or in local currency, but watch that you are not being deliberately confused and short-changed.

Post

You can buy stamps (*marke*, singular *marka*) at *pošta* of the HPT Hravtska, announced by a yellow spiral with a stripy triangle on its tail, but far easier is to purchase them from newsagents and tobacco kiosks, then pop postcards into canary-yellow post boxes: delivery within the EU takes around five days. Allow two weeks to send transatlantic. Letters are priced according to weight, airmail (*avionska pošta*) costs extra, and staff must inspect parcels before you seal them. At some post offices, too, you can also buy telephone cards and make international calls, and change travellers' cheques and money.

Working and Employment

With high unemployment and limited opportunities for non-Croatian speakers, you may not find it easy to find work. The best opportunities are in freelance work, investment and employment within the tourist industry, which requires English-speakers, particularly in Zagreb and along the Dalmatian coast. Volunteer work is a popular option for foreigners, and possible throughout the country. Programmes are run by organisations such as the **Croatian Heritage Foundation** and **Suncokret**.

Education

The war has taken its toll on the state of education in Croatia. Only a fraction of children currently go to **pre-school**. **Elementary school** lasts eight years and consists of two elements: instruction as a class with a single teacher, initially, and then specialised classes. Around three-quarters of the schools are small village or island schools with just one or two teachers. **Private schools** have only recently been made legal, so there are not many in the country.

Elementary schools in particular have been criticised for their lack of openness and autonomy, but improvements have been made in all areas. There are various types of **secondary schools**, as well as **trade schools**, **art schools** and **international schools**. In Croatia, as many as 95 per cent of pupils continue their education beyond the elementary level. The country has a developed system of **university** education, with four universities – in Zagreb, Rijeka, Split and Osijek.

Health and Emergencies

Ambulance services can be reached by dialling **t** 94.

Croatia's reciprocal arrangement with the EU provides EU citizens with free consultation and emergency care on the presentation of a passport or E111 or new European Health Insurance Card (EHIC; both available from post offices); the deal does not cover medical repatriation, private care or dental treatment. If you have to pay for any treatment, get a receipt for reimbursement later.

Health facilities in Croatia have had severe budgetary constraints since the war, and some medicines are in short supply in public hospitals and clinics. There is a large number of private medical and dental practitioners, and private **pharmacies** stock a variety of medicines which may not be easily available through public health facilities. Some healthcare facilities, doctors and hospitals may require immediate cash payment and do not normally accept credit cards. A list of English-speaking physicians and dentists is available from the British Embassy.

Accidents aside, Croatia is no health hazard. Standards of public health are high, tap water is drinkable everywhere and the most common complaint is sunburn. Having said that, swimmers should keep a wary eye for sea urchins on rocky shores of wild beaches and serious hikers of mountains woods should consider the vaccination for tick-borne encephalitis recommended by the US and British embassies. Inland, mosquitoes around lakes are annoying.

Social Services and Welfare Benefits

Your social security rights in Croatia are the same as those that apply in the UK. If you start work in Croatia, you will contribute to the Croatian social security system and, consequently, gain the right to benefits.

Cars and Taxis

If you plan to drive in Croatia, a **driving licence** valid for up to six months from entry into the country is required. Those staying longer need to apply for a **Croatian licence** (international driving licences are not valid in Croatia). Road conditions in and around main cities and towns are generally fine. However, minor roads are usually unlit at night.

A new law states that all drivers use dipped headlights at all times, even during the day. The country has a zero tolerance approach to drink driving. There is a speed limit of 60kph in urban areas, 80kph on standard roads, 100kph on highways and 120kph on motorways. If you break down, the Croatian automobile club (HAK) has a 24hr emergency service (**t** 987).

Taxis are generally plentiful, but agree a fare or make sure the meter (with the correct tariff) is used.

Crime and the Police

Police, t 92.

Compared with most of Europe, the crime rate in Croatia is very low, although the usual commonsense rules about looking after yourself and property apply. Police are courteous and helpful, businesslike without being effusive, although their low level of English can overcomplicate brushes with the law.

If possible, carry one official proof of identity to simplify matters.

Safety

Although Croatia has only recently come out of a war, there is practically no danger to tourists. There are few reminders of the war, and even Dubrovnik, which was heavily shelled, has been completely restored. In some areas inland, it is wise to take local advice about unexploded mines.

A large number of visitors come to Croatia to sail its clear waters, but make sure you follow the rules of the sea. Croatia has recently brought in a law which states a zero tolerance towards alcohol consumption for those in charge of yachts and other boats, with harsh penalties for those who fail to comply.

Food and Drink

The Venetians may have retreated back across the Adriatic, and the Austrian Habsburgs returned north, but both former rulers left behind a little piece of themselves in Croatia's contradictory cuisines. Pastas and risottos abound on coastal menus full of Mediterranean dishes, seafood is exquisite, and everything comes with herbs and garlic and soused in olive oil; but go inland, north and east, and you will instead find pork and paprika, goulash and beans.

Croatian menus tend to be somewhat limited. Fish (particularly in the south), squid, pasta, pizza and risotto can be found in most restaurants serving tourists. Croats themselves tend to eat fairly simple food. In all areas, produce is fresh and carefully prepared. A food enhancer known as Vegeta, which is actually a vegetable seasoning, is commonly used to flavour Croatian food.

Menus are often in German in the south, although English translations are usually given on request. The price for fish is given per kilo, which can make it sound expensive – e.g. €24 for a kilo – but as a rough guide one person would eat a quarter of a kilo – 250g – and so the total would be €6 – about £4.

Croatian **beers** are good – particularly Ozujsko pivo from Zagreb, or Tuborg, brewed under licence in Croatia. **Wines** are of a high standard, too, and very reasonable; *see* below. Only the hard-stomached should also try the lethal brandy *sljivovica*, made from plums, which really does taste like firewater. *Maraskino* is a more palatable and less potent liqueur made from Dalmatian cherries. Daytime drinking takes place in a café (*kavana*) or a pâtisserie

> ## Hamming it Up
> *Pršut* is a home-cured ham produced in Istria and Dalmatia and Croatia's delicious answer to prosciutto. Often local families keep a few pigs in order to make ham and sell to large suppliers. There is something of a traditional art involved. The pigs are killed in autumn and their back legs – from which *pršut* is made – are carefully washed before being covered in salt and squashed either in a press or between rocks to get rid of all the blood. This procedure may have to be repeated several times. Finally the meat is tied outside to dry out in the coastal wind and then hung inside the house until the next summer.
>
> The Dalmatian version is smoked, while the Istrian version traditionally is not. *Drnis Pršut*, made in the town of Drnis around 70 miles north of Dubrovnik, has long been considered by gourmands as one of the best meats in the world. In fact, the Habsburg emperors are reported to have insisted on it, and it was even served up at the ceremony for the coronation of Queen Elizabeth II.

(*slasticarnica*). Coffee is usually served black unless specified otherwise – ask for milk (*mlijeko*), although in many places popular with tourists cappuccino is the norm. Tea is widely available, but is herbal or drunk without milk.

Fine Wines

It is no surprise that wine is a part of everyday life in a country which basks in over 2,400 hours of sunshine in an average year and where vines have been tended as far back as Roman times. Croatia produces a large number of bottles of wine – over 50 million annually; 70 per cent of the country's 620 wines are Quality standard and only two bottles in ten are plain old plonk. The wine region on the coast runs all along the Adriatic from Istria in the north to Dalmatia in the south and is divided into two main areas, coastal and continental. Fine grapes are grown on estates on the islands and green hills. Istria specialises in red wines varieties such as Merlot and Cabernet Sauvignon, while Dalmatia is home to a wide range of mostly white wines, many of them with names that are hard to pronounce. On the Dalmatian coast, look for red wines such as Faros, or try a dry white like Posip.

Croatia: References

Directory of Contacts and Resources

Embassies

- **Croatian Embassy**, 21 Conway St, London W1P 5HL, UK, **t** 0870 005 6709/ **t** (020) 7387 1790/**t** (020) 7387 1144; **www.croatiaembassyhomepage.com.**

- **British Embassy**, Ivana Lucica 4, Zagreb, **t** + 385 1 6009 100 (switchboard); **t** + 385 1 6009 122 (Visa and Consular); **f** + 385 1 6009 111 (British Embassy), **british.embassyzagreb@fco.gov.uk**

Information and Resources

- **Croatian Tourist Office, t** (020) 8563 7979, **www.croatia.hr**. The site of the national tourist board has contacts for offices in countries around the world. There is good, basic information about regions, culture, climate.
- **www.visit-croatia.co.uk**. Lots of information on many aspects of Croatia.
- **www.slavophilia.net**. Information on all the Slavic countries.
- **www.mvp.hr**. Croatian Ministry of Foreign Affairs, with links to national embassies.
- **www.hgk.hr**. Croatian Chamber of Economy.
- **www.istria.com**. Covers the area of Istria, which in many ways is very different from the rest of the country.
- **www.croatica.net**. Online magazine.
- **www.dalmacija.net**. Information on all the Dalmatian Coast.
- **www.tzzz.net**. Information on the Zagreb region.

Property Companies and Estate Agents

- **Adriatic Maritime**, **www.croatiaproperty.ie.**
- **Avatar International, t** 08707 282827, **www.avatar-international.com**. An estate agent with offices in the UK and Dubrovnik.
- **Ballymaice House**, Bohernabreena, Co. Dublin, Ireland (agents are in Croatia), **t** + 353 86 805 5402, **adraiticmaritime@hotmail.com**.
- **Broker Nekretnine, t** + 385 2154 7004, **www.broker.hr.**
- **Croatian Sun**, Iva Vojnovica 61A, 20000 Dubrovnik, **t** + 385 20 312 228, **f** + 385 20 312 226, **info@croatiansun.com**, **www.croatiansun.com**. Will arrange personalised inspection visits for potential buyers – their offices are based in Dubrovnik but they cover the entire country – and offers a full service including design and build.
- **Dubrovnik Nekretnine**, Dordiceva 4, 20000 Dubrovnik, **t** + 385 98 178 7877, **dalmacija-nekretnine@du.hinet.hr.**
- **Hvar Property Services**, Jelsa, Hvar Island, **info@hvarpropertyservices. com, www.croatianhouse.com.**
- **Homes in Croatia, t** (020) 7502 1371, **www.homesincroatia.com.**
- **KPMG Croatia, t** + 385 1466 6440, **www.kpmg.hr.**
- **My Home, t** + 385 5178 1575, **www.agencija-myhome.com.**

Removal Companies

- **1st Move International Removals Ltd**, International House, Unit 5B Worthy Rd, Chittening Industrial Estate, Avonmouth, Bristol BS11 0YB, **t** (0117) 982 8123, **f** (0117) 982 2229, **info@shipit.co.uk**, **www.shipit.co.uk**.

Holiday Companies

- **Transun, t** 0870 444 4747, **f** 0870 444 2747, **www.transun.co.uk.** Wide coverage, including Poreč and Rovinj in Istria, the islands of Brač, Hvar, Korčula, and Dubrovnik, Mlini and Cavtat.
- **Croatia for Travellers, t** (020) 7226 4460, **f** (020) 7226 7906. Caters for independent travellers, offering island hopping, fly-drive holidays and yacht charter.
- **Crystal Croatia Reservations, t** 0870 888 0224, **www.crystalcroatia.co.uk**. Upmarket holidays in good resorts across the country.
- **Dalma Holidays, t** (020) 8677 2655, **f** (020) 8769 6450, **www.dalma holidays.co.uk**. A flexible and personalised service and a wide range of self-catering accommodation.

Also *see* pp.169 and 170 for specialist tour operators.

Administrative Departments

Croatia is divided into 20 regions and the city district of the capital, Zagreb, for the purposes of administration: Bjelovar-Bilogora, Dubrovnik-Neretva, Istria, Karlovac, Koprivnica-Križevci, Krapina-Zagorje, Lika-Senj, Medimurje, Osijek-Baranja, Požega-Slavonia, Primorje-Gorski Kotar, Šibenik-Knin, Sisak-Moslavina, Slavonski Brod-Posavina, Split-Dalmatia, Varaždin, Virovitica-Podravina, Vukovar-Srijem, Zadar, Zagreb.

Time

Croatia is one hour ahead of GMT (two hours in summer).

Public Holidays

1 January	New Year's Day
March or April	Easter
1 May	Labour Day
10 June	Corpus Christi
22 June	Anti-Fascist Resistance Day
5 August	Victory Day and National Thanksgiving Day

15 August	Assumption
8 October	Independence Day
1 November	All Saints' Day
November (Muslim community)	End of Ramadan
25–26 December	Christmas

Further Reading

Croatia: A History, Ivo Goldstein, Nikolina Jovanovic – good, albeit brief overview of the history of the country by a professor at the University of Zagreb, who is at his best when writing about the 20th century

Lovers and Madmen: A True Story of Passion, Politics and Air Piracy, Julienne Eden Busic – fascinating story of four Croats and an American woman who hijacked a plane in America in 1976 to publicise the Croatian fight for independence

The Bone Woman: A Forensic Anthropologist's Search for Truth in the Mass Graves of Rwanda, Bosnia, Croatia, and Kosovo, Clea Koff – harrowing and personal account by a forensic anthropologist who worked on seven missions with the UN War Crimes Tribunal.

Climate Charts

Average Temperature in Zagreb (°C)

Jan	Feb	Mar	April	May	June	July	Aug	Sept	Oct	Nov	Dec
33	35	43	52	60	65	73	69	62	50	43	34

Average Days of Rain in Zagreb

Jan	Feb	Mar	April	May	June	July	Aug	Sept	Oct	Nov	Dec
7	6	10	13	11	14	8	11	10	9	12	9

Average Number of Rainy Days per Month in Dubrovnik

Jan	Feb	Mar	April	May	June	July	Aug	Sept	Oct	Nov	Dec
13	13	11	10	10	6	4	3	7	11	16	15

Average Daily Maximum Temperature in Dubrovnik (°C)

Jan	Feb	Mar	April	May	June	July	Aug	Sept	Oct	Nov	Dec
12	13	14	17	21	25	29	28	25	21	17	14

The Czech Republic

12

Why Buy in the Czech Republic?

The landlocked Czech Republic is bordered by Poland, Slovakia, Austria and Germany, enjoying a position that is in many ways at the heart of Europe. There is relatively easy access to the Czech Republic from Western Europe and the country has a long tradition of welcoming tourists. In fact, unlike many of the other countries covered in this book, the Republic, or at least its capital, which is conveniently located around halfway between Berlin and Vienna, could be said to be experiencing overdeveloped tourism.

The Czech Republic has experienced a phenomenal tourist boom since 1989, largely because of the fairytale romance of its capital, Prague – although the high-quality, low-cost Czech beer could also be a factor. The city is undeniably beautiful year-round, with its seven hills crowned with castles and churches on a lovely bend in the Vltava River. Its stunning architecture, set around pretty squares, includes Gothic cathedrals and Art Nouveau cafés which appeal to history buffs and young people alike. At night, its cavernous bars come alive serving cheap local beer to tourists from all over the world. 'The City of One Hundred Towers and Spires', as it is sometimes known, is a UNESCO World Heritage Site. Prague managed to survive the effects of war and, more recently, the terrible floods of 2002. The Czech Republic has just over 10 million residents, yet it hosts an annual influx of 17 million tourists, and the capital city can be horribly crowded during peak season; however, Prague's popularity is not recent, and as a result it has a great infrastructure and receives a wide range of visitors, making the buy-to-let market relatively buoyant.

The countryside is attractive, too. The ancient lands of Bohemia and Moravia are dotted with castles, châteaux and beautifully preserved medieval towns. Generally hilly, it has well-known spa towns such as Karlovy Vary and Mariánské Lázně, and scenic mountains which offer skiing and hiking.

The Czech Republic has deep musical traditions which are reflected today in its variety of music festivals. Apart from the world-famous Prague Spring Festival and the concerts of the Czech Philharmonic, there are all manner of other celebrations and even a Czech association of music festivals (**www.czech-festivals.cz**). The Karlovy Vary Festival of Early Music takes place in the last week in July, the International Piper Festival in Luby in August, and the international singing competition in České Budějovice in August and September.

In 2002 the country was devastated by floods, which were the worst it had seen in over 200 years. The waters caused millions of pounds' worth of damage and were a tremendous blow for the country's economy and tourism. With the World Heritage Site cities of Prague and Český Krumlov completely under water, many architectural treasures were destroyed and thousands of people had to be evacuated from their homes.

Visas and Permits

UK citizens do not need a visa for tourist stays of up to **six months**. Other Western Europeans are allowed 90 visa-free days, US nationals 30 visa-free days. Canadians need a visa.

EU citizens can apply for a **temporary residence permit** if they intend to stay in the Czech Republic for more than three months. They can apply for a **permanent residence permit** if they are employed in the Czech Republic and are in the country for more than three uninterrupted years, or do business there.

You can apply for **citizenship** of the Czech Republic if you have:

- **been a permanent resident for at least five years in the Czech Republic.**
- **proof that you have ceased to have citizenship at home.**
- **had a clean criminal record for the past five years.**
- **a good knowledge of the Czech language.**

Kafka

Franz Kafka's is the country's most famous son, and arguably one of the world's greatest 20th-century writers. Although Kafka wrote in German and was a citizen of the Austro-Hungarian Empire at birth in 1883, his writing was inextricably linked with his home town of Prague. His most well-known works, such as *Metamorphosis* and *The Trial*, have a universal resonance expressing the alienation of the modern person; they are from a tradition of Jewish storytelling and deeply rooted in his native land. Some even go so far as to say that the Old Town Square in Prague was Kafka's front yard.

One of his more well-known quotations comes not from his works of fiction, but his journals:

'A book should serve as the axe for the frozen sea within us.'

Profile of the Czech Republic

Recent History and Poliitcs

The Czech kingdom was once part of the Holy Roman Empire, and under Charles IV (1346–78), King of Bohemia and Holy Roman Emperor, Prague grew into one of the largest cities in Europe. During this time it acquired striking Gothic features such as Charles University, Charles Bridge and St Vitus' Cathedral. The Republic's second great ruler was the emperor Rudolf II during the second half of the 16th century. The city became even more wealthy, acquired great collections of works of art and became the seat of the Habsburg Empire. The Czech kingdom remained a part of the Habsburg monarchy until 1918 and the Czechoslovak Republic was proclaimed. Czechoslovakia's 'Velvet Revolution' took place in November 1989 and was so-called because it was the most peaceful rejection of Communism in Eastern Europe. However, only three years later, on 1 January 1993, to the shock of the international community, the country was divided in two, and the Czech Republic came into being as a separate democratic state.

In 2003, when Vaclav Havel's term as president ended, it was the end of an era. The man who was a dissident playwright and had led the Velvet Revolution was the first president of post-Communist Czechoslovakia. Havel had seen off the final spectre of Soviet military power in 1999 when the Republic was given full membership of NATO. Vaclav Klaus of the conservative Civic Democratic Party succeeded Vaclav Havel in the largely ceremonial role of president. Klaus named Stanislav Gross as prime minister in July 2004.

The Czech Republic joined the EU in 2004 after some controversy within the country. Havel had brought his country to the brink of EU membership, dogged by criticism of the Republic's treatment of its 300,000 Roma, or Gypsy, population, which suffers extremely high levels of unemployment, illiteracy and

What's in a Name?

From 1918 to 1938 and 1945 to 1960 the country was called the Czechoslovak Republic. Between 1938 and 1939 it was known as the Czecho-Slovak Republic. From 1960 to 1990 it was the Czechoslovak Socialist Republic. In April 1990 'Czechoslovak Federative Republic' was the Czech version and 'Czecho-Slovak Federative Republic' was the Slovak version. This eventually became the Czech and Slovak Federative Republic, with the short forms being Czechoslovakia in the Czech version and Czecho-Slovakia in the Slovak form.

In 1993 the Czech Ministry of Foreign Affairs announced that the name Czechia was to be used, but this hasn't caught on. Czech businessmen have become frustrated in their search for a more catchy name to brand their goods. One common short name is Cesko but it ignores Slovakia and sounds rather too much like the supermarket 'Tesco'.

poverty. In 2000, the firing of the Temelin nuclear power plant was internationally controversial, as was the Czech Republic's refusal to revoke the post-war expulsion of around 2.5 million ethnic Germans and Hungarians.

Religion

Around 39 per cent of the population is Roman Catholic. Other Christian churches include the Orthodox Church and Protestant denominations such as the Evangelical Church of Czech Brethren and the Czechoslovak Hussite Church. Few people who declare themselves members of religious organisations actually go to church, however. In the past, 1 per cent of the population was Jewish, but now there are only few thousand Jews living in the country.

Climate and Geography

For such a small country, the Czech landscape is pleasantly varied. The western part of the country is a basin drained by the rivers Elba and Vltava, and surrounded by low mountains like the Krkonose. To the east, the land is hilly and cut through by the Morava and Oder rivers. The country enjoys warm summers with cold and sometimes humid winters. See 'Climate Charts', p.220.

Regional Profile

Prague and Around

The capital's wonderfully eclectic architecture is recognised by UNESCO as a World Heritage Site. Prague managed to escape being bombed in the Second World War and is one of nine cities given the title of 'European metropolis of culture in 2000' by the European Union. Prague has long been noted for its magnificent Gothic, Baroque, Art Nouveau and even Cubist architecture; since the fall of Communism it has gained itself the title 'Paris of the East'.

Goethe called Prague the 'prettiest gem in the stone crown of the world'. The compact city, which is divided unequally by the River Vltava, is made up of five ancient towns. The Old Town features the iconic Charles Bridge, which has best views of the castle and is just one of the ornate bridges spanning the river. The once-walled Jewish Quarter still has six synagogues and a historic town hall, while the area around Václavské náměstí (Wenceslas Square) is the main shopping zone. To the south is Vysehrad, with its Slavin Cemetery honouring the city's intellectuals and artists.

Much of the city's population lives a world away from the pretty centre in typical post-Communist high-rise housing estates, but outside this area is a different world again. Much of the best countryside is only an hour or so away from the capital, making it popular for short trips and the site for second homes

---

Case Study: Alex Brown and Eric Reid

Alex Brown is a successful property developer living in London's Fulham area. Although he has a full-time job working in the city, he makes much more income from the two flats he owns in Brixton. In the last few years, he watched the buy-to-let market in London collapse and looked further afield. In 2002 he bought a one-bedroom flat in the centre of Prague for £50,000 and he has seen his property increase in value by 12 per cent each year since then. Alex says, 'I have seen a good return for my money, and, because the costs are so much lower in Prague, the risks are so much less.'

Eric Reid, a director of the Association of the Retired and Persons over 50, has recently bought a flat in the Czech Republic. He is working there for six months and considering staying on permanently. He advises other retired people on moving abroad and says, 'In general, there are few problems buying property in the EU. In some areas they don't sell to foreigners. If they do it is at an inflated price, up to 20 per cent more with the extra expenses of legal work.'

---

and country retreats. Many retired people spend as much as two-thirds of the year outside the city. Also in the surroundings of the capital are the famous castles of **Karlstejn**, **Krivoklat** and **Konopiste**. The historic silver-mining town of **Kutná Hora** boasts a spectacular Gothic cathedral and once rivalled Prague in terms of cultural and political importance.

South Bohemia

This is a particularly picturesque area, with small medieval towns, old stone farmhouses and large swaths of dense forest. Unlike other parts of the country, south Bohemia has escaped the ravages of industrialisation and enjoys a number of protected areas.

The 13th-century town of **České Budějovice** lies on the confluence of the Vltava and Malše Rivers. Built on a medieval grid plan, the historic buildings include a Dominican cloister with Gothic fresco paintings, a Gothic cathedral and a Gothic-Renaissance Black Tower, which dominates the town. Today České Budějovice is best known for being home to the Budějovice (Budvar) Brewery a couple of miles outside the town, where guided tours are available.

Český Krumlov is a special place that brings visitors back again and again. Its combination of beautiful medieval buildings and special location tucked into a loop of the Vltava River seem to bewitch. Watched over by its awesome castle, this is the most important of the 'Rose Towns' in the region, a term used to describe a series of medieval walled towns which take their name from the black and red roses used as the emblems of the two most powerful dynasties in south Bohemia. Český Krumlov has been declared a UNESCO World Heritage Site and its narrow, winding streets are often full with visitors. It is something of an artist's enclave and the birthplace of Egon Schiele; there is a large gallery devoted to his works. Day-trippers and holidaymakers alike are discovering the town, which is second only to Prague as the country's top tourist attraction. And, like the capital, it is in some ways suffering from its own popularity.

In contrast to the rolling hills of the rest of south Bohemia, **Třeboň** and its surroundings are characterised by flat bog and marshlands. This area is famed for its pretty artificial lakes, which are used for rearing fish in a tradition that dates back to the 15th century; the country's Christmas carp come from here. The medieval spa town is surrounded by some of the largest ponds. Its tiny centre has historic buildings that are dwarfed by a hulking château, next to which is an 'English park'.

The **Sumava** region stretches along the Austrian and German borders, covered by thick pine forests and peat bogs. This wilderness area with a very low population forms the largest national park in the country. Within the park are glacial lakes and the artificial Lake Lipno, which is very popular in summer with tourists from neighbouring countries. Hikers come to enjoy the peace and there is a sports centre for winter visitors.

West Bohemia

This region bordering Germany is known for one thing: its spas. The trio of spa towns – **Mariánské Lázně, Karlovy Vary** and **Františkovy Lázně** – have attracted Czech, German and Russian cure-seekers for hundreds of years. All three are spaciously laid out around their springs, with neat parks and elegant colonnades. Luminaries such as Wagner, Goethe and Edward VII visited Mariánské Lázně, although Karlovy Vary remains the country's most famous spa and welcomes guests from around the world, many of them elderly or sick. Karlovy Vary also has golf and tennis facilities and lively year-round culture.

Plzeň is the second largest city in Bohemia and overwhelmingly industrial. It has a mix of architecture from Gothic to Art Nouveau, a lively student population and Západoceské Galérie, the best art gallery outside Prague. Plzeň is better known to the rest of the world as Pilsner, and birthplace of the legendary Pilsner beer, *see* p.218.

North Bohemia

This area has two, somewhat conflicting characteristics: it has the protected **Jizerske Mountains**, the Labe and Upa rivers, and sandstone 'rock-cities' of spectacular canyons and hulking volcanic rocks around the town of **Děčín**; however, North Bohemia is also a sad example of the effects of ill-considered industrialisation, its forests having been decimated by acid rain. Many villages were destroyed and replaced with coalmines, and the air became thick with the pollution from the local power stations. In the last few years, however, attempts to clean up the region have been partly successful.

East Bohemia

People come here for the variety of scenery. Although it has some of the flattest countryside in Bohemia, it also has some of the Czech Republic's highest mountains – the **Krkonoše** (Giant Mountains) **National Park** with hiking and skiing facilities and the charming **Český Ráj Nature Reserve**, with sandstone formations and quiet forests.

South Moravia

This area southeast of Prague is just across the border from Austria and conveniently located close to Vienna. Its rolling hills and thick forests make its landscape similar to that in Bohemia, but in the south vineyards and orchards give it a different flavour. **Brno** is the main city; it is industrial but a good jumping-off point for the karst region, including the limestone caves of the Moravský kras. Small towns and villages with prettily painted houses and an older population sometimes still wearing traditional folk costumes give the region a bucolic air. **Pernstejn** boasts an almost perfect medieval castle, and the towns of **Telc**, a UNESCO Heritage Site with a Zamec castle, and **Slavonice** both have wonderful examples of Renaissance architecture. **Kromeriz** is a beautiful Baroque town, which can be reached from Prague in a day trip; it has a bishop's palace and elegant water gardens.

North Moravia

Bordering Poland and Slovakia, north Moravia has suffered from industrialisation and ecological problems, but is peaceful and has a landscape that is relatively untouched by tourism. The **Jeseníky Mountains** are a scenic location for skiing in winter and hiking in summer, and there are still traditional communities living in the Beskydy hills, which are rich in folklore and have attractive wooden houses and churches. There is an extraordinary open-air folk museum at **Rožnov pod Radhoštěm**, which is a showcase for the region's rich cultural heritage. **Olomouc** used to be a Soviet garrison but nowadays university students wander the parks and cobbled streets.

Selecting a Property

Getting There

By Air

The national carrier **Czech Airlines** (**t** (020) 7255 1898, **www.czechairlines.com**) flies to Prague from London Stansted and a number of other European cities. **EasyJet** (**www.easyjet. com**) flies to Prague from London Stansted and London

Gatwick, and from regional UK airports such as Bristol, Newcastle and the East Midlands. **British Airways** (**t** 0870 850 9850, **www.ba.com**) flies to Prague from London Gatwick.

By Train

Train services are good in the Czech Republic, making it is easy to get to there from all major European cities. However, in summer international trains tend to be full and you should book your seat at least a few weeks ahead of your journey. Seat reservations are compulsory on all international trains.

For London to Prague, there are two main options, the first taking **Eurostar**, **t** 08705 186 186, **www.eurostar.com**, sleeper and EuroCity trains via Brussels and Berlin. The journey takes 23hrs. Or travel by day to Brussels and Frankfurt, leaving London Waterloo on the Eurostar for Brussels, taking a train from Brussels to Frankfurt, and then the Frankfurt–Prague sleeper. Book via **Rail Europe**, 178 Piccadilly, London W1, **t** 08705 848 848, **www.raileurope.co.uk**.

By Bus

Taking a bus to the Czech Republic from the UK will probably work out no cheaper than buying a ticket on one of the budget airlines. It takes 23hrs on **Eurolines**, **t** 08705 808080, **www.eurolines.com**, from London to Prague, costing around £59 return. There are bus connections from the Czech Republic to and from major European cities several times a week. Most international buses arrive in Prague's main station, Florenc, which has good metro connections.

Getting Around

By Train

Make sure you don't get on a *osobní* train, as they stop at almost every station and travel as slowly as 30kph. The quickest way to travel is on **InterCity** (IC), and **EuroCity** (EC) expresses, which charge a supplement. If you are planning to travel to a neighbouring country, sleepers are the best bet, but you need to book as far in advance as possible and no later then 6 hours before the train departs.

By Bus

Most regional buses are run by the state company, *Česká státní automobilová doprava* (CSAD), which runs buses to most destinations. Private companies like CEBUS provide an alternative on most inter-city routes. Bus stations are usually next to the train station, and if there's no separate terminal you will have to buy your ticket from the driver. It's essential to book your ticket at least a day in advance if you're travelling at the weekend, on a public holiday or early in the morning on a main route. See **www.vlak-bus.cz** for times and information.

By Road

More and more people in the country own cars, making travelling by road less relaxing than it used to be. Roads generally are not in good condition and they suffer from potholes and poor signposting. *See 'Settling In', pp.216–17.*

Choosing a Location

Although Prague is the focus of the vast majority of property investment in the country, there is a certain amount of foreign interest in its border regions, particularly northern Bohemia and northern Moravia. Even this, however, is restricted to very specific areas where there is already tourist interest or where foreigners are living.

Property Types and Prices

A wide range of property is available, from newly renovated or new-build city apartments to rural villas and village houses. Prices in Prague rose by about 35 per cent from 2000 to 2004 although it is still possible to buy apartments for under £40,000. Foreign buyers favour Prague's districts 1, 2 and 6. The most expensive property is close to the historic Old Town (Staré Mesto) in district 1. District 1 also includes the Jewish Quarter (Josefov) and Mala Strana, below the castle. A two-bedroom apartment in a traditional block would currently be around £200,000 and there is very little in the centre under £125,000, although studios are still available for half that. District 2 has a cheaper but very pleasant residential neighbourhood, Vinohrady, while district 6 has the capital's most expensive property, with town houses and villas of £650,000 and more.

Castles in the Air

The Czech Republic has a fairytale selection of dream properties, although few people can afford to put down several million pounds to buy their very own historic castle, manor house or palace. What about a magical palace on its own lake with 60 bedrooms and numerous libraries where the glitterati from around the world have come to get married? Or maybe a Baroque manor house just outside Prague, which is an annexe of a renaissance palace built above the scenic Vltava river? Otherwise there is a castle in its own park land with 20 rooms and a spectacular indoor swimming pool.

Most of us will have to content ourselves with just visiting one of the 1,000 or so castles and ruins in the country. There are several spectacular châteaux and castles around an hour away from Prague. While the major attractions of Karlstejn Castle and Krivoklat Castle are open all the year round, most of the others are only open from the beginning of April to the end of October (May, June, July and August 9–6; April, September and October 10–3).

Case Study: An Isolated Incident

When Tom Aleny decided to buy a remote cabin in the Czech countryside, he had no idea what he was letting himself in for. The small building he bought was surrounded by privately owned land and it transpired that he had no legal right to cross it. 'I had to laugh. I had bought a bargain-priced property that was little more than a shed, yet it turned out I needed also to purchase some kind of light aircraft to access it,' said Tom.

He has since got his lawyer to draw up something called an easement, which allows him to use someone else's land legally.

Every Friday in summer, a mass exodus occurs from Prague as locals escape the city to enjoy their country cottage (*chalupy*) or cabin (*chata*). As is the case in much of this part of the world, there is a long tradition of owning these weekend retreats. While most people in the West regard a second home as an extravagance reserved for the very rich, for Prague residents who may not have luxury city apartments, their 'cottage' may not be much more than a shack, but it is a valued part of their life. Locals try to buy somewhere in the direction closest to the part of the city in which they live so they don't have to cross the city during the rush hour on Fridays.

Germans and Austrians also buy this sort of accommodation, usually close to their border and often near woods or water. Golfers like **Benesov** because it is close to the city and near a good course, while those who ski plump for the **Krkonose** area and cottages in these two locations are most expensive.

Most properties are small and on two levels, with the bedrooms in the smaller attic area, and with some land. Some are in poor condition, as most were built in the 1950s and 1960s; they are in remote locations and reasonably priced. If you are considering buying one of these buildings, make sure that local utilities exist, as some of these places do not have electricity or running water and the cost of installing it may be prohibitive.

It is advisable to look for a place out of season – autumn or winter for a summer cottage, spring for a ski property. If you can, bring someone who knows about wiring and building maintenance to check things over. Finally, bear in mind that you will probably have more contact with your neighbours in the country than you would in the city. Watch out for barking dogs and general unsociable behaviour.

Estate agents will deal with these cottages, but you can widen your choice if you have a Czech-speaking contact and can look at the classified adverts in local papers, such as *Annonce*. There may be a question of land ownership to be resolved, as many of these buildings were constructed on government land during the Communist period. Check also that there are no plans for developments in the area.

Guide Prices

€10,000

- Small shack-like 'cottage' in a rural area such as Znojmo.

€40,000

- Renovated studio apartment on the edge of Prague.

€70,000

- Two-bedroom 1930s villa in a town near Prague built over 80 sq m, on a plot of 500 sq m.
- One-bedroom flat in the centre of Prague with 60 sq m of living space.

€100,000

- One-bedroom flat with open plan kitchen in luxurious and completely renovated Art Nouveau building in outskirts of Prague; includes parking space.
- Renovated one-bedroom flat with a floor area of 64 sq m and basement room in the Holešovice area of Prague.
- Family house with land of 1,120 sq m, 1 hour from Prague; quiet area with outbuildings.

€200,000

- Three-bedroom penthouse on the edge of Prague built on two storeys, over 200 sq m with balcony and underfloor heating.
- 1940s villa in a suburb of Prague converted into three large flats with a shared garden, swimming pool and garage.
- 1930s renovated two-bedroomed house near Hvezda; basement with two rooms and land of 326 sq m with a garage.

€300,000

- Three-bedroom Art Nouveau house with two bedrooms and terrace; near Riegrovy Orchards.
- Three-bedroom house in Nebušice (which has an international school); about 230 sq m of living space and land of 650 sq m; with garage, balcony and independent studio.

€400,000

- Renovated villa with seven rooms, fireplace and security system; one hour from the capital; land of 508 sq m.
- Luxurious villa in the Smíchov area; outdoor pool; land area of 615 sq m.
- Stylish 1940s villa in a quiet location in Nebušice; terrace, good transport connections and tennis courts nearby.

Building from Scratch or Renovation

The Velvet Revolution brought about major changes in the economic life in the Czech Republic, which dramatically changed the housing sector, with major state-funded housing developments being phased out completely by 1992. Since then, the rental and sales markets have undergone a steady metamorphosis, which is mainly to the foreign investor's advantage. Between 1950 and 1990, almost all the present existing housing was constructed – mostly high-rise and pre-fabricated, where more than 40 per cent of the population live. These buildings, including some of the newer ones, are deteriorating rapidly, not only because of the poor construction quality but also because of a lack of maintenance or funds for maintenance, and foreign buyers are buying them for renovation. In rural areas there are a large number of very old houses falling to pieces and needing renovation. In some cases, it makes sense to knock the property down and to build it from scratch, as it can be cheaper than buying empty plots of land with building permission and there is an existing network of sewage, electricity and water services.

Temporary Accommodation

Hotels in Prague are readily available, although they get booked up in peak season. In other parts of the country, facilities for visitors are more limited. Rental property is in short supply, especially in Prague. When renting property, it may either be through an individual or a company, but in both cases check any legal documents thoroughly, preferably with a solicitor. Some contracts may include use of all utilities.

The Process of Buying a Property

Freedom to Buy

When the Czech Republic joined the EU in 2004, some feared that the country would be swamped by eager overseas investors looking for a bargain. But under the terms of a newly brokered deal, citizens from other EU countries have to wait five years before they are able to buy second homes. Those who want to set up a limited liability company, however, are not restricted in the same way and can buy property legally without waiting; *see* pp.69–70. If the property is acquired through a company then the company is subject to Czech corporation tax on net taxable income. The rate is currently 31 per cent. UK corporation tax also has to be paid in the UK on any company profits, i.e. when you sell, or receive rental income. However, tax paid on the property overseas can usually be offset against your British tax bill.

Contracts and Registration

The legal system is similar to that of Britain and ownership is much more clear-cut than in some Eastern European countries. Even so, there have been property disputes, therefore it is important to engage an experienced lawyer to ascertain title. Prague has a central registry of ownership known as the Kadastra to help do this. Many overseas buyers purchase in restored apartment blocks because these are generally not liable for ownership disputes. The property registration process takes about six months. After the buyer and seller have negotiated the sale conditions, typically the purchaser lodges the purchase price in a notarial or escrow account to which the seller will have access when the purchaser has been registered as the new owner.

The Expenses of Buying Property

Estate agency fees vary: some charge the buyer, others charge the seller or both parties. The seller is liable for a property transfer tax of 5 per cent, which the buyer becomes liable for in the event that the seller does not pay up.

Letting Your Property

See the general chapter **Letting Your Property**, pp.117–26.

If you are letting property, make sure that you use a proper **rental contract**. Your lawyer will be able to supply you with a draft that you can change as necessary. Short-term letting to tourists produces the fewest problems in terms of what you can do if the tenant does not pay the rent or refuses to leave. For those considering letting out their property, note that Czech tenants are protected by rent controls; there are no such restrictions on foreign tenants.

Settling In

Learning and Speaking Czech

Czech is a west Slavic language and a difficult language to learn, but English is spoken widely in Prague. Outside the capital, German is more likely to be of use. Moravians speak a slightly different form of the language than that used in Bohemia. Czech is a phonetic language (pronounced consistently according to its spelling) with no silent letters. That's simple enough – the problem is learning how to pronounce the letters in the first place!

Czech Out the Czech Dream

In an extraordinary surrealist hoax, two film students staged a fake opening of the cheapest hypermarket in Prague. Using PR, advertising agencies and crowd psychologists, they fooled over a thousand keen bargain-hunters, who arrived at a location only to find that the shop and the whole marketing campaign was a hoax and that they were standing outside a canvas façade stretched across scaffolding on a piece of derelict land. The exercise was part of a documentary called *The Czech Dream*, which was also the name of the bogus hypermarket. It set out to explore the country's post-Communist obsession with supermarket shopping and consumerism.

Shopping

Over the past decade both the quantity and quality of products have significantly improved, and hypermarkets and western-style shopping malls in the capital stock a wide variety of goods. In the rest of the country, too, the range of consumer goods is growing. However, the Czech people do not have much of a customer-orientated mentality and in some places service with a scowl still rules. In rural shops, customers have to wait for the shop assistant to gather the goods you request, a tradition that dates back to the Austro-Hungarian Empire.

Shops are usually open Mon–Fri 9–7 (sometimes earlier) and may close during lunch hours. The hours are shorter on Saturdays and most shops are closed on Sundays. Some outlets in Prague have longer hours and are also open weekends.

Home Utilities and Services

Electricity, Gas and Water

Register for services *before* the occupation of a property, ashe process can take several days, and sometimes even weeks.

For electricity, register at the service office of the regional distributor for your district. An administrative fee will be charged and sometimes an advance payment for usage. The government sets the cost of electricity for household consumption and an estimated payment must be made in advance every month. Quarterly statements detail your usage and any additional payments.

For gas, there are separate companies for each region. You must register with the one that services your district, for which you will need to provide a copy of your proof of ownership. As with electricity, the government sets the price, and usage is paid for in advance each month. A 'summary of use' statement is normally issued annually.

Property-owners must register with the water and sewerage company in their relevant district.

Telephones

Most public phones only take **phone cards**, which can be bought from post offices and certain shops. These phone cards can be used for both local and international calls. Calls abroad can also be made from post offices.

All Czech numbers now have 9 digits and there is no area code. The international code for the Czech Republic is **t** 420. To call the Czech Republic from abroad, dial **t** 00 420 and then the number. Directory enquiries, **t** 120.

Mobile Phones

It seems as if everyone in the capital, and many in the countryside, own a mobile phone. Using or renting one is a straightforward procedure. Most UK mobiles can be used throughout the Czech Republic, assuming that you've asked your company to activate international roaming.

The Internet

The Internet is commonly available in Prague, and more and more common in major towns, but access can be more difficult elsewhere.

Media

In the 1990s, independent media blossomed and there are now a large number of private radio and television stations. Although in theory press freedom is protected, there is a certain amount of private and political interference.

The *Lidove Noviny*, *Mlada Fronta Dnes* and *Pravo* are all Prague-based national daily **newspapers**; the first was a former dissident publication. The *Prague Post* and *Prague Tribune* are English-language papers; the latter focuses on business and lifestyle in the city.

Sreality (**www.sreality.cz**) is a free **magazine** available from estate agents or online and lists several thousand cottages by location. *Annonce* (**www.annonce. cz**) also has property listings and is available at newspaper stands and online.

There are two major private **television** channels that broadcast nationally, and more than 70 private **radio** stations on air across the country. **Czech TV** is the public broadcaster; operating the mainstream channel **CT1** and cultural channel **CT2**. **TV Nova** and **Prima** are the two main commercial stations. Czech public radio, **Cesky Rozhlas**, operates three national networks and local services.

Money and Banking

Although the Czech Republic has been a member of the EU since May 2004, the euro is not yet used and is not expected to be adopted until 2009. The local currency is the Czech crown, or **koruna** (kc), which is divided into 100 **hellers** or halér (h). Coins come in denominations of 10h, 20h, 50h, 1kc, 2kc, 5kc, 10kc, 20kc and 50kc; notes 20kc, 50kc, 100kc, 200kc, 500kc, 1,000kc, 2,000kc and 5,000kc. In Prague, the plastic revolution is well under way, but **cash** is still ubiquitous. Many shops and restaurants still insist on cash rather than credit cards, although you will find **ATMs** everywhere. When changing money, don't bother with the 'black market'. *Bureaux de change* exist all over town, with 24-hour 'Chequepoints'. Commission is high, and you should try to change your money at a bank, for a 1–2 per cent charge. Easiest of all is to use a credit or debit card in an ATM machine. Holders of MasterCard and Visa cards will probably be charged around 1.5 per cent commission, but the rates will be better than at a bank or *bureau de change*. Debit cards with a Maestro or Cirrus symbol can also be used in most ATMs, with a 2 per cent commission. Cash advances can also be obtained from banks and *bureaux de change* with your card, and major cards can now be used in all the swankier places, but are not accepted everywhere.

The four main Czech banks are Česka sporitelna, Československá obchodni banka (ČSOB), Komerčni banka and Živnostenská banka. Most major international banks are also represented. Banking hours are Mon–Fri 9–5.

Post

Correspondence can take anything from five days to two weeks to reach the UK or USA. There is an Express Service that does not cost much and can halve that time. Stamps (*známka*) can be bought from tobacconists and card shops, as well as post-office counters.

Working and Employment

Citizens of an EU country may be employed in or establish a business in the Czech Republic without having to apply for a work permit or residence permit. However, they must register with the Czech Republic authorities if their stay is to exceed 30 days. Although a temporary residence permit is not a condition of employment in the Czech Republic, it may be useful to obtain one for a number of secondary reasons. The temporary residence permit for the purpose of employment is valid for five years, and may be extended repeatedly.

A Model Example

The Czech Republic is home to one of the largest concentrations of internationally successful models in the world. Eva Herzigova was the first; her long legs, chiselled features and cat-like eyes shot her to fame in the early 1990s. Eva was born in the town of Litvinov to Czech parents; her mother was a secretary, her father an electrician. Striking blond Karolina Kurkova followed quickly in her footsteps and since then several model agencies from the UK have set themselves up in the capital hoping to spot the next big thing.

Education

Because of recent changes in the educational system, schools are no longer exclusively state-run, and there are a number of new **private schools**. Children begin school at the age of six, although they may attend **nursery** before that. After completing nine years of study, pupils can choose to continue their education at a **secondary school** for four years, at a **vocational school** for between two and four years, or through **apprenticeship** training. Most major cities in the Czech Republic have a **university**, many of which offer courses in English. There are also several private **international schools** offering accredited educational courses in English.

Health and Emergencies

Ambulance, **t** 155.

If you hold a British or Irish passport and carry an E111 or EHIC card, you're entitled to the same free emergency medical treatment as Czech citizens. You may have to pay for it upfront and get reimbursed later. E111s and EHIC cards are available from post offices in the UK. All foreigners entering the Czech Republic, however, must demonstrate proof of health insurance. The quality of medical care varies, but there are excellent facilities in Prague. For example, Na Homolce hospital has a foreigner's clinic, where English is spoken, at Roentgenova 2, Prague 5. Emergency numbers: **t** 5292 2043 children, **t** 5721 1111 adults.

Social Services and Welfare Benefits

Foreign employees of Czech companies are treated like Czech citizens in that they are required to pay Czech healthcare and social security contributions. The current rate is 12.5 per cent of their gross salary earned. In some rare instances this requirement does not apply, for example when a working contract falls under employment laws other than those of the Czech Republic.

Foreign employees working for a non-Czech company may also be required to pay local social security and healthcare contributions, depending on the specifics of the Social Security Agreement and EU policies governing social security. If a non-resident is employed by a non-Czech company and works in the Republic for fewer than 183 days, then social security and healthcare payments are usually not required.

Cars, Car Hire and Taxis

Driving in Prague is to be avoided because of potential parking problems, and anyway is not generally necessary. For travel outside the capital, car hire is readily available but you will need a valid driving licence. Most car-hire companies offer unlimited mileage. Local firms tend to offer much more reasonable fees, but make sure you check the small print.

If you intend to drive your own car to the Czech Republic, you should have:

- a valid passport.
- **your national driving licence as well as an international driving permit.**
- **the vehicle registration documents.**
- **insurance cover.**
- **a national identity sticker stuck to the rear of the vehicle.**
- **a first aid kit.**
- **two red warning triangles in case of breakdown.**
- **replacement bulbs for all lights.**

Speed limits are 60kph in towns and villages, 90kph on the main roads and 110kph on motorways, but be aware that the speed limit is reduced to 80kph on motorways in built-up areas. Seat belts are compulsory and children under 12 may not ride in the front passenger seat. Drink-driving is strictly prohibited and enforced with on-the-spot fines. An emergency road rescue service is available by calling t 154. Call t 158 to report any traffic accidents or injuries.

To drive on any motorway in the country, a motorway tax windscreen sticker is compulsory to show you have paid road tolls. The sticker costs around £30 and is valid for one year. Short-term permits are also available. Forms for stickers can be bought at border crossings, petrol stations, post offices and some shops.

Drivers of official taxis are allowed to decide on their own rates for trips from the city centre to the airport and within the city, so you negotiate prices before setting off on your journey. Higher charges are usually made for night services.

Crime and the Police

Crime has risen in recent years and there is some corruption within the police force. The main concerns for tourists are car theft and petty theft such as pickpocketing. In theory, everyone should carry some form of photo ID, which for most British residents means a passport.

Food and Drink

Eating out is relatively inexpensive and hot food is also available from pubs and wine bars. Most eating establishments are open 11–11. Breakfast is likely to consist of cereal or meat and bread. Soups are good and a common starter for lunch. Main dishes tend to be meat-based – often pork or beef and more rarely goose, duck and wild boar. Fish is less commonly available, with carp and trout the most popular types. Additions include dumplings, potatoes and sauerkraut. Desserts include filled pancakes and ice-cream.

> ## Good King Wenceslas
>
> Czech beer is legendary and drunk around the world, but nowhere with more enthusiasm than in Prague. According to some, the secret is that the country's agricultural conditions could not be more perfect for growing hops, which have been cultivated in the republic since the 1st century AD and exported just a few years later. Locals had what were in effect micro-breweries in their own home, until they formed co-operatives that would give them an extract to take home to brew – effectively a medieval home-brew kit. In the 13th century, King Wenceslas persuaded the Pope to end his ban on the brewing of beer and declared that anyone found leaving the country with hop cuttings would be sentenced to the death penalty. By the 16th century, the beer industry was providing as much as 88 per cent of the city coffers.
>
> Probably the two beers best known in the UK are Budweis, which comes from the unpronounceable České Budějovice in south Bohemia, and Pilsner, derived from the place name of the west Bohemian town of Plzeň. For a number of political reasons, Czech beer went into decline after the 16th century and did not fully recover until the 19th century, when country began to reinvent itself after a long period of decline and German influence.

Wines are drunk less frequently than the famous Czech beer, but there are some average-quality labels to be found. *Slivovice* is an incredibly strong plum brandy that should only be tried by the brave and strong-stomached. There is also a local herbal spirit called *Becherovka*, which is often taken as a medicine.

Traditionally, **coffee** is thick and black, but today filter coffee, cappuccino and latte are available in more popular tourist areas. Coffee and cake is an important ritual, particularly on Sundays. A snack might be a pancake or a 'hotdog' – a tinned frankfurter in a roll.

The Czech Republic: References

Directory of Contacts and Resources

Embassies

- **Embassy of the Czech Republic**, 26 Kensington Palace Gardens, London W8 4QY, **t** (020) 7243 1115, **www.czech.org.uk**, **www.czech.cz**.
- **British Embassy**, Thunovská 14, 118 00 Prague 1, **t** 257 530 278, **www.britain.cz**.

Information and Resources

- **Czech Republic Tourist Office**, 320 Regent Street, London W1B 3BG, UK, **t** (020) 7631 0427; **www.czechtourism.com**.

- **www.myczechrepublic.com**. Country information and destination guide.
- **www.czech.cz, articles**. With sections on working and studying.
- **www.czech-slovakia.travel-information.org**. Travel forum.
- **www.musica.cz**. Comprehensive online Czech music information centre.

Poperty Companies and Estate Agents

- **Apollo Real Estate Agency**, **t** 224 222 587 or **t** 603 560 000, **f** 224 222 641, info@apollosro.cz, **www.apollorec.cz**.

- **Continental Realty, s.r.o.**, Namesti Miru 15, 120 00 Prague 2, Vinohrady, Czech Republic, **t** 222 517 105, **f** 222 517 078, **realty@continental.cz**, **www.continental.cz**.

- **EHS, t** 257 328 281; **www.ehs.cz**.

- **Lexxus, t** 224 812 611; **www.lexxus.cz**.

- **www.praguerealestate.cz**. Site in English, prices in local currency.

- **www.pragueproperty.co.uk**. A British company based in London; it does not put properties on its website because it claims they are selling too fast.

Removal Companies

- **Westward Freight Ltd**, Leigh House, 7 Station Approach, Bexleyheath, Kent DA7 4QP, **t** (020) 8304 6388, **f** (020) 8301 6944, **info@westwardfreight.com**, **www.westwardfreight.com**.

Holiday Companies

- **www.pragueholiday.cz**. A range of accommodation in Prague.
- **www.iglu.com**. Ski and villa holidays in the Czech Republic.
- **www.barrheadtravel.co.uk/holiday-destinations/europe/ czech-republic**. 25 years of experience.

Administrative Departments

The Czech Republic consists of 13 regions for the purposes of administration: Prague (capital: Praha), Central Bohemian Region (capital: Praha), South Bohemian Region (capital: České Budějovice), Plzeň Region (capital: Plzeň), Carlsbad Region (capital: Karlovy Vary), Ústí nad Labem Region (capital: Ústí nad Labem), Liberec Region (capital: Liberec), Hradec Kralove Region (capital: Hradec Kralove), Pardubice Region (capital: Pardubice), Olomouc Region (capital: Olomouc), Moravian-Silesian Region (capital: Ostrava), Zlin Region (capital: Zlin), Vysocina Region (capital: Jihlava).

Public Holidays

1 January	New Year's Day
March/April	Easter
1 May	May Day
8 May	Liberation Day
5 July	Day of the Apostles St Cyril and St Methodius
6 July	Anniversary of the Martyrdom of Jan Hus
28 September	Czech Statehood Day
28 October	Independence Day
17 November	Freedom and Democracy Day
24–26 December	Christmas

Further Reading

Prague: A Traveler's Literary Companion, Paul Wilson – Prague has been the inspiration for a lot of great literature; this is an anthology of 23 Prague stories by authors such as Franz Kafka, Jan Neruda, and Ivan Klima.

The Trial, Franz Kafka – famous early 20th-century work by Prague's best-known author.

The Unbearable Lightness of Being, Milan Kundera – wonderfully readable account of modern 20th-century life and love.

The Spirit of Prague, Ivan Klima – essays charting five critical decades of Czech history: the Nazi occupation, the Stalinist regimes of the 1950s, the 1960s Prague Spring, the 1968 Soviet invasion, Charter 77 and the Velvet Revolution of 1989

Climate Charts

Average Daily Hours of Sunlight in Prague

Jan	Feb	Mar	April	May	June	July	Aug	Sept	Oct	Nov	Dec
2	3	5	6	8	9	8	8	6	4	2	1

Average Rainfall (Millimetres)

Jan	Feb	Mar	April	May	June	July	Aug	Sept	Oct	Nov	Dec
18	18	18	27	48	54	68	55	31	33	20	21

Estonia

12

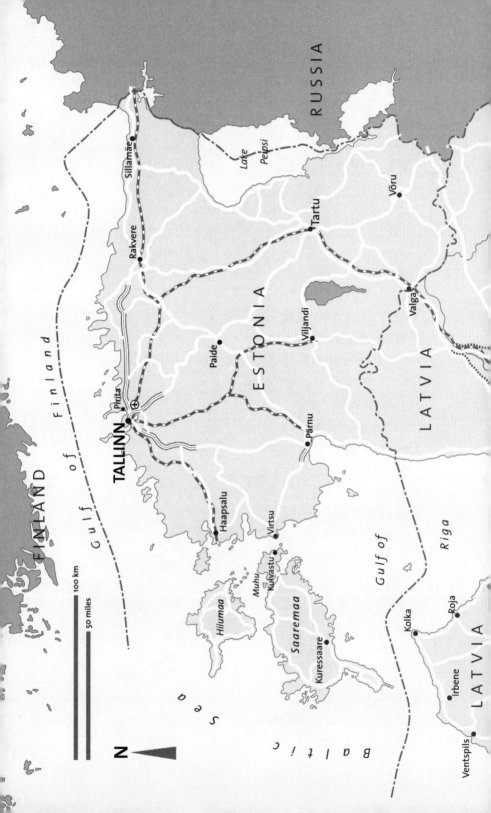

Why Buy in Estonia?

Estonia is a relatively small country. At just over 45,000 sq km it is roughly a fifth of the size of the United Kingdom and five times as large as Cyprus. It is the most northerly of the three Baltic states and the smallest of them. Tallinn, the capital city, has roots going back hundreds of years, and is a very attractive city in the Central European tradition.

There are two important driving forces behind the decision of investors to put their money in Estonia. First, the historic capital city of Tallinn is a gem; people believe that such rarities are likely to increase in value. Secondly, there is a general belief that with the recent entrance of the Baltic states into the European Union there will be increasing pressure on prices. Certainly there has been upward movement over the last couple of years: in 2003 prices increased about 12 per cent and in 2004 about 15 per cent.

This market should, however, be viewed with some caution. Most of the investment in Estonia seems speculative. That is to say, people are investing with the intention of selling on quickly at a profit, and there is some doubt as to who the final buyers will be.

Tourism and the Economy

Estonia, like the other Baltic states, is not ideally placed for trade. Estonia's economy depends largely on telecommunications and its main trading partners are in Scandinavia. It runs a substantial trade deficit of about 14 per cent of GDP. As a city aspiring to be a business destination, Tallinn seems likely only to be the base for trade within Estonia or the other Baltic states and for a certain amount of specialist tourism; there has been a steady increase in the number of tourists in Estonia since 2000. There is currently little reason to locate in Estonia in order to trade there.

The country's prime strength will become clearer when the Russian economy reactivates, but there seems little sign of that happening soon. When it does happen, there may well be businesses that would prefer to locate in the relative security of Estonia rather than in Moscow. In the meantime, there is depopulation, though this is less acute than in some of its Baltic neighbours: the country now has a population of about 1.4 million.

The GDP per capita is roughly half that of the UK, and roughly double that of countries such as Bulgaria or Turkey. As you would expect, the cost of living is considerably lower than in the UK, though, at least in Tallinn, more than half.

The Exchange Rate

The exchange rate in Estonia (*see* chart overleaf) has followed a typical pattern for an emerging market country and is slowly gaining ground.

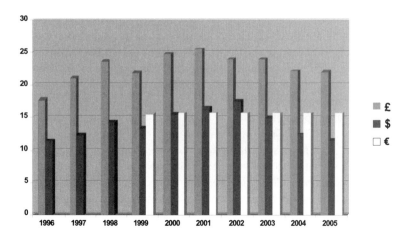

Exchange Rate - Estonian Kroon

Visas and Permits

As Estonia is a member of the European Union, any citizen of a member state can enter the country without a visa for up to **90 days** in the same way as they can enter, say, France or Spain.

After 90 days you need to obtain a **residence document**. This is a relatively painless procedure. After you have held a residence document for three years you can apply for **permanent residence**, subject to certain qualifications.

Profile of Estonia

Recent History and Politics

Over the centuries Estonia's brief periods of independence have been dwarfed by domination by other countries including Denmark, Sweden, Germany and most recently Russia. After the collapse of the Soviet Union, in 1991 Estonia became an independent parliamentary republic in 1991. It has proved keen to embrace the West, and in May 2004 joined NATO and the European Union. EU membership will change this former Soviet state rapidly, with large-scale EU investment improving the infrastructure, and mortgage finance becoming increasingly available to locals, causing prices to shoot up.

Climate and Geography

Estonia has a coastline of over 3,700km and more than 1,500 islands. Within the country are 1,400 large and small lakes. It has the largest proportion of marshes of any country in Europe but nearly 50 per cent of its area is covered by wooded hills and forests. As you would expect from its extreme northerly location, the climate in Estonia is hardly tropical, *see* 'Climate Charts', p.232. From October to March the country is generally very cold and dark, though winter can be lovely around Christmas and January.

During the Soviet era, like many of its neighbours, Estonia suffered from high levels of industrial pollution but this has been reducing sharply.

Regional Profile

The country's capital city is charming medieval cobbled **Tallinn**, home to more than a third of the country's inhabitants. The very best restaurants charge £15 at most; superb opera and ballet costs around £6 a ticket; woodland boasting wolves, bears and elks, and unspoilt beaches, are a ten-minute drive away on the Gulf of Finland. Helsinki in Finland is a boat trip away and St Petersburg a few hours away by car.

The next largest city is **Tartu**, with a population of 150,000, 185km (115 miles) south of Tallinn in the centre of southern Estonia. The Emajõgi river, which connects the two largest lakes of Estonia, Peipsi and Võrtsjärv, flows through its city limits. Another pleasant city is Estonia's 'summer capital', **Pärnu**, long renowned as a spa town by the sea, crisscrossed with lush, tree-lined parks, with a long stretch of white sand beach and a picturesque 17th-century town centre, and a thriving spa industry dating back to the late 19th century.

Selecting a Property

Getting There

Tallinn is served by air by **Estonian Air**, **Air Baltic**, **British Airways** and **easyJet**. A direct return ticket from London for June 2005 is quoted at £283 by Estonian Air. Single tickets are available on easyJet for about £50.

Getting Around

Within the Baltic States, the rail system is sadly out of date, especially in Estonia where domestic rail services suffer from damage to the infrastructure. Buses are faster, cheaper and more frequent than trains. Vehicles are fairly comfortable, and streets and highways are being improved constantly. In Estonia, international bus lines connect Tallinn to Germany, Poland, Kaliningrad, Riga, St Petersburg and Vilnius. For those making ferry-to-bus connections, most Riga- and Vilnius-bound Eurolines buses, **t** 680 0909, **www.eurolines.ee**, stop right at the passenger port before leaving Tallinn. It is advisable to buy all tickets in advance.

For full up-to-date arrival and departure timetables for Baltic ferries, planes, trains and buses, *see* **www.balticsworldwide.com**.

Choosing a Location

Very few foreigners are buying outside Tallinn. Leafy Kadriorg is a pleasant suburb with cheaper prices.

Property Types and Prices

Despite Estonia's small size, there is a wide variety of property types, from city apartment blocks to tall merchant's houses, several thousand manor houses built in the pre-Soviet era, wooden homes in the forests and chalets by the sea. There is a wide range of prices and on the whole you get what you pay for. Prices have been rising rapidly – some purchasers have seen growth of over 20 per cent in the last year. Some sample prices as at January 2005 are:

- **One-bedroom apartment in suburbs in Tallinn, about 10 years old, £30,000.**
- **Three-bedroom house with garden in Tallinn, £37,000.**
- **Two-bedroom traditional terraced house in Tallinn, £42,000.**

The Process of Buying a Property

Freedom to Buy

There are generally no special requirements for foreigners wishing to buy real estate in Estonia, but there are two exceptions to this.

The first is the purchase of either agricultural or forestry land over 10ha. In both these cases for the next few years there are going to remain a number of restrictions, despite Estonia's entry into the European Union. Agricultural or forest land can only be bought by foreigners who have been resident in Estonia for a number of years and who are themselves engaged in agriculture.

The second exception relates to coastal properties, where there are a variety of potential restrictions to trap the unwary.

Initial Steps

First Contracts

Once you have found a property that you want to purchase, you will be expected to sign some form of contract. This will generally either be a reservation contract or a preliminary purchase contract. *See* 'Reservation and Preliminary Contracts', p.75, for an explanation of these concepts. Note that the title preliminary purchase contract is misleading – it is actually a full binding purchase contract. We recommend that, wherever possible, you insist on signing a **reservation contract** rather than a preliminary purchase contract at this stage.

Searches and Enquiries

Once you have signed a reservation contract, your lawyer should make the standard enquiries to check that the contract is fair, that the seller has good title and the right to sell to you, that the area is zoned for residential building and that any building work being undertaken enjoys all necessary planning and building consents. Depending on the circumstances of your case there could well be other enquiries that also need to be made.

In Estonia it is common for work to be started illegally before all of these steps are in place. It is also common for property to have a defective title. Sometimes these problems should put you off being involved in the purchase. On other occasions, the risks are minimal and, provided you go into the transaction with your eyes open, might not put you off buying if you like the property.

Possible Dangers

The main problem associated with buying property in Estonia is the fact that so few people have done it. This inevitably means that the procedures – while relatively straightforward – are applied somewhat variably. Although this tends to be more of an aggravation than a danger, it can make the whole process more time-consuming and frustrating than would be the case elsewhere.

Signing the Contract and Registering the Title

Once your lawyer has checked out the property and found that everything is in order, you are ready to sign the **preliminary purchase contract**. This commits you and the seller to signing the full contract transferring ownership shortly afterwards or, if the property is still under construction, once the property has been built.

The preliminary purchase contract contains most of the clauses you would expect to see in a UK contract. These include a description of the property, a statement of the legal title to the property, the price to be paid, how it is to be paid, the deadline for any deadlines, and what should happen in the event of breach of contract. Many Estonian contracts are badly drafted by UK standards because there is no history in Estonia of drafting contracts for the sale of land. The problem is exacerbated by the fact that many contracts are drafted in

English and are unclear or muddled. Specifications tend to be thin and the contracts lack detail about what happens if anything goes wrong.

At this point you will normally pay a **deposit** of 10 per cent of the price of the property or start to make **stage payments** for off-plan properties, which vary in size and number from property to property. A typical scheme provides for an initial payment of 30 per cent followed by two further payments of 30 per cent as construction progresses, followed by a final payment of 10 per cent on delivery. Occasionally there are schemes where there is only one preliminary payment of, say, 30 per cent with the balance being paid on delivery. This is useful if you are taking out a mortgage.

Once you are ready to take delivery of the property you will sign the **final purchase contract** in front of a notary public. It is at this point that the balance of the money is paid to the notary, who will release it to the seller once the property transfer has taken place. You do not need to be present in Estonia to sign this document, as your lawyer can prepare a **power of attorney** (*see* pp.77–8) under which you can appoint somebody else to sign on your behalf. This is a sensible thing to do, as it saves the need for you to go to Estonia, often at short notice, to sign the final title.

Once you have paid the balance of the price the seller will authorise you to **register your ownership** of the property in the local title register. Once this has been done, you – or the local Estonian company that you have set up to own the property – will be the full legal owner of the property in much the same way as you would be in the UK.

The Expenses of Buying

The main expenses of buying are:

- tax – the equivalent of stamp duty – 0.075 per cent of the price.

- estate agents' fees, if these are not paid by the seller – typically 5 per cent of the price if you are using a local Estonian agent.

- notary's fees – these will vary from case to case but will typically not exceed 1 per cent.

- legal fees – these depend on whether you use a Estonian or an English lawyer; English lawyer's fees will inevitably be higher but you will be able to sue them if they get it wrong and they will be able to give you lots of advice, particularly about the vital issues of who should own the property to minimise your tax and other problems, which the local Estonian lawyer would not be able to help you with; they will range from about £350 if you use a local Estonian lawyer to £1,500 if you use a specialist English lawyer.

- fees to set up a company if you set up a Estonian company; this is likely to cost £500.

Letting Your Property

See the general chapter **Letting Your Property**, pp.117–26. If you are letting your property you should make sure that you use a proper **rental contract**. Your lawyer will be able to supply you with a draft that you can amend as necessary.

Rental yields in Estonia are reasonable. Generally there should be a rental yield (net of all expenses apart from your finance costs and personal taxation) of about 4–5 per cent. In the longer term, demand and supply are both likely to increase, which could cancel each other out and leave yields more or less as they stand today. However, this may change with the rapidly rising price of property. When calculating your rental yield, work it out on the basis of current value, not purchase value, as that will allow you to compare the performance of your investment with opportunities elsewhere.

Taxes

Taxes for Non-resident Property-owners

Local Property Taxes

Local property taxes in Estonia are very low.

Income and Capital Gains Taxes

Private individuals and corporations pay tax at 24 per cent of their relevant income. Only income arising in Estonia is taxed for non-residents. This includes the income from any property in Estonia.

Capital Gains Taxes

These are treated as part of your income.

Wealth Taxes and Inheritance Taxes

There are no wealth taxes, general inheritance or gift taxes in Estonia.

Taxes for Resident Foreigners

This is beyond the scope of this book.

Settling In

Learning and Speaking Estonian

Although the common language spoken is Estonian, Russian is also widely spoken – particularly in the northern part of the country where there are many ex-Russian settlers. English is also spoken by many people in Tallinn.

Shopping

Shops are generally open from 9/10–6/7 on weekdays, and from 9/10–4 on Saturdays. Larger department stores are open daily 10–8, while food shops and supermarkets open 8am–10pm during the week, with some open on Sunday. Shops in rural areas often close for a lunch break and closer earlier in the evening. Most larger stores accept Visa, Mastercard and Eurocard.

Telephones and the Internet

All Estonian phone numbers are 7 digits and there are no area codes; to call from abroad, dial 00, then the **country code (t** 372) and then the number. Within Estonia, you can make local and international calls from card-operated public pay phones. **Telephone cards** costing 30, 50 and 100EEK are sold at news stands (kiosks), post offices, the tourist information centre and most hotels.

Mobile phones can also be rented at local phone shops. If you have a GSM 900/1800, and a phone that is not locked to a network, you can purchase a SIM card package from a local provider.

There are more and more **Internet** cafés opening up in larger cities as well as small towns, as well as small towns. You can get online at tourist offices, libraries, post offices and shopping centres.

Money and Banking

The currency is the **Kroon** (EEK; rhymes with tone; plural krooni), which is pegged to the euro. The kroon is divided into 100 sents. Notes come in denominations of 2, 5, 10, 25, 50, 200 and 500kr. 5kr coins are rare, but are often required in public lockers at train stations, for instance. 1kr coins are in common use, as are the nearly worthless 10, 20 and 50 sent coins. The switch to the euro is planned for 2007–8.

Estonian **banks** such as Sampo, Hansapank and Ühispank have branches in most towns and change cash for a small commission, as well as providing cash advances on most major credit cards. Exchange offices (*valuuta vahetus*) are found in the larger towns near the bus station and city centre. They are usually open longer hours as well as on Sundays, often with lower commission rates than banks. Banks are generally open Mon–Fri 9/10–4/5, and some banks in larger cities are often open on Saturday from 10–2 or 3.

There are **ATMs** all around larger towns. Major **credit cards** can be used in all of the bigger hotels, restaurants, department stores and shops, but don't count on using them at petrol stations outside larger cities, which often take cash only.

Health

Ambulance: **t** 112.

There are some improving private facilities catering to foreigners, and EU members are entitled to **emergency** treatment with an E111 or EHIC card, but if you have a serious medical problem, you might consider leaving the country. Take out good private insurance. If you will be travelling in wooded or coastal areas, immunisation against tick-borne encephalitis is highly recommended.

Although the **tap water** in the Baltics is said to be drinkable, it's safer to stick with bottled water. **Pharmacies** (*apteek*) are usually open 10–7, but in the city some stay open all night.

Crime and the Police

Police: **t** 110 or **t** 112.

Tallinn is not any more dangerous than any other European capital, but foreigners have been known to be targeted. The most common problems are pick-pocketing and car break-ins. It is best, as anywhere, to avoid wandering into unfamiliar streets alone after dark, and be careful who you drink with and how much you consume! Be discreet when using your mobile phone.

Estonia: References

Directory of Contacts and Resources

Embassies

- **Estonian Embassy**, 16 Hyde Park Gate, London SW7 5DG, UK, **t** (020) 7589 3428; **www.estonia.gov.uk**.

- **British Embassy**, Wismari tänav 6, **t** 667 4700, **f** 667 4755, **information@ britishembassy.ee**, **www.britishembassy.ee**.

Information and Resources

- **www.visitestonia.com**. Information on the country.

Property Companies and Estate Agents

- **Ober Haus**, **t** 665 9700, **www.ober-haus.ee**.
- **Raid and Co.**, **t** 627 2080, **www.raid.ee**.
- **Rime Real Estate**, **t** 683 7777, **www.rime.ee**.

Removal Companies

- **1st Move International Removals Ltd**, International House, Unit 5B Worthy Rd, Chittening Industrial Estate, Avonmouth, Bristol BS11 0YB, **t** (0117) 982 8123, **f** (0117) 982 2229, **info@shipit.co.uk**, **www.shipit.co.uk**.

Time

Estonia is on Eastern European Time (GMT/UTC + 2). The 24hr clock is used for flight, train and bus timetables. In summer, the country follows daylight saving, putting clocks forward an hour in spring and back in autumn.

Public Holidays

1 January	New Year's Day
24 February	Independence Day 1918
March or April	Good Friday, Easter Sunday
1 May	May Day
23 June	Victory Day
24 June	St John's Day or Midsummer's Day
20 August	Day of Restoration of Independence 1991
25–6 Dec	Christmas

Climate Charts

Average Maximum Temperatures in Tallinn (°C)

Jan	Feb	Mar	April	May	June	July	Aug	Sept	Oct	Nov	Dec
−4	−4	0	6	13	18	20	18	15	10	3	−1

Average Minimum Temperature in Tallinn (°C)

Jan	Feb	Mar	April	May	June	July	Aug	Sept	Oct	Nov	Dec
−10	−12	−7	0	5	10	12	11	8	4	−1	−7

Average Monthly Rainfall in Tallinn (mm)

Jan	Feb	Mar	April	May	June	July	Aug	Sept	Oct	Nov	Dec
30	30	−20	32	42	40	66	78	70	64	56	38

Average Daily Hours of Sunshine in Estonia

Jan	Feb	Mar	April	May	June	July	Aug	Sept	Oct	Nov	Dec
1	2	4	6	7	10	11	8	5	2	1	0

Hungary

Why Buy in Hungary?

Landlocked Hungary is encircled by its many neighbours – Slovakia, Ukraine, Romania, Serb, Croatia, Slovenia and Austria – and sliced down the middle by the not so blue Danube. The landscape is a mass of rolling plains dotted with lakes. The country has a deep respect for its traditions; despite welcoming membership of the EU with open arms, the people are very much allied to their heritage, and a sensibility that is is one of romance and intellectuality with a strong sense of patriotism. There is a rich tradition of music, particularly folk music using lutes and violins. The redevelopment of 16 castles over the next five years is an important and symbolic gesture. Hungary's national parks are fiercely protected, with more than 2,000 flowering plants, as well as wild deer, hare and boar, and a large number of birds. Its people are proud of the *puszta*, the vast Hungarian grasslands, the firewater brandy known as *pálinka*, and the *csárda*, a characteristically Hungarian country inn and the Hungarians' lively national dance, the *csárdás*.

In many ways, it has therefore been hard for Hungarians to witness the influx of people from other countries. Eva Ferenczi is a 23-year-old who has lived in Budapest all her life. She works in an Irish bar popular with tourists and foreign investors, which has sausage and chips on the menu and English football on the television. Irish men drink Guinness at the bar and in the corner are a stack of *Property Watch* magazines advising English-speaking visitors about where to buy. Eva says people often come to the bar with maps asking her advice about the best places to buy property. 'It's a kind of invasion, and these people are

> *Rural Retreats*
> Hungary has a long tradition of rural living. A large number of natives choose to live in the peace of the countryside and make the commute to the cities to earn their daily crust. Over 50 per cent of Hungary's population takes part in extra-curricular farming as well as their regular work.

buying places at the click of their fingers which I will never be able to afford in my lifetime.'

The Economy and Tourism

The country's economic stance is perhaps the strongest in Central and Eastern Europe. Of all the former Communist countries, Hungary has always been the most Western in its thinking, even if its progress towards market economics since 1989 has been more gradual than in Poland or the Czech Republic. Although Hungary experienced escalating inflation and crippling unemployment in the early 1990s, this difficult chapter of its economic history appears to be over and it is currently enjoying high foreign investment from America, Asia and Europe. Tourism has always been high – the country receives over 14 million foreign visitors annually, nearly as many as Austria – and is gradually increasing.

The Exchange Rate

One of the key indicators of any country where investment is likely to prove successful is either a stable exchange rate against other major currencies or a rate that is slowly improving against other major currencies. A common pattern for emerging market countries is that when they first get their independence

Exchange Rate – Hungarian Forint

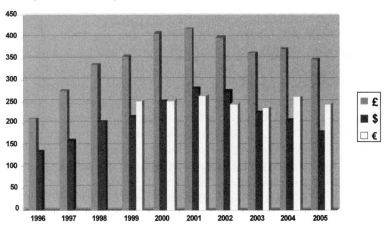

High-flying Hungarians

• **László József Bíró** (1899–1985): the inventor of the ballpoint pen. As a journalist he found that ink could be applied to paper by a pipe and a ball.

• **Ernő Rubik** (1944–): the creator of the infuriating, once ubiquitous Rubik's cube; he is believed to own weekend property near Lake Balaton.

• **Joseph Pulitzer** (1847–1911): became an American newspaper man and journalist. The Pulitzer Prizes, first awarded in 1917, were provisions in his will.

• **Harry Houdini** (1874–1926): the stage name of Ehrich Weiss, one of the most famous magicians and escapologists of all time.

• **Zsa Zsa Gabor** (1917–): known less for her acting than for her love of expensive jewellery and serial matrimony.

• **Dennis Gabor** (1900–79): an electrical engineer who won the Nobel Prize for Physics in 1971 for his invention of holography.

• **William Fox** (1879–1952): the founder of Fox Film Corporation, now 20th Century Fox, which he set up in 1915.

• **Count Istvan Szechenyi** (1791–1860): a writer, statesman and reformer who is considered one of the great Hungarians.

the exchange rate sinks rapidly, then it improves slowly and then stabilises or, if the country is doing well, slowly gains ground. If the exchange rate is rising against the pound or the dollar the effect is that, in addition to benefiting from any increase in the value of the property you have bought, you also benefit from the increase in value of the currency. The reverse is, of course, also true.

Visas and Permits

UK and EU visitors to Hungary can visit without any type of visa for up to **90 days**. They can only do this once in any six-month period. If you wish to visit for longer than 90 days or more often than once every six months you can obtain a visa from the Hungarian consulate in the country where you live. You can download an application form from **www.hungarianembassy.org.uk**.

There are two sorts of **residence permit**, both of which are pretty easy to obtain after a certain amount of paperwork. The first permit is a **temporary permit** that lasts for one year. In order to obtain such a permit you need to obtain a visa from the Hungarian consulate in your country of residence before you travel to Hungary. You need to show proof of health insurance and that you have sufficient funds to support yourself in Hungary, which generally requires you to demonstrate that you have about £1,000 deposited in a Hungarian bank. This permit can be renewed annually. After five years it can be converted into a **permanent residence permit**.

To apply for Hungarian **citizenship** you must have:

- been resident in Hungary for eight years preceding the application.
- a clean criminal record.
- proof of income in the country.
- passed an examination in Hungary in basic constitutional knowledge.

Profile of Hungary

Rcent History and Politics

Hungary was under Communist rule from 1948 until 1988, when demonstrations brought about the fall of the old Communist regime. The Hungarian Republic was declared in 1989 and in 1990 the first democratic parliamentary elections were held. When the old Soviet-style economy disintegrated in the late 1980s, it pulled the Hungarian Socialist Party down with it. Hard-line leaders were dismissed in 1988, a multi-party system was introduced in October 1989, and Hungary's first free elections in more than 40 years were held in 1990. Free elections do not automatically solve all social problems, of course, and unemployment and inflation have continued. However, Hungary's economic growth is the second-highest in the former Soviet Bloc nations. The country became part of NATO in 1999, and joined the EU in 2004.

Religion

The population is 68 per cent Roman Catholic, 21 per cent Reformed (Calvinist) Protestant, 6 per cent Evangelical (Lutheran), 5 per cent other, including Jews.

A Haunting History

Hungary currently has Eastern Europe's largest Jewish population, of 60,000–100,000. In April 2004, the first Holocaust museum in Central Europe opened in Budapest on the 60th anniversary of the day Hungary's pro-Nazi regime started rounding up Jews. An estimated 600,000 Hungarians perished in the Holocaust, most of them Jews. In 1944 more than 437,000 Jews were deported to Nazi death camps in less than two months.

In the courtyard is a haunting memorial wall featuring 40,000 names of those who died in the Holocaust, which is being added to all the time. Historians have criticised the building, claiming that it should have been built in the countryside where most of the Jews lived in pre-war times, or in the former area of the ghetto in the capital. But the museum is impressive, and chillingly portrays this chapter in history with audio-visual displays and filmed testaments from the victims.

> ## Lost Property
> It was only in 1989 that Communism was overthrown. During that period, it was the Hungarian way to work on large farming co-operatives and in factories in return for a small wage and housing, and a great deal of private property was confiscated by the state. Thanks to a law in 1991 people were finally given some compensation for their 'lost property'.

Climate and Geography

Hungary is flat as a pancake; rolling plains cover almost the whole of the country, with low mountains on the Slovakian border to the north. The country is divided by two rivers, the Danube, which cuts the country in half east and west, and the Tisza, which further divides the eastern half. The Great Plain, with its grassland and horses, lies to the east of the Danube and covers almost half the country. The Little Plain runs along the country's northwestern border. West of the Danube is the Transdanubia, which has more varied geography, with mountains in the south and smaller plains in the northwest, with Lake Balaton is in its centre.

Temperatures in summer and winter vary widely; spring and summer can be wet and snow often falls in winter when the Danube freezes over, although the climate is generally dry. The 'shoulder' months of May/June and September are the perfect time, because of the weather and relatively fewer crowds, although the weather can be decidedly 'cool' during this time. *See* 'Climate Charts', p.262.

Regional Profile

Budapest

In many ways, Budapest *is* Hungary. In the dead centre of the country, the capital is physically and psychologically its navel. You will hear that the city is 'The Paris of the East' and for once this is not some shallow cliché; Budapest, although smaller than Paris, is a city of sophisticated beauty. Like an old queen who has survived historical and personal turmoil, watching her family fight with outsiders for the control of Central Europe's main waterway, Budapest has aged gracefully.

Potentially schizophrenic, the capital is made up of its twin sisters (Budapest is undeniably feminine): Buda and Pest. In 1873 the three cities of Óbuda, Buda and Pest joined to form what we now know as Budapest. The gracious and mighty Danube divides the two, which are linked by nine connecting bridges. Buda is hilly and to the west. Despite being almost completely destroyed during the Second World War, it retains its narrow cobbled streets and a combination of medieval and neoclassical buildings. Pest is to the east, a wonderful melting

The Buda Tunnel: A Labyrinth of Legends

There are all kinds of stories associated with the Buda Tunnel, which seems to fire people's imaginations. According to some theories there are ventilation drains behind the grids, while others insist there is an undiscovered secret system of tunnels built by the German occupation army in the Second World War. The tunnels were used for military operations during the Cold War, but they were formed by nature: water seeping into the limestone of the Buda Hills created these caves, which the original inhabitants of Buda dug out to create the labyrinth which still exists.

Today, tourists come to gaze at the permanent exhibitions in the caves. The Palaeolithic Labyrinth shows copies of the most famous cave paintings in Europe. The Historical Labyrinth presents an overview of the history of Hungarians from the great migrations to the middle ages. The Labyrinth of the Other World is a display of articles from an imaginary civilisation.

pot of styles testament to its Venetian, Turkish and Art Nouveau influences. Largely laid out during the 19th century along the lines of Paris, with *arrondissiments*, *grands boulevards* and straight avenues, it has always been a business and entertainment centre, featuring parliament, theatres and opera houses.

Budapest is set for huge changes over the next ten years as major plans for redevelopment and the building of new Danube bridges take shape. Former industrial areas such as Váci út on the city's outskirts have already been transformed into a sought-after shopping and commercial district. Another scheme is planned to create thousands of flats in Foka harbour, while the redevelopment of unused fields on northern Csepel sziget looks set to take place. New four- and five-star hotels will be completed in 2005 and 2006.

The Danube Bend

A trio of historic towns where the Danube snakes northwards from Budapest are all within an hour from Budapest and easily accessible by public transport.

Hungry for Facts? Four of the Biggest and Best

• The Danube is the second-longest river in Europe. It flows through Germany, Austria, Slovakia, Hungary, Croatia, Serbia, Romania, Bulgaria, Moldavia and the Ukraine.

• Hungary's highest point is Mount Kekes in the Matra Mountains.

• Lake Balaton is not just Hungary's largest lake, but the largest in Central Europe.

• Hungary is the fifth most important producer of thermal waters in the world, after New Zealand, Japan, Italy and Iceland.

Szentendre (St Andrew) can be reached in summer by boat when it swarms with daytrippers from the capital. The town has orthodox churches, museums and opportunities for cycling and canoeing.

Visegrad has a citadel and castle built by the Hungarian kings after the 13th-century Mogul invasion.

Esztergom was the country's capital for nearly 250 years. It was the seat of Roman Catholicism for a millennium and was where Marcus Aurelius wrote his famous *Meditations* as a Roman emperor in waiting in the 2nd century.

Lake Balaton

Bounded by the Danube and the Alps, the milky green, waist-deep waters of Lake Balaton form an expanse 50 miles long by 10 miles wide, the largest lake in Europe. This is 'Hungary's Sea', and it holds an almost mythic status in the hearts of Hungarians. As one of Europe's largest freshwater lakes, this is what parks are to Londoners, and the sea to Australians – a place of recreation but also somewhere to cling to for sanity. Hungarians sunbathe, horse-ride, sail, walk and relax in the many thermal pools, but most of all Lake Balaton is a place to breathe.

There has long been a history of holidaying here, beginning with the Romans. In the 18th century, the wealthy built villas and the nobility of the Austro-Hungarian Empire came to escape from Vienna, 180km away. Then came the Communists; the palaces were taken over by the Party and the lake became hideously polluted. It has been less than twenty years since the fall of Communism, but it didn't take long for the aristocratic families to repossess the historic buildings and for the Germans, Austrians and even the Dutch to move in. Needless to say, there are few real bargains to be had here, and prices have shot up in recent years. However, a fair number of Germans have sold up as the recession in Germany takes hold, which has revived the market.

Balatonfured is one of the major resorts on the lake, with a long tradition of sailing and 'taking to the waters'. The first yacht association in the country was established in Balatonfured, and it attracted members of the upper classes who built their villas here in the 19th century. **Keszthely** is the oldest settlement, which was an important commercial centre in Roman times: it features mansions, châteaux, the remnants of a fortress and several museums.

The North–South Divide

There is a north–south divide at Lake Balaton to rival London's. The north shore is the upmarket part, reaching its zenith at the stunning Tihany peninsula (which, incidentally is a national park and therefore cannot be purchased by foreigners). The south shore, especially round Siofok, is brasher and cheaper. While the north shore is sedate, the south is the centre for hedonism, with its rash of hotels built in the 1970s.

Western Transdanubia

Northwest of Lake Balaton, Western Transdanubia is a sandwiched between the watery Danube and the snowy Alps, dotted with charming small towns. **Gyor** was a Roman town where the splendid houses of its prosperous residents still stand, along with its enormous Baroque City Hall, cathedral and bishop's castle; it is a joy to wander around the town's pedestrianised winding streets. On the outskirts, standing sentinel on a hill, is the working monastery of Pannonhalma Abbey, which is now a World Heritage Site. In terms of historic buildings, though, **Sopron** beats Gyor. Sitting out of the way on the Austrian border, it escaped the Turks and Mongols, so that most of its medieval architecture remains intact.

Southern Transdanubia

Pécs is a 2,000-year-old city at the foot of Mount Mecsek, with flea markets, charming houses and nearby hiking. Christian churches, domed Turkish mosques and Roman tombs are some of the remnants of its rich past. More modern attractions are art galleries, museums and an exhibition of natural sciences. **Szekszárd** is small town circled by seven hills where Ferenc (Franz) Liszt composed a number of well known works. There is a House of Arts in a former synagogue and the town is famous for its production of the red wine of the same name. A wine route from Villany takes visitors to eight centres of wine production, with tastings on the way.

Lake Tisza

Lying in the centre of the Great Plain, Lake Tisza is an important centre for recreation, with camping, watersports and open-air baths. The whole area forms a nature reserve. **Karcag** is a market town renowned for its pottery, lace-makers and folk artists, and a museum displays these rich traditions. **Tiszafured** is one of the most popular areas for recreation on the lake. Small boats ply the backwater of the river, and visitors relax on the sands of the river beach and in the waters of the thermal baths

Northern Hungary

Eger, a thousand-year-old episcopal seat full of Baroque history, boasts the second-largest church in country as well as a museum of astronomy, a castle and synagogue. **Bukk National Park** is to the north of the city, offering riding and walking in a protected area. For Hungarians, it is perhaps best loved as the home of Bull's Blood, a full-bodied, even fiery red wine, which can be tasted and bought in one of the many cellars.

Another tiny town with a big reputation for its wine is **Tokaj**. It is one of 28 towns and villages known as Tokaj-Hegyalja, which was made a World Heritage

Site in 2002. This wine region in the north of the country is home to the country's highest mountain, and its smallest village. French king Louis XIV called Tokaj the 'wine of kings and the king of wines' but not everyone finds the sweet, sherry-like product to their taste.

Northern Great Plain

This enormous area of flatlands borders the Ukraine and Romania. **Debrecen** is the third largest city in Hungary in the heart of the Tisza region, the birthplace of Hungarian Protestantism and the centre for education – with a number of universities, colleges and professional schools. **Hortobagy** is a large, protected area where Hungarian stud horses, prized cattle and buffalo graze in open pastures. The **Hortobagy National Park** is a World Heritage Site and distinctly pastural area, with a shepherd museum, an animal park and a rich tradition of folk art. **Nyiregyhaza** is a sedate town dotted with flower-filled squares; it has an Art Nouveau palace and houses covered in Art Nouveau mosaics, and a health resort just outside the town.

Southern Great Plain

This is prairie country crossed by the River Tisza. The port town of **Baja** was once wealthy and still has highly decorated buildings. Locals go to the nearby island of **Sugovica** to relax, and feast on the local delicacy of fish soup. Another

Turkish Delight

Hungary's very own Center Parc was built in the summer of 2003 at a cost of nearly US$10 million. Debrecen, the country's third-largest city, is home to the first indoor thermal water park. In typical scenes, children splash and scream in the pools and water slides underneath a 99,000 sq ft glass dome, which also covers whirlpool baths and an underground water cave.

But this culture is not new to the country. Hungary's thermal water culture, where its natives have cleansed themselves and relaxed in the minerals of the thermal waters in the belief that it benefits muscles, skin and nervous system, spans two millennia. Many drink the thermal water to ease gastric and respiratory problems. The Romans were the first to capitalise on Hungary's thermal waters in the 1st century AD, when they built baths on the banks of the Danube; others were built by the Turks in the late 16th century.

Today, there are more than a hundred spas and bathhouses across Hungary, though many of them are badly in need of major renovation. Over the past two years, the country has spent about US$118 million on spa development, including a US$39.1 million spa complex in the northern wine region of Egerszalok. In 2004 an Aqua Park, claimed to be Central Europe's biggest, was opened at Zalaegerszeg and has already had 250,000 visitors.

village famous for its local dish is **Bekescsaba**, from where the tasty Csaba sausage takes its name. A large number of Slovaks live here, and there is a Slovak museum. Famous food features again in **Gyula**, a peaceful town of rose gardens and a 15th-century Gothic castle. The pastry shop and tea room called Hundred Year Old Confectionery is actually nearly 170 years old; it also acts as a small museum. The town also has a sausage, known as the Gyula sausage. These are just some of the villages that make up the area of the Southern Great Plain.

Selecting a Property

Getting There

By Air

Most people will arrive in Budapest, at one of the two terminals of Ferihegy airport, which is around 28km from the city centre.

- **easyJet (www.easyjet.com)** flies daily to Budapest from a number of European cities, including Luton, Gatwick and Heathrow airport in London and Newcastle. Their prices are among the most competitive, as well as offering an efficient service and some of the most frequent flights to the capital.

- **Malev Hungarian Airlines (www.malev.hu)** flies direct to Budapest from the UK (daily from Heathrow and twice daily from Stansted) and from most cities in Continental Europe.

- **Wizz Air (www.wizzair.com)** operates flights from London's Luton airport to Budapest.

- **Air Berlin (www.airberlin.com)** flies to Budapest from a number of European airports, including Stansted in London.

- **Sky Europe (www.skyeurope.com)** was the first low-cost airline to fly from the UK to Budapest and currently operates from London Stansted and other European airports to Budapest.

- **British Airways (t 0870 850 9850, www.ba.com)** flies to Budapest twice daily from Heathrow and daily from Gatwick from £98.60 including taxes, plus £15 if tickets are booked by phone.

By Train

The state railway is **Magyar Allamvasutak (www.mav.hu)**, which offers direct rail links between Hungary and 16 European cities along with around 50 international trains daily to Budapest. If travelling from London, you can choose to take a route either via Paris or Brussels.

> ## *Building Bridges*
> Across the Danube from Esztergom is the Slovak town of Sturovo, once linked by the Mária Valéria Bridge, which was blown up the Germans in the Second World War. Until recently, all that remained was a curious stump, along with four unconnected pylons in the river. Many locals on both sides of the river campaigned for its reconstruction because travel between the two countries is mostly by boat. The campaign was helped along by the friendship between the Hungarian prime minister and the Slovakian president and in 2001 it was finally rebuilt. The new bridge is symbolic not only because it was the last one on the Danube destroyed by the Germans to be reconstructed, but because the relationship between the two countries has not always been easy.

By Bus

International buses are mostly run by **Eurolines** (**www.eurolines.com** or **www.gobycoach.com**) or its Hungarian partner, **Volánbusz Rt** (**www.volanbusz.hu**). They operate services from London's Victoria Station (26 hours) most days a week, as well as other major European cities, such as Amsterdam, Berlin and Paris. It is also possible to travel by bus to and from most of Hungary's neighbours – most services start from Budapest.

By Road

Eurotunel (**www.eurotunnel.co.uk**) runs daily train through the Channel Tunnel between Folkestone in Kent (with direct access from the M20) and Calais in France. All vehicles from motorcycles to campers can be accommodated. Eurotunnel operates 3–4 passenger trains per hour at peak times. The journey takes approximately 35 minutes. There are plans to open four new motorways to connect Hungary with neighbouring countries; the M3 to Ukraine and Slovakia is nearly complete, and the M4 to Romania and M5 to Yugoslavia and M7 to Croatia are under construction.

By River

For an unusual alternative to road or rail, you might consider taking a scenic trip on the very fast hydrofoil service (**www.mahartpassnave.hu**) between Vienna, Bratislava and Budapest. April–Oct only, the journey takes 5–6 hours.

Getting Around

By Train

Generally, rail is the ideal way to travel within Hungary. The country has a good system of trains, which are very reasonable and reliable. However, you will find it difficult to travel around unless your journey starts or finishes in the capital.

To avoid a painfully slow journey, try to get on a fast train (*gyorsvonat*) rather than a local train (*személyvonat*). Intercity trains are the fastest and most comfortable and usually require a seat reservation.

By Bus

The bus system is extensive and cheap, but you will have to be dedicated to do any significant amount of travel in Hungary by bus – the best bet is to use buses only for short, rural trips. Vehicles are invariably crowded, and usually the only connecting point is Budapest. If you do decide to brave it, buy your ticket on board and get there early if you want to get a seat. In some big cities it is possible to purchase tickets in advance and you may even get a seat reservation.

By Road

The country has a handful of good motorways, with additions being built and planned. Some are toll motorways, where tokens can be bought from bigger petrol stations and post offices in advance. *See* 'Settling In', pp.256–7.

Public Transport in Budapest

Metro, Tram and Bus

The city's three underground lines run from 4.30am to 11pm and their efficiency puts London's system to shame. The M1 line (Milleniumi Földalatti Vasút, MFAV – Millennium Underground Railway) was built in 1896, and is the oldest underground in Europe. Tickets are valid for one ride only; a new ticket must be used every time you change lines and you cannot buy your ticket on board. Buy them at machines at the station and punch them in the orange boxes in the station entrance to validate them.

Buses with red numbers are express buses, which are great if you want to get somewhere quickly, but there are few stops so don't get on the wrong one! Night buses have a letter E attached to the number.

Daily, weekend, weekly, bi-weekly and monthly passes are also available at discounted prices. On trolleybuses and some buses you can buy a ticket from the driver, but this is more expensive. Generally, you buy a ticket on board for a tram or a bus and validate them by punching them in a machine on board.

Other Public Transport

Budapest has some quirky means of public transport which are used for novelty value rather than high-speed travel. The **Sikló** is a funicular railway which opened in 1870 and runs between Clark Ádám tér at the Buda end of the Lánchíd and the southern part of Buda Castle between 7.30am and 10pm.

The **Children's Railway** is a narrow-gauge railway operated by children aged 10–14 under the supervision of adults. It runs along a 7-mile forested route from the terminal Huvösvölgy from March to October. A **chair lift** runs to 262m

(86oft) to the János-hegy from May to September. The journey takes 15 minutes on average and provides unforgettable views from the top.

Choosing a Location

Most foreigners are buying in either the capital or on the shores of beautiful Lake Balaton. In Budapest, the best areas for investment – both for residential and commercial property – are Pest's V, VI, VII and XIII districts, and the I, II, III and XI districts in Buda. Property on Lake Balaton is very expensive, but venture into the hinterland away from the water and prices drop. They also fall the further you go from Budapest. Although there are a number of agents dealing with this area, most of them speak German and very little English, but this is changing fast.

Property Types and Prices

There is a large variety of property available, from city apartments and villas in new-build developments to larger, older, more run-down rural properties.

Guide Prices

€20,000

- Studio on the edge of Budapest in need of work.
- One-bedroom flat in Pécs in the south of the country.

€50,000

- Small villa on the south shore of Lake Balaton, but inland.
- One-bedroom apartment in a modern block on the outskirts of Budapest.

€100,000

- Charming 19th-century farmhouse with outbuildings near Balatonfured in the Kali Basin.
- Five-bedroom house in Kaposvar, 30-minute drive from Lake Balaton.

€200,000

- Historic five-bedroom villa on north shore of Lake Balaton.
- Two-bedroom, fully renovated apartment in the nicest part of Budapest, on the Pest side.

€500,000

- New four-bedroom villa near Balatonfured with lake views.
- 95,000 sq m of land 60km from Budapest.
- Four-bedroom house with pool and sauna in Buda part of Budapest.

€1,000,000
  • Building of three apartments in luxury area of Budapest.

Buying to Let

In some respects the bottom has fallen out of the rental market. After the fall of Communism, many multinational companies moved in, bringing their own workforce. Once the local people were trained and took over senior positions, the expatriate community shrank and the demand for well-appointed property along with it. If you are planning to let out a property, bear in mind that rental income is taxed at 20 per cent. It is worth bearing in mind, too, that there is an 'apartment mafia': groups of local people will put pressure on an elderly person to sell their flat at a reduced rate in return for a more convenient modern property. They then sell it on – often to overseas buyers – at a vastly inflated price. In some cases the family gets to hear of it and takes the new owner (not the mafia) to court and gains repossession of the property.

Building from Scratch or Renovation

The majority of buildings in the centre of Budapest are 19th-century. Because of severe lack of investment during the Communist period, some of these are in a bad state of repair. David White from Budapest Properties says, 'There is a lot of Hungarian-American investment in Budapest, particularly in the buy-to-let market. Many of these people are looking to renovate the once exquisite, grand 19th-century apartments in the city. Usually, permission to carry out the work has been granted and in some cases the exterior work has been completed. We recommend builders and electricians to our clients, as finding them in a foreign country without the language can be a daunting task.'

But an awful lot of thought is necessary before buying an old property. The cost of rewiring and re-plumbing a building with walls a metre thick can be as

---

Case Study: An Irish Invasion
Declan Miller has been working with an Irish company in Budapest for the last year. 'You wouldn't believe how many phone calls I get from friends of friends at home asking me about property. They call up and say, "Declan, I've bought this place in this district – what do you think?" I say, "Well, have you been out to see it?" "Nah," they say. I tell them they're crazy. This one lady called me up. She has a big mortgage at home and three kids. She bought a property in Budapest and is really happy because she will make the mortgage back on the rental income – what the estate agent told her. When I tell her the average wage is a quarter of what she is hoping to get back in rent, she goes quiet and I can't really think of what else to say to her. It's too late then.'

much as the original price of the property. Many experts are suggesting buyers look at the newer properties, which may not be as beautiful but are much more practical than the gorgeous 19th-century apartments.

There are also many properties on sale in Hungary in the rural areas that need huge amounts of work. As yet there is not much of a market for these properties. The problems associated with the renovation project can be huge. Not least will be your probable inability to speak Hungarian. If you are contemplating a renovation project it is vital to get good advice right at the outset. As is the case with many countries, it is very easy to find that once you have finished your project the cost of buying the property and the work you have undertaken is more than the value of the property as it stands.

Temporary Accommodation

Because of the large foreign business community in the capital, Budapest is well served for serviced apartments, which can be rented by the week, month or year. Online guides are a good source of information for all temporary accommodation needs; many have detailed information on private accommodation facilities including paying-guest accommodation places and rural tourism in holiday houses, rooms, flats and apartments.

The Process of Buying a Property

There is a lot more risk associated with buying property in Hungary than if buying in France or the UK, as there is a lot of property with either bad title or defective planning consent. Legal advice is essential, unless you take the view that the amount you are investing is so small you can afford to write it off.

Freedom to Buy

You can buy land, buildings or apartments in Hungary. If you wish to buy land or buildings attached to land (but not apartments), however, you will need to do so through a local Hungarian company, which will be the owner of the property. This is because only Hungarians are currently allowed to own land and buildings in Hungary. By owning through a Hungarian company the property is treated as being owned by a Hungarian, even if the company itself is 100 per cent owned and controlled by foreigners. This rule may change soon under EU regulations.

You are already free to buy an apartment in your own name, without the intervention of a Hungarian company. This is because, technically, the form of ownership of an apartment is slightly short of 100 per cent ownership of land. It is not the same as an English leasehold interest where you only have the rights over the apartment for a limited number of years – your rights as the owner of an apartment in Hungary are much fuller, but still not quite the same as the rights you enjoy when you own the land itself.

Initial Steps
First Contracts

Once you have found a property that you want to purchase, you will be expected to sign some form of contract, generally either a reservation contract or a preliminary purchase contract. *See* p.75. Note that the 'preliminary purchase contract' is actually a full binding purchase contract. We therefore recommend that, wherever possible, you insist on signing a **reservation contract**.

Searches and Enquiries

Once you have signed a reservation contract, your lawyer should make various enquiries, such as checking that the contract is fair, that the seller has good title and the right to sell to you, that the area is zoned for residential building and that any building work being undertaken enjoys all of the necessary planning and building consents. Depending on the circumstances of your case, there could well be other enquiries that also need to be made.

Structural Guarantees on New Property

These benefit from a 10-year guarantee.

Declared Values

It is common for the value declared in the title to be less than the true value. This is technically illegal but almost universal practice. The reason for this is that the declared value is the value used by the tax office to determine the taxes payable for the purchase.

You should avoid going along with this if possible. The tax payable by you, the buyer, on the purchase (the equivalent of stamp duty) is very low; the main benefit accrues to the seller, who will avoid paying capital gains tax. You will be removing a burden from the seller and landing yourself with a potential capital gains problem later on if you make a significant under-declaration and then, when you sell, your buyer refuses to do the same for you.

Bank Guarantees

Bank guarantees under which you are repaid the money you have invested if the builder is unable to complete the project are still very much a rarity in Hungary. A few developers are now providing them. They are worth having if you can get them.

Some Problems

The main problems in Hungary are defective title and defective planning consents. However, there is a new category of problems that is only just beginning to emerge: problems generated by greed. Some developers are trying to raise a large charge for the right to use the land on which the apartment stands. They have, no doubt, borrowed this idea from the English concept of a lease and ground rent. Some developers are also trying to charge substantial sums for managing the apartment complex and are trying to tie in the owners of the apartments to using their services for a number of years.

Signing the Contract and Registering the Title

Once your lawyer has checked out the property and found that everything is in order, you are ready to sign the **preliminary purchase contract**. This commits you and the seller to signing the full contract transferring ownership on an agreed date shortly afterwards, or, if the property is still under construction, once the property has been fully built.

The preliminary purchase contract contains most of the clauses you would expect to see in a UK contract. These will include a description of the property, a statement of the legal title to the property, the price to be paid, how it is to be paid, the deadline for payment and any other deadlines applicable, what should happen in the event of breach of contract and so on. Many Hungarian contracts are badly drafted, because there is really no history in Hungary of drafting contracts for the sale of land. The problem is exacerbated by the fact that many contracts are drafted in English, which is clearly not the first language of the person doing the drafting. As a result they are unclear or muddled. Specifications tend to be very 'thin'. The contracts tend to be lacking in detail as to what happens if anything goes wrong.

At this point you will normally pay a **deposit** of 10–20 per cent of the price of the property and apply for a buying permit from the local council. If the permit is refused, the deposit is forfeited. In the case of a property under construction ('off-plan') you will start to make **stage payments**, which will vary in size and number from property to property. A typical scheme would provide for an initial payment of 30 per cent followed by two further payments of 30 per cent as construction progresses, followed by a final payment of 10 per cent on delivery. Occasionally schemes are found where there is only one preliminary payment

Foreign Currency

There is a long tradition of American investment in Hungary, partly because so many Hungarians emigrated to the USA in the 20th century. But more recently Irish real estate investors have been stepping into central Budapest. The Irish are looking to Hungary in anticipation of a similar property boom to that experienced by Ireland after it joined the European Communities in 1973.

of, say, 30 per cent with the balance being paid on delivery. This is obviously very useful if you are taking out a mortgage.

Once you are ready to take delivery of the house you will sign the **final purchase contract**. This is signed in front of a notary public. It is at this point that the balance of the money is paid across to the seller. You do not need to be present in Hungary to sign this document, as your lawyer can prepare a **power of attorney** (*see* pp.77–8) under which you can appoint somebody else to sign on your behalf. This is a sensible thing to do, as it saves the need for you to go to Hungary, often at short notice, to sign the final title.

Once you have paid the balance of the price the seller will authorise you to **register your ownership** of the property in the local title register. Once this has been done, you – or the local Hungarian company that you have set up to own the property – will be the full legal owner of the property in much the same way as you would be in the UK.

The Expenses of Buying Property

The main expenses of buying are:

- stamp duty, legal costs and estate agency fees – together average around 10 per cent of the purchase price.
- fees to set up a company – likely to cost £500.

Letting Your Property

See the general chapter **Letting Your Property**, pp.117–26.

If you are letting out your property you should make sure that you use a proper **rental contract**. Your lawyer will be able to supply you with a draft that you can amend as necessary. Letting out short-term to tourists produces the least problems in terms of what you can do if the tenant does not pay the rent or refuses to leave.

Taxes

Taxes for Non-resident Property-owners

Local Property Taxes

Local property taxes in Hungary are very low.

Income and Capital Gains Taxes

The Hungarian rules for income tax are in the process of being reviewed. Foreign investors can invest in properties in Hungary either directly, in their own name, or through a local company.

Capital Gains Taxes

There is currently no capital gains tax but an increasing likelihood that it will be reintroduced.

Wealth Taxes

There are no wealth taxes.

Inheritance Taxes

This is progressive and dependent on the size of the estate and the relationship between donor and recipient.

Taxes for Resident Foreigners

This is beyond the scope of this book.

Settling In

Learning and Speaking Magyar

Magyar is the language of Hungary, and it is so unlike every other tongue in the world that even its closest relative, Finnish, is less like it than Italian is like German. This means that there will be very few words that you will recognise. It is a difficult language to learn, as even native speakers admit. The younger generation in Budapest is becoming increasingly more familiar with English, and children learn it at school, but you will find that older members of the population only speak German. It is worth remembering that one source of confusion is that in Hungary surnames are put before first names.

The queen of all Hungarian language schools is the Summer University in Debrecen. It offers intensive, residential 2- and 4-week courses (which include culture and history lessons) in July and August and 80-hour advanced courses in winter. For more information, contact the **Debreceni Nyari Egyetem**, PO Box 35, Debrecen 4010, **t** +36 5232 9117.

Shopping

Outside the capital you will be hard pushed to find many of the goods you would get at home. Having said that, Budapest's range of shops has gone through a mini-explosion recently. Here you will find international chains and many new shopping malls, which are mostly on the edge of the city. If you are looking for furniture for your newly bought property, you can do no better than one of the city's flea markets, which attract dealers from all over Europe, if not the world. The best is probably **Petõfi Csarnok** (open weekends 7am–2pm); **Ecseri Piac** tends to be more expensive but is open Monday to Friday. If you do buy antiques, keep the receipt to show to customs if you ever want to bring it back to the UK, and if you are after real finds, get there early before the best bargains are halfway to Venice.

Wine (Bull's Blood or Tokaj), porcelain and food products all make good souvenirs. Hungarian folk art is very collectable, including embroidered clothing – although watch out for fakes – the simpler pieces are the most likely to be authentic. Paprika, a very popular spice in Hungarian cooking, is easy to take home, as are the colourful dried peppers and chillis.

Shops are open Mon–Fri 10–6, Sat 10–1. Many food stores have longer hours – 8–6 or even later, especially in Budapest. You can usually find a 24-hour shop serving alcohol, cigarettes and some food in the centre of Budapest.

Home Utilities and Services

Gas and Electricity

Most Hungarian households cook with gas, so domestic 220V electricity is mainly used for lighting and appliances. If meters are installed within your home, the monthly bills will be an estimate. Once a year, the suppliers will visit the apartment to take readings and then issue a bill for any difference. With the removal of government subsidies over the past decade, gas and electricity prices have risen significantly. Electricity costs are now comparable to those in the UK, and gas just is a just a little cheaper than in this country.

Before moving in, ensure that the previous tenant has contacted the utility companies to take final readings, and ask to see final statements of account.

Water

Water prices increased 15-fold recently after subsidies were removed. Supplies are metered, and a household should expect to pay about €180 per year. In smaller villages, the construction of an expensive sewer system is uneconomical, and so homes are connected to local drainage pits.

Telephones

Blue or silver public phones take 20, 50 and 100 Ft coins, but are generally best avoided for their tendency to act as slot machines. The best option is to buy a **phone card** from post offices and kiosks.

The **international code** for Hungary is t 36. The code for Budapest is t 01, which is not necessary to dial if you're there. To dial Hungary from abroad, dial t 00 36 and drop the 0 from the area or city code. For long-distance calls, numbers need a t 06 prefix before the city code. You also have to dial t 06 before calling mobile phones. Operator, t 191; directory enquiries, t 198; international, t 199.

Mobiles

There is GSM dual band 900/1800, coverage throughout Hungary. Network operators include **Pannon GSM Telecoms** (**www.pannongsm.com**), **Westel Mobile Telecommunications Company** (**www.westel900.net**) and **Vodafone** (**www.vodafone.hu**).

Internet

Of all the former Communist countries, Hungary has the second-highest (after Estonia) proportion of homes connected to the Internet. Internet access in major cities is now reliable and cheap (broadband from €18 per month through **www.keystone.hu**). It takes approximately two to three weeks to get a connection. Broadband connections are usually restricted to larger towns and cities, but most villages have public access computers with satellite connection. These can be rented by the hour and are fairly cheap. Pay-as-you-go dial-up access is widely available for the cost of a local call.

Media

The *Budapest Business Journal* (**www.bbj.hu**) is a weekly newspaper that covers much more than just commerce. The general weekly news publication the *Budapest Sun* (**www.budapestsun.com**) has been in operation since 1993. The *Budapest Week* (**www.budapestweek.com**) is the oldest of the expat papers, focusing mostly on entertainment and art.

The **BBC World Service** (**www.bbc.co.uk/worldservice**) and **Voice of America** (**www.voa.gov**) are the main English-language radio services.

Money and Banking

The official unit of currency is the **forint** (Ft or HUF) and **fillér** (100 fillér = 1 Ft, though officially out of use). Notes come in denominations of Ft 200, 500, 5,000, 10,000 and 20,000. The US dollar is widely used for quoting property prices, as is the euro.

Currency can be exchanged at all the usual outlets – banks, *bureaux de change*, airports, railway stations, travel agencies and even some restaurants. ATM machines are available in Budapest and other main tourist centres. Unlimited currency can be taken in and out of the country, but only 50 per cent of forints can be reconverted, and even then only with exchange receipts.

If you intend spending a longer period in Hungary – or decide to live in the country – you will want to open a bank account. Strangely, the country's biggest and most widespread **banks** – **OTP** and **Postabank** – rarely have English-speaking staff. You would be better off going to the Russian owned **Általános Értékforgalmi Bank** (**ÁÉB**), the German **Magyar Külkereskedelmi Bank** (**MKB**) or the **American CitiBank**.

Working and Employment

Online agencies can provide information about job opportunities in the country. A number of areas of industry seek out UK workers, particularly in fields that require English speakers. UK nationals have the right to live and work in Hungary without a work permit and those from the UK working in Hungary have the same rights as Hungarian nationals in terms of pay, working conditions and access to training, social security and trade union membership. For more information on moving to Hungary contact the **Hungarian Embassy**, *see* p.259. Jobcentres and Jobcentre Plus offices in the UK have details of vacancies and employment services in Hungary.

Education

Pre-school education is compulsory for children at age six. There is also optional provision available for children between ages three and six. Compulsory education lasts from age six to age 18. **Elementary education** lasts for eight years from age six in primary schools. After elementary education pupils enter **secondary education**, which is offered in a variety of schools.

British families moving to Hungary with children have two main options: to educate their offspring within the Hungarian system or to send them to an international school, where they may be able to follow a UK or international curriculum. The best source of additional information on all aspects of education in Hungary is the **European Commission PLOTEUS (www.europa. eu.int/ploteus)**. The **British International School Budapest (www.bisb.hu)** offers an education in English based on the national curriculum of England and Wales, for children aged three to 16. As an accredited International Baccalaureate (IB) World School it also offers students over 16 the internationally respected IB programme.

Higher education is provided by state-run and private institutions. There are two types of institution: universities offering courses of four years' duration and colleges offering courses lasting three years.

Health and Emergencies

For an ambulance, call **t** 104 or **t** 350 0388. If English is not spoken, dial **t** 112.

No vaccinations are required to enter Hungary. Medicines can be obtained with prescriptions written abroad, and most common over-the-counter drugs are available. Foreign citizens are entitled to first-aid and emergency ambulance treatment free of charge if injured. EU citizens are now entitled to free treatment to the same extent as Hungarian citizens with an E111 or EHIC card (available from post offices), but insurance is still recommended. Medical treatment in Hungary is of a reasonable standard, with well-trained doctors,

> ### *Touchy Subject*
> As a general rule, Hungarians are not uninhibited like the Romanians or the sentimental Slavs, who will laugh or cry at the drop of a hat – or more likely a drink. There are not too many rules governing personal relationships for a foreigner to watch, but if you are invited to someone's home, bring a bunch of flowers or a bottle of good local wine. You can discuss just about anything except money, which is considered impolite.

some of who speak English (mostly in Budapest). However, emergency services are sometimes lacking. Both doctors and hospitals usually expect immediate cash payment for health services, which is reimbursed later.

Social Services and Welfare Benefits

In the Hungarian social system, services are provided by three main sectors: the state, local governments and the civil or non-profit sector. The legislation is based on a constitutional authorisation, according to which the Republic of Hungary provides care for those who need it with extensive social measures, and citizens have a right to social security, which right is enforced through social insurance, and partly through the system of social institutions.

Rights to social security are the same as those as those in the UK. If you start work in Hungary, you will contribute to the Hungarian social security system and as a result gain the right to any benefits. If you have been claiming Job Seeker's Allowance for at least four weeks in the UK before arriving in Hungary, you may continue to receive it for up to three months while you actively seek work. You must, however, first inform your Jobcentre Plus office or Jobcentre in the UK where you are registered of your intention to look for work in Hungary well in advance of your departure date. Your Jobcentre Plus office or Jobcentre will then advise the DWP Pensions and Overseas Benefits Directorate, who will decide whether you have satisfied certain conditions and send you form E303. Take this to the Hungarian employment service as soon as possible after your arrival in Hungary.

Cars

If you are taking a car to Hungary, make sure you have adequate pan-European insurance as well as a well-serviced cooling system, especially during the hot summer months. Having recently joined the EU, Hungary has invested a great deal in recent years to improve and extend its motorway (*autópálya*) network. A valid, full UK licence is needed to drive in Hungary – old format, 'green' UK licences are accepted only if accompanied by an international driving permit. The following equipment is compulsory:

- a first aid kit.
- a warning triangle.
- spare bulbs.
- headlamp converters for right-hand drive vehicles.
- a nationality plate.

Most petrol stations are open from 6am to 10pm, with an increasing number offering a 24hr service.

If you are bringing a vehicle from home, you will need a vehicle licence and country sign along with third-party insurance.

The rules of the road are generally the same as at home: seat belts and child seats are compulsory and mobile phones can only be used with headsets. There are a couple that may catch you out, though. First, there is a total alcohol ban when driving, and this rule is very strictly enforced; with even just 0.008 per cent alcohol in your blood, you will probably be fined, and higher levels will result in your arrest. Secondly, dipped headlights must be used at all times, even in daylight. Speed limits are: 50kph (31mph) in built-up areas; 90kph (50mph) on main roads; 110kph (62mph) on highways; 130kph (75mph) on motorways.

Crime and the Police

Police: **t** 107 or **t** 112.

There are three levels of enforcement, national, country and local (the last of which can include district or municipal). By law, tourists must carry their passports or a form of photo ID with them at all times. Residents must be in possession of their apartment card, showing their residency, photo ID and their car papers and licence if they own a car.

Food and Drink

Check the prices of the menu – if there aren't any, then leave. The story of the Danish tourist in 1997 who was stung with a whopping US$6,000 bill in Budapest may be just that – a story – but do you want to risk it?

Just because a restaurant has a credit card sticker on its window, it doesn't mean it will accept them. Ask first. The *prix-fixe* (literally, fixed-price) menus

Ancient Cuisine

Magyars are the original settlers of Hungary. This nomadic people arrived between 892 and 896 AD after agreeing with Emperor Arnulf, a ruler of a nearby kingdom, to help him conquer his enemies in return for land. It was a good deal, as the area was rich with fish and game and ideal for rearing livestock and growing crops. The Magyars used large cauldrons called *bogrács* over open fires, which are still used today to cook dishes such as goulash.

Food Fashion

A massive change has taken place in the last few years in Budapest, and the city now boasts stylish restaurants dishing up delicate, imaginative food. Contemporary Asian cuisine is all the rage, and sushi bars abound. Many restaurants feature food with a foreign influence, such as French duck or Indian curry. Goa is an achingly cool eatery filled with carved stone features and bamboo screens. Handsome waiters serve Asian fusion cuisine to a beautiful clientele. Tom George has a funky DJ and a menu that features *tom yam* and *mee goreng* along with scallops and risotto with a vodka and tomato sauce.

offered in many restaurants are the best value. Don't expect bargains in Budapest – a meal in a good restaurant will cost you the same as in London: £3 coffees are not unusual and main courses are around £10.

Confusingly, *gulyas* is soup, not goulash. What we know as goulash is actually *porkolt*, a kind of meat with papikra-spiced gravy. Hungarian dishes tend to feature lots of sour cream or grated cheese. Traditional options are Wiener schnitzel (though usually made of pork, not veal), roast goose or duck with cabbage, paprika chicken (*paprikascsirke*), steak with goose liver, stuffed peppers (*toltott paprika*) and fish stew (*racponty*). *Foie gras* features heavily on every menu, and often a whole page is devoted to the dish. Even if you don't order it, you may find a big dollop of it on your steak or other dish or delivered to you on a spoon as an unasked for starter.

In Budapest there is a surprising range of restaurants. It is easy to find French, Russian, Greek, Japanese and Indian restaurants side by side, and even in the countryside you can usually find a pizzeria. Budapest is big on fast food, with all the hideous international chains. For a cheap, quick snack, try a Hungarian speciality instead – the *étkezde* is a lunchtime diner where customers sit at shared tables and tuck into wholesome, home-cooked food. Hungarian desserts may surprise you. The country has taken the best from Viennese sweets: and offers *dobos torte* (sponge cake with caramel), *szomloi galuska* (custard cake with rum and chocolate), or a chocolate and raspberry crêpe.

The Hungarians have an expression, '*sírva vigad a magyar*', which translates roughly as 'crying when you are happy'. Some would say that a look at the history of their wine industry is enough to make you sob into your Bull's Blood. The collapse of the Soviet Union at the beginning of the 1990s, followed by the rest of the Eastern Bloc, brought the industry to its knees as most of its exports were to these countries, but it is picking up again.

Ironically, Hungary is best known for its red **wines**, but it is actually much better at producing inexpensive whites. The most famous Hungarian wines are the red Bull's Blood and the honey-sweet white Tokaj wines. Fruit schnapps (*pálinka*) are a national speciality. The very best red wine, however, comes from the Villany region in the far south (near Pecs) – try their merlot and cabernet sauvignon. A glass of Hungarian champagne will be on a menu for £2 but

French Moët et Chandon will be there too. The quality of wine in Hungary has improved dramatically in recent years, and the best place to buy it in Budapest is direct from the Budapest Wine Society shop on Batthyány Utca.

Local **beers** are good and imported beer is available everywhere. Szalon sor, brewed in Pecs, is a good German-style wheat beer. Don't clink beer glasses – Hungarians haven't done this since the Austrians hanged the Hungarian generals leading the revolution of 1848 and toasted the executions with beer.

Hungary: References

Directory of Contacts and Resources

Embassies and Cultural Centres

- **Hungarian Embassy**, 35 Eaton Place, London SW1X 8BY, **t** (020) 7201 3440/7235 4448, **f** (020) 7823 1348, **www.huemblon.org.uk**, **http://hungary.embassyhomepage.com**.

- **Hungarian Cultural Centre**, 10 Maiden Lane, London WC2E 7NA, **t** (020) 7240 8448, **f** (020) 7240 4847, **culture@hungary.org.uk**. Established by the government of the Republic of Hungary. It acts as an envoy of Hungarian culture, art and social sciences, in a way similar to the British Council in Budapest.

- **British Embassy**, Harmincad utca 6, Budapest 1051, **t** + 36 1 266 2888, **www.britishembassy.hu**.

Information and Resources

- **British Consulate** (Hungary), **t** 1266 2888. Can provide a list of reliable English-speaking lawyers.

- **Hungarian Tourist Board**, 46 Eaton Place, London SW1X 8AL, UK, **t** (020) 7823 1032, **www.hungarywelcomes-britain.com**.

- **www.budapestinfo.hu**. Budapest's official home page.

Coffee Houses

Daily life in Budapest is still punctuated by the consumption of black coffee drunk from little glasses, though cappuccinos and white coffee are becoming ever more popular. These quintessentially Central European coffee breaks are less prolonged these days than before the war, when Budapest's coffee houses were both social club and haven for their respective clientele. Free newspapers were available to the regulars – writers, journalists and lawyers for whom the cafés were effectively offices or to posing revolutionaries. Today's coffee houses and pâtisseries are less romantic but no less important to daily life.

- **www.budapest.hu**. A site maintained by the mayor's office.
- **www.livebudapest.com**. Articles and listings.

Property Companies and Estate Agents

- **Aquarius Properties**, 2A Main Street, Rock House, Blackrock, Co. Dublin, Ireland, **t** +353 01278 2900, **f** +353 01706 0414, **info@aquariusproperties. com, www.aquariusproperties.com**.
- **Aquavista Property Consultants Ltd**, Longleys, Rye Road, Sandhurst, Cranbrook, Kent TN18 5PG, **t** (01580) 850170, **f** (01580) 850186, **info@aquavistaproperty.com, www.aquavistaproperty.com**.
- **Harlon Property Management**, 48 Wimbledon Stadium Business Centre, Riverside Road, London SW17 0BA, **t** (020) 8944 9538, **www.harlon.co.uk**. A small owner-run organisation based in Wimbledon and operating in southwest London and Surrey. It specialises in providing a personal but professional service for tenants' associations, owners of investment property and other landlords, including landlords residing abroad.
- **Hungarian Real Estate Association (HREA)**, Margit krt. 43–45, H-1024 Budapest, **t** +36 1 326 7776, **f** +36 1 315 1038, **http://webcei.com/hrea.htm**.
- **Hungary Property**, **t/f** (01293) 541 667, **www.hungaryproperty.net**. Claims to be the largest property brokerage in Hungary.
- **Properties in Budapest**, **t** +353 87 245 6357, **www.propertiesinbudapest. com**. Specialises in new properties solely for investment (the property must be capable of achieving at least 5 per cent rental yield per year)
- **Budapestproperties**, **www.budapestproperties.co.uk**. Based in west London. Specialising in Budapest, can arrange builders for renovation work.
- **Lavan French**, **t** (Ireland) +353 021 485 8400, **www.lavanfrench.com**. Deals with all types of property, including off-plan, re-sale, rural and front-line.

Removal Companies

- **Corstjens**, Erik Christiaensen, Bogancsvirag U. 5-7, 1106 Budapest, **t** +36 1 261 2651, **f** +36 1 260 1055, **info@corstjens.hu, www.corstjens.com**.
- **Excess International Movers**, 4 Hannah Close, Great Central Way, London NW10 0UX, **t** 0800 783 1085 (freephone) or **t** (020) 8324 2066, **f** (020) 8324 2095, **sales@excess-baggage.com, www.excess-baggage.com**.

Holiday Companies

- **Archers Direct**, **www.archersdirect.co.uk**. Touring holidays in Hungary.
- **Sunvil**, **www.sunvil.co.uk**. A well-established, award-winning company specialising in responsible tourism.

Administrative Departments

Hungary is subdivided administratively into 19 areas, in addition to the capital city of Budapest: Békéscsaba, Debrecen, Dunaújváros, Eger, Győr, Hódmező-vásárhely, Kaposvár, Kecskemét, Miskolc, Nagykanizsa, Nyíregyháza, Pécs, Salgótarján, Sopron, Szeged, Székesfehérvár, Szekszárd, Szolnok, Szombathely, Tatabánya, Veszprém, Zalaegerszeg.

There are also 22 so-called urban counties (singular *megyei jogú város*), listed below, together with the name of the county capital: Bács-Kiskun (Kecskemét), Baranya (Pécs), Békés (Békéscsaba), Borsod-Abaúj-Zemplén (Miskolc), Csongrád (Szeged), Fejér (Székesfehérvár), Győr-Moson-Sopron (Győr), Hajdú-Bihar (Debrecen), Heves (Eger), Jász-Nagykun-Szolnok (Szolnok), Komárom-Esztergom (Tatabánya), Nógrád (Salgótarján), Pest (Budapest), Somogy (Kaposvár), Szabolcs-Szatmár-Bereg (Nyíregyháza), Tolna (Szekszárd), Vas (Szombathely), Veszprém (Veszprém), Zala (Zalaegerszeg).

Time

Winter time is GMT + 1hr. Summertime, from early March to late October, is GMT + 2hrs, Eastern Standard Time + 7hrs, Pacific Standard Time + 10hrs.

Note that Hungarians represent times in a way which can be confusing to Westerners: ½ 8 ('half-eight') means 7.30.

Public Holidays

1 January	New Year's Day
15 March	Anniversary of 1848–49 Revolution
March/April	Easter Monday
1 May	Labour Day
End May	Whit Monday
20 August	St Stephen's and Constitution Day
23 October	Anniversary of 1956 Revolution
1 November	All Saints' Day
25 and 26 December	Christmas

Further Reading

The Budapest File, George Szirtes (Bloodaxe Books) – a collection of poetry devoted to the author's complicated and often sad relationship with the country he left as a child.

Living in Hungary, Jean-Luc Soule with photographer Alain Fleischer – Hungary's rich legacy of architecture and design is explored.

Culture Shock!: Hungary, Zsuzsanna Ardo (Culture Shock! Guides) – an insight into the country's etiquette and culture.

Easter Sprinkling

Easter is a two-day-long holiday in Hungary, when an unusual ritual takes place. On Easter Monday boys and men visit all women relatives, friends and neighbours in a tour that lasts all day. They recite humorous poems to the girls and women and sprinkle them with cologne. The women give the men food and drink and often hand-painted eggs. Women compete to see who gets the most 'sprinklers', and they may be wearing more then a dozen types of cologne by Monday evening, while the men may have indulged in the same number of alcoholic drinks. In the past, the sprinkling was more of a soaking and done with water, particularly in rural areas. Boys often dragged girls to a well and poured water on them from a bucket or threw them in a river. It is thought that this tradition stems from the belief in the healing effects of water as well as its ability to improve fertility.

Budapest 1900, A Historical Portrait of the City and its Culture, John Lukacs – a thoughtful, illustrated portrait.

I Have Lived a Thousand Years: Growing Up in the Holocaust, Livia Bitton Jackson – a true story.

Historic Coffeehouses: Vienna, Budapest, Prague, Carol Dittrich.

Climate Charts

Daily Mean Temperature in Budapest

	Jan	Feb	Mar	Apr	May	Jun	Jul	Aug	Sep	Oct	Nov	Dec
°C	0.2	3.4	5.8	11.9	15.8	18.9	24.8	21.0	15.4	12.9	3.3	1.1
°F	32	34	42	53	60	66	77	70	60	55	38	34

Average Daily Max and Min Temperatures in Budapest (°C)

	Jan	Feb	Mar	Apr	May	Jun	Jul	Aug	Sep	Oct	Nov	Dec
Min	−4	−2	2	−4	11	15	16	16	12	7	3	−1
Max	1	4	10	17	22	26	28	27	23	16	8	4

Average Monthly Rainfall in Budapest (mm)

Jan	Feb	Mar	April	May	June	July	Aug	Sept	Oct	Nov	Dec
38	44	39	42	70	66	58	38	42	58	68	44

Average Daily Hours of Sunshine in Budapest

Jan	Feb	Mar	April	May	June	July	Aug	Sept	Oct	Nov	Dec
6	7	3	7	8	9	10	9	9	5	3	1

Latvia

14

Why Buy in Latvia?

Latvia is a relatively small country. At just over 64,500 sq km it is roughly a quarter of the size of the UK and seven times as large as Cyprus. It is the centre of the three Baltic states and the middle also in terms of size.

Investment in Latvia has been driven by a number of factors. First, the economy has been doing well. Local wealth has generated demand for property, and that demand is likely to press prices ever higher. Secondly, the Latvian government appears to have brought inflation (previously running at nearly 1,000 per cent per annum) under control, to the extent that it is now less than 3 per cent per annum. The boom in foreigners considering Latvia as a place to invest in real estate coincided with that inflationary control. Thirdly, there has been a realisation that, of all of the Baltic states, Latvia has the most cosmopolitan capital city, the one with the strongest Russian links, and thus possibly the greatest potential for growth on the back of an expanding Russian economy. Property prices in Latvia, and in Riga in particular, have been rising steadily at around 20 per cent per annum and look likely to continue to rise for a few years to come.

Tourism

There has been a steady increase in the number of tourists in Latvia since 2000, and some investors are also seeking to tap into the increasing popularity of the attractive capital city, Riga, as a short-break holiday destination. Since the arrival of Ryanair and cheap flights, the growth in this market has been startling. Latvia receives around half a million international visitors annually, and the number of foreign visitors in the first quarter of 2004 was 15 per cent up on the equivalent quarters of 2002 and 2003.

The Economy

Latvia's economy recovered well from the 1998 Russian financial crisis as the country gradually reorientated its exports towards EU countries, lessening Latvia's trade dependency on Russia. The majority of companies and banks have been privatised. Latvia officially joined the World Trade Organization in February 1999, and the EU, a top foreign policy goal, in May 2004. Banking and internal government deficits remain major concerns, but the government's efforts to increase efficiency in revenue collection may lessen the budget deficit. A growing perception that many of Latvia's banks facilitate illicit activity could damage the country's vibrant financial sector.

GDP per capita is roughly half that of the UK, and double that of countries such as Bulgaria or Turkey. Latvia has seen a steady decline in its population (10 per cent in 10 years), mainly through emigration. The population today is 2.3

million. As you would expect, the cost of living is considerably lower than in the UK, though, at least in Riga, it runs at more than half the cost.

The Exchange Rate

See the graph below for an analysis of the movement in exchange rates over the last few years. Latvia follows a pattern common in Eastern Europe.

Exchange Rate – Latvian Lats

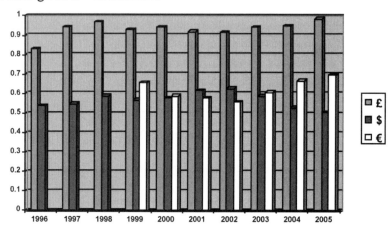

Visas and Permits

As Latvia is a member of the European Union, any citizen of a member state can enter the country without a visa in the same way as they can enter, say, France or Spain. They can stay for up to **90 days** in any six-month period. After 90 days they need to obtain a **residence permit**, a relatively painless procedure.

Profile of Latvia

Recent History and Politics

From 1944 to 1991 Latvia was occupied by Russia; although it became independent in 1991, 30 per cent of the population is of Russian extraction and over half is native Russian-speaking. The Republic of Latvia is a parliamentary democracy. It has proved keen to embrace the West, and joined NATO and the European Union in May 2004.

Climate and Geography

Latvia has a coastline of only about 530km. As you would expect from its northerly location, the climate is hardly tropical. The summer temperatures are acceptable at about 20°C but the winters can be seriously cold, with temperatures hovering around freezing. In the inland towns to the east, winter lasts about six weeks longer than the coastal towns in the western part of the country. *See* 'Climate Charts', p.276, for more details of the temperature and rainfall patterns.

Regional Profile

Riga, the capital city, on a flat plain divided by the Daugava river, has roots going back hundreds of years. It is a beautiful and cosmopolitan city in the Central European tradition and, superficially at least, has many similarities with areas of Prague, though hampered somewhat by its geographical location and (particularly winter) climate. It is the largest city in the Baltic states and over half the population of Latvia lives within its borders. It is also the centre of the Latvian economy; its booming business life is evident in the many new office blocks and large hotels, though it has a quaint old centre as well. It has become a tourist destination at least partly because of its thriving nightlife.

A 20-mile stretch of white sand beach called **Jūrmala** stretches east from the city, with dunes backed by pine forests and countless historic wooden houses of the 19th and 20th centuries, designed by top architects of the period.

North and west, the country has a dramatic Baltic Sea **coastline** with historic towns such as **Kurzeme** and **Liepāja**. **Inland** are areas of forest, bog and farm-land studded with castles, and many new nature parks are being created.

Selecting a Property

Getting There

Riga is served by **Air Baltic, British Airways, SAS (Scandinavian Airlines)** and **Ryanair**. A direct return ticket from London, departing June 2005, is quoted at £230 by **British Airways**. Single tickets are available on **Ryanair** for about £50.

Getting Around

Within the Baltic States, the **rail** system is sadly out of date. Baltic **buses** are faster, cheaper and more frequent than trains. Vehicles are fairly comfortable, and streets and highways are being improved constantly.

Choosing a Location

There has been a steady trickle of interest in foreigners buying property in Latvia. In the last year or so this has increased significantly, though the numbers in absolute terms are still small. The main focus of activity by foreign buyers is in Riga and on the coast.

Riga

Most people buying in Riga are buying historic properties in the centre of the old town, but as these become more expensive and less available they are also looking to buy in some of the newer developments designed for the emerging middle classes.

The Coast

The coast of Latvia has a number of seaside resorts that are blessed with good sandy beaches and a pleasant summer climate. These are not yet greatly in favour with the investor from outside the region and the weather in these resorts is not such as to make them attractive to a person seeking their own holiday accommodation.

Property Types and Prices

For a small country, there is a wide variety of property types, from city apartment blocks to tall townhouses, country manor houses and wooden homes in the forests and chalets by the sea. The attractive capital, Riga, is as cheap to buy in as it is to live in. Elsewhere, property prices are much lower.

Prices have been rising rapidly. Some people have seen growth of over 30 per cent in the last year, though 20 per cent would probably be more typical in Riga.

Guide Prices in January 2005

Place and Type of Property	Low	Mid	High
Centre of Riga, one-bedroom apartment, 60 sq m		£67,000	£100,000
Centre of Riga, two-bedroom apartment, 100 sq m		£80,000	£120,000
Suburbs of Riga, three-bedroom villa, 175 sq m			£176,000
Cottage in countryside on 45 sq m	£27,000		
Beach (Jūrmala), three-bedroom house in central location			£170,000

Building from Scratch or Renovation

There are many historic properties on sale in Latvia – in rural areas and in Riga – that need huge amounts of work. Some of the properties have not been touched for over 60 years. As yet there is not much of a market for these properties. The problems associated with a renovation project can be huge; not least will be your probable inability to speak Latvian, so if you are contemplating a renovation project it is vital to get good advice right at the outset. Building costs are low, however, and a full restoration project is likely to cost about £250 per square metre.

Skilled workers are in short supply in Latvia as there is a great demand for their services for repair work and for the large amount of new property that is under construction. This is despite the fact that Latvia has an official unemployment rate of nearly 10 per cent.

As is the case with many countries, it is very easy to find that once you have finished your project the cost of buying the property and the work you have undertaken is more than the value of the property as it stands. Keep control.

The Process of Buying a Property

Legal advice is essential unless you take the view that the amount you are investing is so small that you can afford to write it off.

Freedom to Buy

You can buy buildings or apartments in Latvia. Buying land requires permission from the local municipality. Alternatively, you can choose to buy the property (whether land, a building or an apartment) via a Latvian company. This has a number of tax and other consequences. For some people it can significantly reduce their tax liabilities, but for other people it can increase them substantially. Take advice.

Initial Steps

First Contracts

Once you have found a property that you want to purchase, you will be expected to sign some form of contract. This will generally either be a reservation contract or a preliminary purchase contract. *See* 'Reservation and Preliminary Contracts', p.75, for an explanation of these concepts. Note that the title 'preliminary purchase contract' is misleading; it is actually a full binding purchase contract. We recommend that, wherever possible, you insist on signing a **reservation contract** rather than a preliminary purchase contract at this stage.

Searches and Enquiries

Once you have signed a reservation contract, your lawyer should make the standard enquiries to check that the contract is fair, that the seller has good title and the right to sell to you, that the area is zoned for residential building and that any building work being undertaken enjoys all of the necessary planning and building consents. Depending on the circumstances of your case there could well be other enquiries that also need to be made.

In Latvia it is common for work to be started illegally before all of these steps are in place. It is also common for property to have defective title. Sometimes these problems should put you off being involved in the purchase. On other occasions, the risks are minimal and, provided you go into the transaction with your eyes open, might not put you off buying if you like the property.

Possible Dangers

Defective title and defective planning consents are common in Latvia, as in all former Eastern Bloc countries. There have been some property disputes, particularly where multiple members of a family all claim to be the genuine owners of a valuable city centre property that has passed down through the family for several generations.

Signing the Contract and Registering the Title

Once your lawyer has checked out the property and found that everything is in order, you are ready to sign the **preliminary purchase contract**. This commits you and the seller to signing the full contract transferring ownership shortly afterwards or, if the property is still under construction, once the property has been built.

The preliminary purchase contract contains most of the clauses you would expect to see in a UK contract. These include a description of the property, a statement of the legal title to the property, the price to be paid, how it is to be paid, the deadline for any deadlines, and what should happen in the event of breach of contract. Many Latvian contracts are badly drafted by UK standards because there is no history in Latvia of drafting contracts for the sale of land. The problem is exacerbated by the fact that many contracts are drafted in English and are unclear or muddled. Specifications tend to be thin and the contracts lack detail about what happens if anything goes wrong.

At this point you will normally pay a **deposit** of 10 per cent of the price of the property or start to make **stage payments** for off-plan properties, which vary in size and number from property to property. A typical scheme provides for an initial payment of 30 per cent followed by two further payments of 30 per cent as construction progresses, followed by a final payment of 10 per cent on delivery. Occasionally there are schemes where there is only one preliminary payment of, say, 30 per cent with the balance being paid on delivery. This is useful if you are taking out a mortgage.

Once you are ready to take delivery of the house you will sign the **final purchase contract**. This may be signed in front of a notary public, or you may simply present the contract signed by the parties to the Latvian Land Registry. It is at this point that the balance of the money is paid across to the seller.

You do not need to be present in Latvia to sign this document as your lawyer can prepare a **power of attorney** (see pp.77–8) under which you can appoint somebody else to sign on your behalf. This is a sensible thing to do as it saves the need for you to go to Latvia, often at short notice, to sign the final title.

Once you have paid the balance of the price the seller will authorise you to **register your ownership** of the property in the local title register. Then you – or the local Latvian company that you have set up to own the property – will be the full legal owner of the property in much the same way as you would be in the UK. It is likely to take 2–6 weeks for the registered title deeds to be made available to you. How long will depend how busy the registry is in the place where you are buying. With the current explosion of demand, these periods are getting longer.

The Expenses of Buying

The main expenses of buying are:

- tax – the equivalent of stamp duty – 2 per cent of the price.

- any estate agent's fees.

- notary's fees – these will vary from case to case but will typically not exceed £300.

- legal fees – these depend on whether you use a Latvian or an English lawyer; English lawyer's fees will be higher but you will be able to sue them if they get it wrong and they will be able to give you lots of advice, particularly about the vital issues of who should own the property to minimise your tax and other problems, which the local Latvian lawyer would not be able to help you with; they will range from about £500 if you use a local Latvian lawyer to £1,500 if you use a specialist English lawyer.

- fees to set up a Latvian company if you decide this is best; this is likely to cost £500.

Letting Your Property

See the general chapter **Letting Your Property**, pp.117–26.

If you are letting your property, make sure that you use a proper **rental contract**. Your lawyer will be able to supply you with a draft that you can amend. Offering short-term lets to tourists is the lowest risk. The law in Latvia presents a reasonable balance between the interests of the landlord and the interests of the tenant; in general, it is not difficult to remove an unsuitable tenant.

At the moment one can expect to see a **rental yield** (net of all expenses apart from your finance costs and personal taxation) of about 5 per cent on the coast and perhaps 6–7 per cent in Riga.

Taxes

Taxes for Non-resident Property-owners

Local Property Taxes

Property taxes are the equivalent of UK council tax and are low in Latvia. The fees are calculated by reference to the official value of the property, which is usually somewhat different from (much less than) the real commercial value of the property. The local property taxes are 1.5 per cent of the assessed value of the property.

Income Taxes

Foreign investors can invest in properties in Latvia either directly, in their own name, or through a local company. The tax paid depends on the choice.

• **Rental income on company-owned property.**

The basis of the taxable income of a company investing in Latvian property is the gross income from the property less any tax-deductible expenses and depreciation. These expenses include any management costs, repairs, maintenance, insurance, etc., and interest on any loans used to buy the property. The corporate tax rate is a flat rate of 15 per cent – due to be reduced to 12.5 per cent in 2006.

• **Rental income on individually owned property.**

For non-residents, at present, there is a 25 per cent tax rate. This can be set off against your UK tax liabilities on the same income.

Capital Gains Taxes

Capital gains taxes are treated as part of an individual's income. The gain is tax-free for a private individual who has owned a residential property for a period of at least one year. For a company, the gain is completed as part of its income for tax purposes. For a non-resident foreign company that sells land or buildings in Latvia there is a deduction of 2 per cent from the price of the property that must be filed as a payment of tax.

Wealth Taxes
There are no wealth taxes in Latvia.

Inheritance Taxes
There is no general inheritance or gift tax.

Taxes for Resident Foreigners
This is beyond the scope of this book.

Settling In

Learning and Speaking Latvian
The language spoken is Latvian, though Russian is also common as there are many ex-Russian settlers. The language belongs to the Baltic branch of the Indo-European language family. Many people, particularly in Riga, speak English.

Shopping
Shops are generally open from 9/10–6/7 on weekdays, and from 9/10–4 on Saturdays. Larger department stores are open daily 10–8, while food shops and supermarkets open 8am–10pm during the week, with some open on Sunday. Shops in rural areas often close for a lunch break and closer earlier in the evening. Most larger stores accept Visa, Mastercard and Eurocard.

Telephones and the Internet
All Latvian phone numbers are 7 digits and there are no area codes; to call from abroad, dial 00, then the **country code** (**t** 371) and then the number.

Public **payphones** are common, but not many take coins. Cards can be purchased for 2, 3 or 5Ls from kiosks and post offices.

Mobile phones can also be rented at local phone shops. If you have a GSM 900/1800, and a phone that is not locked to a network, you can purchase a SIM card package from a local provider.

There are more and more **Internet** cafés opening up in larger cities as well as small towns, as well as small towns. You can get online at tourist offices, libraries, post offices and shopping centres.

Money and Banking

Latvia's currency, the **lats** (Ls; plural lati) is divided into 100 **santimi**. Lati come in 5, 10, 20, 50,100 and 500 lats notes, and 1 and 2 lats coins. Santimi come in 1, 2, 5, 10, 20 and 50 cent coins.

Major **banks** such as Hansabanka, Latvijas Krajbanka and Unibanka will change money, give advances on major credit cards and cash traveller's cheques. There are also a number of currency exchange offices (*valutas maina*), which are either found in the centre of town or in a food shop or gambling arcade. Some of them in Riga are open 24 hours.

Banks are generally open Mon–Fri 9/10–4/5, and some banks in larger cities are often open on Sat from 10–2 or 3.

There are **ATMs** all around larger towns. Major **credit cards** can be used in all of the bigger hotels, restaurants, department stores and shops, but don't count on using them at petrol stations outside larger cities.

Post

Postal services have improved considerably in the Baltics, with mail arriving in 7–10 days to North America and within 2–5 days to Western Europe. Main post offices (*pasts*) are located throughout the city, and are usually open 9–6 on weekdays and 9–1 on Sat. Stamps can also be bought at some hotels.

Health

Ambulance: **t** 03 or **t** 112.

There are some improving private facilities catering to foreigners in each country, and EU members are entitled to **emergency** treatment with an E111 or new EHIC card, but if you have a serious medical problem, you might consider leaving the country. Take good travel insurance. If you will be in wooded or coastal areas, immunisation against tick-borne encephalitis is recommended.

Although the **tap water** in the Baltics is said to be drinkable, stick with bottled water. **Pharmacies** are usually open 10–7, but some stay open all night.

Crime and the Police

Police: **t** 02 or **t** 112.

Riga is not any more dangerous than any other European capital, but foreigners have been known to be targeted. The most common problems are pick-pocketing and car break-ins. It is best, as anywhere, to avoid wandering into unfamiliar streets alone after dark, and be careful who you drink with and how much you consume! Be discreet when using your mobile phone.

Latvia: References

Directory of Contacts and Resources

Embassies

- **Latvian Embassy**, 45 Nottingham Place, London W1U 5LR, **t** (020) 7312 0040, **f** (020) 7312 0042, **t** (020) 7312 0125 (Consular Sect), **embassy@ embassyoflatvia.uk**.

- **British Embassy**, Alunana 5, **t** + 371 777 4700, **f** + 371 777 4707, **british. embassy@apollo.lv**, **www.britain.lv**.

Information and Resources

- **www.latviatourism.lv**. Information on the country.

Time

Latvia is on Eastern European Time (GMT/UTC + 2). The 24hr clock is used for flight, train and bus timetables. In summer, Latvia follows daylight saving, putting clocks forward an hour in spring and back in autumn.

Public Holidays

1 January	New Year's Day
16 March	Latvian Legion Day
25 March	Deportations of 1949
March/April	Good Friday, Easter Sunday, Easter Monday
1 May	Labour Day
4 May	Declaration of Independence of the Republic
8 May	Memorial Day for Victims of World War Two
2nd Sun in May	Mother's Day
14 June	Remembrance Day for Victims of Communist Terror
4 July	Remembrance Day of Jewish Genocide
23–4 June	Ligo Day/Midsummer's Day
11 November	Soldiers' Memorial Day
18 November	Proclamation Day of the Republic of Latvia
24–6 December	Christmas
31 December	New Year's Eve

Climate Charts

Average Temperatures in Riga (°C)

Jan	Feb	Mar	April	May	June	July	Aug	Sept	Oct	Nov	Dec
−4	−3	2	10	16	21	22	21	17	11	4	−2

Average Daily Hours of Sunshine in Riga

Jan	Feb	Mar	April	May	June	July	Aug	Sept	Oct	Nov	Dec
1	2	4	6	7	11	10	9	6	3	1	1

Lithuania

15

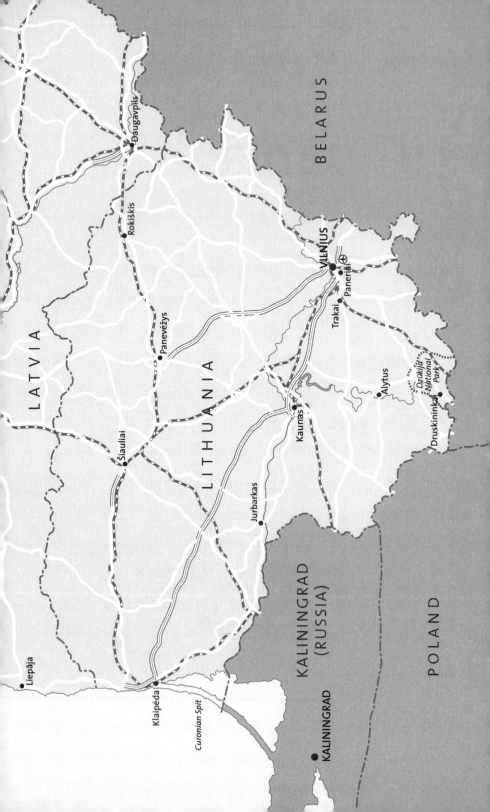

Why Buy in Lithuania?

Lithuania is a relatively small country, though it is the largest of the three Baltic states in terms of area. At just over 65,000 sq km it is roughly a quarter of the size of the United Kingdom and seven times as large as Cyprus. Lithuania is the most southerly of the three Baltic states and has very little coastline.

The driving force behind the explosion of investment in Lithuania (and in Vilnius in particular) has been the huge success of the local economy coupled with the defeat of the rampant inflation that characterised the immediate post-Soviet era. This, together with the belief that entry to the European Union would increase prices and opportunities, has led to the high levels of growth seen over the last few years. Some of the investors are professional investors. Increasingly, however, amateur investors are enthused by the potential returns and who like the idea of Vilnius, the capital city, as an attractive place to have a *pied à terre* for occasional holiday use.

Tourism

Tourist numbers in Lithuania have been steadily rising in the last five years, with almost 1.5 million foreign visitors staying at least one night. There is a 12% increase annually, consisting entirely of arrivals by air.

The Economy

Lithuania, the Baltic state that always conducted the most trade with Russia, has slowly rebounded from the 1998 Russian financial crisis. Unemployment dropped from 11 per cent in 2003 to 8 per cent in 2004. Growing domestic consumption and increased investment have furthered recovery, and trade has been increasingly orientated towards the West. Lithuania gained membership in the World Trade Organization in May 2004. The privatisation of the large, state-owned utilities, particularly in the energy sector, is nearing completion; overall, more than 80 per cent of enterprises have been privatised. Foreign government and business support have helped in the transition from the old command economy to a market economy. Economic growth is, arguably, the highest in Europe (8.9 per cent in 2003, 6.6 per cent in 2004).

GDP per capita is roughly half that of the UK, and roughly double that of countries such as Bulgaria or Turkey. Lithuania's population is the largest in the Baltic states at 3.5 million, but it has seen a steady decline (7 per cent in 10 years), mainly through emigration.

The Exchange Rate

The chart overleaf shows the exchange rate in Lithuania for the last 10 years.

Exchange Rate – Lithuanian Lita

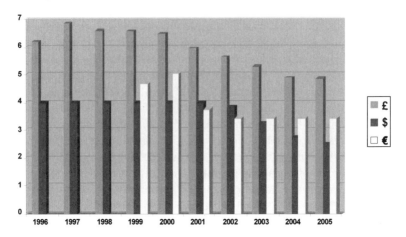

Visas and Permits

As Lithuania is a member of the European Union, any citizen of a member state can enter the country without a visa in the same way as they can enter, say, France or Spain. You can stay for up to **90 days** in any six-month period. After 90 days you need to obtain a **residence permit** – a relatively painless procedure.

Profile of Lithuania

Recent History and Politics

From 1920 until 1939 the capital of Lithuania, Vilnius, was annexed to neihbouring Poland. The country was under Nazi occupation from 1939 until 1944, and then from 1944 to 1990 Lithuania was occupied by Russia. Lithuania declared its independence in 1990 (the first of the Baltic states to do so; it led the push for Baltic independence) but this was not recognised until 1991. The Republic of Lithuania is a parliamentary democracy. It has proved keen to embrace the West and in May 2004 joined NATO and the European Union.

Climate and Geography

Lithuania has a coastline of only about 100km and most of the country comprises farmland. As you would expect from its location, the climate is hardly tropical. The summer temperatures are acceptable at about 20°C but the winters can be seriously cold. *See* 'Climate Charts', p.288, for more details of the temperature and rainfall patterns.

Regional Profile

Vilnius, the capital city, has roots going back hundreds of years. It is a very attractive historic city – probably the prettiest in the Baltic states – in the Central European tradition. Today, in this 'town of 100 churches', the impressive skyline is pierced with spires, domes and crosses; the Old Town was declared a UNESCO World Heritage Site in 1994. Modern Vilnius is now a mix of old and new architecture, with Gothic and Italian Baroque buildings, as well as the bleak structures influenced by the former Soviet Union. The famous skyline has been changing rapidly and expanding north across the river Neris, where high-rise structures are starting to dominate this newly developing area of a city that is home to 600,000 people.

Lithuania's second city, **Kaunas**, is equally pleasant, with a vibrant main drag full of trendy bars and cafés charging 1970s prices. The rest of the country is mainly farmland, with five national parks and various reserves. The old Lithuanian capital of **Trakai** is around 30km west of Vilnius. The small stretch of coastline is home to the busy industrial port of **Klaipėda**.

Selecting a Property

Getting There

Vilnius is served by air by **Air Baltic**, **Lithuanian Airlines, SAS** and **British Airways**. A direct return ticket from London, departing June 2005, is quoted at £180 by the **British Airways**.

Getting Around

Within all the Baltic States, the rail system is sadly out of date, with damage to the infrastructure. Buses are faster, cheaper and more frequent than trains; they are fairly comfortable, and highways are constantly being improved.

Choosing a Location

The only real place where there is any activity by the foreign buyer is in **Vilnius**, the capital city.

Property Prices

Prices have been rising rapidly. Some of our clients have seen growth of over 20 per cent in the last year. The table below attempts to show some general indication of prices as at January 2005.

Property Prices in Vilnius, January 2005

Place and Type of Property	Low	Mid	High
Vilnius – one-bedroom apartment in historic centre (60 sq m)		£45,000	£58,000
Vilnius – two-bedroom apartment in historic centre (100 sq m)		£80,000	£130,000
Vilnius — two-bedroom apartment in historic centre (156 sq m)			£250,000
Vilnius – three-bedroom villa in suburbs (160 sq m)			£350,000

Building from Scratch or Renovation

There are many properties on sale in Lithuania that need huge amounts of work and there is not much of a market for these properties. The problems associated with a renovation project can be huge; not least will be your probable inability to speak Lithuanian. If you are contemplating a renovation project it is vital to get good advice at the outset. Building costs are low, however; a full restoration project is likely to cost about £250 per square metre.

The Process of Buying a Property

Legal advice is essential unless you take the view that the amount you are investing is so small you can afford to write it off.

Freedom to Buy

You can freely buy land, buildings or apartments in Lithuania.

Initial Steps

First Contracts

Once you have found a property that you want to purchase, you will be expected to sign some form of contract. This will generally either be a reservation contract or a preliminary purchase contract. *See* 'Reservation and Preliminary Contracts', p.75, for an explanation of these concepts. Note that the title 'preliminary purchase contract' is misleading; it is actually a full binding purchase contract. We therefore recommend that, wherever possible, you insist on signing a **reservation contract** rather than a preliminary purchase contract at this stage.

Searches and Enquiries

Once you have signed a reservation contract, your lawyer should make the standard enquiries to check that the contract is fair, that the seller has good title and the right to sell to you, that the area is zoned for residential building and that any building work being undertaken enjoys all of the necessary planning and building consents. Depending on the circumstances of your case there could well be other enquiries that also need to be made.

In Lithuania it is common for work to be started, illegally, before all of these steps are in place.

Some Problems

In Lithuania there is a danger of property having defective title and planning consents. This is true of most of the old Eastern Bloc countries. Many older properties, though very attractive, are also in a very poor state of repair. You should not underestimate the cost and complexity of restoring these.

Sometimes these problems should put you off having any involvement in the purchase. On other occasions the risks are minimal and, provided you go into the transaction with your eyes open, might not put you off buying if you really like the property.

Signing the Contract and Registering the Title

Once your lawyer has checked out the property and found that everything is in order, you are ready to sign the **preliminary purchase contract**. This commits you and the seller to signing the full contract transferring ownership shortly afterwards or, if the property is still under construction, once the property has been built. The preliminary purchase contract contains most of the clauses you would expect to see in a UK contract, including a description of the property, a statement of the legal title to the property, the price to be paid, how it is to be paid, the deadline for payment and any other deadlines applicable, what should happen in the event of breach of contract and so on. Many Lithuanian contracts are badly drafted because there is no history in Lithuania of drafting contracts for the sale of land, and they can be unclear or muddled because of language difficulties. Specifications tend to be thin and the contracts lack detail about what happens if anything goes wrong.

At this point you will normally pay a **deposit** of 10 per cent of the price of the property or start to make **stage payments** for off-plan properties, which vary in size and number from property to property. A typical scheme provides for an initial payment of 30 per cent followed by two further payments of 30 per cent as construction progresses, followed by a final payment of 10 per cent on delivery. Occasionally there are schemes where there is only one preliminary payment of, say, 30 per cent with the balance being paid on delivery. This is useful if you are taking out a mortgage.

Once you are ready to take delivery of the property you will sign the **final purchase contract** in front of a notary public. It is at this point that the balance of the money is paid to the notary, who will release it to the seller once the property transfer has taken place. You do not need to be present in Lithuania to sign this document, as your lawyer can prepare a **power of attorney** (*see* pp.77–8) under which you can appoint somebody else to sign on your behalf. This is a sensible thing to do as it saves the need for you to go to Lithuania, often at short notice, to sign the final title.

Once you have paid the balance of the price the seller will authorise you to **register your ownership** of the property in the local title register. Once this has been done, you will be the full legal owner of the property in much the same way as you would be in the UK. It is likely to take 2–6 weeks for the registered title deeds to be made available to you; exactly how long will depend on how busy the registry is in the place where you are buying. With the current explosion of demand these periods are getting longer.

The Expenses of Buying

The main expenses of buying are:

- **tax** – the equivalent of stamp duty – 1 per cent of the price.

- **estate agents' fees**, if these are not paid by the seller – typically 5 per cent of the price if you are using a local Lithuanian agent.

- **notary's fees** – these will vary from case to case but will typically not exceed £100.

- **legal fees** – these depend on whether you use a Lithuanian or a UK lawyer; UK lawyer's fees will inevitably be higher but you will be able to sue them if they get it wrong and they will be able to give you lots of advice, particularly about the vital issues of who should own the property to minimise your tax and other problems, which the local Lithuanian lawyer would not be able to help you with; fees will range from about £350 if you use a local Lithuanian lawyer to £1,500 if you use a specialist UK lawyer.

- **fees to set up a company** – if you are buying a piece of land or a house on a piece of land (but not an apartment) you will need to set up a Lithuanian company; this is likely to cost £500.

Letting Your Property

See the general chapter **Letting Your Property**, pp.117–26.

If you are letting out your property you should make sure that you use a proper **rental contract**. Your lawyer will be able to supply you with a draft that you can amend as necessary. Offering short-term lets to tourists is the safest. In general terms, landlord and tenant law in the Baltic states offers a fair balance between the interests of the landlord and the interests of the tenant.

Taxes

Taxes for Non-resident Property-owners

Local Property Taxes

Local property taxes in Lithuania are very low. They are assessed on the basis of the official tax value of property which, in itself, is normally only about half the true value of your property. The normal rate of local property tax is 1 per cent of the official value.

Income Taxes

A foreign investor can invest in properties in Lithuania either directly, in his own name, or through a local company. The tax paid depends on the choice.

• **Rental income on company-owned property.**

The basis of the taxable income of a company investing in Lithuanian real estate is the gross income from the property less any tax-deductible expenses and depreciation. These expenses include any management costs, repairs, maintenance, insurance and so on, and interest on any loans used to buy the property. The corporate tax rate is a flat rate of 15 per cent.

• **Rental income on individually owned property.**

For non-residents, tax is payable on income derived in Lithuania or from real estate located in Lithuania. The rate of tax depends upon the nature of the income. Tax on rental income is at 20 per cent. This can be set off against UK tax liabilities on the same income.

Capital Gains Taxes

Capital gains taxes are treated as part of your income and non-residents are taxed at 10 per cent on the capital gain arising from the sale of all real estate, however long that real estate has been owned for. For a resident, the gain is tax-free provided only one piece of real estate is sold in each year.

Wealth Taxes

There are no wealth taxes in Lithuania.

Inheritance Taxes

There is a general inheritance or gift tax, usually 10 per cent. Gifts between parents and children or spouses are exempt from tax.

Taxes for Resident Foreigners

This is beyond the scope of this book.

Settling In

Learning and Speaking Lithuanian

The language spoken is Lithuanian, though Russian is also widely spoken. You will find some people who speak English in Vilnius, but probably not elsewhere.

Shopping

Shops are generally open from 9/10–6/7 on weekdays, and from 9/10–4 on Saturdays. Larger department stores are open daily 10–8, while food shops and supermarkets open 8am–10pm during the week, with some open on Sunday. Shops in rural areas often close for a lunch break.

Telephones and the Internet

To call Lithuania from abroad, dial the **country code** (**t** 370), then the area or city code (Vilnius = 5), then the number. To call a local number once you are in Lithuania, omit the area code. To call one city from another in Lithuania, or any number (even local) from a mobile phone, you should dial 8, wait for a tone, and then dial the area code and number. Lithuanian public telephones work using a card-only system; **telephone cards** cost 9Lt, 13Lt, 16Lt and 30Lt and may be purchased at Lietuvos Spauda kiosks and post offices.

Mobile phones can also be rented at local phone shops. If you have a GSM 900/1800, and a phone that is not locked to a network, it will work out cheaper to purchase a SIM card package from a local provider.

There are more and more **Internet** cafés opening up in larger cities as well as small towns, as well as small towns. You can get online at tourist offices, libraries, post offices and shopping centres.

Money and Banking

The unit of currency in Lithuania is the **litas** (Lt; plural **litų**), which was introduced in 1994. It comes in notes of 10 Lt, 20Lt, 50Lt, 100 Lt, 200 Lt and 500Lt, plus

1, 2 and 5Lt coins, as well as a few other weightless **centų** coins that are worth only the space they take up in your pocket. **Banks** are generally open Mon–Fri 9/10–4/5, and some banks in larger cities are often open on Sat from 10–2 or 3.

There are **ATMs** all around larger towns. Major **credit cards** can be used in all of the bigger hotels, restaurants, department stores and shops.

Post

Postal services have improved considerably in the Baltics, with mail arriving in 7–10 days to North America and within 2–5 days to Western Europe. Main post offices (*pasts*) are located throughout the city, and are usually open 9–6 on weekdays and 9–1 on Sat. Stamps can also be bought at some hotels.

Health

Ambulance: **t** 03 or **t** 112.

There are some improving private facilities catering to foreigners in each country, and EU members are entitled to **emergency** treatment with an E111 or the new EHIC card, but if you have a serious medical problem, you might consider leaving the country. Take good travel insurance. If you will be in wooded areas, immunisation against tick-borne encephalitis is highly recommended.

Although the **tap water** in the Baltics is said to be drinkable, stick with bottled water. **Pharmacies** (*apteek*) are usually open 10–7, but some stay open all night.

Crime and the Police

Police: **t** 02 or **t** 112.

Vilnius is not any more dangerous than any other European capital, but foreigners have been known to be targeted. The most common problems are pick-pocketing and car break-ins. It is best, as anywhere, to avoid wandering into unfamiliar streets alone after dark. Be discreet when using your mobile phone.

Lithuania: References

Directory of Contacts and Resources

Embassies

- **Lithuanian Embassy**, 84 Gloucester Place, London W1H 3HN, **t** (020) 7486 6401, **amb.uk@urm.lt**.

- **British Embassy**, Antakalnio 2, **t** (5) 246 2900 or **t** (5) 246 2901, **www.britain.lt**.

Information and Resources

- **www.tourism.lt**. Information on the country.

Time

Lithuania is on Eastern European Time (GMT/UTC + 2). The 24hr clock is used for flight, train and bus timetables. In summer, the country follows daylight saving, putting clocks forward an hour in spring and back in autumn.

Public Holidays

1 January	New Year's Day and National Flag Day
16 February	Independence Day
11 March	Restoration of Independence Day
March/April	Palm Sunday, Easter Sunday and Monday
1 May	International Labour Day
14 June	Day of Mourning and Hope
24 June	St John's Day or Midsummer's Day
6 July	King Mindaugas' Coronation (Day of Statehood)
15 August	Assumption
23 August	Black Ribbon Day
8 September	Crowning of Vytautas the Great
25 October	Constitution Day
1 November	All Saints' Day
25–6 December	Christmas

Climate Charts
Average Maximum Temperature in Vilnius (°C)

Jan	Feb	Mar	April	May	June	July	Aug	Sept	Oct	Nov	Dec
−5	−4	−1	12	17	21	23	22	17	11	4	−3

Average Monthly Rainfall in Vilnius (mm)

Jan	Feb	Mar	April	May	June	July	Aug	Sept	Oct	Nov	Dec
28	38	37	40	82	66	49	97	60	48	62	39

Average Daily Hours of Sunshine in Vilnius

Jan	Feb	Mar	April	May	June	July	Aug	Sept	Oct	Nov	Dec
1	2	4	6	7	10	10	9	6	3	1	1

Montenegro

Why Buy in Montenegro?

Tiny Montenegro is the size of Wales, with a population of just 600,000. Formerly part of Yugoslavia, it escaped much of the devastation faced by other former Yugoslav countries during the civil war of the 1990s. Montenegro is now part of the union of Serbia and Montenegro, a loose political alliance which gives both countries a great deal of autonomy. The country has suffered economically as a result of the conflict; it is desperately trying to pick itself up again and is undergoing much change.

Montenegro benefits from all the charms of Croatia without the prices – property here is around a third cheaper. Dubrovnik is the undeniable star of

Croatia's southern coast, with prices reaching their peak in the city, and Montenegro is only a few hours to the south by road. In future it will be even easier to travel between the two countries; many visitors already fly into Dubrovnik and drive across the border. A new six-lane border crossing costing £1.3 million has just been confirmed; starting at Debeli Brijeg, just north of the property hotspot of Herceg Novi, it is predicted to cut travelling time in half.

Montenegro has the advantage of being relatively unexplored by British people, with many people not even knowing exactly where it is. That makes for more unspoilt countryside, greater property choice and perhaps greater profit margins. Bear in mind, though, that the rest of Europe has already discovered Montenegro: visitors from Russia, Austria and Germany have been holidaying here for years and some of them have already bought properties. Also, there is a greater risk attached to this country, which in some ways is still an unknown quantity – a purchase there is something of a gamble.

While British property-buyers have in the main ignored Montenegro in favour of countries like Turkey, Croatia and Bulgaria, this looks set to change. The country's charms are undeniable, and even though its appeal in terms of overseas property investment is certainly in its infancy, its future popularity seems sure to take off.

Montenegro is not nearly as advanced as Croatia as a place in which to invest or even to buy a holiday or retirement property. The whole process is more complicated. The system is less reliable. This does not mean to say that it cannot be done. Those who do it are likely to find that they have acquired an asset that will perform very well in investment terms over the next five to 10 years. Do not, however, expect immediate returns or a bonanza in Montenegro; it is not yet ready for that, and is dependent on political developments that may or may not come later. Certainly Montenegro has a wealth of natural beauty and some magnificent historic cities to offer to the property-buyer.

No Smoke Without Fire

In a surprise move, the parliament in Montenegro has passed a law banning smoking in all public places as well as forbidding any form of tobacco advertising and smoking on television. What makes the ban so bizarre is the fact that, along with Serbia, Montenegro has the third-highest rate of smoking in Europe. Only people in Turkey and Greece smoke more.

In Montenegro 40 per cent of the population smoke and at the moment they are allowed to do so just about anywhere, whether at work, in restaurants or in trains. What also makes the ban seem even odder is that an investigation by the European Union has resulted in the Montenegrin government being accused of large-scale cigarette smuggling. It is thought that the idea has come from the country's commitment to bringing itself in line with more developed countries in Europe.

Celebrity Visits

In the 1950s the country was in its heyday, when sophisticated celebrities such as Elizabeth Taylor, Richard Burton and Sophia Loren fell in love with the place. And even in the 19th century Lord Byron, the romantic poet, wrote, 'At the birth of our planet, the most beautiful encounter between the land and the sea must have happened at the coast of Montenegro. When the pearls of nature were sown, handfuls of them were cast on this soil.'

Sveti Stefan is Montenegro's mini-Mont St-Michel. A thin causeway links a former fishing village to the mainland – all of which was taken over to form a luxury hotel in the 1960s. A hundred or so stone cottages are the guest rooms, set among landscaped gardens and flower-filled walkways. Princess Margaret stayed here, and more recently Jeremy Irons. The island resort was said to be the original planned destination for Prince Charles and Princess Diana's honeymoon before the news was leaked to the press.

The celebrities may now be conspicuous by their absence, but Montenegro retains the grandeur and old-world charm that drew them there, and, as overseas property buyers become more adventurous – as well as possessing a keener eye than ever for a bargain – Montenegro looks set to enjoy the popularity of its past once again.

Tourism

Tourism was obviously very limited during the war – a period of around 10 years – but visitors from around the world are starting to return. Before its onset, the country welcomed around half a million foreign tourists annually. That figure has shrunk to 150,000, but British companies are once again featuring Montenegro in their brochures.

Although Montenegro's tourist infrastructure is not highly developed, with its few larger hotels remnants of the Soviet era or rather monstrous holiday complexes, this has its advantages. Private enterprise has been slow to take a grip, so in most villages there are just a handful of bars, shops and restaurants.

Russian Villages

In September 2004, estate agencies and other companies having inter-national dealings were reminded by the head of Montenegro's anti-money-laundering office, Predrag Mitrovic, to inform the authorities of any suspicious financial dealings. It is thought that Russian companies have been laundering money in the country by purchasing properties and companies. Although it is hard to know how much of their involvement is down to speculation, Russians do have a history of dealings in the country. Way back in 1998, they leased two hotels in Kotor and have since bought further facilities on the coast. They have also been buying plots of lands in prime sites on the sea, to the extent that locals have dubbed one particular settlement 'Russian Village'.

The Economy

The country suffered greatly in the 1990s as a result of its association with Serbia and Slobodan Milošević's mismanagement of the economy. Economic sanctions and the war damaged both countries' industry considerably, reducing output to half that of 1990. In 2005 it is stable, and Yugoslavia's renewal of its membership with the IMF in 2000 brought funding, debt relief and a certain amount of recovery, although unemployment remains a big problem.

Exchange Rate

One curiosity in Montenegro is that, although it is not yet part of the European Union, and has been given no dates are joining, the currency in use is the euro. This is simply because it used to use the Deutschmark.

Visas and Permits

British citizens do not require visas for visits up to **90 days**. For further details check the **Embassy of Serbia and Montenegro** website (*see* p.307).

For the latest information on obtaining **residency** in Montenegro, contact the **Honorary British Consulate** in Podgorica (*see* p.307).

The notion of **citizenship** in the country was only established in 1999. At present, applicants must have been resident for ten consecutive years. For further information, contact the **Embassy of Serbia and Montenegro** (*see* p.307).

Profile of Montenegro

Recent History and Politics

The natives of Montenegro secured a victory over Byzantium as far back as 1042 and were the only people in the region to defend themselves against the Ottoman Turks, who conquered much of southern Europe in the 14th century. Successive attempts by the Turks were foiled, partly through Montenegro's alliances with Venice and then with Russia. For 300 years Montenegro was the seat of the 'Bishop-Kings' who led the country in a continuing struggle against the Ottoman Empire, invading from the East. By the mid-19th century they had evolved into a fully fledged if short-lived monarchy, with King Nikola Petrovich I ruling from 1860 until he was deposed in 1918. Alfred, Lord Tennyson even wrote a poem called 'Montenegro' in 1877 in which he praised the 'race of mightier mountaineers'.

More recently, this tiny corner of the former Yugoslavia (created in 1929) had pressure put on it by Slobodan Milošević, who in 1991 took his army over the border and into its neighbour Croatia, where villages were destroyed and the ancient city of Dubrovnik heavily shelled. Some say they were tricked – they were told that the Croatian army was about to invade so they were forced to take action.

In the 2000 elections, Vojislav Koštunica, a law professor, won the presidency amid reports of fraud and intimidation. In 2001 Miloševic was turned over to the United Nations International Criminal Tribunal for the former Yugoslavia in The Hague, charged with genocide and crimes against humanity. In February 2003 the Federal Republic of Yugoslavia was renamed Serbia and Montenegro. This new country has two capital cities: Belgrade (overall) and Podgorica, which has administered the Republic of Montenegro since 1991. The new government is a loose arrangement, sharing only a small administration responsible for defence and foreign affairs. Montenegro will be able to hold a referendum on independence after three years. The prime minister of Serbia, Zoran Djindjić, who helped bring about the fall of Miloševic, was assassinated in March 2003. In May 2003 Filip Vujanović, a strong supporter of Montenegrin independence, was elected Montenegro's president.

Montenegro's continuing union with Serbia is a major concern. Some experts say the problem in the past was that the two countries were trying to act as one. Despite peace in the region, there are many unresolved disputes between Montenegro and Serbia, with some arguing that EU membership will arrive much more quickly if the two countries separate. It is unlikely that there will be a referendum in Montenegro about EU membership before 2006; only after that – if the country joins the EU – will the economic benefits of predicted membership start to take effect.

Montenegro is already looking ahead to its day of independence and has chosen its new national symbols. The country's new flag will feature a gold coat of arms of a two-headed eagle under a royal crown and a shield with an engraved lion, which will replace the much more straightforward red, blue and white flag. The new national day of 13 July celebrates the date in 1878 when the Berlin Congress recognised Montenegro as the world's 27th independent state. This was also the day in 1941 when Montenegrins rebelled against Nazi occupiers. 'Oh Bright Dawn' will be the national anthem.

Meanwhile, in March 2004 there was an escalation in inter-ethnic violence in the northern parts of Kosovo and British troops were sent in. Although the town has been calm since then, it is wise to take advice from the British embassy, as the situation can change at any point.

Religion

The majority of the population (65 per cent) is Eastern Orthodox, 19 per cent is Muslim Orthodox, 4 per cent Roman Catholic, and 1 per cent Protestant. There is a small Jewish population.

Climate and Geography

In the southern part of the Balkans, Montenegro has 200km of Adriatic coastline and much of the land is covered by mountain ranges cut through with deep gorges, with some lowland areas. The miniature Balkan state benefits from a gorgeous coastline, with expansive beaches composed of rock and small pebbles as well the finest golden sand. The coast is backed by enormous limestone mountains, while its inland area features glacial lakes, crystal-clear rivers and deep canyons. The country has not been subject to mass tourism, and the overwhelming sense is of a rural area punctuated with fishing villages and deep rolling hills dotted with olive trees.

The country as a whole has a Mediterranean climate, with warm summers and mild winters and a high level of rainfall. The climate is essentially divided into three regions. The coastal area has long dry summers with mild winters. The central part is continental, with high average temperatures. The mountain region has a sub-alpine climate, with mild summers and cold winters with regular snowfall. The *bora* is a cold wind which blows in winter for days.

Regional Profile

Crna Gora is the indigenous title for Montenegro. Both names mean Black Mountain, because the country's mountains are covered in dense black pine trees. Located in southeastern Europe, Montenegro is on the Adriatic Sea, north of Albania, south of Croatia, opposite the 'heel' of Italy and sharing borders with Bosnia-Herzogovina and Serbia.

As with the climate, the towns in Montenegro can be divided into three main areas – the coast, the plains and the highlands. Those on the coast – Herceg Novi, Kotor, Budva and Bar – are significant for the economy as tourist centres. Behind the mountains on the plains are the commercial towns of Podgorica, Danilovgrad and Nikšić on the River Zeta, and to the south is the Cetinje. In the highlands are towns such as Kolasin, Plav, Savnik, Bijelo Polje and Rozaj.

The coast stretches for nearly 300km from Herceg Novi in the north to Ulcinj in the south; it features 117 different beaches, from hidden rocky coves only accessible by boat to long open expanses of sand. The green, transparent waters of the Adriatic lie against a backdrop of dark mountains and rolling countryside of olive and orange groves and pine forests.

Podgorica

Because so much of the country is covered by mountains and forests, most of the communities are centred around towns, and the country only has one city. Podgorica, which was previously called Titograd, is the administrative and commercial centre of country and has a small international airport. As a university town it has a lively, young population of over 20,000. Although it has seen better days, its wide, tree-lined streets, once-splendid public buildings and *fin de siècle* mansions that were home to foreign embassies are reminders of its former glory. There's an old stone theatre and a former royal palace, which is now the National Museum.

Kotor

Kotor is a surprise. Not only is it at the head of one of the biggest fjords in Europe and its lovely walled town a UNESCO World Heritage Site, but its port was once one of the most important in the world. Situated against a backdrop of high mountains, in the southwest of the country, circled by well-preserved ramparts, Kotor has had a long association with seafaring. The town's long history is represented by a splendid 9th-century cathedral along with a collection of medieval and Renaissance buildings, including a 6th-century clock tower, Prince's Palace and Napoleon's Theatre. Between 1420 and 1797 Kotor and its surroundings were under the rule of Venice and the maritime city's influence can still be seen. The fjord or bay is known as Boka Kotorska, which literally means Bay of Kotor, and is made up of four smaller bays, named after the towns of Kotor, Tivat, Herceg Novi and Risan.

Prcanj is a small village in the Bay of Kotor. Founded in the 16th century, it was long used by pirates as a hideaway. By the end of the 18th century, it had become more reputable and had a large fleet of trading ships and a number of private schools for ship's captains and sailors. In 2003 a four-star hotel opened in the village, where international package tourists stay.

Bar

Bar is essentially a modern administrative and transport centre with little to attract the visitor. It has good links north and south by rail, and ferry connections to Bari and Ancona in Italy. Although it is swamped by cement architecture from the Soviet era, there are some reminders of its earlier history, such as a 6th-century church. The surrounding area includes the lovely **Skadar Lake**, which is in a landscape of small villages and old monasteries surrounded

Killing Fields

The country's rural areas, as well as the coastline, rather disturbingly serve as hunting-grounds where wild duck, moorhen, turtle-dove, quail and partridge are shot. The mountain areas have traditionally provided for the shooting of bear, boar and wolf among other animals. Trout, perch and carp are fished in the sea and rivers of the country. With Montenegro keen to bring itself in line with other European countries and conservation groups slating the practice, it seems unlikely that the current situation, in which local travel agencies proudly advertise hunting tours on the Internet, will continue.

by cattle-raising country and scenic vineyards. The great lake – over 30 miles long and 10 miles wide – is home to nearly 300 species of birds, including pelicans and black ibises. Nearby are the Rumija Mountains, around which are springs and watering fields of edible produce and local flowers.

Budva

Budva dates back 2,500 years and is one of the oldest towns in the Mediterranean. The ancient part of the town is surrounded by ramparts, and the medieval fortification on a peninsula has been beautifully restored. Within the town walls is a network of narrow streets leading on to pretty squares. Nearby are modern hotels and a large number of bays with beaches and limestone cliffs, making Budva the country's biggest beach resort.

Other Small Towns

The town of **Herceg Novi** is the administrative and cultural centre for Montenegro. Dating back 600 years or so, it has a number of fortresses, palaces and churches, including the significant Savina Monastery. The coastal town of **Igalo** is joined to Herceg Novi by a 7km-long promenade, and is home to the well-known Igalo Spa, which offers medicinal and beauty treatments.

Cetinje is perched high above Budva. The old capital has an undeniable romance and is still the cultural heart of the country. The subject of many patriotic poems, it boasts palaces, museums and monasteries. The star of its attractions is the 15th-century Cetinje Monastery, which contains the hand of St John the Baptist in a jewel-encrusted casket. The hills around the town are known for hiking.

The attractive and unspoilt coastal resort of **Petrovac** was formerly a fishing village, and now has pretty gardens, shops and restaurants lining the front and a 16th-century fortress, Kastel Lastva. There is a tiny harbour in an area of olive trees and vineyards.

Although its origins go back to the 3rd century, **Tivat** is basically a modern town with a naval base, harbour and an airport where most visitors arrive in summer. Essentially an administrative centre, it boasts a lovely park with exotic ornamental plants and trees planted by local sea men. The suburb of Lepatane has a car ferry, which connects with the other side of the Boka Kotorska.

One of the oldest towns on the coast of Montenegro, **Ulcinj** has a three-millennium-year-old history. Reached via one of two gates, it is a charming mix of east and west, old and new; the old town features traces of old stone buildings, ancient ramparts and towers, while modern hotels line the beaches. Velika plaza ('Big Beach') is – at 12km long – aptly named. Nearby, on the banks of the River Bojana, traditional fishing methods and old wooden huts can still be seen. The river is full of delicious fish, and on its shores are the remains of the old town of Svac.

Selecting a Property

Getting There

You can enter Montenegro directly through the international airports in Podgorica, Tivat and Čilipi (Croatia) as well at the following land border crossings: from Croatia: Debeli brijeg; from Bosnia and Hercegovina: Vilusi, Vracenovici, Scepan polje and Metaljka; and from Albania: Bozaj. The sea border crossings are Bar, Kotor, Budva and Zelenika.

When entering Montenegro through the territory of Serbia, check with the nearest Yugoslav Embassy to see whether you need a visa for entering Serbia before starting your trip. This is also advisable if you are planning to continue your trip from Montenegro to Serbia.

By Air

- **Montenegro Airlines, t** + 381 81 405 500/501, **www.montenegro-airlines.cg.yu.** The national carrier operating scheduled flights at the two international airports, Tivat and Podgorica.
- **British Airways, t** (0870) 850 9850, **www.ba.com.** Flies between Heathrow and Belgrade and Dubrovnik.
- **JAT Yugoslav Airlines, www.jat.com.** Operates a flight from Heathrow to Tivat in Montenegro.

By Sea

Montenegro has good ferry connections, with regular services on routes to Bar from Bari and Ancona in Italy.

By Bus

Travelling overland to Montenegro from neighbouring European countries is not straightforward and the country does not have good international connections. For example, at the time of writing there was only one bus a day from Croatia into Montenegro. See **www.eurolines.co.yu/Eng** for more information about international services.

By Train

The passenger trains on the Bar–Belgrade line are connected with international trains to Budapest, Vienna, Bucharest, Athens, Moscow and other cities.

Getting Around

By Air
Because of the size of the country, internal air travel is not always practical. The national carrier, **Montenegro Airlines** (**www.montenegroairlines.cg.yu**), flies from the airports of Podgorica, Nis and Tivat, as well as Skopje in neighbouring Macedonia.

By Rail
The main railway line goes from Bar to Belgrade (Bar–Podgorica–Belgrade) with branches towards Nikšić and another towards Skadar in Albania. There are five passenger trains on the Bar–Belgrade route per day: three-express trains, one business, one auto-car and one train with sleeping cars. On the Bar–Subotica line there is one daily express train with sleeping cars.

By Bus
Bus services can be irregular and, although scenic, rather tortuous in the mountains. The best services run between Subotica, Novi Sad, Belgrade, Nis, Priština and Skopje. Unless you have a car, travelling along the Montenegrin coast is the only way to travel. Try to book a seat ahead in the high season.

By Car
The road network totals 5,174km. The two major roads in Montenegro are the Adriatic motorway from Igalo to Ulcinj and the motorway that links the south and the north of the country, from Pertovac, across Podgorica and Kolasin to Bijelo Polje. In general, however, the roads are in appalling condition. Hefty tolls are charged for vehicles registered abroad, which may also be targets for carjackers. The major cities and airports have car hire companies. Should you drive into Croatia, take note that a new law there demands that dipped headlights should be used at all times.

Choosing a Location

Montenegro is Croatia ten years ago. It is much poorer. It has a tiny population of only about 700,000 people. It lives in an uneasy relationship with its bigger partner, Serbia, which seems only to be held together because the Serbians allow the Montenegrins almost total independence. The border of Montenegro is only about 30 minutes from Dubrovnik airport, and it is the area just over that border that has received most attention. If anything, Montenegro is even more beautiful than southern Croatia. Look out, in particular, for the Kotor inlet (a real fjord), the city of Kotor, the amazing collection of 17th-century summertime palaces at Perast and the town of Bar.

Property Types and Prices

Properties for sale are a mixture of old stone houses, and increasingly new-build apartment blocks, particularly in Bar and other cities on the Adriatic coast. The country has a huge amount of land (particularly ex-army plots) and larger properties that is being sold off.

Predictably, the coast is catching the eye of potential investors. The northern section of coastline – the part closer to Croatia – is the most sought-after, but in the south prices are more competitive. Travel inland even just a few miles and see the prices drop. Further inland, there are activities such as fishing and skiing, with rural retreats and mountain villas.

There are many hotels, restaurants and bars for sale up and down the coast that are currently available for the right investor. Podgorica has a range of new apartment blocks, houses and office buildings.

The main deciding factor when it comes to coastal property prices is the building's proximity to the sea. Buildings within 100 metres or so from the coast retail for around €1,000 per square metre. Many properties in this kind of position have land, berths for boats and even their own beach, all of which will boost the price. Newly constructed apartments near to the sea but not on the beach go for around €800 per square metre, with houses retailing for anything from €35,000 to €1 million.

Guide Prices

€20,000

- Two-bedroom house over 60 sq m in Herceg Novi.

€30,000

- Small one-bedroom flat with no outside space in the popular seaside resort of Budva.
- Land with two ruins on 2,000 sq m with sea views.

€50,000

- Four-bedroom house in the mountains overlooking the fjord of an Adriatic inlet.
- Apartment in Budva with two bedrooms and a terrace.
- Two-bedroom apartment in the old town of Kotor.

€80,000

- Modern two-bedroom apartment with sea views in Herceg Novi.

€100,000

- House that could be converted into four apartments with views over Budva and a large terrace.
- Five-bedroom, two-bathroom old stone building in Kotor.
- Stone-built terraced house on the water's edge, Perast.
- Three-storey house with a large terrace and furniture on the Boka-Kotorska bay not far from Herceg Novi.

€200,000

- Stone house on three floors on the sea front in Herceg Novi-Kumbor, built on 190 sq m with a beach 6m away.
- House in Petrovac with 500 sq m of land; ground floor of two bedrooms, kitchen and bathroom; first floor with living room, bedroom and bathroom; and second floor with two bedrooms and a bathroom.
- Old stone-built house with six bedrooms on 2,000 sq m plot; needs renovation, in Kotor.

€500,000

- House with three bedrooms and two living rooms in upmarket Sv. Stefan.
- Four-floor house with 10 rooms, 25 bedrooms and six bathrooms on the plaza of Petrovac; overlooking the beach, it is built over 400 sq m, with land of 100 sq m.

Temporary Accommodation

Because of its small size and relatively undeveloped tourist industry, Montenegro has a limited range of temporary accommodation. Short-term flat rentals are available in the capital, while elsewhere private self-catering villas, hotels and private rooms can be rented. The tourist office can give information.

The Process of Buying a Property

Although finding an English-speaking agent can be difficult, this is changing and the whole process of buying property is becoming much less over-whelming. The Montenegrin government is keen to encourage foreign investment and to make it as easy as possible for overseas buyers.

Freedom to Buy

British people can buy land, buildings or apartments in Montenegro (other nationalities can only buy land in Montenegro if their country allows

Montenegrins the right to buy land in their country). Foreigners may never buy agricultural land or forestry land, and buying cultural monuments or certain other categories of land requires special procedures.

Initial Steps

First Contracts

Once you have found a property that you want to purchase, you will be expected to sign some form of contract, generally either a reservation contract or a preliminary purchase contract. The name 'preliminary purchase contract' is misleading: it is actually a full binding purchase contract. We therefore recommend that, wherever possible, you insist on signing a **reservation contract** rather than a preliminary purchase contract at this stage.

Searches and Enquiries

Once you have signed a reservation contract, your lawyer should make various enquiries, such as checking that the contract is fair, that the seller has good title and the right to sell to you, that the area is zoned for residential building and that any building work being undertaken enjoys all necessary planning and building consents. Depending on the circumstances of your case there could well be other enquiries that also need to be made.

The main problems in Montenegro are defective title and defective planning consents, as the land registry has not always been as stringent as elsewhere.

Signing the Contract and Registering the Title

Once your lawyer has checked out the property and found that everything is in order, you are ready to sign the **preliminary purchase contract**. This commits you and the seller to signing the full contract transferring ownership on an agreed date shortly afterwards, or, if the property is still under construction, once the property has been fully built.

The preliminary purchase contract contains most of the clauses you would expect to see in a UK contract. These will include a description of the property, a statement of the legal title to the property, the price to be paid, how it is to be paid, the deadline for payment and any other deadlines applicable, what should happen in the event of breach of contract and so on. At this point you will normally pay a **deposit** of 10–20 per cent of the price of the property. In the case of a property under construction ('off-plan') you will start to make **stage payments**, which will vary in size and number from property to property.

Once you are ready to take delivery of the house you will sign the **final purchase contract**. This is signed in front of a notary public. It is at this point that the balance of the money is paid across to the seller.

Case Study: Registration

Elaine and Peter Donaldson went on holiday to Montenegro way before the conflict and were keen to go back. They were not disappointed and decided to buy a house where they could spend their retirement. 'It was a bit daunting,' said Elaine. 'We didn't really know what we were letting ourselves in for. But we fell in love with a huge house which would accommodate all our family when they came to stay. It had views of both the sea and the mountains so we couldn't resist.' All went to plan, and very smoothly, but it was only later that the Donaldsons discovered to their horror that the property had not been registered in the right way. They have since registered their property with the help of the lawyer and are happier than ever.

Once you have paid the balance of the price the seller will authorise you to **register your ownership** of the property in the local title register. Once this has been done you will be the full legal owner of the property in much the same way as you would be in the UK.

Settling In

Learning Montenegrin

Although Montenegrin shares the same origins as the Serbian, Croatian and Bosnian languages, it is linguistically separate and even has 33 letters in its alphabet while the others only have 30.

The language has its roots in an ancient Slavic language and, despite the size of the country, the language has several dialects.

Shopping

To get all your provisions, you will normally find yourself having to visit a number of shops, as most outlets are either small shops or markets. In larger towns and cities there are shops specialising in either clothing or electronics, for example. Delis are common for local cheeses and meats. Bakeries are generally good, with fresh bread and cakes.

Home Utilities and Services

Gas and Electricity

Nearly all Montenegrin households have electricity and meters. Prices increased by 23 per cent in 2003, at the behest of the IMF, and household bills now average about €22 per month. Power is single-phase and three-phase, 220 volts, 50 HZ. Some electrical appliances need transformers adapters if not provided with built-in switches. There is a central gas supply system available, mostly in Vojvodina.

Water

In the past, water supply and sanitation services were well developed in the Republic of Montenegro. However, the situation has deteriorated considerably because of the limited capital investment over the last 10 years.

As a result, the republic's water and sanitation is in poor condition, especially in the coastal areas, which suffer from regular supply shortages, poor water quality and environmental degradation, all exacerbated during the summer season when tourism more than doubles the area's population to over 500,000.

Telephones

Montenegro's country code is **t** 381.

The two **cellular** operators in Montenegro are **Pro Monte GSM** and **Monet GSM**. Roaming services are available in almost all European countries and bigger countries throughout the world.

Internet

There are a number of private Internet providers who offer dial-up access at 56kbps, for €15–25 monthly. Internet penetration, at only 7 per cent, is very low compared with 58 per cent in the UK. Broadband connections are not common.

Media

During the last years of Miloševic rule, Montenegro enjoyed greater media freedom than Serbia. Since then, international organisations have set up a number of support programmes for independent media. The UN-supervised **Blue Sky Radio** aims to provide a multi-ethnic audience with impartial news in Kosovo.

The privately run daily **newspaper** *Vijesti* has the highest circulation in the country. *Pobjeda* is a pro-government daily and the oldest running newspaper. There are no English-language newspapers.

Money and Banking

The country's official currency is the **euro**, which replaced the Deutschmark in early 2002. An unlimited amount of foreign currency may be brought into the country but there are limits on how many euros may be taken out. Euros in

Montenegro, just like euros everywhere, come in notes of 5, 10, 20, 50, 100, 250 and 500 euros. The coins come in 1, 2, 5, 10, 20 and 50 cents and 1 and 2 euros.

As is the case with so much in Montenegro, the currency exchange situation is rapidly improving. Although **credit cards** are not yet widely accepted, bigger hotels, shops, restaurants and travel agents sometimes take them, and again this situation is getting better. Diner's Card is the most common, then Visa. Few banks offer cash advances against credit cards, but there are ever more cash machines in Montenegro. **Banking hours** are weekdays 9–7, Saturdays 8–1.

Working and Employment

Foreigners must obtain a work permit in order to undertake employment legally. This is available from the Ministry of Police in Serbia and Montenegro.

Education

Few children attend pre-school. Education is compulsory between the ages of seven and 15. There are some private foreign language schools in Montenegro as well as several international schools. Further education is optional but in Montenegro is only provided at university level.

Health and Emergencies

There are a growing number of private clinics in Montenegro, and many of the doctors speak English and are overseas-educated. As a foreigner, you do not have access to the domestic national health system, so taking out private health insurance is strongly recommended. The standard of care in medical clinics in Montenegro is generally of a high standard. A large number of private pharmacies offer a good supply of drugs.

Social Services and Welfare Benefits

Your social security rights in Montenegro are the same as those that apply in the UK. If you start work in Montenegro, you will contribute to the country's social security system and consequently gain the right to benefits. If you are entitled to the contributory part of JSA and have been claiming this for at least four weeks in the UK, you may continue to receive it for up to three months in Montenegro, while you actively seek work. You must first tell your Jobcentre Plus office or Jobcentre in the UK (where you are registered) of your intention to look for work in Montenegro well in advance of your departure date.

Cars

UK driving licences are accepted in Montenegro. The conditions of roads, particularly outside major towns, can be very bad and involve tortuous mountain routes. For this reason, driving at night is not advisable.

Taxis are often expensive especially for foreigners. If you use them make sure you have agreed a price before getting into the car, or insist that the driver uses his or her meter.

Crime and the Police

Montenegro has been a hangout for the Italian mafia since the early 1990s, smuggling cigarettes, drugs and arms back to Italy across the Adriatic, mainly from Bar. As a result of international pressure, the government has taken action to clamp down on the criminal gangs. In dramatic scenes, some gangsters were deported to Italy to stand trial while others managed to escape in a fleet of 100 high-speed power boats. Montenegro has since signed an agreement with Italy and the presence of these modern-day pirates is much less noticeable.

Smuggling is not restricted to the water, however. Every international car thief worth his salt knows that Montenegro is the place to go, because the international police have no authority here. Shiny Mercedes go for half the price they would in Germany, as the happy taxi-drivers know, and the same applies to Audis, BMWs and Porsches, although most of them find their way into countries further east.

Food and Drink

In many ways it is impossible to distinguish Montenegro's cuisine from that of its neighbours, because the borders are relatively newly defined. Its food is typically Balkan, with lots of rich soups, meaty stews and grilled meat. In fact, Montenegrins love meat, whether it's duck, hamburgers, pork or sausages. Its coastal position, however, means fish is plentiful and popular. It is usually grilled, although is also used to make soups.

Vegetables include peppers and cabbage, which are often stuffed. Salads are made up of onions, beans, cucumbers and sometimes sauerkraut. Vegetarians will find it hard going, though, as even bean soups are made with meat stock. *Burek* – a cheese- and meat-stuffed pastry – is a ubiquitous snack, which is often eaten for breakfast.

Kebabs and stuffed vine leaves echo the cuisine of nearby Greece.

Wine and beer are commonly drunk and inexpensive. Plum and grape brandy is strong, as is the coffee.

Montenegro: References

Directory of Contacts and Resources

Embassies and Consulates

- **Embassy of Serbia and Montenegro**, 28 Belgrave Square, London SW1X 8QB, **t** (020) 7235 9049, **f** (020) 7235 7092, **www.yugoslavembassy.org.uk**.
- **British Embassy**, Resavska 46 11000 Belgrade, **t** + 381 11 2645 055, **www.britishembassy.gov.uk**.
- **Honorary British Consulate in Podgorica**, Njegoseva 5, 81000 Podgorica, **t** + 381 81 243 672, **f** + 381 81 622 166.

Information and Resources

- www.turizamcg.com.
- www.visit-montenegro.com.
- www.montenegro.com/links/Regions.html.

Removal Companies

- **Allied Pickfords Montenegro**, ul. Zarka Obreskog 23, **t** +381 11 848 7744, **f** +381 11 848 6868, **movers@alliedpickfords-yu.com**, **www.alliedpickfords-see.com**.

Property Companies and Estate Agents

- **Montenegro Living**, **t** (020) 8407 0740, **www.montenegro-living.com**.
- **Montenegro Properties**, **www.montenegroproperties.co.uk**.
- **Montenegro Smiles**, **www.montenegrosmiles.com**.
- **Dream Property Montenegro**, 5–6 High St, Windsor, Berkshire SL4 1LD, **t** (01753) 831182, **info@DreamMontenegro.com**, **www.dreammontenegro.com**.
- **Europe Property Plus**, 203 Dunchurch Road, Rugby, Warwickshire CV22 6HP, **t (01788) 814139**, **info@europepropertyplus.com**, **www.europepropertyplus.com**.

Holiday Companies

- **Holiday Options**, **t** 0870 420 8386, **f** (01444) 242 454, **www.holiday options.co.uk**. Flight-only and packages to the major resorts.

• **Montenegro Holidays**, t + 381 86 402 522. A locally based company offering hotel accommodation, transport and excursions.

Administrative Departments

Montenegro has 21 municipalities: Andrijevica, Bar, Berane, Bijelo Polje, Budva, Cetinje, Danilovgrad, Herceg Novi, Kolašin, Kotor, Mojkovac, Nikšić, Plav, Plužine, Pljevlja, Podgorica, Rožaje, Šavnik, Tivat, Ulcinj, Žabljak.

Public Holidays

1 January	New Year
11 and 12 April	Easter, including Easter Monday
27 April	Constitution Day of Socialist Republic of Yugoslavia
1 May	International Workers' Day
13 July	National Day
29 November	Republic Day
25 and 26 December	Christmas

Further Reading

Montenegro: The Divided Land, Thomas Fleming – fascinating account of a country divided by its geography, religion and war.
The Falcon and the Eagle: Montenegro and Austria-Hungary, 1908–1914, John D. Treadway – academic study of a very specific period in Montenegro's history and its relationship with its neighbours on the eve of the First World War.
Nikola and Milena, King and Queen of the Black Mountain: The Rise and Fall of Montenegro's Royal Family, Marco Houston – a well-researched and illustrated book that looks at the country's royal family through history.

Climate Charts

	Jan	Feb	Mar	April	May	June	July	Aug	Sept	Oct	Nov	Dec
Coastal Area												
Max (air) (°C)	11.9	12.4	14.8	18.7	22.3	26.1	28.6	28.8	25.8	21.6	13.7	13.2
Min (sea) (°C)	4.5	5.1	7.1	9.7	13.6	16.8	19.3	19.2	16.6	13.1	9.3	6.1
Hours sunshine (total for month)	116	119	165	194	254	289	338	312	248	192	121	106
Mountain Area												
Max (air) (°C)	2	4.1	8.1	12.4	17.8	20.8	23.3	23.5	20	14.9	8.8	3.2
Hours sunshine (total for month)	83	96	136	159	192	204	262	245	194	159	97	75

Poland

17

Why Buy in Poland?

Poland is a relatively large country, compared with the other countries featured in this book. At just over 312,000 square kilometres it is nearly half as big again as the United Kingdom. Yet with a population of less than 40 million it has only two-thirds the number of people.

Investors seem attracted by a higher than average growth rate in the Polish economy (over 6 per cent in 2004) and by the prospect of heavy investment from the European Union since membership in 2004, leading to greater prosperity and rising property prices. Warsaw attracts because, as the capital city, there is a wide range of rental markets available. Kraków attracts because of its inherent beauty and its emerging status as a tourist destination.

The Economy

Poland has pursued a policy of economic liberalisation throughout the 1990s and today stands out as a success story among transition economies. Even so, much remains to be done, especially in bringing down unemployment. The privatisation of small- and medium-sized state-owned companies and a liberal law on establishing new firms has encouraged the development of the private business sector, but legal and bureaucratic obstacles and persistent corruption are hampering further development. Poland's agricultural sector remains handicapped by surplus labour, inefficient small farms and lack of investment. The restructuring and privatisation of sensitive sectors such as coal, steel, railroads and energy have stalled. Reforms in healthcare, education, the pension system and state administration have resulted in larger-than-expected fiscal pressures. Further progress in public finance depends mainly on the privatisation of Poland's remaining state sector, the reduction of state employment, and an overhaul of the tax code to incorporate the growing black economy – and farmers, most of whom pay no tax. The government has introduced a package of social and administrative spending cuts to reduce public spending by about $17 billion to 2007, but only about half of this has been approved by the legislature, and the remainder could be trumped by election-year politics in 2005.

Poland joined the EU in May 2004, and surging exports to the EU contributed to Poland's strong growth in 2004, though its competitiveness could be threatened by the zloty's appreciation against the euro. Poland stands to benefit from nearly $17 billion in EU funds, available up to 2006. Farmers have already begun to reap the rewards of membership via higher food prices and EU agricultural subsidies.

Poland has seen a slow but steady growth in its population. GDP per capita is roughly half that of the UK and roughly equals that of the three Baltic states.

The Exchange Rate

The chart below shows the exchange rate in Poland from 1996 to 2005.

Exchange Rate – Polish Zloty

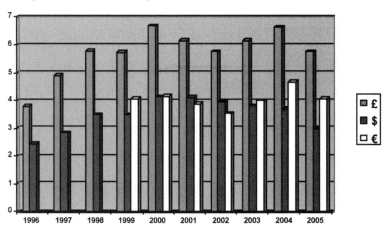

Visas and Permits

As Poland is a member of the European Union, any citizen of a member state can enter the country without a visa and stay for up to **90 days**. For purely historical reasons, British citizens can stay for up to six months. After that period has passed, they need to obtain a **residence permit**.

Profile of Poland

Recent History and Politics

The country has been much meddled with. From the middle of the 18th century until after the Second World War its borders have constantly been moved and it has been carved up between first one country and then another. The Republic of Poland is a democracy and a member of the European Union since May 2004.

Climate and Geography

The summers are hot, the spring and autumn pleasant and the winters cruel. *See* 'Climate Charts', p.318, for details of the temperature and rainfall patterns.

Regional Profile

Poland has a coastline of only about 500km and almost half of the country comprises farmland. **Warsaw**, the capital city, has roots going back hundreds of years. It is, in part, a very attractive historic city in the Central European tradition. Other parts of the city reflect the industrialisation of Eastern Europe in the Soviet era. It is also a modern, sophisticated city. Outside Warsaw there are large historic towns, many small villages and modern industrial cities. The main attraction of **Kraków** is that it was largely undamaged during the Second World War and thus retains more of its authentic characteristics than Warsaw, where most of the city had to be rebuilt. Kraków has become a tourist destination, particularly for weekend breaks.

Selecting a Property

Getting There

Kraków and Warsaw are served by air by **Lot Polish Airlines** and **British Airways**. A direct return ticket from London, departing in June 2005 is quoted at £96 by Lot. **EasyJet** flies to Kraków and Warsaw, with single fares at about £50.

Getting Around

The public transport system is comprehensive and very cheap, but often achingly slow and usually overcrowded. In general, trains are faster and more useful, while buses come into their own in rural areas which are not on the train network. Polish trains are run by Polish Increasingly, private coach operators such as Polski Express (**www.polski express.pl**) are offering more luxurious services between the major cities. Information from **www.pekaesbus.com.pl**.

Choosing a Location

The main focus of activity by foreign buyers is in Warsaw, Kraków and Zakopane. The main investments in **Warsaw** are in the prime historic parts of the city. Other people are looking at some of the new up-and-coming areas occupied by the emerging middle classes. Although property in the capital, Warsaw, is very good value by western European standards, the city is widely regarded as ugly and overpriced, and property is considerably cheaper in **Kraków** than in Warsaw; a typical apartment is about half the price of its equivalent in the historic part of Warsaw. Rental yields are good, as this is a year-round destination. **Zakopane** has only recently been discovered by the British investor and it is accessible as it is only a short distance from Kraków and prices are much higher than you will find elsewhere. As soon as you leave the cities, beautiful properties in need of renovation are available in spellbinding country-side for unbelievably low prices.

Property Types and Prices

Propeties for sale range between anything from city apartments to sprawling rural detached villas. Prices have been rising rapidly. Some of our clients have seen growth of over 25 per cent in the last year. The table below attempts to show some general indication of prices as at January 2005.

Place and Type of Property	Low	Mid	High
One-bedroom apartment in historic Warsaw (26 sq m)		£40,000	£54,000
One-bedroom apartment in historic Warsaw (60 sq m)		£63,000	£95,000
Two-bedroom apartment in historic Warsaw (100 sq m)		£100,000	£166,000
Three-bedroom apartment in historic Warsaw (160 sq m)			£350,000
Two-bedroom apartment in historic Warsaw		£63,000	
Three-bedroom villa in historic Kraków (100 sq m)		£87,000	
Wooden cottage in countryside (42 sq m)	£11,000		

Bulding from Scratch and Renovation

There are many properties on sale in Poland that need huge amounts of work and there is not much of a market for these properties currently. The problems associated with the renovation project can be huge. A full restoration project is likely to cost about £200 per square metre.

The Process of Buying a Property

Legal advice is essential.

Freedom to Buy

You can buy land, buildings or apartments in Poland, either in your own name or via a company you control, as you choose.

Initial Steps

First Contracts

Once you have found a property that you want to purchase, you will be expected to sign some form of contract, generally either a reservation contract or a preliminary purchase contract. The latter is binding, so, wherever possible, insist on signing a **reservation contract**.

Searches and Enquiries

Once you have signed a reservation contract, your lawyer should make various enquiries, such as checking that the contract is fair, that the seller has good title and the right to sell to you, that the area is zoned for residential building and that any building work being undertaken enjoys all of the necessary planning and building consents. Depending on the circumstances of your case there could well be other enquiries that also need to be made. In Poland it is common for work to be started, illegally, before all of these steps are in place.

Possible Dangers

The main problems in Poland are defective title and defective planning consents. In particular, be aware that there are various different types of 'ownership' for buildings and apartments. Some do not have an independent registered title but are owned collectively. Some property is subject to serious disputes, many dating back half a century or more, and a lot of property is in poor condition. Do not estimate the complexities and expense involved in taking on a project of this kind.

Signing the Contract and Registering the Title

Once your lawyer has checked out the property and found that everything is in order, you are ready to sign the **preliminary purchase contract**. This commits you and the seller to signing the full contract transferring ownership on an agreed date shortly afterwards, or, if the property is still under construction, once the property has been fully built. The contract contains most of the clauses you would expect to see in a UK contract. These will include a description of the property, a statement of the legal title to the property, the price to be paid, how it is to be paid, the deadline for payment and any other deadlines applicable, what should happen in the event of breach of contract and so on.

Many Polish contracts are badly drafted and the problem is exacerbated by the fact that many contracts are drafted in English, which is not the first language of the person doing the drafting. As a result they can be unclear or muddled. Specifications tend to be very 'thin'. The contracts tend to be lacking in detail as to what happens if anything goes wrong. At this point you will normally pay a **deposit** of 10–20 per cent of the price of the property. In the case of a property under construction ('off-plan') you will start to make **stage payments**, which will vary in size and number from property to property.

Once you are ready to take delivery of the house and have obtained a **certificate** from the Ministry of Foreign Affairs that you are entitled to own property in Poland, you will sign the **final purchase contract**. This is signed in front of a notary public. It is at this point that the balance of the money is paid across to the seller. You do not need to be present in Poland to sign this document as your lawyer can prepare a **power of attorney** (*see* pp.77–8) under which you can appoint somebody else to sign on your behalf. This saves the need for you to go to Poland, often at short notice, to sign the final title.

Once you have paid the balance of the price the seller will authorise you to **register your ownership** of the property in the local title register. Once this has been done, you – or the local Polish company that you have set up to own the property – will be the full legal owner of the property in much the same way as you would be in the UK. It usually takes 2–6 weeks.

The Expenses of Buying Property

- tax – the equivalent of stamp duty, at 2 per cent of the price.
- VAT on new property at 22 per cent – sometimes included in quoted price.
- estate agent's fees, if these are not all paid by the seller, which are 5 per cent of the price if you are using a local Polish agent.
- notary's fees – these will vary but will typically not exceed £200.
- legal fees – English lawyer's fees will be higher but you will be able to sue them if they get it wrong and they will be able to give you lots of advice;

fees will range from about £350 if you use a Polish lawyer to £1,500 if you use a specialist English lawyer.

• fees to set up a Polish company; this is likely to cost £500.

Taxes

Taxes for Non-resident Property-owners

Local Property Taxes

Local property taxes in Poland are very low, and are assessed on the basis of the official tax value of property; this in itself is normally only about a part of the true value of your property. The maximum rate is 38 Zloty per square metre.

Income Taxes

Foreign investors can invest in properties in Poland either directly, in their own name, or through a local company.

• **Rental income on company-owned property.**

The basis of the taxable income of a company, investing in Polish real property is the gross income from the property less any tax-deductible expenses and depreciation. These expenses include any management costs, repairs, maintenance, insurance, etc., and interest on any loans used to buy the property. The corporate tax rate is a flat rate of 19 per cent.

• **Rental income on individually owned property .**

For non-residents, tax is paid at rates that increase with your income in Poland (this includes the income from renting real estate in Poland, whether or not income is paid to you in Poland) and vary from 19 per cent to 40 per cent, which can be set off against your UK tax liabilities on the same income.

Capital Gains Taxes

Capital gains taxes are treated as part of your income. However, the capital gain made on the sale of real estate is charged to income tax at 10 per cent of the sale price. No tax is paid if you have owned the real estate for over five years.

Wealth Taxes

There are no wealth taxes in Poland.

Inheritance Taxes

Inheritance taxes are being abolished for most gifts. They only apply to your assets in Poland.

Taxes for Resident Foreigners

This is beyond the scope of this book.

Settling In

Learning Polish

The language spoken is Polish. It uses a Latin-based alphabet which includes letters with the addition of daunting little dots and hooks (called diagraphs and diacritics) which change the pronunciation of the letter. Away from major cities, English is not widely spoken.

Telephones and the Internet

The Polish national telephone network has developed rapidly since the end of the Communist regime, but remains unreliable. Perhaps as a result of this, the mobile phone market has exploded and coverage is excellent.

When calling Poland from abroad, dial the **country code** (t 48) and drop the first zero in the area code. When calling within a city, you don't need to dial the area code (e.g. Warsaw **t** 022, Kraków **t** 012).

Public **telephone boxes** which actually work are thin on the ground, although you can usually find functioning phones at post offices. All are now operated with **phone cards** (available from newsagents or post offices).

There are **Internet cafés** in all the major cities and it is common in homes also.

Money and Banking

The currency is the **Zloty** (PLN), which is broken broken down into 100 **groszy** (gr). Prices, particularly for smarter restaurants, often appear in euros.

Cash is still king in Poland: **credit cards** are accepted in the major cities only. **ATMs**, called Bankomats, are everywhere in larger towns, but rare in provincial areas. You can change money in banks and exchange offices (*kantors*), which charge between 1 and 2% commission. **Banks** are usually open Mon–Fri 8–5, with larger branches also opening on Saturday mornings from 9–1.

Health

Ambulance: **t** 999 or **t** 112.

In theory, reciprocal agreements with the UK mean that basic and emergency healthcare is free if you carry an E111 or the new European Health Identity Card (EHIC) which is gradually replacing it (available from post offices), but Poland's public health service is very poor and you are should take out private insurance.

Poland: References

Directory of Contacts and Resources

Embassies and Consulates

- **Polish Embassy**, 47 Portland Place, London W1B 1JH, **t** 0870 774 2700, **www.polishembassy.org.uk**.
- **UK Embassy**, al. Róži, Warsaw, **t** (022) 311 0000, **www.britishembassy.pl**.

Information and Resources

- www.www.visitpoland.org.

National Holidays

1 January	New Year's Day
March/April	Easter Monday
1 May	Labour Day
3 May	Constitution Day
May/June	Corpus Christi
15 August	Assumption Day
1 November	Feast of All Saints
11 November	Independence Day
25–6 December	Christmas Day/Boxing Day

Climate Charts

	Jan	Feb	Mar	April	May	June	July	Aug	Sept	Oct	Nov	Dec
Warsaw												
Max (°C)	0	0	6	12	20	23	24	23	18	13	6	2
Min (°C)	−6	−6	−2	3	8	12	15	14	10	5	1	−3
Rainfall (ave monthly, mm)	24	30	25	38	43	66	75	62	41	38	30	42
Sunshine (ave daily hours)	2	2	3	5	8	8	7	7	5	4	2	1

Romania

18

Why Buy in Romania?

Romania is roughly the same size as the United Kingdom but has only one-third the number of people (22 million). Romania is a democracy and wishes to join the EU and was accepted as an accession state in 2004, with a hoped-for joining date of 2007/8 – though much work needs to be done before that is definite.

The reason that Romania remains much less developed as a market than Bulgaria and the other Eastern European countries is that the political and economic situation is much less stable. Accordingly, an investment in Romania seems more of a risk than elsewhere. The reason that people are looking at the market at all is that they have seen what has happened to other countries as they get closer to entry to the European Union, and they expect a similar explosion of interest and prices to take place in Romania.

The Economy

Romania began the transition from Communism in 1989 with a largely obsolete industrial base and a pattern of output unsuited to the country's needs. The country emerged in 2000 from a punishing three-year recession thanks to strong demand in EU export markets. Despite the global slowdown in

2001–2, strong domestic activity in construction, agriculture and consumption have kept growth above 4 per cent. Recent changes have done little to address Romania's widespread poverty, however, while corruption and red tape continue to handicap business. Romania has seen a slow but steady reduction in its population, which is now about 22 million. GDP per capita is roughly one-third of that of the UK and roughly equal to that of Bulgaria or Turkey.

The Exchange Rate

The graph below shows the exchange rate in Romania from 1996 to 2005.

Exchange Rate – Romanian Lei

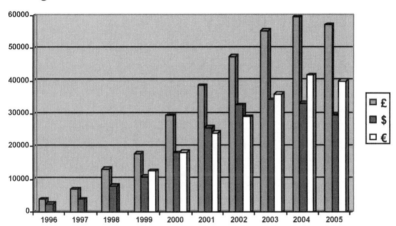

Visas and Permits

As Romania is a not a member of the European Union, visas are generally needed to enter, though British people do not need visas for visits of under **90 days**. Your passport must be valid for at least six months after your departure date. Longer visits require residence papers.

Profile of Romania

Romania has a coastline of only about 200km, almost half of which comprises farmland. Bucharest, the capital city, has roots going back hundreds of years. It is, in small parts, a very attractive historic Central European city; other parts of the city reflect the worst aspects of the industrialisation of Eastern Europe in the Soviet era. Outside the city there are the dramatic forested mountains of Dracula country, the Transylvanian Alps, and vast fertile plains. Transylvania is home to medieval villages including Sibiu, Prejmer, Nasaud, Bistrita, Harman and Sighişoara, which has a UNESCO-protected historic centre. Winter-sports centres in the region include Poiana Braşov, Predeal, Sinaia and Busteni. The beautiful Black Sea coast is hard to beat; the city of Constanţa has an easygoing atmosphere and lively cultural life.

The population is 87 per cent Romanian Orthodox, 5 per cent Roman Catholic, 6 per cent Protestant and 1 per cent Greek Orthodox, with small Muslim and Jewish communities.

The summers are hot, the spring and autumn pleasant and the winters cruel. *See* 'Climate Charts', p.326, for details of the temperature and rainfall patterns.

Selecting a Property

Getting There

Buccarest is served by air by **TAROM** (Romanian Airlines) and **British Airways**. A direct return ticket from London in June 2005 is quoted at £148.

Choosing a Location

There is, as yet, relatively little activity on the property market in Romania, though there has been some interest in the capital, Bucharest. There are other signs of the beginnings of interest in the Black Sea coast. This has been largely fuelled by the fact that Constanţa is only about 200km from the Bulgarian resort of Varna, yet is substantially cheaper.

Building from Scratch and Renovation

There are many properties on sale in Romania, particularly in the rural areas and in Bucharest, that need huge amounts of work. As yet there is not much of a market for these properties and the problems associated with the renovation project can be huge, even though building costs are low. Not least will be your probable inability to speak Romanian. If you are contemplating a renovation project it is vital to get good advice right at the outset.

The Process of Buying a Property

The most important thing to stress about buying a property in Romania is that there is a lot more risk associated with it than buying in, say, Spain or England. There is a lot of property with either bad title or defective planning consent. Legal advice is essential, unless you take the view that the amount you are investing is so small you can afford to write it off.

Freedom to Buy

You can buy land, buildings or apartments in Romania, but if you wish to buy land you will need to do so through a local Romanian company that is the owner of the property. This is because only Romanians are currently allowed to own land and buildings in Romania. By owning through a Romanian company the property is treated as being owned by a Romanian, even if the company itself is 100 per cent owned and controlled by foreigners. This rule will change no later than 2007/8 if Romania enters the European Union.

Initial Steps

First Contracts

Once you have found a property that you want to purchase, you will be expected to sign some form of contract, generally either a reservation contract or a preliminary purchase contract. The latter is binding, so, wherever possible, insist on signing a **reservation contract**.

Searches and Enquiries

Once you have signed a reservation contract, your lawyer should make various enquiries, such as checking that the contract is fair, that the seller has good title and the right to sell to you, that the area is zoned for residential building and that any building work being undertaken enjoys all of the necessary planning and building consents. Depending on the circumstances of your case there could well be other enquiries that also need to be made.

Possible Dangers

The main problem in Romania are defective title, defective paperwork and defective planning consents. These are endemic: enormous care is needed when investigating the purchase of a property in Romania.

Signing the Contract and Registering the Title

Once your lawyer has checked out the property and found that everything is in order, you are ready to sign the **preliminary purchase contract**. This commits you and the seller to signing the full contract transferring ownership on an agreed date shortly afterwards, or, if the property is still under construction, once the property has been fully built. The contract contains most of the clauses you would expect to see in a UK contract. These will include a description of the property, a statement of the legal title to the property, the price to be paid, how it is to be paid, the deadline for payment and any other deadlines applicable, what should happen in the event of breach of contract and so on.

Many Romanian contracts are badly drafted and the problem is exacerbated by the fact that many contracts are drafted in English, which is not the first language of the person doing the drafting. As a result they can be unclear or muddled. Specifications tend to be very 'thin'. The contracts tend to be lacking in detail as to what happens if anything goes wrong. At this point you will normally pay a **deposit** of 10–20 per cent of the price of the property. In the case of a property under construction ('off-plan') you will start to make **stage payments**, which will vary in size and number from property to property.

Once you are ready to take delivery of the house you will sign the **final purchase contract** in front of a notary public. It is at this point that the balance of the money is paid across to the seller. You do not need to be present to sign this document as your lawyer can prepare a **power of attorney** (*see* pp.77–8) under which you can appoint somebody else to sign on your behalf.

Once you have paid the balance of the price the seller will authorise you to **register your ownership** of the property in the local title register. Once this has been done, you – or the local Romanian company that you have set up to own the property – will be the full legal owner of the property in much the same way as you would be in Britain. It usually takes 2–6 weeks.

The Expenses of Buying

The main expenses of buying are:

- tax – the equivalent of stamp duty – 2 per cent of the price.

- estate agent's fees, if these are not paid by the seller – they vary across the country, from 2 per cent to 6 per cent.

- notary's fees – these will vary from case to case but will typically not exceed £200.

- legal fees – these depend on whether you use a Romanian or an English lawyer; English lawyer's fees will inevitably be higher but you will be able to sue them if they get it wrong and they will be able to give you lots of advice, particularly about the vital issues of who should own the property to minimise your tax and other problems, which the local Romanian lawyer would not be able to help you with; they will range from about £350 if you use a local Romanian lawyer to £1,500 if you use a specialist English lawyer.

- fees to set up a company if you set up a Romanian company; this is likely to cost £300.

Taxes

Taxes for Non-resident Property-owners

Local Property Taxes

Local property taxes in Romania are very low and for most people amount to no more than £100 per year.

Income Taxes

Foreign investor can invest in properties in Romania in their own name or through a local company. Romania has a unified tax system, with a unified rate of 16 per cent.

• Rental income on company-owned property

The basis of the taxable income of a company, investing in Romanian real property is the gross income from the property less any tax-deductible expenses and depreciation. These expenses include any management costs, repairs, maintenance, insurance and so on, and interest on any loans used to buy the property. The corporate tax rate is a flat rate of 16 per cent.

• Rental income on individually owned property

For non-residents, at present, there is a 16 per cent tax paid on 75 per cent of gross rental income. This tax can be set off against your UK tax liabilities on the same income.

Capital Gains Taxes

Capital gains taxes are treated as part of your income.

Wealth Taxes

There are no wealth taxes in Romania.

Taxes for Resident Foreigners

This is beyond the scope of this book.

Settling In

Learning Romanian

Romanian is spoken everywhere. English is not widely spoken outside the cities.

Telephones

The country code for Romania is **t** 40.

Money and Banking

The currency is the **leu** (ROL), plural lei, divided into 100 **bani**.

Romania: References

Directory of Contacts and Resources

Embassies and Consulates

• **Romanian Embassy**, Arundel House, 4 Palace Green, London W8 4QD, t (020) 7937 9666, **www.roemb.co.uk**.

Estate Agents

• **Elion, t** 241 508 217, **www.elion.ro**.
• **www.viviun.com**. A selection of Romanian properties for sale.

Climate Charts

Average Maximum Temperature in Bucharest (°C)

Jan	Feb	Mar	April	May	June	July	Aug	Sept	Oct	Nov	Dec
1	4	10	18	23	27	20	30	25	17	10	4

Average Monthly Rainfall in Bucharest (mm)

Jan	Feb	Mar	April	May	June	July	Aug	Sept	Oct	Nov	Dec
44	23	26	60	78	120	53	42	42	26	35	24

Average Daily Hours of Sunshine in Bucharest

Jan	Feb	Mar	April	May	June	July	Aug	Sept	Oct	Nov	Dec
2	3	5	6	8	9	11	10	8	5	2	2

Slovakia

19

Why Buy in Slovakia?

Slovakia is centrally positioned in Europe, bordered by Austria, the Czech Republic, Poland, Ukraine and Hungary. Many visitors coming overland from Western Europe tend to bypass the capital, and indeed the country, so focused are they on what has been called the 'golden triangle' of the cities of Vienna, Budapest and Prague. Bratislava has much smaller crowds than these three cities, although during the weekends large numbers of Austrians tend to visit.

There have been budget flights to Bratislava from the UK since 2004, and there is likely to be a steep increase in British tourists as a result. As it is close to Vienna, when border controls are dropped Bratislava expects to see a growing number of people who work in the Austrian city and commute from Slovakia.

The natural heritage of the country is protected within nine national parks, and some of the country's most spectacular natural beauty is found in the karst region of limestone caves and canyons. These included the Ice Cave and the Aragonite Cave in Ochtina, both of which are recognised as UNESCO World Heritage Sites. Slovakia's history is reflected in medieval towns, ancient castles and unique folk architecture.

Almost every town in Slovakia has its own folk festival. Often taking place in the run-up to the September harvest, these celebrations involve traditional food, dancing and costumes. There are also a number of activities all year round, ranging from dance events to opera seasons and craft fairs. International festivals may centre on anything from film to ghosts and spirits. Easter is a time for the ancient art of egg-painting and Christmas brings its own traditions.

Tourism

Slovakia receives around a million foreign visitors annually, a figure which is gradually increasing. It has lots of different experiences to offer.

A Healing Tradition

With over one thousand healing springs – both mineral and thermal – and significant supplies of curative substances in the form of peat and mud, Slovakia has a long spa tradition, and its spa towns feature hotels and facilities for the visitors who want to take to the waters. As in other countries in Eastern Europe, these people are likely to be ill or elderly, rather than the luxury-seekers associated with the spas of more contemporary resorts in other parts of the world. But these spas have seen the likes of illustrious guests right back to the days of the esteemed Roman emperor Marcus Aurelius.

Ancient Architecture

There are around 200 castles and fortifications in Slovakia. The oldest is pretty Bojnický Castle, while Bardejov and Banská Štiavnica are architecturally significant enough to be World Heritage Sites. Most were built before the second half of the 15th century.: just after the Tartars invaded in the 13th century, there was a great deal of building of stone castles. The Turks did not start attacking again until the latter half of the 16th century, when a new wave of fortifications appeared. The Habsburg royalty commissioned Italian builders; by

Hungarians in Slovakia

Hungarians make up over 10 per cent of the population and live mostly in the western part of the country. There is a certain amount of friction between them and the rest of the population, which has become more pronounced since the creation of separate Czech and Slovak republics. Slovakia, then known as the Upper Lands, was for many years part of Hungary, with the Slovaks very much the poorer peasant class and their culture and language repressed. This continued until 1918, when the new republic was created and 750,000 Hungarians remained on the Slovak side of the Danube. Nationalism on the part of the Slovaks increased after the Velvet Revolution (*see* pp.331–2) and the relations remain strained.

A new green metal bridge across the Danube now connects Slovakia and Hungary, and Slovaks can walk across the construction to reach greater work opportunities on the other side. The European Union funded half of the €20 million it cost to build the bridge, which is greatly symbolic for this sleepy part of the east of Slovakia. Spanning the two countries, the bridge represents the greater opportunity, integration and prospects that the country hopes to see as a result of being part of the Union.

> ## Spelunking
> Spelunking is the sport of lowering oneself on a rope into an abyss. Slovakia's caves in the Slovenský Raj and Slovensky Kras regions, with their glittering stalagmites and stalactites, attract subterranean sportsmen who may just content themselves with caving. Various companies arrange trips into the country's cave systems. A book called *Show Caves*, published by the Slovak Caves Administration, includes information and photos of 12 spectacular caves.

the 17th century the military necessity for castles had disappeared and aristocrats began to depart for more homely manor houses.

More unusual are the country's wooden churches, which reflect the Orthodox, Catholic and Protestant religions, but were originally created by the Rutherians (*see* p.334). They are rare in this part of Europe, and most of them are found in the east of the country. These lovely wooden constructions blend in with the surrounding countryside and were usually built without either nails or metal; they are still used as places of worship today.

Take to the Hills

The countryside of Slovakia has thousands of miles of marked footpaths. Some are gentle strolls while others, such as in the High Tatras, are closer to mountain climbs, and require walking boots. The paths are easy to follow, using colour-coded markers every 100 metres or so with distances to the next destination. English walking guides and detailed maps are available.

The Economy

After the collapse of Communism in 1989 and Slovakia's split from the Czech Republic in 1993, the economy suffered because the country had been involved in heavy industry, which was largely dependent on the Eastern Bloc countries, and found it hard to adjust to a market economy. In the last few years Slovakia has managed to boost and modernise its economy and has privatised much of its industry. However, it suffers from some the highest unemployment in Europe – as much as 13 per cent in 2004, but this represented a drop from 18.5 per cent in 2002.

Visas and Permits

EU citizens do not need a visa to enter Slovakia for up to **90 days**, but they must have a passport valid for at least six months from date of return.

An application for a **long-term-stay permit** is required if you intend to work or study in the Slovak Republic. It should be accompanied with documentation of acceptance for study or employment. Information on applying for work and residency permits can be obtained from the Slovak Embassy.

Slovak **citizenship** is dependent on having:

- **had permanent residence in the country for at least five years.**
- **a command of the Slovak language.**
- **no criminal record within the last five years.**

Profile of Slovakia

Recent History and Politics

Then Governor George W. Bush famously told a Slovak journalist, 'The only thing I know about Slovakia is what I learned first-hand from your foreign minister, who came to Texas.' Bush had in fact met the minister of Slovenia, not Slovakia, and many people tend to confuse the two. In some ways Eastern Europe's poorest cousin, Slovakia suffered when it separated from the Czech Republic in 1993. The western half of former Czechoslovakia bagged the tourist mecca of Prague and a buoyant economy, while Slovakia got the industrialised areas and many of the poorer communities. This is, of course, not without its advantages; the country has great swaths of mountains, rural communities and an altogether tranquil air.

The events known today as the 'Prague Spring' were the culmination of an increasingly vocal grass-roots independence movement in what was then Czechoslovakia. During the 1960s, locals had begun to campaign for more autonomy, and in the end became so vocal that tanks had to be brought in. When the reform-committed Alexander Dubcek became Secretary of the

The Woman who Would be King

Maria Theresa was an empress at age 24, and between 1740 and 1780 she ruled an empire that covered Austria, Hungary and Bohemia. Many Hungarian aristocrats were opposed to having a woman as 'king', and her father assumed she would always give the real power to her husband, which never happened. He gave her no information about the intricacies of government and she was forced to work out the job on her own. She often held court in the castle of Bratislava and implemented the beginning of the city's golden age, being responsible for many of the city's more splendid buildings. Some even say she was the saviour of the Habsburg Dynasty as she worked to transform her empire into a modern state. Others maintain that her title of 'enlightened monarch' was put into question by her staunch Catholicism. Sadly her son Josef II, the eldest of her 16 children (one of whom was Marie Antionette), did not continue her good work.

> **What's in a Name?**
> Slovakia is the country's official name, although this is not always used. A Slovak is an inhabitant or native of Slovakia, but also refers to the language of Slovakia. Slovak can also be used as an adjective; Slovakian can also be used in this context but is less formal.

Czechoslovak Communist Party he put the desire for change into action. In a radical move he openly criticised the strict policies of the Communist Party, which had been in place since 1948, declared basic human rights for all and condemned political persecution. When the now famous '2,000 words' article by Ludvik Vaculik was published, it dramatically rallied the country's citizens to protest against what was wrong in society.

The Soviet Communists in Moscow were not amused. In August 1968 Warsaw Pact troops in tanks rolled into Czechoslovakia and a brutal regime ensued. Those who had supported the Prague Spring were stripped of their jobs, and nearly 2,000 people escaped to the West. In the 1970s and '80s the Communists introduced an approach in Czechoslovakia known as Normalisation, actually one of the strictest regimes of all the Communist countries. Although the country was effectively under occupation, and the movement had been pushed underground, however, the convictions of those involved remained, and the spirit of independence lived on. In protest a student killed himself in Prague and in Bratislava supporters protested in front of oncoming tanks.

Czechoslovakia's 'Velvet Revolution' took place in November 1989 and was so-called because it was the most peaceful rejection of Communism in Eastern Europe. However, only three years later, on 1 January 1993, to the shock of the international community, the country was divided in two, and Slovakia came into being as a separate democratic state.

The new country joined NATO in March 2004 and the EU in May 2004. The Slovak head of state is the president, who is elected for a five-year term. Almost all executive power is held by the head of government, the prime minister. The current president, Ivan Gašparovič, law professor and once member of the Communist Party, founded the Movement for Democracy Party in 2002. He came to power on 15 June 2004 when he gained nearly 60 per cent of the vote.

Representation of all parties is decided by proportional representation. There is a wide range of political parties, including a number of social democratic parties and the nationalistic Slovak National Party (SNS). The highest legislative body is the 150-seat National Council of the Slovak Republic. The country's highest judicial body is the constitutional court.

Religion

Over 60 per cent of the population are Roman Catholic, with over 8 per cent Protestant. Just under 10 per cent of people in Slovakia are atheist.

Climate and Geography

Slovakia has rugged mountains in its central and northern regions, while the southern part of the country consists mostly of fertile low-lying lands. The River Danube forms a natural border with Hungary. Other rivers include the Váh, Hron and Nitra. The country is more hilly than the Czech Republic and in general the weather within the country does not vary greatly. There is snow and cold easterly winds in winter, while spring and summer can be wet. *See* 'Climate Charts, p.348.

Regional Profile

Bratislava

The capital of Slovakia overlooks the Danube, backed by vineyards on the slopes of the forested Carpathian Mountains, with the Austrian border only 10 miles away. Despite having a rich history, the city does not have the number of historic buildings of somewhere like Prague, and the outskirts are blighted by the familiar Eastern European concrete blocks constructed to house the working classes.

A world away from these Communist remnants is the Old Town, which is slowly being restored. Sadly, a major road and suspension bridge was built right through the centre of this area, which all but destroyed the old Jewish quarter and isolated the recently restored castle area from the rest of the historic streets. In fact, in many ways the city has two very different faces. The old town is an example of Habsburg Baroque, and its newer incarnation a dreary display of post-war architecture, with more buildings having been destroyed since the war than were bombed during it.

As a result of its central position in Europe, Bratislava has suffered from being used as a pawn of surrounding empires, and until 1918 it was more Hungarian and German than Slavic. In fact, it was only called Bratislava after the First World War; until that point it had been known as the Germanic Pressburg. Once a Celtic community, Bratislava was then a Roman outpost before becoming the hub of a medieval Slavic empire and capital of Hungary. The city benefits from its close neighbours, its proximity to Austria and Hungary and its student population lend it a cosmopolitan atmosphere.

West Slovakia

This is a land of castle and spas. **Devín**, with its well-known ruined castle, is just six miles from Bratislava. The first Slavs settled in **Nitra**, which is the agricultural capital of the country today. Its ruined castle is reached by a walk past statues of saints and two dramatic gateways, but as the third-largest city in the country, its historic centre is somewhat lost. The mountains known as the

Small Carpathians reach northwards from Bratislava to form an important wine-growing and walking area. **Trnava** retains its medieval wall and character and was the centre for Hungarian Church for 200 years from the 16th century.

The **Danube Basin** is the closest the country gets to resort towns, with some of the warmest temperatures and numerous rivers, ponds and springs. The town of **Senec** is particularly popular, being just 20 miles or so east of the capital. Two important spa towns on the Váh River are **Piešt'any**, with its opulent late-19th-century Thermia Palace Hotel drawing visitors from around the world to its healing waters, and **Trenčianske Teplice**, best reached by narrow-gauge railway. Also on the river, **Trenčin** is home to the largest castle still standing today outside Bratislava, although it has its share of modern high rises.

East Slovakia

More than anywhere else in Slovakia, this region was an important crossroads, influenced from all directions. Culturally very mixed, this part of the country is the main home for Slovakian Roma who live in shanty towns on the edge of communities. Other populations are the Rusyn (or Rutherian) people and Hungarians in the south. Much of this region is rural, but **Košice** is a city second only in size to the capital. It made its fortune by the trading of salt, and has a fine cathedral and several museums.

Medieval towns in the Spis region include the walled town of **Levoča** and **Kežmarok**, which has a notable wooden Protestant church. Walled **Spišská Kapitula** has an interesting Romanesque cathedral, and Spis Castle is the biggest medieval castle in central Europe. The Slovenský Raj (Slovak Paradise) National Park features pine forests and waterfalls, and Europe's oldest ice cave at Dobšiná – its surroundings were turned into a popular tourist spot for swimming and hiking when a reservoir was created.

Towards Poland, the Saris region is home of the Rusyn minority. **Bardejov** is an almost perfectly preserved walled medieval German town, which today acts mostly as a commercial centre. Nearby is the spa town of **Bardejovské Kúpele**, once the luxurious playground of Hungarian and Russian nobles but today a shadow of its former self.

Central and Mountain Region

Slovakia's central region is the true heart of the country, the cradle of national folklore and identity, where the Slovak language was first codified. Its forests were home to the nation's very own Robin Hood and the Slovak National Uprising, a movement of anti-fascists in the Second World War, was born here. **Bojnický** has the country's most splendid and popular castle, with pseudo-Gothic towering spires, a moat and supposedly its own ghost.

The old German mining town of **Banská Bystrica** is surrounded by mountain ranges, which appear at first sight to be an unattractive collection of industry;

Čičmany, Fairytale Folk Village

Fewer than 400 people live in the mountain village of Čičmany, in the green hills in the north of the country. It is an extraordinary village – a living open-air museum and the world's first folk architecture reserve. The houses are the reason for its acclaim: two-storey wooden cottages intricately decorated with traditional designs. The unique homes were created in the 13th century when the Tartars were ransacking villages and locals were forced to flee.

The Čič family, from who the village takes its name, sought sanctuary in this isolated valley surrounded by forested peaks. The tiny houses would often be home to as many as 25 people. Living a rural life, the men were farmers and shepherds while the women became adept at embroidery and transferred these decorative skills to their homes, using symbols such as crosses and animals, clover leaves and hearts. Two of the houses have been made into a museum, which tells the story of the village, and others have been converted into miniature hotels.

Despite the fact that the original intention of the settlers was to escape persecution and find peace, the hamlet has had more than its fair share of drama. A fire completely destroyed the town in 1921, and the villagers had to re-build and redecorate their homes. Then the Nazis burnt the whole lot down again during the Second World War. More recently, a government programme funded the rebuilding of the village once again.

however, at the centre of the town there is a medieval marketplace, which still serves as the focal point. There are a number of burgher houses here, such as the Venetian House and the beautifully decorated Thurzo Palace, which is the town museum. Other historic buildings include the town hall, remains of the castle, an art gallery and the country's grandest SNP square, with SNP museum.

While the east and west of the country are relatively flat, the central region is characterised by the Carpathian Mountains, made up of the Low and High Tatras, both parts of national parks. Deeply symbolic as the protectors of freedom, they are represented in the Slovak flag, which depicts a Gothic shield and cross rising above a trio of mountains. The High Tatras are locally known as the 'Little Giant Mountains', because, while they are condensed into a small area, six of its peaks are over 2,500 metres high. Below is a green landscape sliced through by blue streams and rivers and dotted with tiny villages built around traditional wooden churches. Dense forests are home to brown bears, deer and wolves. There are more than 80 clear mountain lakes and a good range of tourist facilities. Although there is great hiking in this area, for over half the year footpaths are closed because of snow and summer can be crowded. The Low Tatras are really a smaller, more isolated version of their grander sibling.

The mountains here are dotted with ski and winter sports resorts such as **Tatranská Lomnica**, **Štrbské Pleso** and **Smokovce**, which also is a grand old spa town. The Low Tatras National Park in the western Carpathians has more ski and

Musical History

Musical life in Slovakia is inseparable from its history. From the start of the 19th century, its folk heritage became part of an important musical tradition which has influenced both the country's classical and folk styles. Its traditional music is the most original and dates back to the 9th century, later drawing on chamber music. Folk instruments include Slovak versions of a long flute and bagpipes. During Hungarian rule, folk songs were important for preserving the Slovak language. Music is very important culturally today in Slovakia and it is home to the Philharmonic Orchestra of Bratislava and Košice, the Symphonic Orchestra of Bratislava Broadcast and the Slovak Chamber Orchestra.

recreation resorts including **Jasna**, and the **Demänová Valley**, with its extensive ice-cave system. The **Pieniny National Park** is partly in Poland, 20 miles northeast of the High Tatras, its deep gorges making it perfect for rafting, trips which are more scenic than white water. The **Malá Fatra National Park** was designated because of the area's gorgeous valleys and rich wildlife.

Selecting a Property

Getting There

By Air

Slovakia is served by **Aeroflot, Air France, Air Slovakia** (**www.airslovakia.sk**), **British Airways, Czech Airlines, Delta, KLM, Lot, Lufthansa, Sky Europe** and **Slovak Airlines** (**www.slovakairlines.sk**).

By River

It is possible to arrive in Slovakia by hydrofoil, with international connections on the Danube from Austria, which joins the Black Sea as well as the Rhine. Services operate either from Vienna or Budapest (**www.mahartpassnave.hu**).

By Bus

Eurolines buses link Bratislava and other important towns to major cities such as London, Munich, Paris, Venice and Vienna. For further information, contact **Eurolines**, t 08705 143219, **www.eurolines.com** or **www.nationalexpress.com**.

By Train

The most convenient route to Slovakia from Western Europe is via Prague or Vienna. Slovakia's network also has direct connections with Berlin, Bucharest, Budapest, Hamburg and Moscow.

By Road

Slovakia is easily accessible from Western Europe and there is a good motorway system from Austria to Bratislava. The motorway link between Bratislava and Prague is also useful. Some roads require that a toll is paid, in which case you have to buy and display a sticker or stamp, the price of which varies according to the weight of your vehicle. The stamps are either for the whole calendar year or for a period of 15 days. You can buy them on border crossings, petrol stations or post offices. *See* Settling In', pp.344–5.

Getting Around

By Rail

The national rail company is **Slovak Railways** (Zeleznice Slovenskej Republiky or ZSR; **www.zsr.sk**). There are two types of trains: *rychlik* trains are the fastest and stop only at major towns, and *osobní* , or local trains, which stop at every station and travel only at around 30kph. To travel to neighbouring countries, try to book a sleeper as far ahead as possible.

By Bus

Most buses are run by the state bus company and tickets can usually be purchased from the driver. Try to book your ticket ahead of time if travelling at weekends on popular routes.

By River

There are a couple of thousand miles of navigable waterways. The Danube is the main artery for transport by ship, and it has tourist cruises as well as regular passenger transport.

Choosing a Location

The best areas for investment are the country's capital, Bratislava, and the second city, Košice, or near ski areas or natural parks if you plan to let to tourists.

Property Prices

Guide Prices

€30,000

- **Two-bedroom villa in Low Tatras.**

€60,000

- Luxury three-bedroom cottage with pool and sauna in Kysuce-Cadca, 5 miles from the largest ski resort in Slovakia.
- Luxury apartment in a 16th-century château in need of restoration in the spa town of Piešt'any.

€100,000

- New-build two-bedroom apartment on outskirts of the capital.
- New villa in High Tatras with eight bedrooms, four bathrooms, swimming pool and mountain view.

€200,000

- 18th-century château one mile from Slovak paradise national park; 15 rooms in château and 13 rooms in an additional building.
- Six-bedroom villa with garden and pool in Hamuliakovo near Bratislava.
- Nine-bedroom château in need of renovation in Tatra Mountains with garden and pool.

€500,000

- 19th-century château in Kovarce, in Tatra mountains with lake view.

€1,0000,000

- Two-storey manor house to be reconstructed into an 88-room hotel-casino in an arboretum park in a recreation area.
- Commercial property in Tatra mountains consisting of three ski lifts, a ski resort, new hotel and a ski hire company.
- Three-star luxury hotel with nine bedrooms in the east of country with river and mountain view.

Building from Scratch or Renovation

Older properties in need of renovation tend to be in the rural areas of the country, but consider carefully before renovating. Finding local workers and arranging procedures from home can be difficult and you may find the whole process frustrating.

If building from scratch, take into account the cost of applying for building permission and installing connections to utility services.

Temporary Accommodation

In rural areas temporary accommodation may be more difficult to find, and, even in the capital, bear in mind that the choice is still relatively small and standards may not be what you would expect at home. The website **www. accommodation-online.biz/slovenia.html** features a whole range of accommodation, including apartments, camping, hostels and hotels.

The Process of Buying a Property

There is a lot more risk associated with buying property in Slovakia than when buying in Italy or the UK, as there is a lot of property with either bad title or defective planning consent. Legal advice is essential, unless you take the view that the amount you are investing is so small that you can afford to write it off.

Initial Steps

First Contracts

Once you have found a property that you want to purchase, you will be expected to sign some form of contract, generally either a reservation contract or a preliminary purchase contract, *see* p.75. Note that the title 'preliminary purchase contract' is misleading; it is actually a full binding purchase contract. We therefore recommend that, wherever possible, you insist on signing a **reservation contract** at this stage.

Searches and Enquiries

Once you have signed a reservation contract, your lawyer should make various enquiries, such as checking that the contract is fair, that the seller has good title and the right to sell to you, that the area is zoned for residential building and that any building work being undertaken enjoys all of the necessary planning and building consents. Depending on the circumstances of your case, there could well be other enquiries that also need to be made.

Signing the Contract and Registering the Title

Once your lawyer has checked out the property and found that everything is in order, you are ready to sign the **preliminary purchase contract**. This commits you and the seller to signing the full contract transferring ownership on an agreed date shortly afterwards, or, if the property is still under construction, once the property has been fully built.

The preliminary purchase contract contains most of the clauses you would expect to see in a UK contract. These will include a description of the property, a statement of the legal title to the property, the price to be paid, how it is to be paid, the deadline for payment and any other deadlines applicable, what should happen in the event of breach of contract and so on. Many Slovakian contracts are badly drafted, because there is really no history in Slovakia of drafting contracts for the sale of land. The problem is exacerbated by the fact that many contracts are drafted in English, which is clearly not the first language of the person doing the drafting. As a result they are unclear or muddled. Specifications tend to be very 'thin'. The contracts tend to be lacking in detail as to what happens if anything goes wrong.

At this point you will normally pay a **deposit** of 10–20 per cent of the price of the property and apply for a **buying permit** from the local council. If the permit is refused, the deposit is forfeited. In the case of a property under construction ('off-plan') you will start to make **stage payments**, which will vary in size and number from property to property. A typical scheme would provide for an initial payment of 30 per cent followed by two further payments of 30 per cent as construction progresses, followed by a final payment of 10 per cent on delivery. Occasionally schemes are found where there is only one preliminary payment of, say, 30 per cent with the balance being paid on delivery. This is obviously very useful if you are taking out a mortgage.

Once you are ready to take delivery of the house you will sign the **final purchase contract**. This is signed in front of a notary public. It is at this point that the balance of the money is paid across to the seller. You do not need to be present in Slovakia to sign this document, as your lawyer can prepare a **power of attorney** (*see* pp.77–8) under which you can appoint somebody else to sign on your behalf. This is a sensible thing to do, as it saves the need for you to go to Slovakia, often at short notice, to sign the final title.

Once you have paid the balance of the price the seller will authorise you to **register your ownership** of the property in the local title register. Once this has been done, you – or the local Slovakian company that you have set up to own the property – will be the full legal owner of the property in much the same way as you would be in the UK.

Letting Your Property

See the general chapter **Letting Your Property**, pp.117–26.

If you are letting out your property you should make sure that you use a proper **rental contract**. Your lawyer will be able to supply you with a draft that you can change as necessary. Letting out short-term to tourists produces the least problems in terms of what you can do if the tenant does not pay the rent or refuses to leave.

Settling In

Learning Slovak

Slovak is a Slavic language like, for example, Czech, Russian, Polish, Bulgarian and Serbo-Croat. It is not an easy language for an English-speaking person to learn: accents can be confusing and indicate a slight change in pronunciation, but are quite consistent.

Culture Clashes

It is worth learning a few cultural tips before you go to Slovakia:

- The concept of 'ladies first' does not apply; men always lead when going into a bar or restaurant. Some say it is to protect the women in case there is a fight inside!

- If giving flowers, make sure they are an odd number, as even numbers are only given for funerals.

- Shoes are big here, in that they must always be very clean, in good condition, and removed before going into someone's house. Often you will be presented with a pair of slippers as temporary replacement.

- Drinking is taken very seriously by Slovaks. Say '*na zdravie*' for 'cheers', and as you clink glasses, look your companion in the eye. Sometimes drinkers carry out a choreographed move in which they clink the top of their glasses, then the bottom and finally the table.

- Confusingly, Slovaks count with the thumb to mean one and the thumb and index finger to mean two. So be careful when ordering anything with sign-language as you may end up with more than you bargained for.

- Spending a penny in Slovakia can be quite a literal process. Many establishments make a small charge to use the toilet and you may be charged for toilet paper too.

Home Utilities and Services

Gas and Electricity

The cost of electricity and gas for households increased dramatically in recent years. Prices are still set by government decree, and the residential markets are subsidised. Peak tariff costs about €0.40 (3 SKK) per kwH and off-peak €0.14 (1 SKK) per kwH (the equivalent UK tariff would be €0.09/kwH).

Around 90 per cent of Slovakians have access to mains gas, and because of the poor insulation in many existing properties, domestic gas consumption is high.

Water

Slovakians are gradually learning to control their consumption of water, with the progressive elimination of subsidies, and consequent increase in prices. Water supply costs vary across the regions. In Bratislava average bills are €140 per annum, compared with €250 in Košice.

Telephones

To call Slovakia from abroad, use the **country code t** 421 and drop the first zero in the area code. The Bratislava area code is **t** 02. Directory enquiries: **t** 120 or 121.

You can make cheap local calls from any phone, but for international calls it's best to use a **card phone**. Some coin phones exist in Slovakia, but most take cards (*telefonná karta*), a variety of which can be bought from post offices and tobacconists. With international cards, ask for the booklet listing international toll-free access numbers. These cards can also be used to make local calls.

Mobile phones from the UK and other countries in Western Europe should function in Slovakia and local use is more widespread than you might expect.

The Internet

The internet is not as common in Slovakia as it is in some other countries in Eastern Europe. In Bratislava there are some Internet cafés, and a few others in major cities.

Media

The English language paper **www.slovakspectator.sk** is available online. News in English is also provided by the *Hospodarske Noviny* daily newspaper. *Novy Cas* and *Pravda* are two daily newspapers in Slovak.

Markiza TV is the national commercial TV station, **STV** the Slovak public TV station, and **TA 3** is the Slovak news channel. The main cable operator in Slovakia is **UPC**, which broadcasts news services of the **BBC** and **CNN**.

Radio Slovakia International has news in English, German, French and Russian. **Blue Danube Radio** is the English programme of **Austrian Radio FM 103.8**, which can be received in Bratislava.

Money and Banking

The currency in Slovakia is the **Slovak crown** or **Slovenská koruna** (abbreviated to Sk), which is divided into 100 **halier** (h). Coins come as 10h, 20h, 50h, 1Sk, 2Sk, 5Sk and 10Sk; notes as 20Sk, 50Sk, 100Sk, 500Sk, 1,000Sk and 5,000Sk.

The easiest way to withdraw currency is to use an **ATM**, but there are exchange offices in major hotels and department stores. **Credit cards** are accepted in most hotels and restaurants and some shops, though sometimes there is a minimum amount. Banks and exchange offices also exchange hard currency, and there is no limit to the amount of foreign currency that may be imported into Slovakia. Avoid exchanging money on the street. Most banks are open from 8 or 9am to 4 or 5pm; exchange offices tend to keep longer hours.

Post

Most post offices (*pošta*) are open weekdays from 7 or 8am to 5 or 8pm, and till noon at weekends. It is also possible to buy stamps (*známky*) from some tobacconists (*tabák*) and street kiosks.

Airmail from Slovakia is reliable up to a point. Parcels over 2kg need to be sent from a customs office; ask postal workers where the nearest one is.

Working and Employment

UK nationals have the right to live and work in the Slovak Republic without a work permit and have the same rights as Slovakian nationals with regard to pay, working conditions and access to housing, training, social security and trade union membership. Families and immediate dependants are entitled to join them and have similar rights. For more information on moving to the Slovak Republic contact the Slovakian Embassy (*see* p.346).

In the Slovak Republic citizens can find employment through the **Office for Labour, Social Affairs and Family** (*Ministerstvo prace, socialnych veci a rodiny*; **www.employment.gov.sk**). Some UK employment agencies that deal with work abroad are registered with the **Recruitment and Employment Confederation** (REC; 36–38 Mortimer Street, London W1W 7RG, **t** (020) 7462 3260, **f** (020) 7255 2878, **www.rec.uk.com**), which is a trade association of recruitment agencies that may be able to recommend an agency to help you in your search for work. REC can provide a list of suitable agencies if you write to them outlining the type of employment you are looking for.

Education

The education system in the Slovak Republic is based on a three-tier system (primary, secondary and higher education). Children are required to attend school between the ages of six and 15. The first stage runs from age six to 10, the second from age 10 to 15. Further education, including vocational training, is available in specialised schools such as gymnasiums, specialised secondary schools, conservatories and vocational secondary schools. Higher education institutions have the exclusive right to award academic degrees.

Health and Emergencies

Ambulance, **t** 155 or **t** 112; Slovak Rescue System, **t** 154.

The UK has a reciprocal agreement with the Slovak Republic for the provision of full hospital treatment at reduced cost or even free (produce your E111 or EHIC card), though medicines must be paid for. It is necessary to choose one of the five health insurance companies to which a doctor will charge for healthcare provided. In case of illness, consult a clinic (*poliklinika*) or hospital (*nemocnia*). If you are given a prescription take it to a pharmacist (*lekárem*). Pharmacies are the first place to go for minor ailments. Some prescription drugs are still subsidised. In most towns at least one pharmacy is open 24 hours a day.

Medical facilities are adequate in the country, but the number of doctors who speak English is limited. Doctors and hospitals will require cash payment for health services. Medical prescriptions issued in the UK are not valid in the Slovak Republic; you will need a local doctor to issue a prescription.

Social Services and Welfare Benefits

The Slovak Republic's welfare system is currently being overhauled, meaning, for example, that benefits are being cut by half for capable citizens who remain voluntarily unemployed. Pension reform directly links benefits to contributions as a way of trying to increase work incentives. Child and family benefits are to be distributed partly as tax bonuses in order to reward legal earnings. Registration for unemployment, a condition for getting access to welfare benefits, is being made more difficult.

Social security rights in the Slovak Republic are the same as those that apply in the UK. If you work in the Slovak Republic, you will contribute to the Slovakian social security system and, consequently, gain the right to benefits. If you are entitled to the contributory part of Job Seekers' Allowance, and have been claiming this for at least four weeks in the UK, you may continue to receive it for up to three months in the Slovak Republic, while you actively seek work there. Tell your Jobcentre Plus office or Jobcentre in the UK (where you are registered) of your intention to look for work in the Slovak Republic well in advance of your departure date. Your Jobcentre Plus office or Jobcentre will advise the DWP Pensions and Overseas Benefits Directorate who will determine whether conditions are satisfied and send you form E303 before you leave. Take this form, which secures the payment of your unemployment benefit in the Slovak Republic, to the Slovakian employment service as soon as possible.

Cars

Car ownership is still relatively low, so traffic levels are pretty contained. Slovak roads are in reasonably good condition, with road signs that follow European standards. There are few stretches of motorways, but a pass must be purchased to travel on them. That said, many main roads have only a single carriageway in each direction, making overtaking difficult, and some road markings can be hard to see, especially in bad weather. Speed limits on motorways are 130kph, 90kph on roads and 50kph in towns and cities. Drinking any amount of alcohol before driving is illegal and safety belts must be worn at all times. Cars are obliged to have their lights on even during the day from 15 October to 15 March, and failure to do so may result in a fine.

If you bring your car over from home, make sure that you have valid motor insurance. Bear in mind that right-hand drive cars cannot be registered in the country, which makes it very difficult to get insurance. It is possible to drive on a UK driving licence for up to six months.

There are a number of international car rental companies in Slovakia, but Slovak companies are likely to charge a much more reasonable price. Watch out for local drivers who use the horn instead of a brake and tend to accelerate on blind curves.

Crime and the Police

Police, **t** 158 or **t** 112.

Although there has been a rise in crime in Slovak Republic recently, the crime rate is still much lower than in the UK and most of Western Europe. It mostly takes the form of petty theft and pickpocketing, so take all the normal precautions. You are required by law to carry some form of photo ID, such as a driving licence or a passport, and in theory police can stop you to check that you are carrying such identification. The **national police** (*polícia*) wear green uniforms, while the **municipal police** (*mestská polícia*) wear various different uniforms depending on the area. If you need to report a crime, it will be to the municipal police. There are also private police, employed mostly by hotels and banks, who are authorised to carry guns but have no legal powers of arrest. You should carry your passport with you at all times, though you're highly unlikely to get stopped.

Food and Drink

There is no Slovak cuisine as such. The national dish is a kind of gnocchi served with a thick sheep's cheese sauce and bacon. Goulash is common, although it is much less spicy than the Hungarian version. Main dishes are meat-based, with pork and beef the most common ingredients. Fish such as trout and carp are usually on offer. Vegetables and other greens are not common and vegetarians will have a tough time. Although potatoes, cow's and sheep's cheese, cabbage, onions and garlic are the bases of many dishes in Slovakia, meat will almost always be added.

There are soups everywhere, and they are usually good. Stand-up canteens are popular for cheap snacks, especially a kind of hot dog known as the *párek*. In the Bratislava region, the snack *treska* – a cold salad made of codfish, mayonnaise and vegetables – is very popular. Office workers commonly grab some five ounces of *treska* and two rolls for lunch. In the capital you may find some international food, such as Chinese cuisine or Italian pizzas, as well as fast-food burger bars.

Traditionally **coffee** is drunk as a strong espresso. The south of the country has some decent white **wines**. **Brandy** is much loved, particularly the firewater plum brandy known as *slivovice*. Because of its position next to the Czech Republic, beer is a national drink, but less ubiquitous.

Slovakia: References

Directory of Contacts and Resources

Embassies

- **Slovak Embassy**, 25 Kensington Palace Gardens, London W8 4QY, **t** (020) 7313 6470 or 7243 0803, **f** (020) 7313 6481, **www.slovakembassy.co.uk**.
- **British Embassy**, Panská 16, 811 01 Bratislava, Slovak Republic, **t** + 421 2 5998 2000, **f** +421 2 5998 2237, **www.britishembassy.gov.uk**.

Information and Resources

- **www.government.gov.sk**. An official government site.
- **www.slovakia.org/sk-faq.htm**. An interesting tourist site.
- **www.sunshineestates.net**. Good information in English.
- **www.hosmanek.com/slovak**. Claims to have the world's largest collection of Slovak links.
- **www.czechcottages.cz**. Lists over 1,000 cottages, chalets, cabins and similar for rent.
- **www.slovakia-slovakia.com**. Personal travel guide with accommodation.
- **www.slovakheritage.org**. A wide range of articles.

Property Companies and Estate Agents

- **The National Association of Real Estate Offices of Slovakia (NARKS)**, **www.narks-real.sk/goals.htm**. Has a list of links of members.
- **www.reality.sk**. With an English version.
- **www.slovakia-property.com**.
- **www.sunshineestates.net**.

- **Slovak Real Estate**, Panska ul. 3–5, 81101 Bratislava, **t** + 421 2 5910 3236 or **t** 904 988 540 (mobile), **f** + 421 2 5443 2321, **info@slovakrealestate.sk, www.slovakrealestate.sk.**

Removal Companies

- **UK & International Movers**, Grove Barns, North Road, South Ockendon, Essex RM15 6SR, **t** 0800 954 6474 (freephone) or **t** (01708) 854545, **f** 08700 940149, **relo@askmonarch.com, www.yourpersonalmover.com**.

Holiday Companies

- **www.slovakiagreentours.com**. A family-run company with an English owner, offers city breaks and country tours.

Administrative Departments

For administrative purposes, Slovakia is subdivided into eight regions, each of which is named after its principal city: Banská Bystrica, Bratislava, Košice, Nitra, Presov, Trenčin, Trnava, Zilina.

Time

Slovakia is in the Central European time zone: GMT + 1 hour (+ 2hrs Mar–Oct). It is six hours ahead of Eastern Standard Time and nine hours ahead of Western Standard Time.

Public Holidays

1 January	New Year's Day and the Establishment of Slovakia
6 January	Epiphany
March/April	Good Friday and Easter Monday
1 May	May Day
8 May	Victory Day (the end of the Second World War)
5 July	Holiday of Saints Cyril and Methodius
29 August	Anniversary of the Slovak National Uprising
1 September	Day of the Constitution of Slovakia
15 September	Our Lady of the Seven Sorrows
1 November	All Saints' Day
24–26 December	Christmas

Further Reading

A History of Slovak Literature, Peter Petro, Liverpool University Press – academic approach to history of Slovakia from the Middle Ages to the present.

Czech, Moravian and Slovak Fairy Tales, Parker Fillmore (Hippocrene Books, Inc) – 15 classic regional fairytales with illustrations.

Crossing Borders: Contemporary Czech and Slovak Photography (Aperture Foundation Inc) – fascinating collection of photographs with essays.

Slovak Republic, Kummerly and Frey (International Road Map).

Climate Charts

Rainfall and Sunlight in Košice

	Jan	Feb	Mar	Apr	May	Jun	Jul	Aug	Sep	Oct	Nov	Dec
Rainfall (mm)	−30	30	26	38	57	84	84	80	47	41	49	39
Sunlight (hours)	−7	3	4	6	8	8	8	8	6	4	2	1

Rainfall and Sunlight in Bratislava

	Jan	Feb	Mar	Apr	May	Jun	Jul	Aug	Sep	Oct	Nov	Dec
Rainfall (mm)	43	47	42	42	42	61	64	73	69	54	55	59
Sunlight (hours)	2	3	5	7	9	9	9	9	7	5	2	1

Slovenia

20

Why Buy in Slovenia?

Little Slovenia is nestled between Italy, Austria, Hungary and Croatia and has only a tiny stretch of Mediterranean coast. Few visitors come to Slovenia for its beaches; what is special is the countryside, which is astonishingly varied considering its size. It is sometimes referred to as mini-Switzerland because of its mountains, and because it is one of the richer countries of the former Yugoslavia. In fact, it is one of the most prosperous and stable countries of all Europe's former Communist countries, and the only country in the former Yugoslavia to join the EU in May 2004.

Slovenia's position makes it easily accessible from a number of countries. For the coast and the capital, cheap flights into Italy's Trieste are ideal. Those who want to get to the skiing area in the northwest of the country can conveniently fly into Graz's airport in Austria, and easyJet now flies into Slovenia's capital city of Ljubljana.

Although Slovenia experienced a huge drop in the number of tourists because of the Yugoslav conflict, concerns were unfounded and the country was as safe as ever. Like so many of these countries, Slovenia has a long history of welcoming foreign tourists and is waiting patiently for them to return in the same numbers as before the conflict.

The property market in Slovenia is currently fairly undeveloped, but it has been opening up rapidly over the last few years. Prices here are closer to those in its richer neighbours such as Italy and Austria and may not offer the bargains you expect, but are still very good value.

Tourism

Slovenia receives just under a million foreign visitors annually, a figure which is gradually increasing. It has lots of different experiences to offer.

Health Spas

Slovenia has a long history of spa resorts, which can be traced back as far as Roman times. Their healing and restorative powers have been recognised throughout the country and across Europe since that time. In recent years, the spas have gone through something of a renaissance, with existing resorts being renovated and expanded and new complexes constructed. Some have a wonderful *fin-de-siècle* feel about them, some have waterslides and beauty parlours, while others feel like municipal swimming pools with the old and ill taking the waters – so check before you go; these spas have their roots in medicine and may not have the atmosphere of luxury and decadence you might expect. There are 15 health spas in total, including the Radenci spa, whose mineral water was sent to the Vienna's imperial court as well as the Vatican's papal court. The tourist office is very keen to promote the spas to international visitors; its website (**www.terme-giz.si**) has more detailed information.

A Sporting Nation

Slovenia's mountains, rivers, lakes and forests have spawned a rich sporting tradition. Way back in the 17th century, the first encyclopaedic writings of Slovenia outlined climbing, boating, skiing and caving activities in the country, part of which forms the oldest written record of skiing in central Europe. Mountaineering has a long history as a traditional Slovene sport – the Julian and Kamnik Alps are particularly popular. In the 19th century priest Jakob Aljaz was so alarmed by the rapid influx of foreign visitors in the Slovene mountains that he bought the Triglav Peak and Kredarica for five guilders. He built a turret at the summit, which he then gave to the Slovene Alpine Society. The **Slovene Mountaineering Association (www.pzs.si)** organises adventure holidays.

Going Downhill Fast

The skiing season lasts from December to March. The slopes are fairly small compared with the more dramatic areas in countries like Switzerland and Italy. Maribor is by far the biggest ski resort in the country and plays host to several international ski competitions. The resort itself is compact and set among stunning alpine scenery; there is a ski school and night skiing with flood-lighting. Kranjska Gora offers low-level skiing and the resort itself is modest, although it benefits from being easily accessible from Austria and Italy. Kravavec is perhaps the best-equipped ski resort and very popular with locals, as it is less than an hour away from the capital.

In a 10-day trip, you could pretty much cover all of the country's highlights and travel to its four corners. Slovenia's roads are excellent and generally quiet. Six different routes, romantically named Amber, Wind, Emerald, Golden Horn, Peddler and Sun, have been outlined by the tourist office in an illustrated brochure.

Anyone for Golf?

Even as recently as a few years ago, golf was uncommon in Slovenia because it was seen as a bourgeois activity. Things could not be more different now, and the country has eight courses. Bled Golf and Country Club was founded way back in 1937 to cater to the diplomats who came to Bled because the king of Yugoslavia had his summer residence there. Like some stately dame, the club lies in splendid Alpine countryside near romantic Lake Bled, with 27 holes and a new lake course that has been added in recent years. Other courses include Lipica, home of white Lipizzaner horses, Arboretum Volčji Potok near the capital, Mokrice with a lovely castle, Moravske Toplice in an area of thermal waters, the newest course in the ancient town of Ptuj, Slovenske Konjice surrounded by vineyards, and Podčetrtek near the Olimja Health Resort. If the rumours are true, a number of new golf courses are currently on the drawing board.

A Walk in the Park

From reindeer safaris and strolls in landscaped parks to serious mountain-climbing, Slovenia offers walking opportunities galore. It has over 7,000km of trails, including two European hiking trails and the Slovenian alpine trail, which was opened in 1953. Via Alpina 2000 passes through Slovenia, Austria, Germany, France and Italy, among other countries, and is a 150-day trail following the Alps all the way from Trieste to Monaco; it is due for completion in 2006.

The tourist office is keen to encourage walking tourism, and has an excellent website (**www.slovenia-tourism.si/intro**), even if it is rather over-zealous in the number of walking trails, tours and routes it is keen to promote. Heritage trails take visitors to places of natural beauty, ethnological points of interest and attractive towns and cities. There are also trails exploring Slovenia's history,

If You Go Down to the Woods Today

Slovenia is the only place in the world where bears live in forests just 20 miles from a capital city. The country was one of the first in Europe to protect its indigenous brown bear population by declaring it a protected species after the Second World War. It is thought that during the Balkan conflict a number of animals escaped to peace across the borders. There may today be as many as 700 bears living in the woods of Slovenia, which cover more than half the country. Every year a quota is determined of the number of bears that should be slaughtered and there was a huge increase in this figure in 2002–3, which brought protests from animal protection organisations.

Fine Wines

Slovenia's wine tradition dates back to the Roman times and today the country's 14 wine-growing regions produce some high-quality varieties. Around the town of Ptuj are a number of fine white wine vineyards. For example, the Haloze Hills towards the border of Croatia is a landscape of corn, sunflowers and vines, and is featured on the Haloze Trail. To take some of bottles home with you, call in at one of the specialised wine shops (*vinoteka*) which can be found in most major towns and wine-growing regions. Vinoteka Bradesko in the City Fairground in Ljubljana offers the biggest selection and offers examples from many smaller producers. Apart from the 800 or so vintages, the shop has a bar for sampling as well as a restaurant. Another memorable *vinoteka* is in the Water Tower in the centre of Maribor with a huge wine-tasting hall. Most connoisseurs have their favourite private suppliers and in some areas, such as the Podravje region, viticulture is a common pastime, especially in retirement.

such as the Cultural Heritage Path in Žirovnica, which connects the birthplaces of important Slovenians, and another which explores the country's literary past.

Wine Routes

The more hedonistic could embark on a wine route, although these are as much about scenic landscapes as fine tipples. Calling in at traditional inns (*gostilnas*) allows you to experience Slovenia's rich culinary traditions. *Gostilnas* are usually family-run and provide home-cooked food typical of the region and, of course, local wines. There are 13 routes identified on the tourist office's website (**www.slovenia-tourism.si**), with attractions and host restaurants.

The Economy

Slovenia was one of the wealthiest parts of the former Yugoslavia. Its standard of living is considerably higher than in Croatia and even higher than in Montenegro. The prices of attractive, well-positioned property reflect this. However, it is possible to buy property inland at Croatian prices. Slovenia's links to the West are stronger than those in its neighbours and it is already a member of the EU.

Visas and Permits

Those holding a UK passport which is valid for six months after the planned date of leaving Slovenia do not require a visa to visit Slovenia and no special permits are required for periods up to **90 days**. If you are intending to work in Slovenia, a **temporary residence permit** is required, which is issued for periods of up to one year at a time by the Ministry for Internal Affairs. Those who wish to retire in Slovenia with **permanent residence** must have proof of health insurance, statements indicating income and a permanent address.

To obtain **citizenship** of Slovenia, individuals must have been resident for at least 10 years, and for at least five years without interruption. They must also have a fixed residence, means of supporting themselves and a demonstrable working knowledge of the Slovenian language.

Profile of Slovenia

Recent History and Politics

Until 1918 Slovenia was part of the Austro-Hungarian Empire, but it always kept a clear sense of its own identity; in many ways it is more closely allied with Central Europe than with the east, and the country managed to avoid much of the conflict that its neighbours to the east experienced, although it took part in the Ten Day War to bring about its independence from Yugoslavia in 1991.

It had taken less than 80 years for Yugoslavia to be created and then dissolved. The country was only formed after the First World War when the Croats, Serbs and Slovenes got together to create a new kingdom. After the Second World War, under Marshal Tito, Yugoslavia was transformed into an independent Communist state. When Slovenia and Croatia asserted independence in 1991, the once kingdom was fragmented.

Since splitting from the former Yugoslavia, Slovenia has enjoyed a stable, multi-party, democratic political system and an excellent human rights record. In its government, power is shared between an elected president, a prime minister, and parliament. Milan Kučan was the man who led his people to independence in 1991; he became the first president of independent Slovenia in 1992 and elections in 1997 resulted in his being elected again. Janez Drnovšek from the Liberal Democratic Party of Slovenia (LDS) was re-elected prime minister in the 2000 parliamentary elections. He then won the second round of presidential elections in December 2002, when he stepped down as prime minister. He also played a key role in Slovenian politics since independence. Slovenia is now a member of the EU and NATO.

Timeline

1990   National referendum in which 88 per cent vote for the independent republic of Slovenia.

1991   Slovenia declares its independence from Yugoslavia, removes Yugoslav border signs and sends 2,000 soldiers to occupy the border. Ten Day War lasts 27 June to 6 July. Fewer than 100 people die. In December, independent Slovenia gets a new, democratic constitution.

1992　In January all members of the European Economic Community recognise Slovenia as a state. In May Slovenia becomes a member of the United Nations. In December the first presidential elections are held and Milan Kučan becomes president.

1997　The second presidential elections are held in November and Milan again becomes president until 2002.

1998　Slovenia becomes non-permanent member of the UN Security Council.

2002　The European Commission of the EU announces that Slovenia is one of 10 countries to meet its criteria to become a member of the EU.

2002　The third presidential elections are held in December; Janez Drnovšek becomes president.

2003　Referenda are held for Slovenia joining the EU and NATO, both positive.

2004　Slovenia joins NATO in March and the EU in May.

Religion

The vast majority of Slovenes (almost 70 per cent) are Roman Catholics, 1 per cent of population are Lutheran and 1 per cent Muslim. There are around 30 other religious communities, spiritual groups, societies and associations registered in Slovenia.

Climate and Geography

Slovenia has four distinct seasons. There is a Mediterranean climate on the Adriatic coast, with mild winters and sunny summers. Because of the mountains, which back the coast, rainfall in summer and winter can be heavy and the *bora* often blows in this area. Away from the coast, the weather is more obviously Eastern European, with cold winters and very warm, wet summers.

See 'Climate Charts', p.371.

Regional Profile

Although most of the population work in towns, much of the country is rural and retains many of its traditions. Even close to major towns, old farm buildings such as wooden barns, raised granaries, pigsties and beehives can be seen. In wine-growing areas you can see traditional wine houses where farmers store wine and retreat to sample it. The farmed landscape features strip fields, pastures and vineyards, bordered by woodland.

Ljubljana

Claims that this lovely, compact city on a river could be the next Prague are probably exaggerated. Yes, it has charming old buildings with red tile roofs, cobblestoned streets and romantic castle, but Ljubljana has its own personality. In fact, with a population of only around 300,000 and a positively laid-back air, it hardly seems a city at all. The Ljubljanica River snakes through the centre of the city, crossed by a number of decorative bridges. On one side is the old town with a lively outdoor market and dramatic castle. On the other side are the bulk of the city's sights, including the Opera House, the defunct Tivoli castle, the shopping streets and the Baroque town hall. Many of the older buildings were destroyed in an earthquake in 1895, but several remaining structures show Roman and Baroque influences.

Just west of the city, Vrhovci has a number of newer buildings, many dating back to the 1970s but recently restored to keep up with demand. North, the suburb of Brod is green and quiet, with views of the Julian Mountains. A farmhouse in a rural location is accessible only around 30 miles out of the capital, with prices nearly half of those in the centre.

Around the Julian Alps

The two stars of the Julian Alps and indeed the whole of Slovenia are the beautiful lakes Bled and Bohinj. **Lake Bled** has a medieval church on a wooded island and, overlooked by a castle, it appears like a scene from a fairytale. It is no surprise that it has been popular with visitors around the world for years. It is possible to rent a rowing boat or gondola to go out to the island in summer; in winter you will need ice skates. **Lake Bohinj**, just to the south, is quieter and is a mecca for skiing and hiking.

Mount Triglav, Slovenia's highest mountain, forms **Triglav National Park**, an area of looming mountains cut through with deep gorges that is home to important plant and wild life. **Trenta** is the focus for the park, with an information office and botanical gardens. Below are the Soča and the upper Sava river valleys. The **Soča Valley**'s green rivers attract adrenaline-seekers who raft and kayak their waters, while hang-gliders and parachutists take to the air. **Bovec** is a small resort in the upper part of the valley, which lies at the foot of towering mountains in a wide wooded valley created by the winding Soca River. Mount Kanin is a ski centre reached from the valley with a range of hotels and restaurants. The Upper Sava Valley features the popular ski resort of Kranjska Gora, which provides for hiking, riding and fishing in summer, and skiing, sledging and mountaineering in winter.

Velike Planina

Dubbed the Great Highlands, this area reaches a height of 1,666 metres and is serviced by a cable car. This is a region of dairy farming where distinct round buildings with cone-shaped roofs and traditional shepherd huts dot the country and shepherds wearing traditional green-felt hats sell curd, milk and cheese. Walking and skiing are popular activities here.

Maribor Pohorje Area

In the northeast of the country, **Maribor** is closer to Austria and Hungary than it is to the capital (50 miles away), and is easily accessible from both countries. Although it is Slovenia's second largest city, the centre of the country's wine industry and home to the country's second university, it has more of the atmosphere of a large provincial town. The old town, known as Lent, on the north bank of the River Drava has well-preserved Renaissance architecture. In the region nearby is scenic **Brestrniško Jezero Lake** and numerous wine roads. Maribor is the gateway to the skiing and recreational area of Maribor Pohorje. **Pohorje** has well-developed skiing facilities, including a snow stadium, an adrenaline park and a thermal spa.

Ptuj Area

Ptuj is Slovenia's oldest city and home to an imposing hilltop castle, a regional museum and the country's oldest wine cellar. It has a medieval centre on the banks of the fast-flowing Drava River. Ptuj Thermal Spa has indoor and outdoor pools, tennis courts, massage facilities and beauty treatments, while **Ptujsko Jezero Lake** is a popular recreational area with fishing, rowing and sailing opportunities. Nearby are wine-growing regions including the Haloze Hills, one of the best in the country.

In the run-up to Shrove Tuesday there is an 11-day carnival in Ptuj. The star of the event is the Kurent, a bizarre-looking animal with antlers, a long red nose and tongue. Residents dress up in sheepskins as this character and walk through the streets to chase away winter by brandishing two feathered sticks and to welcome spring by ringing enormous cow bells. The ancient origins of this pagan festival are obscure and traditionally the Kurenti did not leave the Ptuj area, although today they visit other Slovenian towns and even travel abroad. Another festival is Cerknica, which features a procession of frogs and boars, devils and witches, as well as a giant and a lake monster. In fact, Slovenia is home to more than 170 different traditional characters and masks.

The Coast

The country only has 25 miles of coast, sometimes rather hopefully called the Slovene Riviera. Here, on the northern edge of the Istrian peninsula, are the resorts of the former Yugoslavia. Lovely **Piran** is set on a peninsula on the Adriatic, tucked in underneath Italy's coast. With its well-preserved Venetian architecture, it is a historical jewel. Understandably popular, it becomes very crowded, even overrun, in summer. In town is a maritime museum within a 17th-century palace, Venetian houses and historic churches such as the tower of the parish church, which is a copy of St Mark's. Nearby are a number of rocky beaches.

Famous Farm

The Lipica Stud Farm was founded in 1580 by Charles, the Archduke of Vienna, and remained the property of the Vienna Court until 1918. The stud farm continues to breed some of the best horses in the world today; there are 3,000 left of them. The Lipizzaner horses are dark at birth and lighten to a bright white with age. Only authentic Lipizzaner horses sport an 'L' branded on their left cheek. Visitors can take tours of the farm to see the horses perform dancing movements once used for warfare, and people (no children under 12 years) of all riding abilities can take lessons. The farm, known as Kobilarna Lipica, is located at Lipica 5, 6210 Sežana, Slovenia, **t** + 386 5 739 1580.

Lipica itself is just across from the Italian border. Its name means 'little linden' because of the many trees in the surrounds. Apart from the stud farm, the area has become something of a resort and relaxation location. There are nature trails for walking and cycling, as well as a golf course and tennis courts.

Portoroz is Slovenia's bold, brash beach resort; its very own Blackpool. Enjoying 150 years as a seaside destination, 'the Port of Roses' has casinos and accommodation ranging from high-rise hotels to the 1891 Palace Hotel with its mud and brine baths. Despite its being very developed, there are wooded hills behind the coast and it has the biggest sandy beaches in the country.

Koper is a working port that attracts few tourists, but get past its huge container ports and sprawling industry and you will find a preserved medieval core. The seaside area of Ankaran has a tourist complex and there are some tourist facilities on the border with Italy.

Postojna

Postojna is known for just one thing: its caves. The spectacular grottoes in the karst region form one of the largest cave systems in the world, with 15 miles of impressive rock formations, stalagmites and stalactites.

Karsts are formed by the meeting of limestone and water, creating sinkholes, springs and caves, and Slovenia has an extraordinary underground network of over a thousand karst caves and potholes, 20 of which are open to tourists. The Postojna Cave, with miles of passages and gleaming stalagmites and stalactites, is the most visited cave in Europe; an electric train takes tourists through the special underworld past its clear lakes. The **Škocjan Caves**, in the centre of of the Rakov Škocjan Regional Park, became a UNESCO World Heritage Site in 1986. The cave's miles of passages formed by the Reka River make up one of the largest underground caves in Europe.

Selecting a Property

Getting There

By Air

Adria Airways (Kuzmičeva 7, 1000 Ljubljanatel, **t** + 386 1 369 1000, **f** + 386 1 436 9233, **www.adria.si**) is Slovenia's national carrier. It offers regular scheduled flights to Ljubljana from most major European cities, including London, Manchester, Amsterdam, Barcelona, Brussels, Dublin, Frankfurt, Munich, Paris, Vienna and Zurich. **EasyJet** flies between London Stansted and Ljubljana.

By Bus

Slovenia can be reached from neighbouring countries by bus. International bus transport is well organised and relatively inexpensive.

By Train

International rail connections with Slovenia are good, with direct connections from Austria, Croatia, Hungary, Italy, Macedonia and Yugoslavia. Most trains are relatively modern and prices are reasonable.

By Car

You can reach Slovenia via one of the border crossings with Austria, Croatia, Hungary or Italy, or you can hire a car from a rental agency. Slovenia's roads are good and clearly signposted; beside the roads you will find rest stops and overnight accommodation. *See* 'Settling In', pp.367.

Getting Around

By Rail

Slovene Railways (*Slovenske železnice*) runs the national service. Where possible, avoid *potniški* trains, which are slow and stop at every halt. Intercity (IC) trains are faster and more expensive. Some of the intercity services, known locally as green trains, require advance reservations.

By Bus

Slovenia's bus network consists of a large number of small local companies, with normally well-organised services. Ljubljana, Maribor and Koper have bus stations with full facilities and computerised booking facilities where you can buy your tickets hours in advance; this is recommended if you're travelling between Ljubljana and the coast in the summer. In other places, get onto the bus and pay the driver or conductor. You will normally be charged an extra fee for large pieces of baggage, which must be stored in the hold.

By Sea

Slovenia has ports at Izola, Koper, Piran and Portoroz.

Choosing a Location

For most people, Slovenia is a mountain destination rather than a coastal destination, but there are developments being sold on the coast, with particular interest around Koper, Piran and Portoroz. Be aware that parts of the coast are fairly industrial and spoiled by some low-grade developments carried out many years ago.

The jewels in Slovenia are to be found inland. Slovenia has largely unspoilt alpine terrain. The main focus at the moment is in the capital, Ljubljana, in Bled (in the hops to the northwest of the country), and in the Soča Valley.

In popular Ljubljana, some experts predict price rises of 30 per cent each year until 2010. Because Slovenia is such a small country, even living in the capital gives easy access within a few hours to the rest of its delights, and there is a limited supply of housing, and restrictions on development. The increase in international tourism and business will bring an increase in demand.

Property Types and Prices

Because Slovenia is incredibly small (drive more than two hours in any direction and you'll end up in a different country), and the population very low, the choice of properties is limited. When looking for somewhere to purchase, it is advisable to be as flexible as possible, rather than setting your heart on a specific kind of property in a precise location.

Buyers can choose from luxury modern apartments to historic villas. The atmospheric old town next to the scenic river, with narrow streets and a café culture, is predictably the most desirable area and prices reflect this. Another favourite part of town is Rozna Dolina, close to the green of Tivoli Park. This area has many old houses in need of renovation.

Guide Prices

€80,000

- **Three-bedroom country house in good condition.**
- **Modern top-floor flat in Kranjska Gora with 40 sq m of living area.**

Case Study: A Rude Awakening

Attracted by the sound of £5,000 for a property – fuelled by the optimistic hype of newspaper reports and television programmes – Angela Johnson took a trip out to Slovenia. How could she go wrong at that price? she thought. It was less than the cost of her car. But when she arrived, agents laughed at her and asked about her DIY skills. They explained that those sort of prices were for somewhere dilapidated, without running water, in a rural area. If she wanted to move to the country and spend time repairing the property or deal with local builders, she would have a full-time job on her hands.

Angela was clear that she wanted to rent the property out to cover the mortgage and have it as an investment. The agent pointed out that most holidaymakers in Slovenia want to be in the ski resorts, the spa towns or the capital and these areas are where the rental potential is. Angela managed to put her romantic idea of a house surrounded by wildflowers aside and bought a brand new purpose-built block in a ski resort in the north.

€150,000

- Two-bed apartment in a good area of Ljubijana.
- Modern two-bedroom in the centre of Ljubljana with 80 sq m of living space with parking and a balcony.
- Detached three-bedroom house near Lake Bohinj

€200,000

- Four-bedroom designer flat in Ljubljana with 150 sq m of living space.
- Three-bedroom house 10 minutes from capital in a wooded area with 180 sq m of living space and 180 sq m of land.
- Two-bedroom apartment in Piran, overlooking the sea.

€260,000

- 50-year-old house on beach in Peljesac; 70 sq m on 300 sq m plot.
- Farm, 10ha, 50km from Ljubljana, superb situation and quality.

€300,000

- Traditional three-bedroom villa in the centre of the capital.

€400,000

- Large villa (400 sq m of construction) in Portoroz, with six bedrooms.

€700,000

- Fully renovated traditional style family villa on the riverfront in the old town of Ljubljana.

Building from Scratch or Renovation

Most areas outside the capital are rural, and this is where the bulk of land for building new properties and houses in need of renovation is found. There are also city apartments for renovation. Although these have obvious appeal and a relatively low price tag, the cost of repair needs to be fully considered, along with the logistics of employing and communicating with workmen. Some agents take on this responsibility – for a significant fee, of course – but even then there are no guarantees, and anyone considering this option should go in with their eyes fully open. Whether starting from scratch or improving an existing building, take into account the time and money involved. You may very well make money on your investment, but you will not 'get rich quick'.

Temporary Accommodation

It is possible to rent accommodation in the Slovak Republic, although renting a flat is more common than renting an entire house. Accommodation for rent is advertised in the daily newspapers, on the Internet, and by estate agencies in all towns. Estate agents charge for their services and this type of accommodation is expensive. The cost of renting is, predictably, higher in the capital Bratislava than in the smaller towns, and there is also less availability. Utility bills are additional costs and the rent is usually paid monthly with a deposit of a few months' rent.

The Process of Buying a Property

Freedom to Buy

In Slovenia, EU citizens can buy apartments, buildings and land, although they do still have to register their interest in doing so before making an offer on a property.

Initial Steps

First Contracts

Once you have found a property that you want to purchase, you will be expected to sign some form of contract, generally either a reservation contract or a preliminary purchase contract. *See* p.75. Note that the title 'preliminary purchase contract' is misleading – it is actually a full binding purchase contract. We therefore recommend that, wherever possible, you insist on signing a **reservation contract** at this stage.

Searches and Enquiries

Once you have signed a reservation contract, your lawyer should make various enquiries, such as checking that the contract is fair, that the seller has good title and the right to sell to you, that the area is zoned for residential building and that any building work being undertaken enjoys all the necessary planning and building consents. Depending on the circumstances of your case, there could well be other enquiries that also need to be made.

Signing the Contract and Registering the Title

Once your lawyer has checked out the property and found that everything is in order, you are ready to sign the **preliminary purchase contract**. This commits you and the seller to signing the full contract transferring ownership on an agreed date shortly afterwards, or, if the property is still under construction, once the property has been fully built.

The preliminary purchase contract contains most of the clauses you would expect to see in a UK contract. These will include a description of the property, a statement of the legal title to the property, the price to be paid, how it is to be paid, the deadline for payment and any other deadlines applicable, what should happen in the event of breach of contract and so on.

At this point you will normally pay a **deposit** of 10–20 per cent of the price of the property and apply for a buying permit from the local council. If the permit is refused, the deposit is forfeited. In the case of a property under construction ('off-plan') you will start to make **stage payments**, which will vary in size and number from property to property. A typical scheme would provide for an initial payment of 30 per cent followed by two further payments of 30 per cent as construction progresses, followed by a final payment of 10 per cent on delivery. Occasionally schemes are found where there is only one preliminary payment of, say, 30 per cent with the balance being paid on delivery. This is obviously very useful if you are taking out a mortgage.

Once you are ready to take delivery of the house you will sign the **final purchase contract**. This is signed in front of a notary public. It is at this point that the balance of the money is paid across to the seller. You do not need to be present in Slovenia to sign this document, as your lawyer can prepare a **power of attorney** (*see* pp.77–8) under which you can appoint somebody else to sign on your behalf. This is a sensible thing to do, as it saves the need for you to go to Slovenia, often at short notice, to sign the final title.

Once you have paid the balance of the price the seller will authorise you to **register your ownership** of the property in the local title register. Once this has been done, you – or the local Slovenian company that you have set up to own the property – will be the full legal owner of the property in much the same way as you would be in the UK.

Letting Your Property

See the general chapter **Letting Your Property**, pp.117–26.

If you are letting out your property you should make sure that you use a proper **rental contract**. Your lawyer will be able to supply you with a draft that you can change as necessary. Letting out short-term to tourists produces the least problems in terms of what you can do if the tenant does not pay the rent or refuses to leave.

Settling In

Learning Slovenian

The Slovenian language is very difficult for most English speakers. Even having a knowledge of other languages such as French or German will not help you much, and you are unlikely to recognise any words. Because of the tradition of German tourists coming to the country, many locals speak German, but English is widely taught in schools.

Shopping

Shopping in Ljubljana can be a Western experience, with some international outlets and department stores. Slovenians have a saying about the shops in their small towns which translates as 'you can buy anything from a needle to a steam train', and these places with their community feel are definitely worth a visit. Whether in the country or the city, you will find markets with wonderfully fresh produce, although prices are not as low as they once were. Shops are generally open weekdays 8–8 and Saturdays 8–2.

Home Utilities and Services

Gas and Electricity

There are five regional public companies supplying electricity: **Elektro Ljubljana**, **Elektro Maribor**, **Elektro Celje**, **Elektro Promorska** and **Elektro Gorenjska**. Households buy their electricity from one of these companies, and prices are almost the same as in the UK.

Geoplin is the country's natural gas supplier and transmission utility, but many homes rely on oil-fired boilers for heating.

Water

All domestic water connections are metered and billed by consumption.

Telephones

Post offices and telephone centres are the best places to make international phone calls. They are quieter and cheaper than public telephones. If you want to use a public phone, you will need to buy a card from a post office or local shop.

To call Slovenia from abroad, dial the **country code** (t 386), omit the first zero of the area code, then dial the number.

For **mobile phones**, Slovenia's GSM 900 network is compatible with the rest of Europe (although not with North America). Check with your provider before you leave that you have international roaming, and ask about charges, which can be extortionate. You may want to consider renting a mobile in Slovenia.

Internet

The Internet is only available in large towns and tourist centres. Many libraries in Slovenia offer free access, although you may be limited to half an hour and may have to wait. More and more hotels provide access to the web.

Media

Dnevnik and *Delo* (the most popular) are two daily newspapers based in Ljubljana. *Vecer* reports from Maribor and is published daily. *Slovenske Novice* is a daily tabloid; *Mladina* is a weekly newspaper. Most of them can be viewed online, but not in English. International publications are available in some places in the capital.

Slovenia Weekly is one of the few magazines in English and really a newsletter covering business topics. *Ljubljana Life* is a free bimonthly magazine with listings for entertainment and dining, based mostly on advertising.

RTV Slovenia is a public broadcaster incorporating two national TV channels, regional services and radio. **Pop TV** and **Kanal A** are two big commercial stations.

Money and Banking

The euro was introduced in Europe in 2002, and in Slovenia both the tolar and the euro are used. In some shops and on buses only tolars are accepted, but in larger establishments you can pay in euros. The **tolar** is divided into 100 virtually worthless **stotini**. Coins are in denominations of 50 stotini and 1, 2, 5 and 10 tolars; and there are notes of 10, 20, 50, 100, 200, 500, 1,000, 5,000 and 10,000 tolars. Prices are usually followed by the initials SIT.

Banks are usually open Monday–Friday 8.30–12.30 and 2–5 and Saturday 8.30–12 noon. Money can be changed in tourist offices, post offices, travel agencies and exchange bureaux, which tend to have longer hours than the other options. **Credit cards** are widely accepted, and you can use them to get cash advances from **ATMs** and in the bigger banks.

Post

Look for canary-yellow signs emblazoned with a curled bugle when locating offices of the Posta Slovenije, which are rarely crowded and a model of queuing etiquette. Here you can buy stamps and telephone cards, send faxes and exchange money. Stamps (*znamike*) are also sold at newsagents.

Working and Employment

Foreigners in Slovenia must obtain a work permit before they apply for work. These are usually issued on application by the potential employer and are granted depending on the local job market. They are valid for up to one year. On reapplication, the procedure of checking whether there are local candidates for a job takes place once more. *See* 'Social Services and Welfare benefits', below.

Education

Children must attend school between the ages of six and 15. *Gimnazija*, technical secondary schools and vocational upper secondary schools (offering short-term vocational programmes) provide further education. Higher education facilities in the country comprise two universities, faculties, art academies and professional colleges.

Health and Emergencies

Ambulance **t** 112.

Slovenia has a decent standard of healthcare, and citizens of the EU are entitled to free healthcare in Slovenia with an E111 or the new European Health Identity Card (EHIC) that replaces it from December 2005; both are available free from UK post offices. **Pharmacies** (*lekarna*) usually have normal shopping hours, with a rota system covering night-time and weekend opening; details are posted in the window of each pharmacy. These pharmacies can provide prescription medications and over-the-counter drugs.

Social Services and Welfare Benefits

Your social security rights in Slovenia are the same as those that apply in the UK. If you start work in Slovenia, you will contribute to the Slovenian social security system and, consequently, gain the right to benefits. If you are entitled to the contributory part of JSA and have been claiming this for at least four weeks in the UK, you may continue to receive it for up to three months in Slovenia, while you actively seek work. You must first tell your Jobcentre Plus office or Jobcentre in the UK (where you are registered) of your intention to look for work in Slovenia well in advance of your departure date. Your Jobcentre Plus office or Jobcentre will advise the DWP Pensions and Overseas Benefits Directorate who will determine whether you have satisfied conditions and send you form E303 before you leave.

Cars

Slovenia's roads are good and, because of the lack of vehicles and small distances, driving is generally enjoyable. Certain stretches of the main Ljubljana–Koper, Ljubljana–Maribor and Ljubljana–Jesenice routes are classed as motorways, which are part dual carriageway – where tolls are charged.

If you break down, the **Slovene Automobile Club** has a 24hr emergency service (**t** 987). Because relatively few residents own cars, **hitchhiking** is pretty common, especially on the main Ljubljana–Maribor, Ljubljana–Koper and Bled–Bohinj routes.

Full national **driving licences** are needed for EU members. An international green card for non-EU members can be bought at the border. International car insurance is obligatory except for members of the EU.

Various rules apply to driving in Slovenia:

- **Speed limits are 50kph in built-up areas; 90kph outside built-up areas, 100kph on highways and 130kph on motorways.**
- **Seat belts are compulsory, front and back.**
- **The legal blood alcohol limit is 50mg (0.05 per cent).**
- **Moving vehicles must use headlights at all times.**
- **Buses have priority when leaving a bus stop, so be careful when overtaking them.**
- **The minimum age for drivers is 18.**
- **Children must be at least 12 to sit in the front seat.**
- **Dimmed headlights must be turned on at all times while driving, even during the day.**

Crime and the Police

Police, **t** 113.

Maybe thanks to the fact that its population either lives in or retains strong ties to pastoral communities, Slovenia is safe to the point of complacency, even in small-town capital Ljubljana, with a population of just 300,000. It is therefore unlikely you will have to contact the Slovene police (*policija*), who are unlikely to speak English.

Everyone should take the normal precautions against theft. Pickpockets tend to work in crowded places, such as markets or transport. If you lose your passport, report it instantly to the police and the British embassy.

Food and Drink

Local cheeses and meats available from most supermarkets make good picnic ingredients. Snack bars are good for fillers and breakfast items such as *burek*, a flaky pastry filled with cheese or meat, sausages and hot dogs. In restaurants, choose from roast meats, schnitzels and pork, and you may be surprised to find offal: liver and fried brains. Fish, mussels and squid are not hard to find.

Every Slovenian region has its own various types of bread. There are also many flour-based dishes, often made with buckwheat. Other traditional dishes include goulash and Slovenian-style ravioli. There are few dishes that would appeal to vegetarians, but many national dishes are made from cabbage, beans and potatoes. Everywhere you go you will find Italian food and burger bars. In common its neighbouring countries, Slovenian desserts include fruit-filled strudel, pancakes or dumplings.

Cakes are much loved and are available in most cafés and even bars. **Coffee** is traditionally drunk black with a glass of mineral water. **Tea** is not very good, and again usually served black. **Beer** halls and **wine** cellars dish out local and international beers and wines. Both red and white wines (including sparkling) in general are good and sold abroad. The local firewater is *slivovka*, a plum brandy, and a pear brandy.

Slovenia: References

Directory of Contacts and Resources

Embassies

- **Slovenian Embassy**, 10 Little College Street, London SW1P 3SJ, **t** (020) 7222 5400, **f** (020) 7222 5277, **http://slovenia.embassyhomepage.com**.
- **United Kingdom Embassy**, Trg Republike 3/IV, Ljubljana, **t** + 386 1 200 3910, **f** +386 1 425 0174, **info@british-embassy.si**, **www.british-embassy.si**.

Information and Resources

- **www.slovenia-tourism.si**. The tourist board site.
- **Slovenian Tourist Office**, The Barns, Woodlands End, Mells, Frome, Somerset BA11 3QD, **t** (01373) 814 233, **info@slovenian-tourism.co.uk**.

• **www.sigov.si/mk**. The Ministry of Culture site, with lots of links to museums and galleries.

• **www.slovephilia.net**. Includes detailed directory of resources with links.

• **www.e-uprava.gov.si/e-uprava/en/portal.euprava**. The state portal of the Republic of Slovenia.

• **www.uvi.si**. Government PR portal, with an excellent country overview and links.

• **www.matkurja.com/en**. A network of Slovenian connections.

Property Companies and Estate Agents

• **www.realestate-slovenia.com**. Slovenia-based company with information in English.

• **Euroburo, t** + 43 6137 20099, **www.euroburolimited.co.uk**. Austrian-based company acting as sales agent for firms estate agents in different parts of Slovenia and Croatia.

• **Likof Agency, t** + 386 1 500 5050, **www.agencija-likof.si**. The site lacks information in English, but has good photos and some staff speak English.

• **Slovenia Cottages**, Ozka ulica 18, 9000 Murska Sobota, Slovenia, **t** +386 2 521 1865, **f** +386 2 531 1892, **m.m.s@siol.net**, **www.sloveniacottages.com**.

• **Slovenian Properties**, enquiries@slovenianproperties.com, **sales@slovenianproperties.com** or **rental@slovenianproperties.com**, **www.slovenianproperties.com**.

Removal Companies

• **1st Move International Removals Ltd**, International House, Unit 5B Worthy Road, Chittening Industrial Estate, Avonmouth, Bristol BS11 0YB, **t** (0117) 982 8123, **f** (0117) 982 2229, **info@shipit.co.uk**, **www.shipit.co.uk**.

• **Relocation Enterprises, t** +39 0682 4060, **www.relocationenterprises. com**. An upmarket company that relocates people around the world.

• **Westward Freight Ltd**, Leigh House, 7 Station Approach, Bexleyheath, Kent DA7 4QP, **t** (020) 8304 6388, **f** (020) 8301 6944, **info@westwardfreight.com**, **www.westwardfreight.com**.

• **Excess International Movers**, 4 Hannah Close, Great Central Way, London NW10 0UX, **t** 0800 783 1085 (freephone) or **t** (020) 8324 2066, **f** (020) 8324 2095, **sales@excess-baggage.com**, **www.excess-baggage.com**.

• **UK & International Movers**, Grove Barns, North Road, South Ockendon, Essex RM15 6SR, **t** 0800 954 6474 (freephone) or **t** (01708) 854545, **f** 08700 940149, **relo@askmonarch.com**, **www.yourpersonalmover.com**.

Holiday Companies

- **www.balkanholidays.co.uk**. Established Balkan specialist.
- **www.crystallakes.co.uk**. Brochure includes multi-centre breaks.
- **www.slovenijapursuits.co.uk**. Offers two-night breaks in Ljubljana including scheduled flights from Gatwick.

Administrative Departments

The country has 13 regions for administrative purposes: Gorenjska, Goriška, Jugovzhodna, Koroška, Notranjsko-kraška, Obalno-kraška, Osrednjeslovenska, Podravska, Pomurska, Savinjska, Slovenija, Spodnjeposavska, Zasavska.

However, the government was preparing a plan for a new system at the time of writing (summer 2005).

Time

Slovenia operates within the Central European time zone, one hour ahead of GMT, six hours ahead of Eastern Standard Time and nine ahead of Western Standard Time. Clocks go forward one hour in the early hours on the last Sunday in March, and back one hour on the last Sunday in October.

Public Holidays

1–2 January	New Year
8 February	Preseren Day (Slovenian Cultural Day)
March or April	Easter Sunday and Monday
27 April	Resistance Day
1–2 May	Labour Day Holiday
25 June	National Day
15 August	Assumption
31 October	Reformation Day
1 November	All Saints' Day
25 December	Christmas Day
26 December	Independence Day

Further Reading

Brief History of Slovenia, Janko Prunk – a good overview.
Discover Slovenia, updated annually – deals with the country's cities, geography and history.
Greetings from Slovenia – illustrated guide.

Climate Charts

Normal Daily Temperature Ranges in Ljubljana (°C)

	Jan	Feb	Mar	April	May	June	July	Aug	Sept	Oct	Nov	Dec
Min	−4	−4	0	4	9	12	14	14	11	6	2	−1
Max	2	5	10	15	20	24	27	26	22	15	8	4

Average Monthly Rainfall in Ljubljana (mm)

Jan	Feb	Mar	April	May	June	July	Aug	Sept	Oct	Nov	Dec
88	89	76	98	121	133	113	127	142	151	131	114

Index

Page references to maps are in *italics*.